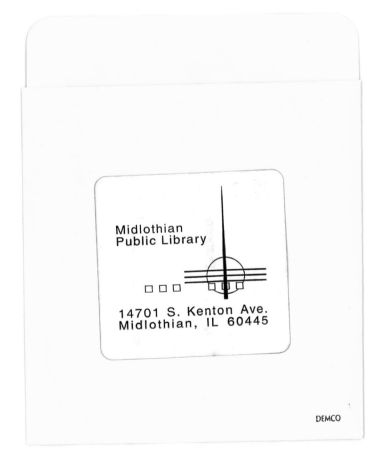

The World Encyclopedia of Comics

Edited by Maurice Horn

VOLUME 5

THE CONTRIBUTORS

Manuel Auad (M.A.), *The Philippines*
Bill Blackbeard (B.B.), *U.S.*
Gianni Bono (G.B.), *Italy*
Joe Brancatelli (J.B.), *U.S.*
MaryBeth Calhoun (M.B.C.), *U.S.*
Javier Coma (J.C.), *Spain*
Bill Crouch (B.C.), *U.S.*
Giulio Cesare Cuccolini (G.C.C.), *Italy*
Mark Evanier (M.E.), *U.S.*
Wolfgang Fuchs (W.F.), *Germany*
Luis Gasca (L.G.), *Spain*
Robert Gerson (R.G.), *U.S.*
Denis Gifford (D.G.), *Great Britain*
Paul Gravett (P.G.), *Great Britain*
Peter Harris (P.H.), *Canada*
Hongying Liu-Lengyel (H.Y.L.L.), *China*
Maurice Horn (M.H.), *France/U.S.*
Pierre L. Horn (P.L.H.), *U.S.*
Slobodan Ivkov (S.I.), *Yugoslavia (Serbia)*
Bill Janocha (B.J.), *U.S.*
Orvy Jundis (O.J.), *The Philippines*
Hisao Kato (H.K.), *Japan*
John A. Lent (J.A.L.), *Asia*
Richard Marschall (R.M.), *U.S.*
Alvaro de Moya (A.M.), *Brazil*
Kalmán Rubovszky (K.R.), *Hungary/Poland*
Ervin Rustemagić (E.R.), *Yugoslavia*
John Ryan (J.R.), *Australia*
Matthew A. Thorn (M.A.T.), *Japan*
Dennis Wepman (D.W.), *U.S.*

The World Encyclopedia of Comics

Edited by Maurice Horn

VOLUME 5

Chelsea House Publishers
Philadelphia

Acknowledgments

The editors of *The World Encyclopedia of Comics* wish to extend their sincere thanks to the following persons: Bill Anderson, Jerry Bails, Larry Brill, Mary Beth Calhoun, Frank Clark, Bill Crouch, Leonard Darvin, Tony Dispoto, Jacques Glénat-Guttin, Ron Goulart, George Henderson, Pierre Horn, Pierre Huet, S. M. "Jerry" Iger, Jessie Kahles Straut, Rolf Kauka, Heikki Kaukoranta, Roland Kohlsaat, Maria-M. Lamm, Mort Leav, Vane Lindesay, Ernie McGee, Jacques Marcovitch, Victor Margolin, Doug Murray, Pascal Nadon, Harry Neigher, Walter Neugebauer, Syd Nicholls, Tom Peoples, Rainer Schwarz, Silvano Scotto, Luciano Secchi, David Smith, Manfred Soder, Jim Steranko, Ernesto Traverso, Miguel Urrutía, Jim Vadeboncoeur, Jr., Wendell Washer, Peter Wiechmann, Mrs. John Wheeler and Joe Willicombe.

We would also like to thank the following collectors who donated reproductions of art from their collections: Wendy Gaines Bucci, Mike Burkey, Tony Christopher, Russ Cochran, Robert Gerson, Roger Hill, Bill Leach, Eric Sack, and Jim Steranko.

Special thanks also to Michel Mandry, Bernard Trout, José Maria Conget of Instituto Cervantes in New York, Four-Color Images Gallery, Frederik Schodt, David Astor, Alain Beyrand, Manuel Halffter, Dominique Petitfaux, Annie Baron-Carvais, Janice Silverman.

Our appreciation also to the following organizations: Associated Newspapers Ltd., Bastei Verlag, Bulls Pressedienst, Comics Magazine Association of America, Editions Dupuis, ERB Inc., Field Newspaper Syndicate, Globi Verlag, The Herald and Weekly Times Ltd., Kauka Comic Akademie, King Features Syndicate, Marvel Comics Group, San Francisco Academy of Comic Art, Strip Art Features, Walt Disney Archives and Walt Disney Productions.

Finally, we wish to thank Don Manza for his photographic work.

Chelsea House Publishers
1974 Sproul Road, Suite 400
P.O. Box 914
Broomall PA 19008-0914

Typeset by Alexander Graphics, Indianapolis IN

Library of Congress Cataloging-in-Publication Data

The world encyclopedia of comics / edited by Maurice Horn.
    p. cm.
    Includes bibliographical references and index.
    ISBN 0-7910-4854-3 (set). — ISBN 0-7910-4857-8 (v. 1). — ISBN
0-7910-4858-6 (v. 2). — ISBN 0-7910-4859-4 (v. 3). — ISBN
0-7910-4860-8 (v. 4). — ISBN 0-7910-4861-6 (v. 5). — ISBN
0-7910-4862-4 (v. 6). — ISBN 0-7910-4863-2 (v. 7)
    1. Comic books, strips, etc.—Dictionaries. I. Horn, Maurice.
PN6710.W6 1998
741.5'03—dc21

97-50448
CIP

NAGAGUTSU NO SANJŪSHI (Japan) *Nagagutsu no Sanjūshi* ("The Three Musketeers with Boots on Their Heads") was created by artist Suimei Imoto and scriptwriter Taisei Makino. It made its first appearance in book form in August 1930.

Nagagutsu featured the exploits of Denko Denyama, a modern and brave girl; Tonkichi Hesoyama ("a lion at home and a mouse abroad"); and Saru, a monkey who had once been a vassal of Momotarō (the hero of a famous Japanese tale who had conquered the ogre Oni). The trio embarked on a long journey in a Zeppelin, but it crashed in a storm. On the island of Oni the ogre they tried to steal the ruby of life but were caught by Oni, who sentenced them to wear boots on their heads (hence the title). In vain efforts to get rid of the boots, the trio tried standing on their heads and hanging from tree branches, but all was useless. So they went back to school and their schoolmates' taunts.

One sunny spring day, the trio discovered a strange bamboo shoot in which was concealed Princess Kaguya (a famous fairy-tale heroine); from Kaguya the trio learned that their boots would disappear only if they found Murasaki-Zukin ("The Purple Mask"). After one month's training at swordmanship by the American teacher Douglas Farebunks, they set out on their journey. After many adventures in which they encountered a number of fairy-tale characters (the woman who lived in a shoe, the fabled swordsman Isamu Kondo, etc.) the three musketeers finally came upon Murasaki-Zukin, who tried to trick them; but, by luck and pluck, they finally got rid of the boots, which were later enshrined as a tribute to their exploits.

Nagagutsu was more a picture story than a comic strip. There were no speech balloons, but text under the panels. The pace, however, was very brisk, with no redundant panel or sentence. The artwork was simple but effective; the storyline fantastic and highly fanciful. The strip itself enjoyed only moderate success, but it is now considered a classic of Japanese comic literature.

H.K.

NAGAI, GŌ (1945-   ) Japanese cartoonist born September 6, 1945, near Tokyo. After formal studies, Gō Nagai burst upon the comics scene with *Harenchi Gakuen*, which began serialization in *Shōnen Jump* in 1968. *Harenchi Gakuen* ("Shameless School") was exactly what its name denoted: the students cavorted in the nude, the teachers played mah jong during class hours, and the assistants drank beer. "*Harenchi Gakuen* was a fantastical school of bedlam," noted Japanese comics scholar Fred Schodt wrote, "where the main preoccupation of both male students and teachers was not study but catching glimpses of girls' underwear or contriving to see them naked." The series ended (1972) in a set battle, complete with guns, tanks, and missiles, that culminated in the school being razed to the ground.

The same year, Nagai started *Devilman*, a tale of the supernatural involving demons, ghouls, monsters, and a teenaged hero determined to stop them, in *Shōnen Magazine*. He also came out with *Mazinger Z* in *Shōnen Jump*, about a gigantic warrior-robot controlled by yet another teenager (the author knew how to play his public). *Mazinger Z* enjoyed unprecedented popularity on three continents; in 1974 an animated cartoon series began, followed by toys, games, and assorted merchandising.

In the 1980s the enterprise mushroomed into a business empire, and to control it Nagai formed his own corporation, Dynamic Productions, with himself at the helm. Employing more than 50 people, including 13 studio assistants and Nagai's two brothers as corporate executives, Dynamic was to become the prototype of the assembly line comics workshops that have sprouted all over Japan in recent years, with a resulting loss of creativity that is deplored by all observers of the form.

M.H.

NAGASHIMA, SHINJI (1937-   ) Japanese comic book artist born in Tokyo on July 8, 1937. Shinji Nagashima decided very early in life to become a cartoonist. As a schoolboy he particularly cherished two comic books, Osamu Tezuka's *Shin Takarajima* ("New Treasure Island") and Tetsuo Ogawa's *Pikadon Hakase no Dai Hatsumei* ("The Great Invention of Dr. Pikadon"), which he reread many times. At the age of 14, Nagashima decided to drop out of school and go to work while pursuing his dream of becoming a comic book artist. He studied in his spare time by himself, but did not go to art school. In 1952, at the age of 15, he made his professional debut.

In 1961 he created his best work, *Mangaka Zankoku Monogatori* ("The Cruel Story of a Cartoonist") for the Japanese magazine *Deka*. The strip met with great success and was followed by a number of other creations: *Fūten* (about a Japanese hippie) in 1967, the *Minwa* series (adaptations of Japanese folktales) and *Wakamonotachi* ("Young Men") in 1968, and *Dōyō Sanbusaku* (a trilogy of children's songs) in 1971. From 1963 to 1965 Nagashima also worked as an animator at the famous Mushi Productions studio.

Among the major influences on his work, Nagashima lists Osamu Tezuka, André François, Raymond Peynet, and Ben Shahn. He is currently working on a new strip, *Tabibito-kun* ("The Boytraveller") strongly influenced by Schulz's *Peanuts*. *Tabibito-kun* and shorter stories done by the author in the course of the past 20 years have been published mainly in *Big Comic Gold*.

Shinji Nagashima tells his stories warmly and poetically. His art style is not realistic but it has flavor and bite. Regarded as the artist who gave fresh stimulus to the Japanese strip in the 1960s, Nagashima has influenced a great number of Japanese comic book artists

Shinji Nagashima.

such as Eiichi Muraoka, Manabu Ōyama, Tsuguo Kōgo, Hisao Hayashi, and Kazuhiko Miyaya.

H.K.

'NAM, THE (U.S.) In one of their periodic forays into gritty realism, the editors at Marvel came up with a comic book series that would retrace the experiences of ordinary grunts in Vietnam, much as such contemporary movies as *The Deer Hunter, Full Metal Jacket,* and *Platoon* have done. The idea was proposed to Marvel in the early 1980s by Doug Murray, a Vietnam war veteran, and after some hesitation it was accepted. *The 'Nam* first appeared in *Savage Tales* in 1985 before getting its own independent title in December 1986.

The story followed the fortunes of enlisted man Ed Marks: his induction into the U.S. Army, his training during boot camp, and his orders to serve in Vietnam. Once Marks was in the field, Murray's narrative line became even more realistic—and controversial for some readers, as Murray described incompetence at high levels and corruption and malingering in the ranks, showing, for instance, how noncoms doled out cushy assignments at headquarters to those privates who could come up with a bribe. Firefights, ambushes, the burning of villages, and other perils of guerilla warfare were also depicted with unusual candor and a marked lack of romanticism. Murray's scripts were brilliantly complemented by Michael Golden's artwork, which seemed to mesh seamlessly with the author's vision.

The Marvel editors eventually became uneasy with the uncompromising tone of the feature, and early in 1990 Murray was replaced by a string of lesser script-writers, including Chuck Dixon and Herb Trimpe, who introduced such incongruous Marvel heroes as the Punisher into the storylines. This only served to trivialize the series further, and it finally bowed out in September 1993.

M.H.

NANCY (U.S.) Nancy appears to be a small girl, about eight, who is imitating a chipmunk with a case of mumps—but it is precisely her endless cheekiness that much of the mass comic-reading public seems to like. Bright-eyed, chirpy, and simple, Nancy was perhaps the most widely followed strip character of the 1950s and early 1960s; attempts by exasperated feature editors to dump her daily and Sunday gag strip were met with outraged public cries. Among other things, every newspaper executive's mother-in-law seemed to love *Nancy* avidly, along with people with influence generally.

What was it in *Nancy* that brainy people hated and the broad middle-aged public loved? Probably the same thing: incredibly simple points which could be grasped at a glance, acted out by a minimal and unconfusing cast of cute kids, drawn with stark plainess against an unadorned background. (Someone once started the unkind rumor that *Nancy* was turned out by a guy with *Joe Miller's Joke Book* and a set of rubber Nancy and Sluggo stamps; a few episodes of the strip read in succession makes one wonder if it was really a rumor.)

Ernie Bushmiller, the strip's creator, was certainly not to be blamed. When he decided to try a kid strip, and the new strip became an almost overnight gold mine, he is hardly at fault for giving the huge public that loved Nancy more of what it wanted, including closing down his daily *Fritzi Ritz* strip and turning its characters over to *Nancy*. Not that Nancy herself was all that new; she had been appearing as Fritzi's niece in the *Fritzi Ritz* strip since the 1920s but was always in tandem with Fritzi herself in an adult-kid gag sequence. Somehow, putting Nancy on her own, with a pseudo-

"Nancy," Ernie Bushmiller. © United Feature Syndicate.

"Napoleon," Clifford McBride. © LaFave Newspaper Features.

tough slum kid named Sluggo, made an electrifying difference to many readers.

Originally, Nancy's Aunt Fritzi was a brighter-than-average flapper when the *Fritzi Ritz* strip began in the early 1920s. She did a number of adventurous and amusing things in the continued daily strip: driving cross-country at a time when highways were unknown; making the Hollywood scene; getting involved with grisly crime mysteries. All these stories were done with great verve and humor by the young Bushmiller, who had a real gift for quality comic continuity. (It is easy to see the elements that Harold Lloyd noted and liked in Bushmiller's work when he invited the cartoonist to come West to work on his film comedies.) The Sunday Bushmiller page was well drawn, with fine comic touches, and sound, often novel, payoff gags, both in its top half (*Fritzi*) and its bottom section (*Phil Fumble*, about a ne'er-do-well boyfriend of Fritzi's who went his own bumbling way each week.)

Nor did their quality lag as the strips proceeded into the 1930s. More and more newspapers, however, were dropping halves of Sunday pages in favor of a remaining half, to accommodate ads and more comics, and Bushmiller realized that *Fumble* was a weak property in this situation. Deciding to try a fresh feature gambit, he replaced Phil's domain with Nancy's simple-minded world—with results that we all know.

In the late 1970s, Bushmiller became seriously ill and left most of the artwork on *Nancy* to his assistants, Will Johnson and Al Plastino. After Bushmiller died in 1982, the strip was briefly done by Mark Lansky until his own death a year later. Jerry Scott then took it over, giving it a jazzier, less stereotypical look. After he left in 1995, brothers Guy and Brad Gilchrist have been carrying it in close imitation of Bushmiller's tone and style.

Bushmiller's work is best read from his early days until 1940, when *Nancy* began. The remainder will always be on tap at an institution or two for the stalwart and devoted research student; the rest of us would be happier forgetting it.

B.B.

NAPOLEON (U.S.) Easily the finest comic strip built around a man and a dog, Clifford McBride's *Napoleon* began on May 5, 1929, as an episode in an untitled irregular weekly series about a fat, jovial fellow named Uncle Elby. (McBride drew a weekly panelled gag feature about various unnamed individuals, in which Uncle Elby reappeared frequently as the only named character.) The first episode involving Napoleon, the gaunt, huge, ungainly black and white mongrel so familiar on comic pages for a quarter of a century, was titled "Uncle Elby Befriends a Lonesome Dog." The dog struck a popular chord, and reappeared with Uncle Elby on May 12 and again on June 23, 1929. Before long, man and dog were an inseparable pair in the McBride Sunday feature, so popular that the Arthur J. LaFave syndicate urged McBride to highlight them in a regular, titled comic strip.

The first episode of the new daily strip, named *Napoleon and Uncle Elby*, appeared in the *Boston Globe* and other papers on June 6, 1932. Phasing out his Sunday feature on April 2, 1933, McBride opened the Sunday *Napoleon* page in the *Denver Post* and elsewhere on March 12, 1933. Based in part on the antics of a 210-pound St. Bernard named Napoleon that was owned by Clifford McBride's Uncle Elby Eastman (on whom the strip character was largely based), the *Napoleon* strip was essentially an episodic gag feature, although some highly fantastic continuity involving finned mermen and other fabulous narrative elements, in which Elby and Napoleon accompany a grizzled old sailor named Singapore Sam, ran in the Sunday pages of 1933. Unfortunately, the public seemed to want Elby and the dog in more mundane surroundings, and the fantasy element was dropped. Widely distributed, the Sunday page dropped to a half-page in 1944, then to a third a year later, losing appeal as the aging McBride redrew more and more of the old strip episodes in the later 1940s. Carried on by several artists after his death, and bylined by his wife, the daily and Sunday *Napoleon* strips finally dropped from publication in 1960.

Several book collections of the strip were published between 1930 and 1950, notably a Big Little Book-type pair from Saalfield (*Napoleon and Uncle Elby* in 1938, and *Napoleon and Uncle Elby and Little Mary* in 1939); and a comic book collection of the early Sunday pages from Eastern Color in 1942 named for the strip. Delightfully drawn and often hilariously funny, much of the McBride strip calls for republication in permanent form.

B.B.

NARCISO PUTIFERIO (Italy) Narciso Putiferio ("Narcissus Rumpus"), a shop clerk at Stevens General Stores, learns of the death of his grandfather Filippone, an old pirate who left him a huge legacy in his will. Upon receiving the news, Narciso leaves on his grandfather's ship, the *Mermaid of the Seas*, and sails for the Island of Mirages to claim his inheritance. After overcoming the dreaded pirate Skipper Shark in combat and freeing an Indian princess, Narciso again sets sail to find new treasures hidden in the Sargasso Sea that he has learned about from an old parchment.

Thus begins *Narciso Putiferio*, a very original and funny series created in 1954 by Ferdinando Corbella, a clever cartoonist who always filled his work with weird contraptions, paradoxical situations, and an assortment of highly individualized characters made even funnier by his easy and free-flowing line. Corbella, one of the first artists to use the stipple technique in his adventure strips (*Rolan Aquila* chief among them), displayed the best of his comic talents in this feature, in which the individual panels stand out sharply.

The adventures of *Narciso Putiferio* ended abruptly in 1962, after having enthused a whole generation of young readers, when the new editors of the comic weekly *Il Monello* (where *Narciso* had been appearing) made the decision to change the editorial policies of the magazine, forcing Narciso and his mates (Gambadilegno, Occhiodilince, and Uncino among others) to retire.

G.B.

NATACHA (Belgium) In the late 1960s the editors of the weekly comics magazine *Spirou* felt the need for a female protagonist to add to their lineup of all-male heroes. They turned to Francois Walthéry, who was then working in the Peyo studios and had a knack for drawing sexy-but-nice young women. *Natacha* made its debut on February 26, 1970, on a script by Roland Goosens.

Natacha was a stewardess working for an international airline company, and this allowed the spunky, toothsome blonde heroine to roam the globe in search of wrongs to redress, villains to combat, and new thrills to experience. She has gone through hair-raising adventures in India ("Natacha and the Maharajah") and Japan ("Double Flight"), on a mysterious island ("The Island Beyond the World"), and even under the seas ("The Thirteenth Apostle"). The enemies she has faced and conquered include arms smugglers, diamond thieves, skyjackers, and a horde of panting lechers, and there have been plenty of crash landings, car chases, and gun fights to keep the story moving at a brisk pace.

Walthéry often writes his own scripts, but to keep the stories from getting stale he has called on many of his colleagues at *Spirou* to lend a hand in the writing department. Others have helped with the backgrounds. As the author himself declared, "It's a team effort." Walthéry retains overall direction, however, and there

has been great consistency of style and tone from episode to episode.

Mixing suspense and adventure with a welcome dose of humor, designed for adults without talking down to children, and never preaching or overreaching itself, *Natacha* is one of the more winsome creations to come out of the French-Belgian school of comic storytelling in the last quarter-century.

M.H.

NATHAN NEVER (Italy) This peculiar science-fiction series, created in 1991 by the so-called "Sardinian Trio" (Michele Medda, Antonio Serra, and Bepi Vigna) is published in black-and-white book form by the Sergio Bonelli publishing house. In an environment dated 2097, which is clearly reminiscent of *Blade Runner*, the official police forces are inadequate to keep order, so citizens must turn to private organizations for help. Nathan Never is a special agent of Alfa Agency, an organization that guarantees security for a fee. Monstrous aliens are absent from this sci-fi narrative set in the near future where people are dressed up in modern ways and are living in Megalopolis, the architectural structure of which looks like that of the present's most modern buildings.

The world of *Nathan Never* has undergone deep geographic transformations owing to a catastrophe caused by man. The Earth's axis has a new inclination, the sea level is increased, the continents are shaped differently, and Megalopolis has a seven-level structure. In the lower levels live mutants, originally artificial beings expressly created for manual jobs that were later outlawed and left to their own destiny. These mutants, now ostracized, often struggle against humans. The social and political organization of this huge city is undermined by corruption, crime, tensions, and fights; these are the background of many of *Nathan Never*'s plots. Other adventures take place in the colonies orbiting the Earth or in the radioactive desert originated by the wild pollution produced by man.

Nathan Never's stories are made up of many characters that are harmoniously blended. On his missions Nathan is accompanied by a team of colleagues, including Legs Weaver (who, thanks to her success, has given birth to a spinoff series), Sigmund Baginov, an expert in computer sciences, Edward Reiser, the boss of Alfa Agency, and many others. The most interesting feature of Nathan Never is his deeply humane attitude that makes him a very peculiar hero—some of his decisions are mistaken, but he pays for them.

The original "Sardinian Trio" has been supported by other scriptwriters, and the team of drawers counts 24 artists, among whom are Claudio Castellini, Robert De Angelis, Nicola Mari, Germano Bonazzi, Stefano Casin, Mario Alberti, Ivan Calcaterra, and Dante Bastianoni.

G.C.C.

NAUSICAÄ OF THE VALLEY OF WIND (Japan) Any but his most dedicated fans would be hard-pressed to name another comic created by Japan's most popular animator, Hayao Miyazaki, but the one comic he is known for, *Nausicaä of the Valley of Wind*, is without a doubt one of the most important comics ever produced in Japan, and it has generated more than a little controversy.

The story is set a millennium in the future, hundreds of years after survivors of the Seven Days of Fire dragged themselves out of the rubble of industrial civi-

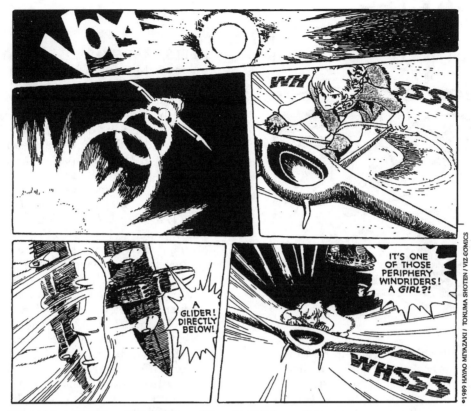

"Nausicaä of the Valley of Wind," Hayao Miyazaki. © Tokuma Shoten.

lization and began to scratch a meager existence from what little usable soil remained on the face of the Earth. In this postapocalyptic world, humanity huddles in villages and kingdoms, coexisting uneasily with the enormous (and growing) Sea of Corruption, a forest of overgrown molds spewing poisonous gases and inhabited by giant insects.

The heroine is Nausicaä, a teenaged girl who seems to be a savior prophesied in ancient writings. Nausicaä, the daughter of the chieftain of a peaceful agricultural community known as the Valley of Wind, struggles to end a war that breaks out between three major powers. In the process, she discovers that the feared Sea of Corruption is in fact cleansing the Earth of a millennium of industrial and military pollution, and that the giant insects are the Earth's ecological conscience.

Nausicaä of the Valley of Wind began as a straightforward environmental cautionary tale, and Miyazaki's hugely popular 1984 animated version was indeed little more, but the comic developed into a complex, often brooding discourse on hubris and moral relativity. Nausicaä, all but flawless in the animated film, becomes a character wracked by doubt and, occasionally, rage or depression.

Nausicaä became controversial when it was revealed that it had been a source of inspiration (one of many, actually) to the Aum Divine Truth cult that was responsible for the tragic sarin gas attack on a Tokyo subway line in 1995. Critics implied a connection between the terrorism and such popular media as comics, animation, and video games, and although no coherent connection was ever made, *Nausicaä's* previously pristine image has been indelibly tarnished by this tenuous link to infamy.

The feature-length animated version was introduced to English-speaking audiences as the notorious *Warriors of the Wind*, a heavily edited version that still invokes anger in those familiar with the original. *Warriors* led creator Miyazaki to adopt a far more cautious approach to granting licenses for foreign-language editions of his films. The first four volumes of the English edition of the comic were translated by Studio Proteus for Viz Comics, and the remaining three volumes were translated by Viz Comics.

M.A.T.

NAYLOR, ROBERT (1910-   ) American cartoonist born February 15, 1910, in New York City. After art studies at the C. N. Landon School, Bob Naylor worked in animation with the Stallings-Nolan studio. He first entered the field of comics as an assistant at King Features Syndicate in 1928 and ghosted for a number of King Features artists, including George Herriman. In 1935 Naylor was promoted to staff artist for advertising, and he later became one in a stable of cartoonists on whom King Features regularly called to take over a strip left vacant by the death or departure of the previous artist.

Bob Naylor received his first byline as the successor to Frank Miller on *Barney Baxter*, an aviation strip that Miller had created in 1935. From 1942-48, Naylor drew and wrote the feature with such ineptitude that the ailing Miller had to come back to try and save the faltering strip. In 1948 Naylor took over Walt Hoban's old gag strip *Jerry on the Job* and promptly ran it down. Nothing daunted, he was given the task in 1954 of continuing Les Fosgrave's anemic strip *Big Sister*, with which he finally found a niche for his modest talents. *Big Sister* was discontinued in 1972, and Naylor retired to Monroe, New York, in the mid-1970s.

Bob Naylor was another sad example of King Features' seniority system at work. His most conspicuous quality (if such it can be called) was blandness; it was

BARNEY BAXTER

Bob Naylor, "Barney Baxter." © King Features Syndicate.

hard to find any personality or conviction in his drawing style, and his writing was a compendium of clichés (his race epithets in *Barney Baxter* were particularly offensive, even for the times). Nevertheless Naylor deserves mention because of his long career in the field and his association with at least two noteworthy features.

M.H.

NEBBS, THE (U.S.) Sol Hess, who had previously written most of the continuity for *The Gumps*, created *The Nebbs* (whose name, Hess once confided to Martin Sheridan, comes from the Jewish "nebbich," meaning a poor sap) for the Bell Syndicate. The strip, written by Hess and drawn by W. A. Carlson, first appeared on May 22, 1923.

In the introductory strip Hess himself described his intentions in the following words: "In presenting the Nebb family, I will try to portray from day to day, in a humorous, human way, the things that happen in everyday life. The Nebbs are just a little family like thousand of other families. While they have their differences, they are good wholesome people and I hope you like them much."

In spite of its stated intentions, *The Nebbs* was an unusual family strip in many ways. Instead of being the stereotyped henpecked husband of comic strip folklore, Rudolph Nebb, in addition to being a troublesome resort hotel operator, was also an unyielding *pater familias* and a confirmed martinet. He bullied and nagged and thundered, running his household in dictatorial (though fully ineffectual) fashion. His wife, the chubby and angelic Fanny, stoically smiled through her husband's tantrums and never as much as talked back. His daughter, the teenaged Betsy, and his son, Junior, obediently listened to their father's homilies while doing their own thing on the sly. The only man who could stand up to Rudy's constant badgering was the rambunctious Max Guggenheim (named after Hess's real-life next-door neighbor), the Nebbs' unofficial adviser and *eminence grise*.

Following Sol Hess's death on the last day of 1941, his daughter and her husband, Stanley Baer, took over the continuity, but they did not possess the creator's

spark and *The Nebbs* slowly lost its popularity, finally disappearing in 1946.

M.H.

NEELS, MARC (1922-   ) Marc Sleen (whose real name is Marc Neels), a Flemish writer, artist, and cartoonist, was born December 31, 1922, in Gentbrugge, and had always felt an urge to write and draw. Therefore, he studied at the Sint Lucasinstituut in Gent in order to find his own style. He finished his studies in 1944 and in the same year debuted as an editorial cartoonist in the newspaper *De Standaard*. In 1947, he started editing the comics magazine *'t Kapoentje*. During the next two years he did three strips for *'t Kapoentje—Stropke en Flopke, De Lustige Kapoentjes,* and *Piet Fluwijn en Bolleke*—all the while continuing to draw newspaper strips. In 1949 the weekly magazine was transformed into a supplement for *Het Volk*. It was edited by Marc Sleen until he left *Het Volk* in 1965.

Sleen created some short-lived comic strips before his enduring *De avonturen van detektief Van Zwam* ("The Adventures of Detective Van Zwam") was published on October 3, 1947, in the Brussels newspaper *De Nieuwe Gids*. Roughly one year later, on September 8, 1948, he started the fourth adventure in this series, but now with former supporting character Nero the star and title of the strip. *Nero* appeared in *De Nieuwe Gids* and, after a merger, in *Het Volk* until 1965.

In 1965 Sleen moved the strip to *De Standaard*, with *Nero* being introduced to the newspaper by "The Story of Nero & Co.," drawn by the Studio Vandersteen. Apart from this one instance, Marc Sleen has done all of his writing and drawing without the help of assistants.

Sleen's ever popular *Nero* strip is reprinted in four albums per year. *Nero* is quite successful because of the wild situations he gets into and because of the spicing of satire to be found throughout the strip. Still a master at cartooning, Sleen sometimes includes caricatures of politicians in his strips. He has tapped a number of adventure genres for the parodistic uses to which they can be put. *Nero* regularly takes part in photo safaris in Africa, just as Sleen does. Since the late 1960s Sleen has devoted all his professional time to *Nero* and all of his extracurricular activities to his African travels; as a board member of the World Wildlife Fund he has had many of his film documentaries broadcast on the Flemish-language programs of Belgian television. And, for all of its long run, the *Nero* strip is still fresh because of good writing, good characterization, and a continued standard of art befitting a humorous strip.

W.F.

NEGRO RAUL, EL (Argentina) Started as *Las Aventuras del Negro Raul* ("The Adventures of Raul the Black Man"), the strip was created by pioneer cartoonist Arturo Lanteri in the pages of the Buenos Aires magazine *El Hogar*, in which it appeared in 1916. Raul lived a life of continuous frustration in a hostile and racist city, where all his efforts were bound to fail. To compensate for the existence of poverty and deprivation which was his real lot, Raul dreamed up a life of princely splendor.

In this work Lanteri did not make use of balloons, but inserted a long text under each panel, usually ending on a morality lesson similar to those in *Buster Brown*. Unlike those in *Buster Brown*, however, Raul's moralities were not funny but as bitter as his life. A

"El Negro Raul," Arturo Lanteri. © El Hogar.

"Nelvana," Adrian Dingle. © Triumph Comics.

nonintegrated and daydreaming character very modern in his predicament, *El Negro Raul* ended his career in the early 1920s when his creator went on to other endeavors such as *Pancho Talero*.

L.G.

NELVANA OF THE NORTHERN LIGHTS (Canada)

Nelvana of the Northern Lights was created by artist Adrian Dingle for an independent wartime Canadian comic book, *Triumph-Adventure*, established in June 1941 by the Hillborough Studio of Toronto. The black-and-white book was absorbed in 1942 by Bell Features and Publishing Company of Toronto and was renamed simply *Triumph Comics*. At the end of World War II, when a Canadian government embargo against the importation of U.S. comic books was lifted, Canadian publishers switched to full-color printing to meet the renewed competition. *Nelvana* then appeared in a new book called *Super Duper Comics*, which was later taken over by F.E. Howard Publications of Toronto. It became the only Canadian comic book title ever to appear under the imprint of three different publishing companies.

Nelvana was a semimythological heroine who received superhuman powers from Koliak, the King of the Northern Lights. Initially her efforts were aimed at thwarting Nazi plans to invade Canada's Arctic regions, but in issue number eight of *Triumph* (by then under the Bell trademark) *Nelvana* began a seven-part serialized adventure in the subterranean world of Glacia, a modernistic city that she finds frozen in a state of suspended animation when she is sent by Koliak to learn the Glacians' secret of undying life. The light of the North Star shining down a deep crevasse and magnified by a great glass dome over Glacia brings life back to the inhabitants after five million years of frozen sleep.

Nelvana later became involved in a running battle between King Rano and his son Targa on one side and, on the other, Vultor the Villainous, who hoped to usurp the Glacian throne. Eventually Vultor was beaten and then, midway through the seventh installment, the narrative abruptly left Nelvana and switched to a Japanese plot to occupy the Arctic.

Nelvana was absent from the strip during the next two installments as Dingle changed his focus to the adventures of Spud Jodwin, an engineer on the Alcan Highway project. It was he who discovers the Japanese plot. Nelvana eventually returned and, in another change of direction for the strip, adopted an alter-ego, that of secret agent Alana North, most of whose adventures took place in the civilized world and not in the frozen north.

After a five-part series called "The Ice-Beam," dealing with efforts of enemy agents to steal plans for a secret weapon, the strip returned to a fantasy theme with Earth facing the threat of war with the Ether People who claimed, as justification for a planned invasion of the world, that man's radio broadcasting was driving them insane. Nelvana journeyed to the world of Etheria and discovered that Vultor the Villainous was masterminding this latest threat to Earth. Using the powers given to her by Koliak, Nelvana defeated Vultor and the great Etherian fleet once and for all. The last chapter of the strip appeared in the third issue of *Super Duper*, dated May 1947.

P.H.

"Nero," Marc Sleen (Marc Neels). © Marc Sleen.

NERO (Belgium) *Nero* is the most popular and most successful creation of Flemish comic artist Marc Sleen. Originally a humorous detective strip titled *De avonturen van detektief Van Zwam* ("The Adventures of Detective Van Zwam"), it started on October 3, 1947, in the Brussels newspaper *De Nieuwe Gids*. As a detective, Van Zwam worked wonders, but his near-perfect character was not very funny. He had a very human assistant, however, whom readers immediately liked. Thus it was that Nero, originally a supporting character, took over the title and the starring role in the fourth adventure, "Het Rattenkasteel" ("The Rats' Castle"), starting on September 8, 1948.

After the merger of *De Nieuwe Gids* and *Het Volk*, four *Nero* albums reprinting his adventures were published per year. In 1965 the strip moved on to yet another newspaper, *De Standaard*, with the first tale to appear there "De Geschiedenis van Nero en Co" ("The Story of Nero and Co."), drawn by the Studio Vandersteen. Apart from this fill-in story, Marc Sleen has worked alone on his strips.

Nero is a globetrotter, following any cue to beckoning adventures and leaving his wife at home. Nevertheless he is a father figure, confronted by the generation gap in the form of his highly talented son, Adhemar. *Nero* also represents strong elements of Flemish folk character without permitting them to become stereotyped. His adventures make humorous use of a number of adventure genres, like fantasy, science fiction, or mystery, as Marc Sleen has tapped almost all sources that lend themselves to parody. He even adds topical material and real-life politicians in order to enable Nero to expound his wishes for world peace. Since 1962, when Sleen started regularly going on photo safaris in Africa, Nero is often seen searching out an African setting for his adventures.

The witty *Nero* comic feature is extremely well written and has a strong cast of characters to add to its enjoyment. This strip tries to teach readers to face each day with a smile. It is still going strong after 50 years of existence.

W.F.

NEUGEBAUER, WALTER (1921-1992) Walter Neugebauer was a German comic artist, born March 28, 1921, the son of German parents, in Tuzla, Bosnia (Yugoslavia). Neugebauer grew up in Zagreb, Yugosla-

via, and got his public and secondary schooling there. He interrupted his studies at the Academy to work full time for the press.

At the age of 12 his cartoons were published in a catholic parish paper; at age 14 he drew the children's page of the newspaper *Novosti* which featured stories and poems (mostly written by his older brother, Norbert, born June 9, 1917). He drew his first comic strip, *Gusarsko Blago* ("Pirate Treasure"), in 1935-36 and, at the same time, started *Nasredin Hodža* for *Oko* ("The Eye"). At 17, together with the journalist Franjo, he founded *Mickeystrip*, the first Yugoslav comic magazine. The title was derived from *Old Mickey*, a Western serial. Here he drew and wrote *Bimbo Bambus*, the humorous story of an African and his white hunter friend.

He continued on *Mickeystrip* until he finished secondary school in 1940, then founded his own magazine, *Veseli Vandrok's* ("The Happy Wanderer"). This magazine contained more funnies and his first attempts at realistic comics: The humoristic *Nasredin Hodža*; the funny snails *Puž and Pužek*, a scouting story; and the realistic Western adventures of *Winnetou*. Text features included a serialized version of "Huckleberry Finn." The magazine folded when Yugoslavia entered the war in 1941. The war years led to some narrow escapes and occasional comic work. After the war, he started working as a cartoonist for the satirical *Kerempuh*. While working there from 1946 to 1948 he became interested once again in animated cartoons. This interest was sponsored by the blossoming *Kerempuh* and finally led to the 21-minute animated cartoon *Veliki Miting* ("The Big Meeting") which told about a meeting of frogs and toads. It was a very successful film that was withdrawn from public showing 10 years later because of Albanian-Yugoslavian quibbling over borderlines.

The film led to the financing of Duga-Film ("Rainbow-Film") which folded in 1952 because of a financial crisis. In 1952-53, Neugebauer introduced the first postwar comic strip to *Pionir*, a children's magazine. The strip told of the adventures of a rabbit and a bear and was called *Priča s Rubašume* ("Tales from the Edge of the Forest"). Next came adaptations of Jules Verne yarns for *Plavi Vjesnik* ("Blue Herald"), a magazine that changed to tabloid size and eventually introduced American and British strips.

In 1954 Neugebauer was back in animated cartoons, working for *Interpublik*, an advertising agency with animated cartoon facilities. While working there, contact between Rolf Kauka and Walter Neugebauer was established. Neugebauer started freelancing for Kauka's *Fix und Foxi* comic books and in 1958 produced a *Munchhausen* cartoon for Kauka, who featured the legendary Baron in his comics of the time. In the following years, Neugebauer helped develop, cocreate, or draw Kauka features like *Fix und Foxi*, *Tom und Biber*, *Mischa*, and *Bussi Bär*.

From 1958 to 1972 Neugebauer held the position of art director at Kauka, although not continuously. In 1970 Neugebauer and Kauka started quarreling over finances and copyrights. The argument was mainly fueled by production of the animated cartoon feature Maria d'Oro. It ultimately led to Neugebauer's breaking with Kauka and leaving the company to freelance for various others, Kauka's fiercest competitor just one of these. Neugebauer drew cover illustrations for Ehapa's *Micky Maus* comic book and, more importantly, produced some 100 animated cartoons for television ads for *Micky Maus*. The 20-second spots usually showed some funny happening that ultimately became the cover issue of the weekly *Micky Maus* magazine.

Neugebauer was known for the speedy delivery of his animated cartoons. Together with six assistants he could crank out two such spots in one week while others took six weeks just to produce one. For a while Neugebauer's studio was the busiest animated cartoon studio in Germany.

Despite his speedy delivery, Neugebauer had a mature, slick style, although it sometimes looked simplistic. On the whole, however, his funny and realistic comic art was always polished and original, and showed his devotion to his two professional loves: comics and animated cartoons. Neugebauer died May 31, 1992, in Geretsried, near Munich, Germany.

W.F.

NEUTRON *see Valentina.*

NEWLYWEDS, THE (U.S.) George McManus tackled the family theme that was to become his hallmark for the first time in *The Newlyweds* (also known as *The Newlyweds and Their Baby*), a Sunday feature which he created in 1904 for Pulitzer's *New York World*.

The plot was simple: Mr. and Mrs. Newlywed (whose first names we never learn, as they are unusually fond of calling each other by such endearing terms as "dovey" and "precious") are inordinately proud and protective of their only child, a rather dull-looking baby. The infant (later christened Snookums) was prone to temper tantrums, and in order to assuage him the Newlyweds would go to any length, such as renting a movie house to show the brat the same Charlie Chaplin picture over and over again, getting Caruso to reprise one of his arias, or having a bum repeatedly kicked out of a saloon, all to the baby's drooling enjoyment.

When McManus left Pulitzer in 1912 to join the Hearst organization, he took *The Newlyweds* with him, mining the same theme again and again in a new version rebaptized *Their Only Child* until the definitive

establishment of *Bringing Up Father* on the Sunday page in 1918.

After a 25 year absence, the Newlyweds and their baby made a comeback in yet another version called *Snookums* in November 1944, as a top to *Bringing Up Father* (replacing *Rosie's Beau*). This third serving of the same theme (which was never as imaginative as the earlier ones) survived its creator by two years, disappearing in December 1956.

The Newlyweds (to use the title by which the strip is best known) was McManus's most popular creation prior to *Bringing Up Father*. A musical comedy, titled *The Newlyweds and Their Baby*, was staged in 1909, and a few years later George McManus collaborated with the famous French animator Emile Cohl to produce the *Baby Snookums* series of animated cartoons based on his strip (1912-1914).

M.H.

NEWMAN, PAUL S. (1924-   ) Paul S. Newman (no relation to the movie actor) bills himself as King of the Comic Book Writers, and he may well be right. Born in Brooklyn, New York, on April 29, 1924, he attended Dartmouth College, majoring in 17th- and early 18th-century drama, before seeing service in World War II. Aspiring to become a playwright, he wrote a number of plays while he was still in his 20s, but none of these were ever produced. In 1947 he received an introduction to National Periodicals (now D.C. Comics) and it wasn't long before he had wrangled his first writing assignment; from then on, there was no stopping him.

Newman's first comic book script was for *A Date With Judy*, based on a then-popular radio show. Thus encouraged, he branched out. "Within three years I was working for 12 different publishers," he relates. His credits during these years included scripts for *Patsy Walker*, *Crime Detective*, *The Two-Gun Kid*, and *Hopalong Cassidy*.

His Western stories finally led to assignment to the title Newman is best remembered for, *The Lone Ranger*. In 1951 he succeeded Fran Striker, the creator of the series, as the main writer on the title, a position he would keep for the next quarter-century. Newman milked every plot and cliché from the Western genre; North and South, from the Canadian border to the Painted Desert, his masked rider and faithful companion Tonto proved the scourge of every lawbreaker who ever rode the West. The stories were always interesting, sometimes gripping, and they earned him the scriptwriter's spot on the *Lone Ranger* newspaper strip in 1961.

In addition to his work on *The Lone Ranger*, he continued to turn out scripts for every possible comic book company. Among the more than 350 titles he contributed to were such now-classic names as *Airboy*, *Archie*, *Captain Marvel*, *G.I. Joe*, *Roy Rogers*, *Superman*, and *Zorro*; he received no credit on any of these. "In the world of comic book writing," Greg Metcalf stated in the *Journal of Popular Culture*, "chances are that Anonymous is Paul S. Newman."

Only in 1976 did he finally receive a credit in an issue of *Turok, Son of Stone*, a title he had been writing for the previous 20 years. Next to *The Lone Ranger*, *Turok* is Newman's most notable achievement. For 27 years he scripted every single issue of the continuing saga of Turok and Andar, two 19th-century Native Americans lost in a primitive world of cavemen and

"The Newlyweds" ("Snookums"), George McManus. © King Features Syndicate.

dinosaurs. In the course of a career that has already spanned half a century, Newman has also written plays, children's stories, radio skits, song lyrics, and newspaper comics (notably *Tom Corbett, Space Cadet* and *Robin Malone*, in addition to *The Lone Ranger*).

Recognition has finally come to the author in the 1990s. He has been interviewed and profiled in several publications, and in 1993 comic book historian Robin Snyder was able to document the fact that to date Newman had written over 4,000 comic book stories for 350 different titles. This incredible fact alone would make him worthy of special mention, had not his writing abilities, solid craftmanship, and sense of humor already earned him a privileged place in the history of the medium.

M.H.

NEW MUTANTS, THE (U.S.) *The New Mutants* were a group spun off from the *X-Men*, and first appeared in a Marvel graphic novel of that title in 1982. The new-comers enjoyed enough popularity in their first solo outing to warrant a comic book line of their own the following year.

The New Mutants were teenage heroes who had acquired their superpowers genetically (instead of getting them from external sources). They formed a heterogeneous phalanx of justice-fighters from diverse social, religious, and ethnic backgrounds who all shared the common bond of being persecuted for their "otherness." They had been brought together for training and mutual support by Professor X, the head honcho of the X-Men. While going through the rigors of a martial education, they also found time to fight a wide assortment of villains and alien menaces.

Chris Claremont created this team of teenaged wonders and endowed the story of their growing together into a close-knit unit with genuine pathos and humor. When *New Mutants* went into a regular monthly title a year after its initial appearance, he created some compelling narratives; consequently, the comic book enjoyed instant, if short-lived, success. The title also had the great luck of attracting top artistic talent to its banner, including John Buscema, Bill Sienkiewicz, Rob Liefeld, and Todd McFarlane. It also had some good writing from Claremont, who produced a clever variation on the tired superhero theme, but after a couple of years he seemed to grow tired himself. After its initial rocket-like takeoff, *The New Mutants* started to come down steadily; it ended neatly with issue number 100 (April 1991).

M.H.

NEWSBOY LEGION (U.S.) After Joe Simon and Jack Kirby launched the first of all comic book kid groups at Timely during the summer of 1941, they moved to National to create their second kid group in April 1942. Beginning in *Star-Spangled* number seven, the *Newsboy Legion* was the first of two superior kid groups the pair invented for National, the other being *Boy Commandos*. The Newsboy Legion was comprised of four ghetto youths: Big Words, the brains of the group; Tommy, the closest of all to the middle-class ideal; Gabby, and Scrapper. They were aided (or monitored) in their exploits by the Guardian, who was really slum policeman Jim Harper.

The strip's origin chronicles the sad tale of rookie policeman Jim Harper, who, during his off-duty hours from the "Suicide Slum" beat, was severely beaten.

Instead of taking the message to cooperate with the powers-that-be of the ghetto, the zealous Harper declared the attack "the last straw," spirited himself into a nearby costume shop and gathered up a blue and gold superhero suit complete with a badge-shaped shield. (Naturally, Harper left payment behind.) Dubbing himself the Guardian, the cop caught his attacker and meted out punishment he could not have employed as a crimefighter within the law.

Later in the original story, Patrolman Harper arrested the Newsboy Legion in the midst of their theft of tools (meant to build their clubhouse), but saved them from a reformatory school by agreeing to be their guardian. Thus, the group and its protector are formed, and, for the next five years, they combated crime blithely. The kids weren't supposed to know that Patrolman Harper, their legal guardian, and the costumed Guardian were one and the same, but they were not easily fooled. They discovered the dual-identity straightaway, but proceeded to keep that fact from Jim Harper throughout the group's career.

The *Newsboy Legion* ran through the 63rd issue of *Star-Spangled* (January 1947) before disappearing with many of its crimefighting compatriots. But when Jack Kirby returned to National in 1971, the second generation *Newsboy Legion* group was introduced in *Jimmy Olsen*. Androids genetically produced from body tissue of the original Legion, the revived group was used as another component of Kirby's complicated "Third World" series.

J.B.

NIBSY THE NEWSBOY (U.S.) A short-lived but very impressive early Sunday strip by George McManus, *Nibsy the Newsboy* (which ran in the *New York World* from April 1905 to July 29, 1906) was originally based on one of the *World*'s street newshawkers that McManus had once seen and liked. Nibsy was a skinny, felt-hatted, shock-haired kid of about 14 who quickly found himself involved in the affairs of a fantasy kingdom he was able to enter as easily as Nemo could dream himself into Slumberland. In fact, it was easier, because Nibsy did not have to dream his way into what McManus called Funny Fairyland, but found

"Nibsy the Newsboy," George McManus.

it around almost any corner of a downtown New York street.

McManus's strip, most often titled in full as *Nibsy the Newsboy in Funny Fairyland*, was a genial takeoff of Winsor McCay's *Little Nemo in Slumberland*, with McManus jovially vulgarizing many of the imaginative elements McCay treated fancifully in his own strip. The boy hero meets a fairy king's daughter turned into a donkey, who is uglier than the donkey when she is retransformed into herself; he uses a magic sword to conjure up an army for the fairy king, but the army falls to fighting among its own members and manages to get the king into the slugfest as well. The king is even able to return Nibsy's visits, as he does in the final episode of the strip, to be trampled in the mob leaving a New York baseball game and run down in automobile traffic. Deliberately crude devices were used to kid McCay's subtle concepts, and McManus continued to draw *Nibsy* at the peak of his graphic imagination. As a result, the strip is one of the high points of comic strip art and vitally in need of reprinting in full, preferably in color.

The troublesome thing about McManus strips like *Nibsy* (and *Panhandle Pete, Spareribs and Gravy*, and others) with their highly colorful narrative, superb comic figures, and constantly inventive graphics that make every large panel an individual visual delight, is that his later successful and more long-lived works like *Their Only Child, Rosie's Beau*, and *Bringing Up Father* seem dull in comparison. One rather resents them for usurping the imagination which might perhaps better have been allowed to continue romping in Funny Fairyland with Nibsy and the ugly enchanted princess.

B.B.

NICHOLLS, SYDNEY WENTWORTH (1896-1977) Cartoonist born 1896 at Frederick Henry Bay, Tasmania, with the surname of Jordan. After his mother remarried, he adopted the name of his stepfather in 1908. Because his stepfather worked on railway tunnels, Nicholls was educated in a number of schools throughout New South Wales and New Zealand. On leaving school in 1910 he attended art classes until he was 21, the last four years being spent at the Royal Art Society, Sydney. His first published art appeared in the *International Socialist* in 1912, and by 1914 his cartoons were accepted by *The Bulletin*.

One of his cartoons for *Direct Action* caused the magazine's editor, Tom Barker, to be jailed for 12 months for publishing material prejudicial to recruiting. In 1917 he began designing art titles and posters for motion pictures and stayed in this field for the next five years. During this time he was responsible for titles and posters for *The Sentimental Bloke* and many Snowy Baker films. He joined the staff of the Syndey *News* and in 1923, as senior artist, was invited to produce a colored Sunday strip to compete with *Ginger Meggs/Us Fellers*, which was proving very popular in the *Sunday Sun*. The result was *Fatty Finn*, first called *Fat and his Friends*, which debuted on September 16. The strip became popular and in 1927 a motion picture, called *Kid Stakes*, was produced using the characters from Nicholls's strip. Three colored *Fatty Finn Annuals* were published during 1928-30. In 1931, the *News* merged with the *Sunday Sun* and *Fatty Finn* was dropped.

Nicholls went to New York where he tried to sell his adventure strip, *Middy Malone*. Developed in 1929, *Malone* was one of the world's first adventure strips created for newspapers. Late in 1931, Nicholls ghosted a number of weeks of Ad Carter's *Just Kids*. Unable to sell his strip, he returned to Australia in 1932. In 1934 he began publishing a tabloid-size comic, *Fatty Finn's Weekly*, but by 1935 he was back designing for the motion picture field, where he stayed until 1940. In 1941 he produced the first of a series of colored books devoted to *Middy Malone*, as well as commencing production on a series of comic books featuring the work of other Australian artists as well as his own.

He founded his own comic line in 1946 which ran until 1950. In 1951, after an absence of 20 years, *Fatty Finn* returned to newspapers when it appeared in the *Sunday Herald*. Following a merger, the strip transferred to the *Sun-Herald* in October 1953 where it continues to appear.

In his formative years, Nicholls was influenced by the work of Will Dyson, Norman Lindsay, Alf Vincent, Dan Smith, and *The Bulletin* school—yet he developed a very distinctive and personalized style of fine line art. His figures generated movement and his detailed linework on sailing ships was not only effective but accurate. His book *About Ships—from the Egyptian Galley to the Queen Elizabeth* is an outstanding work in this area.

Because of his strong antisyndication beliefs, Syd Nicholls and the characters he created were seldom received sympathetically by newspaper managements. He was the first to produce all-Australian comics and, in company with Syd Miller, did more to foster the cause of local artists and writers than any other publisher. He was a former president of the Australian Journalist's Club. Sydney Nicholls died on June 3, 1977.

J.R.

NICK DER WELTRAUMFAHRER (Germany) *Nick der Weltraumfahrer* ("Nick the Spaceman") was the response of Lehning Verlag, a German comic book publishing house, to the sputnik shock of the late 1950s. Science fiction had been one of the staples of dime novels before the first rocket putting a satellite in orbit had been launched. But until then science fiction in comic books was relatively rare in Germany, most of the material being imported. Sputnik came just in time to help launch a science-fiction comic series created, written, and drawn by a very prolific German, Hansrudi Wäscher.

Nick der Weltraumfahrer started on his journeys through space in January 1958 in the piccolo (or Italian) format of $2^{7}/_8 \times 6^{7}/_8$ inches so favored by Lehning Verlag. This first series of books ended after 139 issues in September 1960. This did not ground Nick, however, as the daring black-haired hero had already started additional adventures in a color comic book of more standard proportions in January 1959. This book was titled *Nick. Pionier des Weltraums* ("Nick. Pioneer of Space") and enjoyed a run of 121 books, ending in July 1963. The last 10 books reverted to the title of the original piccolo series but added the subtitle "space magazine." *Nick* reprints appeared in a *Tarzan* comic book in the early 1960s, in *Harry*, in a "piccolo giant" series, and in a *Nick* special.

By and large, Nick was a hero of the late 1950s and early 1960s. He became slightly outdated when his crewcut became obsolete. His disappearance may also have been connected with a growing sophistication in science-fiction stories, something *Nick* was not geared

"Nick," Hansrudi Wäscher. © Hansrudi Wäscher.

for because its space-opera format used the usual threats-of-strange-environments plot (but seemingly took care to avoid the bug-eyed monster routine). The strip held up while it lasted, making many readers devoted fans of science fiction and of the Wäscher style which, although effective telling a story, lacked the visual extravaganza that would have helped to turn the series into a classic.

A first set of reprints was published in 1976. The entire *Nick* material of piccolo-sized comics and regular-sized comic books was again reprinted in 1982. A new series of *Nick* comics also features stories that are not illustrated by Hansrudi Wäscher.

W.F.

NICKEL, HELMUT (1924-   ) Helmut Nickel was born in 1924 in a small village south of Dresden where his father worked as school principal. As a kid he liked visiting the zoo and the Museum of History in Dresden, as well as the museum of German novelist Karl May in Radebeul. There he liked to copy some of the exhibits. Drawing came to him naturally; his only study was an evening course when he was 15.

After graduation from high school, Nickel wanted to become a veterinarian and work in a zoo. Instead he was inducted into the army, spent three years serving in Russia during World War II, and another three years as a prisoner of war. When he returned home to what was now East Germany, he stood no chance of receiving permission to study because he came from a bourgeois family, so he worked in advertising for movies and illustrated children's books.

When he heard that a Free University was being founded in West Berlin, he left the East. Again, however, he could not study to become a veterinarian because there was no faculty of natural sciences at the university, so he studied the history of art. In order to pay for his studies he started working as a freelance graphic designer on the side. This led to contacts with comics publishers in 1952.

The first comic book he wrote and drew was *Die drei Musketiere* ("The Three Musketeers," 1952). He went on to do various other comic books, working for the Western comic book *Hot Jerry* (with scripts by Fritz Klein), and writing and drawing *Don Pedro*, the science-fiction adventures of *Titanus* (the first issue was 3-D), as well as comic features *Francis Drake* and *Peters seltsame Reisen* ("Peter's Strange Voyages"). *Peters seltsame Reisen* was a serialized comics parody along the lines of "The Secret Life of Walter Mitty" that featured a youthful hero, Peter, stumbling through all kinds of comic adventures by meeting comic book heroes like Nick the astronaut or Akim the jungle hero, and later meeting characters from literature. Nickel also created cover illustrations for a *Tarzan* comic book and for a number of pulp novels, and wrote and drew several issues of *Winnetou*, based on the novels of Karl May.

Nickel left the comics field in the early 1960s to take a position with a museum in Berlin. He also earned his doctorate in history. After this he took a position as curator for arms and armor with the Metropolitan Museum of Art in New York, where he worked until he retired in 1988. Although Nickel looks back fondly on his work in the comics, much of which has been reprinted, he never regretted his decision to move to New York. While this move may have been in the best interest of both Helmut Nickel and the Metropolitan Museum, it was a loss for comics published in Germany.

Helmut Nickel always managed to instill into his comics a sense of historic reality and reliability. His heroes, although quite adventuresome, were never musclebound, and his pen-and-ink artwork always stood out because of an intrinsic elegance. Publishers did not always appreciate the amount of talking Nickel's heroes sometimes did, but he always had so much story to tell—and historic background to explain—that he felt he sometimes had to put all the necessary information into dialogue balloons and captions. What made Nickel's comics special were a dose of wry humor and a tendency toward caricature, especially in supporting characters.

W.F.

Helmut Nickel, "Titanus." © Helmut Nickel.

NICK KNATTERTON (Germany) *Nick Knatterton* (one possible literal translation of the name would be "Nick Rattlesound") was created one autumn night in 1950 by Manfred Schmidt in order to satirize *Superman.* Anton Sailer, cartoon editor of the German weekly illustrated paper *Quick,* accepted the adventures of the pointy-headed detective for publication. He felt the feature would not last eight weeks unless it contained lots of well-proportioned females—which it did.

Nick Knatterton was an instant success. Manfred Schmidt had intended to make fun of the comics and, because of the success of the feature, ended up drawing an extremely successful comic feature for ten years. At one time he retired the hero by marrying him off. But his pipe-smoking creation returned to haunt him for some more years until, after more than 500 weekly episodes, Schmidt definitely killed the feature.

In addition to satirizing the likes of *Superman, Dick Tracy,* and *Sherlock Holmes, Nick Knatterton* also offered political satire that was sometimes quoted in the Houses of Parliament of the Federal Republic of Germany. Schmidt used the strip as a vehicle for political satire after the initial idea of satirizing comics had become routine. For much of his work on *Nick Knatterton* Schmidt depended heavily on his cool witticism instead of the brilliance of his art.

The adventures of Nick Knatterton the super sleuth were reprinted in seven album-size comic books and, in 1971-72, in two hardcover volumes. Foreign editions of the strip underwent some surprising changes. In the Netherlands edition in the Amsterdam paper *Volkskrant,* the well-rounded girls had to trim their shapely figures on the altar of chastity, whereas in the Turk paper *Millyet* an artist had to add to the girls' measurements. *Nick Knatterton* was even reprinted in Iron Curtain countries.

The *Knatterton* success led to a movie that was well received by the critics and the public. Based on the *Knatterton* story "Der Raub der Gloria Nylon" ("The Kidnapping of Gloria Nylon"), the motion picture added some comic climaxes like a bar brawl in which Nick Knatterton fights and downs two dozen gangsters to the tune of Mozart's *Kleine Nachtmusik* coming from a jukebox.

Knatterton dolls, card games, coloring books, masks, decals, schnapps, and even orange wrappers turned *Nick Knatterton* into an even bigger commercial success. Manfred Schmidt, after killing off *Knatterton,* continued writing humorous articles for *Quick,* illustrating them in his seemingly simple style.

When the strip's creator had spread out into the field of animated cartoons for advertising he was promptly asked to do his original strips as animated cartoons. Despite some initial misgivings, Manfred Schmidt did start doing *Nick Knatterton* again. The animation actually had the feel of the original strip, because Schmidt's studio did the cartoons, and with Schmidt supplying the narration himself, the animated cartoons have an added dimension the original strips never had: the ironic and sarcastic voice of the feature's creator. The *Nick Knatterton* cartoons were originally made to be aired with continuity, like the original strip. The animated *Nick Knatterton* has since been made available on videocassette.

"Nick Knatterton," Manfred Schmidt. © Manfred Schmidt.

For a comic strip that was originally intended as an anticomic strip, *Nick Knatterton* helped popularize comics in Germany while turning itself into a classic example of the possibilities the comic form offers to satire.

W.F.

"91 Karlsson," Rudolf Petersson. © Rudolf Petersson.

91 KARLSSON (Sweden) *91 Karlsson*, or simply *91:an* ("Soldier No. 91") in the comic book version, is Sweden's most popular comic strip. It was created in 1932 by Swedish artist Rudolf Petersson for the weekly *Allt för Alla*, which had already premiered a number of Swedish strips like Axel Backman's *Burre Busse*, Petter Lindroth's *Jocke, Nicke och Majken* (1921), and Elov Persson's *Kronblom*. The trend had been started by *Allt för Alla* in 1912 with Knut Stangenberg's *Fridolf Celinder*. When *Allt för Alla* merged with *Vårt Hem* in 1933, all strips except *91 Karlsson* were kept. *91 Karlsson* moved on to *Lefvande Livet*. Today, the strip is published in *Året Runt* and has been drawn since 1960 by Nils Egerbrandt. The strip survived its creator, Petersson, who died on April 24, 1970, aged 73. In 1965 Petersson had received the first Adamson, the annual comics Oscar awarded by Svenska Serieakademin, the Swedish Comics Academy. Annuals of *91:an* have been published since 1934; the *91:an* comic book started in 1956.

91 Karlsson started out with a simple farmer's son, Mandel Karlsson, being drafted to serve in the army and, at first, rather realistically showed the troubles he was having adapting to army life in the Halmstad garrison. The strip's creator knew well enough what he was writing about and drawing as he, too, had been in Halmstad during World War I. But after a few years the strip concentrated more on the private aspects of soldiers' lives.

Considerable space was devoted to Karlsson's courting of Elvira, Captain Berån's girl. 91 Karlsson had to compete with his friend and costar, 87 Axelsson, in trying to win Elvira's favors, however. Not unexpectedly,

91 Karlsson is nice, if a bit dense, whereas 87 Axelsson is mean and smart.

The characters of *91 Karlsson* are well rounded and made additionally attractive because of the different stylized dialects which highlight individuality and believability. It is the characterization and the very civilian humor of this parody of army life that ensures continued success for *91 Karlsson* and the *91:an* comic book, as well as for other Swedish strips like *47:an Löken*, which takes up army life in a humorous vein.

W.F.

NINJA BUGEICHŌ (Japan) *Ninja Bugeichō* (subtitled "The Life of Kagemaru") was created by Sanpei Shirato and made its first appearance in a comic book published in December 1959. Seventeen books of *Ninja Bugeichō* were published (its last appearance was in March 1962). *Ninja* soon became the top-selling *kashibonya manga* (comic books published for the exclusive use of lending libraries) of its day; however, these had only a small run and were known only to patrons of the lending library. In 1966 *Ninja Bugeichō* made a reappearance in a series of small comic books published by an important company; it soon became their best seller as well (it was the first time that *Ninja* appeared in a mass-circulation comic book).

The action of the strip took place during Japan's Age of Wars (1560-1588) when the peasants and the ruling samurais were locked in a merciless class war. Kagemaru was a leader of the peasant revolts who enjoyed a charmed life; his invulnerability was due to a dummy created in his likeness, called Kage Ichizoku, that gave him special powers. Kage Ichizoku was destroyed by a female spy, however, and Kagemaru himself was executed by the samurai chieftain Nobunaga, who subsequently made himself master of the realm.

In this long strip Shirato depicted battle scenes with realistic detail, as well as gruesome scenes of death

"Ninja Bugeichō," Sanpei Shirato. © Sanpei Shirato.

(individual or of whole masses of people). The bloody sequences were moderated by romantic interludes. The strip's success was phenomenal, and Shirato achieved a fame comparable to that of Osamu Tezuka.

At the time when *Ninja Bugeichō* was a success as a *kashibon manga* it gave rise to countless imitations (*Ninja Zankokushou* was only one of them). *Ninja Bugeichō* was also made into a motion picture.

H.K.

NIÑO, ALEX N. (1940-   ) Filipino cartoonist born May 1, 1940, in Tarlac. As a child Alex Niño spent many hours just outside of his home drawing on the ground. When he finished, he would erase the drawing and start all over again. He loved to draw, and one of his boyhood dreams was to become a comic book artist. After much perseverance and tribulation, he finally got his chance to work for some of the more obscure titles in the Philippines. Unfortunately, not all of them paid him, but he was happy to be published.

In 1965 he teamed up with Clodualdo del Mundo to do *Kilabot Ng Persia* ("The Terror of Persia") for *Pilipino Komiks*. This was an adventure novel reminiscent of the Arabian Night fables. Later he joined Marcelo B. Isidro to work for *Redondo Komix*. They did *Dinoceras*, a story about a prehistoric creature surviving in modern times. Then in 1966, for *Pioneer Komiks*, he illustrated his own feature, *Gruaga—The Fifth Corner of the World*. This fantasy epic gave Niño a chance to use his fertile imagination and display his artistic ability. During that same period he combined with Virgo Villa on *Tsannga Rannga* for *Espesyal*, and with Amado S. Castrillo, who wrote *Maligno* for *Redondo Komix*.

Eventually Niño began to illustrate for *Alcala Komix*. His stint with this publication produced many memorable artistic achievements. He drew *Mga Matang Nagliliyab* ("The Eyes that Glow in the Dark"), a serialized novel written by Isidro. This title contains some of the most beautiful graphics to ever appear in the comic medium. It combined technical virtuosity with innovative layouts and storytelling. At this stage he developed a calligraphic drawing style that gave his illustrations a rhythmic and flowing quality.

Despite numerous assignments for *Redondo* and *Alcala Komix*, Niño continued to freelance for other companies, among them PSG Publications. At PSG he did a series of short stories dealing with Bruhilda Witch. These short mystery and horror tales enabled him to elaborate and experiment, resulting in some unique visual effects. Because Pablo Gomez's forte was dramatic stories, Alex Niño did many novels in the usual, straightforward manner, but even then he managed to use several drawing styles to add individuality to each story. When many of his collaborations with Gomez were made into motion pictures, Niño started to do movie ads in the realistic mode.

Not content working only for local publishers, Niño also drew for various American publications such as D.C., Gold Key, Peterson, Educational Classics, and Marvel. He penciled the first *Black Orchid* story for National and inked some of the Sunday *Tarzan* strips for United Feature Syndicate. For D.C. he handled *Captain Fear*, *Korak*, *Space Voyagers*, and many mystery and horror stories. He did *Conan*, *Man-Gods*, and the unique short story *Repent Harlequin, Said the Tick Tock Man* for Marvel comics.

Alex Niño, magazine illustration. © Orvy Jundis.

Alex Niño has received numerous awards in the Philippines and the United States. In 1974 the International Science-Fantasy Society, in cooperation with the Philippine Comic Archives and the Philippine Science-Fantasy Society, sponsored Niño on a visit to the United States to attend the World Science Fiction Convention. Unlike many of his compatriots, Niño chose to remain in the United States, where he has enjoyed a solid if unspectacular career. In 1983 he and Trevor Von Eeden created *Thriller* for D.C. Comics; since then he has worked for virtually every U.S. comic book publisher on such titles as *House of Mystery, House of Secrets, Valeria the She-Bat, Bold Adventures,* and *Star Reach Classics.*

O.J.

NIPPER (G.B.) *The Nipper* (who later lost his "The") was created by Brian White as a daily pantomime strip. Rejected by the *London Evening Standard*, it was immediately accepted by the *Daily Mail*, where it ran nationally from August 30, 1933, to July 1947, with a break of a few years during the war.

Nipper, a small boy in frock and diapers, grew slightly older over the years, allowing for a companion to join him in mischief. Called Nobby, this bald baby with but a single hair became Nipper's brother, but was originally a neighbor's child. The other regulars in the strip were Nipper's proud but suffering father and his distraught mother. The gag-a-day format was occasionally varied to permit continuity and the use of speech balloons.

Nipper's popularity rose rapidly as parents recognized in his adventures a genuine humor. In fact, White

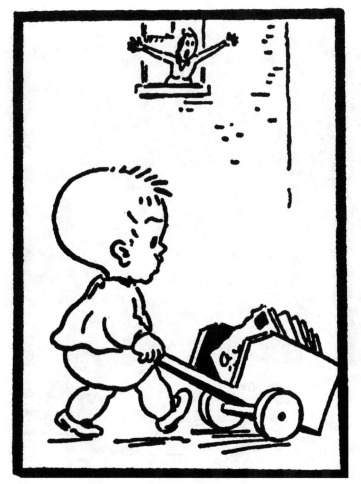

"Nipper," Brian White. © Associated Newspapers Ltd.

based Nipper on his own "nipper," his young son John. A weekly page, *Nipperisms*, was added to his output, and the strips were reprinted annually in a thick paperback, *Nipper Annual*. The first was published on December 7, 1934, the last (dated 1942) in 1941. Altogether there were eight annuals, several with full-color, 16-page sections. (The last two were in reduced format due to wartime paper shortages.) Other spin-offs included *Nipper* postcards in color for valentines, a series of color booklets in the *Merry Miniatures* giveaway comics (1937-39), *Nipper* dolls by Merrythought, *Nipper* figures in china by E. C. Hales, and *Nipper* brooches.

In the postwar period White revived *Nipper* for his own publishing company, having retained the copyright of the character. He reprinted some of the strips in painting books and comic books, and drew new adventures for Road Safety propaganda called *Careful Nippers*. He also produced *Nipper* film strips for home viewers. From March 7, 1959, he drew *Nipper* weekly for *Woman's Day*, until that magazine folded in 1961.

D.G.

NIXON, ROBERT (1935-) Bob Nixon, one of the few modern comic artists permitted to sign his comic pages for the Scottish publisher D. C. Thompson, has a delightfully recognizable style of rounded figures in rapid action; his *King Arthur and the Frights of the Round Table* (1974) for *Whoopee* is masterly in its combination of period and traditional comic style.

Robert T. Nixon was born about 1935 in Southbank, the son of a steelworker. He went to the local Secondary Modern school, where his teachers encouraged his artistic interests, and Bob eventually won a scholarship to Middleborough Art College. He was forced to leave Middleborough after three months because of his father's death, however, and took a job in a printing factory's art department, where he was apprenticed to a lithographic artist. After 10 years, Bob decided to try freelancing to children's comics and sent some samples to *Beano*. Harry Crammond, then the editor, let Bob try his hand at a *Little Plum Your Redskin Chum* strip (created by Leo Baxendale). It was successful enough to warrant a few more fill-ins, and in 1965 Bob decided to freelance full time.

Bob's *Beano* work really began in earnest with *Roger the Dodger*, which he would draw for eight years. Then he took over *Lord Snooty and His Pals* after the death of Dudly Watkins, the strip's creator. Although he succeeded quite well, imitation of another artist's style did not suit Bob's development as an original. Other Thompson work included *Grandpa* for *Beano*, and *Esky Mo* and *Captain Cutler* for *Sparky*.

In the 1970s, Bob moved to the London comic publisher IPC and took over two Reg Parlett series, *Hire a Horror* and *Ivor Lott and Tony Broke*, in *Cor*. Comic horrors suited Bob and he began to specialize in these popular strips for editor Bob Paynter. His work included *Soggy the Sea Monster* (in *Shiver and Shake*), *Frankie Stein* (Bob's favorite character, created by Ken Reid), and *Kid Kong*, about a childlike monster gorilla, based on the Edgar Wallace film, that became the front page star for the *Monster Fun* comic (1975). Soon he was drawing six pages of comic strips per week, as well as special features for the Christmas annuals, summer specials, and other publications. His work included *Kid King* (*Jackpot*), *The Buy-tonic Boy* (*Whizzer & Chips*), *Stage School* (*Whoopee*), *Gums* (a parody of the film *Jaws*,

Claudio Nizzi and Lino Landolfi, "Occhio di Luna." © Nizzi and Landolfi.

in *Monster Fun*), and many others. In addition, he drew cartoon greeting cards, illustrated children's paperbacks, and drew a daily newspaper strip, *The Gems*, for the *Sun*, beginning in 1976.

D.G.

NIZE BABY (U.S.) Milt Gross's first Sunday color page, the funny and inventive *Nize Baby* (1927-29) first appeared in national syndication through the *New York World* on January 2, 1927. It was based on characters Gross had lovingly created more than half a decade earlier in his *Gross Exaggerations* (an illustrated column of comic narrative); these characters had also just appeared in a book based on the column, the bestselling *Nize Baby* (1926).

The comic strip, like the column, featured a first-generation Jewish family of New York called the Feitlebaums. The strip family included the title character, a nefarious infant simply called "Nize baby" by his loving mother; the mother herself, variously called Momma, Mama, and Mom Feitlebaum; her husband, Morris; and Baby's brothers, the six-year-old Isadore and the near-grown Looy Dot Dope. (In the column and book, these people were divided into three different families, living on successive floors of an apartment house; in joining them into one family and dropping various parents here and there, Gross retained only one other family head from the column for occasional use in the strip, Mrs. Yifnif of the second floor.)

Basically, the comedy of the strip evolved out of the hilarious interrelations of the family members, rather than from the ethnic humor and dialogue emphasized in the column and book. Mr. Feitlebaum's failure to persuade the distracted Isadore to take Baby off his hands at vital moments led to slapstick disaster of Keystone dimensions; Looy Dot Dope's brash stupidity led to the collapse of houses and major train wrecks, while Baby's disastrous antics had to be read to be believed. This strip, which would have been a lifetime success for a lesser cartoonist, was dismissed in favor of fresher conceptions by Gross a bare two years after it had been launched, to be replaced by *Count Screwloose of Tooloose* on February 17, 1929. The hundred or so *Nize Baby* pages remain as funny today as ever, and are a major accomplishment in the history of the American comic strip.

B.B.

NIZZI, CLAUDIO (1938-   ) One of the most prolific Italian scriptwriters and comics character creators, born September 9, 1938 in Setif, Algeria. Working as a technician in a tractor factory, in 1960 Claudio Nizzi started contributing short novels to the weekly *Il Vittorioso*. Two years later his first comic adventure, *Il segreto del castello*, appeared, followed by *Safari*, a long series set in Africa and drawn by Renato Polese, which continued up to 1966 when the weekly ceased publication.

For the next three years he wrote novels and short stories that were printed in popular women's magazines such as *Novella*, *Grand Hotel*, *Confidenze*, and *Bella*. In 1969 he went he back to comics and started collaborating with the catholic weekly *Il Giornalino*, for which he created characters such as *Piccolo Dente* (1970) and *Il Colonnello Caster Bum* (1970), both drawn by Lino Landolfi; *Larry Yuma* (1971), drawn by Carlo Boscarato and later by Nadir Quinto; *Capitan Erik* (1972), drawn by Ruggero Giovannini and later by Attilio Micheluzzi; *Il tenente Marlo* (1977), drawn by Sergio Zaniboni; *Rosco & Sonny* (1981), drawn by Giancarlo Alessandrini and later by Rodolfo Torti; *Nicoletta* (1981), drawn by Clod; and others. Nizzi has also adapted in comics form several classic tales like Jules Verne's *The Mysterious Island* and *Un capitano di 15 anni*, Charles Dicken's *Oliver Twist*, Victor Hugo's *Les Miserables*, Robert Louis Stevenson's *Treasure Island*, Lewis Carroll's *Alice in Wonderland*, and Mark Twain's *The Adventures of Tom Sawyer*, as well as *Robin Hood* and *The Adventures of Ulysses*. In 1981 Nizzi began his collaboration with the publisher Sergio Bonelli, for whom he wrote stories for the *Mister No* and *Tex* series, created the criminal series *Nick Raider* (1988), and wrote short novels. At present, he is the official scriptwriter of the western series *Tex* (born in 1948); it is the oldest Italian comic still in existence and one of the most popular.

G.C.C.

NOBODY WANTS BILLY BUNTER *see* Billy Bunter.

NONKINA TOUSAN (Japan) Nonkina Tousan ("Easygoing Daddy"), created by Yutaka Aso, made its first appearance in the *Sunday Hochi* in October 1923. The motivation of the strip was to give hope and comfort to the people of the Kanto district in Japan who had seen their homes destroyed by the great earthquake of September 1, 1923. And indeed the strip did succeed in lifting the spirits of many of its readers.

Nonkina Tousan, a middle-aged, bespectacled man always wearing a splash-pattern kimono and a black Japanese coat, was a kind and cheerful person. Indefatigable, he would crisscross the streets of Tokyo and do his bit for the reconstruction of the city, spreading hope and good cheer in his wake. The strip met unprecedented success, and several books of Nonkina's adventures were published, rapidly becoming bestsellers.

Nonkina Tousan is also credited with bringing the modern daily strip (consisting of four panels across) to Japan. Its debut as a daily took place in January 1924 in the daily edition of *Hochi*, where it continued until October 1925. After that date, *Nonkina Tousan* was carried by a number of Japanese magazines. It folded in 1950.

Nonkina Tousan also inspired several motion pictures, Tousan dolls, and a song, *Non Tou Bushi*, which was very popular in the 1920s.

H.K.

NORAKURO (Japan) Created by Suihou Tagawa, *Norakuro* made its first appearance in the January 1931 issue of the monthly *Shōnen Kurabu* as *Norakuro Nitohēi* ("Private Second Class Norakuro").

Noraini Kurokichi ("Kurokichi the stray dog"), alias Norakuro, was a parentless, homeless little dog; but Norakuro had pledged to become a world-famous general and to this end he joined the Mōken Rentai ("fierce dog regiment") under the command of Buru the bulldog. At first Norakuro made repeated mistakes, but he later rescued regiment commander Buru and his captain Mōru from the enemy Yamazaru ("mountain monkeys"), and saved the battle flag from the pig army. With the passing of time, Norakuro earned his bars and became a professional soldier. Losing all personality, he became the perfect soldier, was promoted to lieutenant, and was twice decorated. The militarism rampant in Japan at the time greatly influenced the development of the strip.

After rising to the rank of captain, Norakuro retired from the army and became a continental pioneer (a euphemism for colonial settler) in Manchuria and Mongolia. He made his last appearance in the December 1941 issue of *Shōnen Kurabu*.

After the war an attempt to revive *Norakuro* in the pages of *Shōnen Kurabu* proved unsuccessful; the feature fared better in the monthly war comic magazine *Maru*, where it has been flourishing since 1958. *Norakuro* also appeared in the monthly *Manga Gekijo* in 1963, and was given his own comic book in 1964. Before the war a series of *Norakuro* hardcover books sold over a million copies; a new series of books was released after the war, starting in 1969. *Norakuro* has also inspired a series of animated cartoons, several motion pictures, and a number of records.

Norakuro is the most famous prewar comic strip, and also the oldest and longest-running feature in the whole history of Japanese comics: Suihou Tagawa and others have been drawing the strip for over 65 years.

H.K.

NORRIS, PAUL (1914-   ) American cartoonist born April 26, 1914 in Greenville, Ohio. Paul Norris studied journalism and art at Midland College in Fremont, Nebraska, and then went on to the Dayton (Ohio) Art Institute. In the late 1930s he started working as an illustrator and cartoonist for the *Dayton Daily News*, before moving to New York in 1940.

In New York, Norris started a career in comic books, first with Prize Publications, where he created and drew *Power Nelson, Futureman* (1940-42), and *Yank and Doodle* (1941-42); from there he went on to National, notably creating (with Mort Weisinger) *Aquaman* in 1941 and working on many other features, including *The Crimson Pirate, The Sandman,* and *TNT*. Norris drew his first newspaper strip in 1942 when he was asked to take over *Vic Jordan* for the New York daily *PM*.

Norris was drafted in 1943 and spent three years in the armed forces. After his return to civilian life, he was hired as a staff artist for King Features Syndicate, drawing the *Jungle Jim* and *Flash Gordon* comic books. Norris's big break at King Features came in 1948 when he was given the *Jungle Jim* Sunday feature. In 1952 he assumed the drawing of the *Brick Bradford* daily strip, and he started drawing the Sunday page in 1957. In the late 1950s Norris also sporadically ghosted Mel Graff's *Secret Agent X-9*. He went into retirement following the demise of *Brick Bradford* in 1987.

A cartoonist of limited artistic range, Paul Norris is one of the most glaring examples of the kind of second-rate workhorses KFS keeps throwing at an unwary public. In Norris's case the offense was compounded by the fact that he was asked to succeed such comic art luminaries as Alex Raymond and Austin Briggs (on *Jungle Jim*) and Clarence Gray (on *Brick Brad-*

"Norakuro," Suihou Tagawa. © Shōnen Kurabu.

ford), thus doing an injustice to both the creators and the readers.

M.H.

NOWLAN, PHILIP (1888-1940) American writer born 1888 in Philadelphia, Pennsylvania. After graduation from the University of Pennsylvania in 1910, Phil Nowlan embarked on a newspaper career in Philadelphia, where he worked successively on the *Public Ledger*, the *North American,* and the *Retail Ledger.* At the same time he started writing for science-fiction magazines (many of his published stories were signed by the pen name "Frank Phillips").

In the August 1928 issue of *Amazing Stories*, Phil Nowlan published a short novel, *Armaggedon 2419 A.D.*, about a 20th-century American pilot named Anthony Rogers who was overcome by toxic gas and reawakened five centuries later. The story was so popular that Nowlan wrote a sequel, *The Warlords of Han* (March 1929), that, together with his earlier story, was later published as a two-part novel under the umbrella title *Armageddon 2419 A.D.* The story also attracted the attention of John F. Dille, who convinced a skeptical Nowlan to adapt it into comic strip form; Dille also changed the hero's name from Anthony to Buck and hired former pilot Dick Calkins as the artist on the strip. *Buck Rogers 2429 A.D.* made its first appearance on January 7, 1929.

In subsequent years Phil Nowlan wrote a few more science fiction stories (for *Amazing* and *Astounding* among others) but his main contribution to the genre was the scenarios of *Buck Rogers*, which he continued to write until his death in Philadelphia on February 1, 1940.

Phil Nowlan was never regarded as a science-fiction author of note (none of his short stories were ever anthologized) and his fame rests solely upon the memories conjured up by the comic strip which he had been so reluctant to originate.

M.H.

NUS (Spain) The weekly collection of comic books published by Salvat Editores under the title "Vector 1" featured on its back cover, *Nus y el Atleta* ("Nus and the Athlete") by Enric Sío, the stylistic counterpart to *Sorang*. It began in October 1968.

Nus aspired to show a double perception of reality: one formed by the apparent, "official" aspect of things; the other "intuitive," consisting in the deductions of truth from appearance. Nus (from the Greek word meaning intellect)—a seer endowed with extra-sensory perception—is capable of divining or intuiting the truth that lies buried under the conventions of normal life.

One day he discovers that his friend, the athlete Quim Fibla, has been abducted by a madman. The pages present panels entirely rendered in black and white, projecting a phantasmic reality, as befits a dream world; this world was re-created from "real" elements, with the utilization of effects produced by the pseudosolarization of photographic negatives, a device previously used by Robert D. Routh and Giovanni Rutelli. When Nus, the protagonist, intuits the truth, this is graphically rendered by means of a color panel. But Sío's treatment is equally phantasmic, aiming at illustrating the mental images picked up by the hero, but not by those surrounding him. In these cases, color—always solarized—stands out all the more from the rest of the page illustrated only in black.

The plot of the strip started with a typical mystery story premise, enriched with connotative references to pop art, photography, posters, movies, and television.

Its plasticity was a forward step in relation to *Sorang*: the violent contrast between color and black-and-white has also been used by Sío for the illustration of record jackets and a Cortázar tale. The incorporation of analytical montages, slow motion, simultaneous representation of several levels of reality—visible, intuitive, etc.—into the narrative language of the comics, the conception of each page as a significant unit (or better, as a macrounit), were at the time absolutely new concepts introduced by Sío.

L.G.

OAKY DOAKS (U.S.) *Oaky Doaks* was launched in 1935 by the Associated Press, and drawn by veteran magazine cartoonist Ralph Briggs Fuller. Although it never forged the comic paths being charted at the time by AP companions Noel Sickles and Milton Caniff, *Oaky Doaks* was a solid entry—genuinely funny, superbly drawn, and well written.

Oaky, an honest, muscular, thickheaded, handsome medieval knight, was the hero, and his Sancho Panza was Cedric—chubby, lazy, bald, and bespectacled. The king, Corny, was a skinny crank, and Oaky's horse, Nellie, rounded out the regular cast; Nellie was trustworthy, often the smartest being in miles, and sometimes capable of supernatural feats.

Almost every episode (beginning in the 1940s) saw Oaky involved with the plight of a pretty maiden, a fringe benefit of knighthood and a great device for establishing bases for continuity and adding some glamour to the strip. Fuller's stories were always well spun and contained a delightful mix of real danger and action with all types of humor—visual, sophisticated, sarcastic, slapstick, and sometimes even topical. His women wisecracked the latest slang and generally—earthy as they were—were more logical and determined than the men in the strip. Each episode averaged four months in the dailies and two to four weeks in the Sundays.

Fuller's art was a thing to behold. For all its comic touches it seemed basically realistic, so accurate was his use of anatomy and composition. He also had a unique sense of action and could heighten that quality by the simple device of splitting up a movement—a sock to the jaw or a jump from a balcony—into two panel frames. His oafs (such as Oaky) were oafish, his women handsome, his villains comically menacing. In all, it was an immensely attractive strip until its demise, along with the AP Newsfeatures service, in 1961.

Oaky's adventures, which retained their strongest traits of witty characterizations and breezy, chummy self-kidding on the part of Fuller, are still enjoyable today. His classic strip was only dropped because the syndicate folded, and Fuller, who died two years later, sincerely wished to continue drawing it.

Oaky Doaks' motto was the pig-Latin "Onay Aday without a Oodgay Eedday," and Fuller's wonderful efforts were indeed a good deed a day to many fans.

R.M.

OBERLÄNDER, ADOLF (1845-1923) Adolf Oberländer, a German painter and cartoonist, was born October 1, 1845, in Regensburg and died on May 29, 1923, in Munich, Germany. After completing public and secondary schools he went to Munich to study art at the academy as a student of Piloty, a fact blissfully unnoticeable by his paintings and cartoons. Oberländer's interest turned toward satire and humorous cartoons. He completed his studies in the heyday of the *Fliegenden Blätter*, and it was only natural that he should join the ranks of that satirical magazine's staff, eventually becoming a kind of "house artist" and, with Wilhelm Busch and Edmund Harburger, one of the *Fliegenden Blätter*'s Big Three. Incidentally, he was not only a "house artist" because he regularly contributed to the magazine, but also because he lived in the house that harbored the offices of the magazine.

The *Fliegenden Blätter*, founded by Kaspar Braun and started on November 7, 1844, was the first German satiric magazine of renown to achieve about a century of regular publication. Published in Munich, the magazine could draw upon the best of the artist colony of Munich to fill its pages with witty cartoons and the best illustrations to be had. Well-known artists like Count Pocci, Moritz von Schwind, Carl Spitzweg, and Eduard Ille were among the regular contributors who questioned the artificial division of art into fine arts and graphic and/or comic arts.

The *Fliegenden Blätter* and similar magazines laid the foundation for the comic strip. Some of the material included in the pages of the *Fliegenden Blätter* no doubt must be counted among the earliest comic strips or, at least, as among the closest predecessors. This can be seen in the work of Busch and Oberländer. In layout and style, much of Oberländer's work looked like later comic strips. Oberländer made use of the German family's foibles and of anthropomorphic animals. He was also one of the artists to use a recurring strip character, the Bavarian Lion. From 1879 to 1901 the work of Oberländer was reprinted in 12 splendid albums. His *Schriebheft des kleinen Moritz* ("Copy-book of Little Moritz") offered humorous highlights of schools of the time.

W.F.

OESTERHELD, HECTOR GERMAN (1919-1977) The medium of comics has had its geniuses and its mountebanks, its noblemen and its toadies, occasionally its heroes, but very rarely has it had its martyrs, which makes Hector Oesterheld perhaps unique in the field. Born in Buenos Aires in 1919, he graduated with a degree in literature and began a writing career in the early 1940s, publishing short stories in the daily *La Prensa* and children's tales for the publishing house Codex. His real calling, however, only became apparent in 1950, the year he joined Editorial Abril, then one of the most important comics publishers in Argentina.

At Abril, Oesterheld worked with some of the most notable artists residing in Argentina at the time. He wrote scripts for Francisco Solano Lopez (*Uma-Uma*, a tale of the Andes, 1953), Carlos Freixas (*Indio Suarez*, another example of his fascination for Indian life and lore, also 1953), and Daniel Haupt (*Hazañas de Tarpon*, a sea adventure, 1954). It was with the transplanted Italian cartoonist Hugo Pratt that he created some of his most notable series, starting in 1952 with *Sargento Kirk*, an anti-Western starring a deserter from the U.S.

Hector Oesterheld and Alberto Breccia, "El Eternauta." © Editorial Frontera.

Cavalry who had joined the Indians. This sweeping epic lasted until the end of the decade.

In 1957, in association with his brother Jorge, Oesterheld set up his own publishing company, Ediciones Frontera. Working principally with Pratt, he created *Ticonderoga* (a tale of the French and Indian wars) and *Ernie Pike*, about an American war correspondent modeled after the actual Ernie Pyle. Among the innumerable series he gave birth to as the editor of Frontera, mention should be made of *Randall*, a more conventional Western; *Capitan Caribe*, a tale of piracy; and especially a number of fascinating and unusual science-fiction stories such as *El Eternauta*, *Sherlock Time*, and *Mort Cinder*. To provide outlets for his abundant production, he founded a number of comics magazines (*Hora Cero*, *Frontera*, *Hora Cero Extra*) and employed the top talent in the business (Alberto Breccia, Arturo Del Castillo, and Carlos Roume, among others).

Following a severe recession in 1968, Oesterheld was forced to close Frontera's doors. He then turned to the Chilean market, turning out a number of potboilers but also some politically sensitive projects, such as a biography of Ché Guevera, the Argentinean revolutionary and brother-in-arms of Fidel Castro. Drawn by Enrique and Alberto Breccia, this comic-strip series appeared in 1968. Among his more conventional creations of the period were *Guerra de los Antartes* (science fiction), *Roland el Corsario* (sea adventure), *Tres por la Ley* (crime stories), and *Kabul de Bengala* (adventures in India).

In the mid-1970s the military took power in Argentina, and every independent spirit in the land became a suspect. On April 21, 1977, Oesterheld was arrested at his home, taken away, and nothing more was heard of him (his four daughters shared the same fate). Alberto Ongaro, an Italian journalist inquiring about his fate during a visit to Argentina in 1979, received the chilling reply, "We did away with him because he wrote the most beautiful story of Ché Guevara ever done."

M.H.

OGON BAT (Japan) *Ogon Bat*, one of the most famous superhero strips in Japan, had a checkered career. Created in 1930 by scriptwriter Ichirō Suzuki and artist Takeo Nagamatsu as a *kamishibai* (comic strip for public narration), it soon became famous and lasted until 1935. Ogon Bat (whose name came from a popular brand of cigarette) was a justice fighter who wore a golden hood and a red cape and could fly in the air. At its peak of popularity (1930-34) *Ogon Bat* inspired a host of imitators. After the Pacific War (1946) *Ogon Bat* again reappeared as a *kamishibai* done by Kouji Kata; Nagamatsu recreated his own version of the character in 1947. Four comic books of Nagamatsu's *Ogon Bat* were published from November 1947 to March 1949. From July 1948 to May 1950 it also appeared in the comic monthly *Bōken Katsugeki Bunko* (later *Shōnen Gaho*).

The new Ogon Bat wore a skull-mask, a broad-brimmed hat, and a musketeer costume. The story was a parable of good and evil as Ogon Bat (who was a demigod rather than a mere human being) and his allies, the private detective Oki, Queen Shima, and the great scientist, Dr. Mōguri, battled the forces of darkness led by Kuro Bat ("the Black Bat"), later rechristened Nazo. Ogon Bat's most terrifying weapon was his sardonic laugh, which instilled fear in the hearts of his enemies when they heard it.

Nagamatsu's style, a cross between the American comic book and the illustrated story, was an oddity in Japanese comics of the time. *Ogon Bat* was made into a series of animated cartoons. In 1967 it was revived briefly in *Shōnen Gaho* and *Shōnen King*, and two *Ogon Bat* comic books appeared in May 1975.

H.K.

OHSER, ERICH (1903-1944) German artist/cartoonist born March 18, 1903, in Untergettengrun near Plauen, Saxony, where he grew up. He studied in Leipzig and started drawing cartoons for the *Sächische Sozialdemokratische Presse* (Saxon Social Democratic Press) in 1928, and continued cartooning for the newspapers *Vorwärts*, *Wahrer Jakob*, *Querschnitt*, and *Neue*

Erich Ohser, "Vater und Sohn." © Südverlag Constanz.

Revue until 1933. In 1934 he came up with *Vater und Sohn* ("Father and Son"), which was published in the *Berliner Illustrirte*. This magazine, like *Das Reich*, also published Ohser's editorial cartoons. At that time Ohser was better known by his pen name E. O. Plauen, derived by adding the name of his hometown to the initials of his real name. Ohser's way to Berlin had been paved by Erich Kästner, world famous for his children's books. From the end of the 1920s, Ohser had been Kästner's satirical brother-in-arms, illustrating Kästner's books.

Ohser's *Vater und Sohn* enjoyed tremendous success. The strip was loved and cherished by millions. It was reprinted in Africa, America, and Australia, and there were even Chinese editions. Exporting *Vater und Sohn* to foreign countries was not much of a problem, as it was a pantomime comic strip in a clearly drawn, easily understandable cartoon style.

In addition to *Vater und Sohn,* the *Berliner Illustrirte* also published another comic strip, *Die fünf Schreckensteiner* ("The five Schreckensteiners," 1939-40) by Barlog, who also did a number of comic features for department-store giveaway children's magazines. These strips in a way prove that the Wilhelm Busch tradition of comic art never died out in Germany. The fact that, with the exception of *Vater und Sohn*, these comic strips are virtually unknown today sheds an interesting light on the kind of esteem Germany has for her comic and cartoon art. After 1974, some of the material reappeared in collectors' circles.

Erich Ohser, despite being adored by his readers, was not treated too well by Third Reich Germany. Following a denunciation for "defeatist remarks in an air-raid shelter," Ohser was arrested, together with a friend, by the Gestapo. This drove him to commit suicide in his cell in March 1944 before he could be brought to trial. His friend was executed.

W.F.

OKAMOTO, IPPEI (1886-1948) Japanese cartoonist and writer born June 11, 1886, in Hakodate, Hokkaidō. After graduation from the Tokyo School of Fine Arts in 1906, Ippei Okamoto took a job as stage painter for one year under Professor Wada.

In 1912 Okamoto made his debut as a cartoonist, working for the newspaper *Asahi*. His talent as a prom-

ising cartoonist was recognized by the famous Japanese writer Sōseki Natsume, after the publication of his first work, *Kuma o Tazunete* ("A Visit to the Bear") that same year. Soon Okamoto displayed great creative activity, and his comic stories for magazines and newspapers were being reprinted in book form as quickly as he could turn them out: *Tanpō Gashu* (his first published work, 1913); *Kanraku* ("Surrender," 1914); *Match no Bou* ("Matchstick," 1915); *Monomiyusan* ("The Sightseeing Picnic," 1920); and *Nakimushi Dera no Yawa* (his most famous story in comic form, "Night Tales at Nakimushi Temple," 1921).

In 1921 Okamoto started on a round-the-world journey that lasted over one year and took him to the United States, England, France, Germany, Italy, and other countries. During his travels he met with foreign cartoonists, visited the offices of *Punch*, and put down many of his observations on paper. Upon his return, he introduced popular American strips, such as *Mutt and Jeff* and *Bringing Up Father*, to the Japanese public. The account of his journey, which appeared in *Asahi* and in *Fujokai* magazine, was released in book form in 1924.

More of Okamoto's works continued to appear: *Yajikita Saikou* ("The Resurrection of Yajikita," 1925); *Ippei Zenshū* (a 15-volume anthology of Okamoto's greatest works, published in 1929-30); and *Shin Mizu ya Sora* (Okamoto's masterwork, a collection of caricatures, 1929) are probably the most famous. Around the same time Okamoto published his famous novel *Fuji wa Sankaku* ("Mt. Fuji is Triangular," 1927).

Ippei Okamoto was the greatest cartoonist of the Taishō era (1912-1926) and the early Shōwa era. He produced many comic strips, humor cartoons, and illustrations; he was also a noted author who wrote several novels and essays. His cartoon creations were dignified and a bit stuffy, but his writings were light and humorous. He contributed mightily to raise the social status of cartoon art, and he was also a pioneer in the use of comics in advertising. He influenced many Japanese cartoonists, such as Shigeo Miyao, Kon Shimizu, Yukio Sugiura, Hidezō Kondō, and others.

Ippei Okamoto's wife, Kanoko Okamoto, was also a famous writer, and his son, Tarō Okamoto, was a noted contemporary painter. Ippei Okamoto died in October 1948.

H.K.

O'KEEFE, NEIL (1893-198?) American cartoonist and illustrator born April 19, 1893, in Galveston, Texas. His father, Colonel John O'Keefe, retired when Neil was still a child and took his family to St. Louis, where the young O'Keefe attended St. Margaret's School, McKinley High, and Washington University. O'Keefe went to work in the art department of the *St. Louis Post-Dispatch* in 1913, going on to the *Chicago Tribune* one year later. In 1918 O'Keefe moved to St. Paul, Minnesota, as a writer for the *Daily News*, also occasionally doing a sports column, *As I Saw It*.

O'Keefe's cartooning really took flight in 1921 when he succeeded such luminaries of the art as Rollin Kirby and Gene Carr on *Metropolitan Movies*. Around the same time he started doing illustrations for the pulp magazines, quickly becoming one of the most noted, and one of the most prolific, pulp artists.

Called in by King Features to replace Lyman Anderson on *Inspector Wade* in July 1938, O'Keefe stayed with the syndicate for the rest of his career. After *Wade* was dropped in 1941, he became one of King's staff cartoonists, moving up to art director of Hearst's Sunday supplement, the *American Humorist*, in 1944. Along with writer Max Trell, O'Keefe created *Dick's Adventures in Dreamland* in 1947. A rather tepid account of great events in American history, it died in 1956. After some more years of illustration, O'Keefe retired in the 1960s. He reportedly died some time in the 1980s.

One of King Features's unsung journeymen artists, O'Keefe deserved better than the second-string features he got. Certainly, he would have made a better *X-9* or *Jungle Jim* artist than either Mel Graff or Paul Norris. His work had the bittersweet quality of a talent deserving of better things.

M.H.

OLD DOC YAK (U.S.)   Sidney Smith's *Old Doc Yak* (which ran from March 10, 1912, to June 22, 1919, as a Sunday page) was one of the three foremost pioneers of the humanized animal strip (with James Swinnerton's *Mr. Jack* at the turn of the century and Dok Hager's *Dippy Duck* of the 1910s), and easily the most successful of its time.

From an early date, Smith had included a goat caricature as a signature accessory or speaking character in many of his sports and political cartoons. By 1908, when he was working on the *Chicago Examiner*'s sports page, Smith elevated the goat to stardom in his first serious attempt at a comic strip, and named him with the strip: Buck Nix. Appearing daily only, Buck moved in a world of other humanized goats and became involved in a series of suspenseful continued adventures, among the first in daily comics (rescuing girlfriend Nanny Millionbuck from kidnappers, etc.), most of which revolved around money and the need for money—vis: the hero's name—and the sporadic, grim advice of an old goat in black spectacles and frock coat called The Old Man of Mystery. Highly imaginative, funny, and enormously entertaining when read today, the popular *Buck Nix* led to Smith's being hired away from the *Examiner* by the *Chicago Tribune*, where he was asked to continue his strip under a new name. To avoid legal problems with the *Examiner*, Buck was changed from a goat to a yak, and the new strip, to be run as a Sunday page feature only, was titled *Old Doc Yak*.

Old Doc Yak was an even more sensational success than *Buck Nix* in Chicago, and gained Smith nationwide syndication, running for eight years in the *Tribune* until the greater impact of Smith's *The Gumps* closed it down after the introduction of the Sunday *Gumps* page in 1919. Smith added other animal characters to his original all-goat cast: hippos, monkeys, tigers, all in a very humanized world centered on Doc Yak's love affair with his sports car (which bore a huge license plate number that became as famous as the strip: 348). Doc Yak also acquired a young son named Yutch, and a recurring rival and enemy in the form of a hairy-eared black bear given several names (Greisheim and Metzler, to name just two) during the course of the strip. Several of Doc Yak's Sunday adventures were as suspenseful and fantastic as the daily escapades of Buck Nix, later narratives being satirically tied into World War I.

Old Doc Yak was revived by Smith on December 7, 1930, as a four-panel Sunday companion strip to *The Gumps*, dealing largely with Doc Yak's verbal and fistic encounters with the bear. It was folded with the last Sidney Smith-signed Sunday page on December 8, 1935.

Old Doc Yak was made into a movie in April 1916.

B.B.

OLD GLORY STORY, THE (U.S.)   In May 1953 the Chicago Tribune-New York News Syndicate debuted a Sunday-only strip that paired the creative team of history writer Athena Robbins and *Chicago Tribune* staff artist Rick Fletcher.

The Old Glory Story focused on the history around the different flags flown in America, beginning with the colonial period. Initially the strip proceeded chronologically through the European settlement of America, the Indian wars, the American Revolution, the War of 1812, and so on. While often featuring military conflict, *Old Glory* also did extended stories on the mountain men of the West and such developments in the East as the Erie Canal. However, more often than not, armed conflict, even if on the level of cowboys and Indians, was deemed necessary to keep this comic strip history lesson lively and interesting.

The strip benefitted by the centennial of the American Civil War (1961-65). The title was modified, to *Old Glory at the Crossroads*, and Sunday after Sunday a wonderful cartoon history of the Civil War was presented. Because of the great interest in the Civil War, circulation of the strip reached its peak during this period. Ironically, once the centennial ended and *Old Glory* returned to a cowboys-and-Indians type story of westward expansion, the strip soon ended, not even finishing out 1965. This might be due in part to Rick Fletcher having become the lead assistant to Chester Gould on *Dick Tracy* beginning in 1963.

Fletcher's representation of the Civil War was definitely a tour de force. Returning to less dynamic subject matter, as *Old Glory*'s circulation slipped, must have seemed anticlimactic. For Fletcher, the relationship with *Dick Tracy* continued until the cartoonist's death in 1983. During that time, Fletcher, who inherited the strip in late 1977 when Gould retired, was instrumental in bringing many technological advances to Tracy's police technique. These current police procedures and techniques were lost from the strip after he died.

The format for *Old Glory* featured illustration with text underneath. Word balloons were not used. Although created in the "politically incorrect" days of telling only one side of America's westward expansion, the scripts still hold up as basic history. Fletcher's research on costumes, uniforms, and the moods of different time periods was as excellent as his artwork. Comics are a visual medium, and *Old Glory*, which has rarely been reprinted, remains a visual treat.

B.C.

OLD TIMER, THE   *see* Snake Tales.

O-MAN (Japan)   *O-Man* was created by Osamu Tezuka for the Japanese comic weekly *Shōnen Sunday* in August 1959.

O-Men were higher creatures than human beings who inhabited an underground city in the Himalayan glaciers. O-Men were descended from squirrels and had a vestigial tail. Rickie was a young O-Man who had been brought up by a Japanese man named called Chikara, and who opposed the evil designs of Daisokān ("the Archbishop"), a leader of the O-Men who dreamed of wiping out the whole human race and taking over the earth. Wanting to make Tokyo his first outpost for conquest, Daisokān unleashed his dreaded Electric Freezing Machine and froze the whole world by error.

Rickie, with the aim of stopping the machine, returned to the O-Men's world, and was befriended by Daisokān's daughter Reeze. After many adventures, a closed-door conference between humans and O-Men, and a raid on the Freezing Machine, Rickie succeeded in stirring up the O-Men against the rule of Daisokān; a revolution ensued and the evil leader was overthrown.

Daisokān did not give up his ambitions, however; while in exile he entered into league with a group of cutthroats whose aim was also world domination. Internal strife brought about their downfall in the end.

O-Man is regarded as one of Tezuka's masterpieces, along with *Tetsuwan-Atom, Jungle Taitei,* and *Hinotori.* The drawings had the brooding, fragile quality of all of Tezuka's creations, while the storyline continually surprised and enchanted with its twists and turns and its inexhaustible inventiveness.

O-Man was reprinted many times in both hardcover and paperback form.

H.K.

O'NEAL, FRANK (1921-1986) American cartoonist born in Springfield, Missouri, on May 9, 1921. Frank O'Neal received a desultory education in schools from Arkansas to California, following his traveling father. After service in World War II, O'Neal attended art classes for three years with noted cartoonist Jefferson Machamer. In 1950 he sold his first cartoon to the *Saturday Evening Post.* Thus encouraged, he decided to embark on a full-time cartooning career, and became a contributor to many national magazines and publications.

In 1956 Frank O'Neal took a job drawing storyboards for television but quit in 1958 when his strip *Short Ribs* (depicting the outlandish doings of a host of nutty characters) was accepted by NEA Service. He worked on the strip for the 15 years until, due to diminishing financial returns, O'Neal abandoned *Short Ribs* to his assistant, Frank Hill, in 1973. He devoted the rest of his life to advertising and commercial art, and died in Pacific Groves, California, on October 10, 1986.

Frank O'Neal ranks higher as a keen observer of the absurdities of life and as an inventive and witty humorist (both in his dialogues and in his situations) than as a cartooning innovator. His drawing style, clean and functional, was perfectly suited, however, to his Martini-dry wit.

M.H.

O'NEIL, DENNIS (1939-   ) American comic book writer and editor born May 3, 1939, in Clayton, Missouri. After a short stint as a Marvel assistant editor in 1965, Denny O'Neil moved to Charlton and wrote for editor Dick Giordano under the pen name Sergius O'Shaugnessey. He worked on a variety of superhero and adventure books, but his best work was *Children of Doom,* a chilling postnuclear holocast tale, and it presaged a long string of O'Neil's later "social consciousness" stories.

When Giordano moved to National in 1968, O'Neil went along and scripted dozens of stories for superhero titles like *Creeper, Justice League, Atom, Hawkman,* and several others. But, like his previous Charlton work, O'Neil's best material came on comic books that later came to be called "relevant." Along with editor Julie Schwartz and artist Neal Adams, O'Neil began producing the *Green Lantern/Green Arrow* series in 1970, and the title became an instant classic due to his sharp, hard-hitting scripts and Adams's inspired artwork. O'Neil took on all the subjects previously taboo in comic books; he did stories on political repression, cultism, Jesus-freaks, slumlords, racism, and many other "touchy" topics. Two highly publicized O'Neil stories cast Green Arrow's sullen young assistant, Speedy, as a heroin addict. Unfortunately, the series folded after two years amidst high praise, low sales, and increasingly antagonistic relationships between the creators.

O'Neil continued to write superhero, mystery, and adventure stories for National, and also became an editor. Quickly becoming one of the most respected writers in the field, he was subsequently asked by National to revamp *Superman* (as a writer) and *Wonder Woman* (as writer/editor); when National revived *Captain Marvel,* O'Neil became the top writer, and he edited and wrote the revived *Shadow* title for National in 1973. Quite different from much of his earlier material, *Shadow* afforded O'Neil an opportunity to create mood and period pieces, and he and artists Mike Kaluta and Frank Robbins produced several outstanding issues despite artistic conflicts and flagging sales. In the course of his decades-long career at DC (formerly National), O'Neil worked on many of the company's titles, but he remains best noted for his contributions to *Batman* in the 1970s and 1980s.

J.B.

O'NEILL, DAN (1942-   ) Dan O'Neill is an American underground comix artist and writer born in 1942. A former Catholic seminarian, O'Neill began his underground career in 1967 when he began producing a strip titled *Odd Bodkins* for the *San Francisco Chronicle.*

Dan O'Neill, "Dan O'Neill's Comics."

Odd Bodkins was different from strips running either in the "straight" newspapers or in the underground newspapers that were beginning to flourish at the time. Basically, it concerned itself with two characters named Hugh and Fred, neither of whom looked the same from one panel to another. Fred had what passed as a beak of sorts, and Hugh was a little taller than Fred, but those were about the only definitions the characters retained. In fact, the whole strip was odd. Characters and backgrounds were always in transition and color came and went in an apparently capricious manner.

The strip itself had a philosophical bent, but most critics and readers found it hard to consistently decipher O'Neill's meanings. One example, a strip entitled "God is a Rock," concerned a repartee between Fred, Hugh, and Lulu the garter snake. Fred tells Hugh that God is everywhere; Hugh therefore decides God must be under a nearby rock because he is everywhere. Under the rock, Hugh finds Lulu the snake, thinks she is God, and then ponders the "fact" that both God and Lucifer are snakelike. In another strip, "100% American Dog in Magic Cookie Land," Hugh decides all he has learned from a long, color-laden adventure is that "Life can be a picnic . . . only if you accept the ants."

O'Neill produced *Odd Bodkins* off and on for the *Chronicle*—and for about 350 underground papers that carried it via the Underground Press Syndicate—until 1969, when he left after a censorship hassle. He later redrew some of the strips for the underground comix market under the title, *Dan O'Neill's Comics and Stories*. Three issues were published by Company and Sons in 1971 and *Odd Bodkins* was also released as a series of Glide books in large, paperback format.

During the *Odd Bodkins* fun, O'Neill infused parodies of Walt Disney characters throughout. Mickey and Minnie Mouse and many others frequently appeared, because, like many cartoonists, O'Neill had been greatly influenced by the old Disney movies and comic strips. In 1971, O'Neill and several other artists produced two comic books—*Mickey Mouse Meets the Air Pirates* and *Air Pirates* number two—that took this Disney parody to its logical conclusion. In short, the books were Walt Disney characters grown up, and some depicted sexual scenes, including a celebrated tableau in which Mickey Mouse and Minnie performed sex acts.

The Disney empire was incensed, of course, and quickly moved to block publication of the third issue. It then sued O'Neill and his associates, Ted Richards, Bobby London, Ron Turner, and Gary Hallgren, for $700,000. The latter two eventually settled out of court, but O'Neill, London, and Richards remained adamant; the trial finally began in August 1975. In the interim, O'Neill garnered considerable publicity from the case and the two issues of *Air Pirates* became collectors' items.

J.B.

In July 1976 the three holdouts issued a four-page illustrated pamphlet, *Walt Disney versus the Air Pirates*, explaining their position and asking for donations to their legal defense fund. Despite this last-ditch effort they eventually lost the case. Outside of an occasional story, O'Neill has largely remained inactive in the field of comix since that time.

M.H.

O'NEILL, ROSE CECIL (1874-1944) Rose O'Neill, the woman who had the genius to give the common choirloft cupid a nickname and who drew her famed *Kewpies* as a comic strip for over a quarter of a century, was born Rose Cecil O'Neill in Wilkes-Barre, Pennsylvania, in 1874. Her father, a merchant, moved his family shortly afterward to Omaha, where his daughter attended the Sacred Heart Convent and won an art competition sponsored by the *Omaha Herald* at the age of 13, drawing a series of weekly cartoons for the paper as a result. By 1889, when she was 15 and the family had moved to New York, Rose O'Neill had sold cartoons and drawings to such major magazines as *Puck, Judge, Life, Truth,* and *Harper's*. Her first, brief marriage at 18 was to a Gray Latham, who died five years later. Four years after his death, she had married the editor of *Puck*, Harry Leon Wilson, later to be famed as the author of *Merton of the Movies*, and illustrated his early novels, such as *The Spenders* (1902) and *The Lions of the Lord* (1903). In 1904, she wrote and illustrated her own first novel, *The Loves of Edwy*. After a trip to Italy and her divorce from Wilson, the writer and artist became a full-time freelancer. She drew her first group of clustered cupids, with curly topknots borrowed from Palmer Cox's popular Brownies, to illustrate some children's verses which she printed in the *Ladies' Home Journal* in 1905. She called them Kewpies, and their public impact was sensational.

Before six months had passed, she was being bid for by the top magazines in the country. *The Woman's Home Companion* paid a small fortune to obtain her Kewpie drawings in 1910, then *Good Housekeeping* paid more. In 1913, George Borgfeldt & Co. of New York manufactured the first of the famed Kewpie dolls that circled the globe in millions over the next two decades. By 1917, Rose O'Neill had drawn, copyrighted, and syndicated a Sunday comic page devoted to verses and drawings of the Kewpies, with a different title each week; it lasted a year and was widely printed, as were her daily *Kewpie* panels of the same period.

Fifteen years later, she was persuaded by King Features to renew her feature, this time as a weekly Sunday page with dialogue balloons and continuity; it appeared early in 1935 and ran until late in the decade. In 1937, however, she retired and left New York to live on a farm in the Ozark Mountains that she had purchased earlier, after an active and Bohemian social life of many years. Here she continued her painting and drawing, but fell into ill health and moved in with nearby relatives in Springfield, Missouri, where she died on April 6, 1944, at the age of 69.

Curiously, no animated cartoons were made of the Kewpies, and only a few books based on them were published, mostly paper-doll and coloring books in paper covers. Two somewhat more substantial titles were *The Kewpies, Their Book* (1911) and *The Kewpie Primer* (1916), but all are now very rare. A contemporary collection of the strips is long overdue.

B.B.

ON STAGE (U.S.) Artist-writer Leonard Starr created *On Stage* for the Tribune-News Syndicate on February 10, 1957.

On Stage's heroine, Mary Perkins, was in the beginning a naive small-town girl who had come to New York to seek her big chance on Broadway. In the first year of the strip she was "discovered" by a deranged stage director, chosen on a bet by star photographer

"On Stage," Leonard Starr. © Chicago Tribune-New York News Syndicate.

Pete Fletcher, picked for an ingenue role in summer stock, lured to Hollywood by a megalomaniacal movie producer, saved from his clutches by a friendly gangster, and was back on Broadway without so much as a missing eyelash.

After that Mary slowed down somewhat, married Pete Fletcher, and went on to make her mark on the stage and in movies. She still kept right on meeting outlandish characters, from the enticing and venomous Morganna D'Alexias to Maximus, "the man without a face," a Phantom-of-the-Opera type. But she matured considerably in the course of the strip and became able to face any situation with cool and aplomb.

On Stage was a stage opera with something extra. The atmosphere, settings, and characters were realistically rendered without excluding humor and even poetry. Starr excelled in the depiction of subtle emotions, furtive expressions, and revealing gestures. Incisive plotting, literate writing, and elegant drawing were some of *On Stage*'s hallmarks, making it one of the best of contemporary comic strips.

Despite its graphic and narrative excellence, *On Stage*, like all story strips, suffered in the 1970s from the growing disaffection of the public toward continuing series, and its circulation slowly eroded. Starr finally abandoned his creation in the fall of 1979, after he had been asked by the syndicate to take charge of the born-again *Annie* strip.

M.H.

OOR WULLIE (G.B.) "Oor Wullie," translated into English, is "Our Willie." He is the scrub-headed star of a Scottish dialect strip that appears on the front page of *Fun Section*, the pullout and foldover comic supplement to the *Sunday Post*, a weekly newspaper published in Scotland by D. C. Thomson. *Oor Wullie*, created by Dudley D. Watkins (who also drew the other full-page dialect strip, *The Broons* ("The Browns"), has appeared continuously since the first issue of the supplement on March 8, 1936.

Wullie begins and ends each adventure sitting on an upturned bucket, and his catchline "Oor Wullie, Your

"Oor Wullie," Dudley Watkins. © Sunday Post.

Wullie, A'body's Wullie" ("anybody's Willie") describes his character, as does the verse that introduces one of his book appearances (to the tune of *Comin' Thro the Rye*): "Gin a body meet a laddie, Fower an' a half feet high./Towsy-heided, rosy-cheekit, Mischief in his eye./Patchit breeks an' bulgin' pockets. Fu' of spirit forbye,/Then like as no' ye've met Oor Wullie, Scotland's fly wee guy."

Wullie divides his time between house and home, one of these being a shaky structure scrawled with the words "Wullie's Shed." In this structure lives his wee moose ("mouse"), Jeemy ("Jimmy"). Friends and acquaintances include Fat Bob, Soapy Soutar, Wee Eck, and P. C. Murdoch, not to mention a particularly human Ma and Pa. He also has very deep pockets in his dungarees, only slightly less capacious than Harpo Marx's, which can be relied upon to provide almost anything in an emergency.

The strips have been reprinted in annual collections since October 1940. They are still running as of 1997.

D.G.

OPPER, FREDERICK BURR (1857-1937) The famed creator of *Happy Hooligan, Maud, Alphonse and Gaston*, and other immortal comic characters, Frederick Burr Opper was born on January 2, 1857, to Austrian immi-

F. B. Opper, magazine cartoon.

"Yes, Willie, this is a rubber toy to amuse you and Teddy. It represents the Working Classes. See how Papa pulls its leg."

F. B. Opper, political cartoon.

grant parents in Madison, Ohio. A prospering crafts-man, Opper's father, Lewis, was the brother of the once-noted newsman Adolphe Opper, who wrote under the name De Blowitz as Paris correspondent of the *London Times* in the 1880s. The young Fred, aware of his considerable cartooning talent, cared little for formal schooling and left high school to go to work on the *Madison Gazette* when he was 14. Eager for recognition, he mailed cartoons to notable magazines of the time; his art was often purchased, and appeared in such titles as *Scribner's, The Century,* and *St. Nicholas.* Encouraged, he left for the east coast before he was 20 and almost at once found a staff artist job on a now-forgotten magazine called *Wild Oats* (managing to make eating money at a dry-goods store job at the same time).

Meanwhile, he continued to freelance work to other magazines, including *Puck* and *Harper's Bazaar,* where Colonel Frank Leslie, publisher of *Leslie's Magazine* (a news publication), saw the young man's work and hired him as a news correspondent, cartoonist, and artist. After three busy years with *Leslie's,* Opper found a better-paying position as *Puck's* leading political cartoonist, a job he held for many years, until William Randolph Hearst hired him in 1899, when Opper was 42, to do weekly humor cartoons for Hearst's American Humorist section of the *New York Journal.* Here the now famed cartoonist and book illustrator (his works included *The Hoosier Schoolmaster,* Bill Nye's *Comic History of the U.S.,* Eugene Field's *Tribune Primer,* and several Twain stories collected in book form) drew additional readers to the Hearst papers in New York and San Francisco—especially when a plump, ragged little tramp with a blue tin-can hat named Happy Hooligan made his first appearance on March 26, 1900. The public loved the tramp, and although Opper tried other characters from time to time, such as a comic farmer named Uncle Si and a practical joker named Mr. Henry Peck, it quickly became obvious that the readers primarily wanted as much Hooligan as possible. They got him almost every week in the Hearst comics, and in a succession of popular reprint collections through the early 1900s. By this time, Opper had fully grasped the potentials of the new comic strip medium and was introducing still more widely popular characters, such as Alphonse and Gaston, and Maud the Mule, all of

whom began appearing in their own strips concurrently with *Hooligan* (often appearing together in the same Sunday section) and in books of their own as well.

In the meantime Opper's competence as a political cartoonist had not gone unnoticed by Hearst, and Opper put in a major daily stint doing topical cartoons for the daily Hearst press from the turn of the century on, a task which delighted Opper, and which he continued side by side with his strip work for the rest of his life. Opper's bloated oil industry tycoons, porcine capitalists, and shrewdly caricatured politicians from Bryan through Hoover were as widely recognized comic figures among the general public as Opper's own strip characters; and he often organized the former into strip sequences with running titles, such as "Mr. Trusty," "The Cruise of the Piffle," and "The Freeneasy Film Co. Presents," which Hearst ran daily on his papers' editorial pages.

Opper did little daily strip work, doing a few spot gag sequences now and again, and attempting a brief daily version of *Happy Hooligan* in the early 1920s. In the Sunday comic section, however, he did as many as three separate full- and half-page episodes a week during the 1900s and early 1910s, finally falling back on a single weekly page dealing with Hooligan, but into which he would periodically reintroduce such popular figures as Maud, Si, Alphonse and Gaston, Gloomy Gus, and others. By the end of the 1920s, he had become recognized as the Dean Emeritus of American strip artists because of his fame, competence, and comparative maturity in years.

Forced by failing eyesight to give up his weekly strip and daily political cartoons in 1932, Opper went into semiretirement, managing to do a bit of special cartooning now and again, at his estate in New Rochelle, New York, where he died of heart trouble on August 28, 1937. His claim to fame is self-evident.

B.B.

ORLANDO, JOE (1927-) American comic book artist and editor born April 4, 1927, in Bari, Italy. He and his family immigrated to the United States in 1929, and Orlando first became acquainted with comic art by reading *Tarzan* in the Italian language daily *Il Progreso*. Orlando attended the High School of Art and Design—classmates were comic book artist Rocco Mastroserio and singer Tony Bennett—and then served in Europe as part of the U.S. Army's occupation. When he returned, he attended the Art Students League, and about this time began his comic book career by illustrating the *Chuck White* adventure strip in the educational *Treasure Chest* comic book.

In 1950, he and Wallace Wood opened an art studio and began producing science-fiction material for Avon, Youthful, Charlton, and Ziff-Davis. When Wood moved to E.C., Orlando briefly went his own way but soon joined E.C. when they were looking for someone to draw in Wood's style. He was assigned to the horror and science-fiction titles, and while publisher Gaines said he was "a little stiff with his interpretations," he was more than adequate. He drew most of his material in a clean, unpretentious, and straightforward manner, and it would have been conspicuously excellent at any other comic group of the 1950s; but at E.C. Orlando had to take a back seat to the likes of Crandall, Ingels, Frazetta, Wood, Williamson, and many others.

When E.C. folded in 1956, Orlando moved on to work for the horror and science-fiction comics published by Stan Lee's Atlas group, and then began drawing for *Mad*. By the end of the decade, however, Orlando was concentrating almost entirely on advertising art and painting, but when James Warren began his black-and-white comic magazine line with *Creepy* in 1964, Orlando was one of the heaviest and best contributors. His artwork had become more stylized and intricate, but it was still amazingly well-paced and fluid; his storytelling and page composition remained deceptively simple.

In 1966, National elevated artist Carmine Infantino to editorial director and Orlando was one of the first new wave of artist/editors he hired. His best book was *Swamp Thing*, a stellar horror title written by Len Wein and drawn by Berni Wrightson. Orlando was named vice president at DC in the late 1970s; he retired in 1996.

J.B.

ORMES, JACKIE (1915-1986) Jackie Ormes holds a special place in the history of American newspaper cartooning as the first African-American woman to create, write, and draw a comic strip that became nationally syndicated. Her strip, *Torchy Brown, From Dixie to Harlem*, was first published by the *Pittsburgh Courier*, a black-owned newspaper, in 1937. The strip was syndicated to other black newspapers. It was not until 1991, when Universal Press Syndicate began to distribute Barbara Brandon's *Where I'm Coming From*, that an African-American woman cartoonist was syndicated by a major mainstream syndicate.

Ormes's romantic adventure strip, featuring sexy black heroine Torchy Brown, predated the debut of Dale Messick's *Brenda Starr* by three years. It is fair to note that while Messick had to battle sexism in her rise to become a mainstream syndicate star, Jackie Ormes had the double whammy of sexism and racism working against her break into the big time.

Torchy Brown's adventures took her from the rural South to the Apollo Theater in New York City. Mixed in with all the romance was a realistic portrait of African-American culture in the 1930s. However, the revenues from the strip were disappointing, and Ormes dropped *Torchy Brown* in 1940, turning to magazine and advertising art to make a living.

In the 1940s Ormes was a newspaper reporter and cartoonist for the black-owned *Chicago Defender*. Her single-panel strip *Candy* starred an African-American maid. *PattyJo 'n Ginger* was a single panel created by Ormes at the request of Smith-Mann Syndicate in 1950. The humor panel, featuring a young African-American girl as its star, even sparked the merchandising of a PattyJo 'n Ginger doll that is now an expensive collectible. Also in 1950, Torchy Brown returned to newspapers, with the feature renamed *Torchy Brown Heartbeats*. It was published through 1955.

The character of Torchy was always a bit more risqué than her white contemporary, Brenda Starr. While Dale Messick used pinups of Brenda to catch the eye of male readers, Jackie Ormes often let her heroine's voluptuous charms be seen in lingerie. Although both Torchy and Brenda shared many heartbreaks, Torchy's boyfriends were always more rough-and-tumble and more sexually aggressive. However, a more significant difference was that while *Brenda Starr* remained basically soap opera fluff, *Torchy Brown* showed in stark realism the problems of racism, bigotry, and even environmental pollution. It would be almost 40 years before mainstream soap-opera strips could even come close to the realism and passion that Ormes presented in these themes.

Jackie Ormes is truly an unsung heroine of American cartooning. During her lifetime her success was unfortunately limited because *Torchy Brown* was only printed in black-owned newspapers and not in a wider market. Still, in Torchy Ormes created a proud, strong African-American heroine, not just the one-dimensional character seen in so many soap-opera strips.

B.C.

OSCAR (Italy) When Oscar was created by Luciano Bottaro in 1959, he was then named Nasolungo ("Bignose"), and slated to appear, along with a host of other characters, in the new monthly publication planned by publisher Angelo Fasani. The name of this comic monthly was to be *Il Musichiere*, also the name of a popular television show of the time. Just as the magazine was due to come out, however, the TV show was dropped, and Fasani decided to change the name of the new publication to *Oscar*. As there was no character by that name in the scheduled features, Bottaro and his scriptwriter Carlo Chendi were asked to write a story in which their Nasolungo character would acquire the nickname "Oscar."

Oscar's first issue came out in 1960. It featured the works of cartoonists G.B. Carpi, Giulio Chierchini, Franco Aloisi, Giancarlo Tonna, and others. Luciano Bottaro, busy as usual, left the drawing in the hands of one or another of his assistants after the 10th episode. The scripts were mostly written by B. Torelli, Carlo Chendi, and Bottaro himself. In the stories—which took place in the African bush country—Nasolungo (alias Oscar) was a professional game warden and an amateur actor in his spare time. Oscar's constant antagonist was Gambacorta ("Shortleg"), a scheming mouse always trying by hook or by crook to kidnap the jungle animals and sell them to some zoo. The series was also enhanced by a rich assortment of characters: an opera-singing hippopotamus afflicted with a terrible-tempered wife; a cowardly octopus; a raven detective; and a worm with a superiority complex, among others.

In the summer of 1961, *Oscar* was reprinted in a splendid four-color gift album, an unusual occurrence in Italy at the time (the practice later became standard among publishers of comics). In this album were also featured two other Bottaro creations: *Piper Maiopi* (about a comic-opera sheriff) and *Lola and Otello*. *Oscar* has also been published in France, in the pages of the magazine *Bravo*.

During the publishing crisis of the mid-1960s, Angelo Fasani retired, leaving his publishing house in the hands of his son Franco, who proved to be more interested in adult magazines than in comics, and he soon ended *Oscar*.

G.B.

OSHIMA, YUMIKO (1947-) Yumiko Oshima made her professional debut in 1968 in Shueisha Publishing's popular weekly girl's comics magazine *Margaret* with the short story *Pora no namida* ("Paula's Tears") while still at student at a two-year college. Although her first story was a melodrama that was typical of the genre of Japanese girls' comics, or *shojo manga*, at the time, Oshima soon carved out an utterly singular niche for herself. In 1970 she stunned readers and gained the attention of critics with *Tanjo* ("Birth," also published in *Margaret*), a story of a teenage girl's pregnancy that probed the most basic questions of existence. In 1973, the ordinarily cliquish Japan Comic Artists Association, Nihon Mangaka Kyokai, presented the young Oshima with their Excellence Award, Yushusho.

Oshima is best known for her only multi-volume work, *Wata no kunihoshi* ("The Country-Star of Cotton"), which tells the story of Chibi, a kitten who believes she will one day grow to be a human being. With a heroine (the kitten) portrayed as a little girl with a kitten's ears and tail wearing a frilly dress, this work is often dismissed as simply "cute," but a close reading reveals serious themes: the fear of becoming physically mature, maternal rejection (a recurring Oshima theme since her debut work), and the inevitability of death. For *Wata no kunihoshi*, Oshima was awarded the Kodansha Comic Award in 1979.

The vast majority of Oshima's work, however, is short stories, a fact which, in the Japanese comics industry, all but precludes popular success. It is a testimony to the power of her work that, in spite of this fact, she is one of the most beloved and influential members of a loosely defined group of groundbreaking women artists known as the *Hana no nijuyonen gumi* ("Magnificent 24-Year Group") because many were born in the year Showa 24, or 1949. (Other "Forty-Niners" include Moto Hagio, Keiko Takemiya, and Ryoko Yamagishi.)

Oshima's power stems from her uncanny talent for exploring the most profound themes through characters, settings, and storylines that seem whimsical: on the first page the reader is laughing, on the last, weeping. There is a dreamlike surrealism to her stories, but never a hint of the irony or cynicism that many in the West consider to be the *sine qua non* of "artistic" works.

The *Oshima Yumiko senshu* ("Selected Works of Yumiko Oshima") spans 16 volumes to date. Two of Oshima's stories, *Shigatsu kaidan* ("April Ghost Story") and *Mainichi ga natsu yasumi* ("Every Day Is Summer Vacation"), were made into feature films, and another, *Akihiko kaku katariki* ("Thus Spoke Akihiko") was made into a movie for television.

M.A.T.

OSOMATSU-KUN (Japan) *Osomatsu-kun* (which can be loosely translated as "the Osomatsu Clan") was created by Fujio Akatsuka and made its first appearance in April 1962 in the pages of the weekly *Shōnen Sunday*.

Osomatsu was one of sextuplets (his five brothers were Choromatsu, Ichimatsu, Jūshimatsu, Karamatsu, and Todomatsu). They were children of a working family, and all exhibited the same characteristics of idleness, uncouthness, and naughtiness embodied in their collective personality called "Osomatsu-kun." The Osomatsu kids had two principal enemies: Chibita, a sneaky, hateful, and gluttonous little boy; and Iyami, a sissified, disagreeable, and cunning prig (modelled after the Japanese actor Tony Tani) who always gave out a little cry, "Shē," when he was surprised by some of the boys' pranks (the cry started a fad among youngsters in Japan at the time).

Some of the other characters included Dekapan (a middle-aged and simple-minded man who always wore oversized drawers); Totoko, the beautiful girl on whom all the sextuplets, as well as their rival Chibita, had a crush; not to mention two weird characters named Dayōn no Ojisan and Hatabō, and the sextuplets' hapless parents. One of the reasons for *Osomatsu-kun*'s continued success was Akatsuka's skill in depicting secondary characters. Another reason was the continually inventive situations that Akatsuka contrived for his characters.

Osomatsu-kun was one of the longer-lasting Japanese humor strips (it was discontinued in August 1969). Although a boys' strip, it was enjoyed by many adults as well. *Osomatsu-kun* was adapted (in animated form) to the television screen in the 1960s.

H.K.

OTOMO, KATSUHIRO (1954-) Japanese cartoonist born in Miyagi Prefecture on April 14, 1954. After high school studies, Katsuhiro Otomo began his artistic career in 1971 as an illustrator for an educational television program. His first comic strip work was *Jusei* ("The Gun Report," 1973), a very loose adaptation of Prosper Mérimée's novella *Matteo Falcone*. After publishing a series of brief, self-contained stories in the mid-1970s (later anthologized in a volume fittingly titled *Short Pieces*), he created several longer narratives, notably the apocalyptic *Sayonara Nihon* ("Farewell Japan"), the science-fictional *Fireball* (1979), and most especially the work that some critics regard as his masterpiece, *Domu* ("A Child's Dream," 1981). A suspense-filled thriller with Hitchcockian overtones, *Domu* opened with a series of suspicious deaths occurring within the same apartment complex. These turned out to have been the work of an embittered old man who used his parapsychological powers to cause his victims to commit suicide; in the end his nefarious designs were thwarted by a child endowed with equally awesome powers.

Otomo delved further into the paranormal with the long-running *Akira*, serialized in *Young Magazine* from

Katsuhiro Otomo, "Domu." © Katsuhiro Otomo.

1982 to 1992. Set in the megalopolis of Neo-Tokyo in the 21st century, it was a dark, dystopian tale involving motorcycle gang wars, a mysterious force code-named Akira ("more powerful than a thousand nuclear bombs"), a sinister government conspiracy, and a cold-blooded, ruthless avenger. *Akira* caused a sensation as soon as it came out in Japan; its success was so great that the author had to form his own studio to supervise the increased production. This was topped in 1987 by the feature-length *Akira* animated film, which was shown in Europe and the United States and resulted in a comic book version that was published around the world. (In the United States it has appeared since 1988 in a colorized version issued by Marvel under its Epic banner.) After *Akira*'s conclusion, Otomo released *Megamex* in 1995, on a script by noted filmmaker Alejandro Jodorowsky.

Otomo, termed by Fred Schodt "the artist who created a revolution in clean-line realism" in Japan, eschews the cartooniness usually associated with *manga* and draws in an illustrative, cursive style much influenced by the French *bande dessinée*. He seems to have bridged the aesthetic gap that has existed between Japanese *manga* and Western comics, a feat not even Osamu Tezuka ever accomplished.

M.H.

OUR BOARDING HOUSE (U.S.) Major Amos Barnaby Hoople was a Fieldsian figure before W. C. Fields himself had developed (via Ziegfeld and the hit play, *Poppy*) his classic con-man character. Hoople, as presented by Gene Ahern in an innovative daily panel strip of 1923, was a short, sag-bellied man of middle age with a lantern jaw and drooping moustache, whose wife, Martha Hoople, presided militantly over the boarding house which was Hoople's sole continuing source of support. Hoople himself did little or nothing to keep the rooming house going, except what he was forced to do by Mrs. Hoople's badgering. Normally he occupied himself with the grandiose development of self-enriching schemes of an almost endless variety—from the ultimate failure or collapse of which he was rescued by either his own good fortune, an accidental element in the scheme which he had overlooked, or by the vigilant and long-suffering Martha and her carefully guarded boarding-house income.

As the strip developed in the early 1920s, Hoople's moustache shortened to a Grouchoesque smear behind his expanded, now-bulbous nose, and his long chin lifted to meet his nose in a near-Popeye profile. Some of the early boarders, such as a Mrs. Church and a prizefighter named Kid Portland, were dropped as the years went by, but a set of basic characters remained: three bachelor boarders named Buster, Clyde, and Mack (whose background comments provided a kind of cynical Greek Chorus for the Major's escapades); the Major's obnoxious 12-year-old nephew, Alvin; and his perennially reappearing black-sheep brother, Jake Hoople. Jake, unlike the Major, was a genuine, unscrupulous con-man who frequently went to jail, and about as frequently got the Major involved in really criminal undertakings—from which the Major, however, normally squeaked out with his usual luck.

The Sunday *Our Boarding House* was a weekly gag page, lacking the continuity of the daily panel, and was for years featured as the front page of the NEA Sunday comic section distributed by many small-town newspapers. Above the main *Boarding House* strip after 1932, Ahern drew a quarter-page weekly feature called *The Nut Brothers: Ches and Wal*. This remarkable strip was

"*Our Boarding House*," Bill Freyse/Gene Ahern. © NEA Service.

"*Our Ernie*," Hugh McNeill. © Knockout Comic.

pure fantasy, preceding the similar but better-known *Smokey Stover* in nutty, surrealistic background. Usually a comic point was made in the successive panels, but the madly shifting backgrounds and their contents were the real focus of attention.

In 1936, Ahern left his NEA strip to begin a new feature for King Features called *Room and Board*, very similar to *Our Boarding House*, with a Sunday companion strip named *The Squirrel Cage*, which paralleled *The Nut Brothers* in content. NEA appointed a talented cartoonist named Bill Freyse to take over the *Boarding House* feature, which he did with great zest and aplomb—so well that very few readers could have been aware of the shift in artists. Ahern's signature vanished, but there was no other sign of his absence until Freyse's signature appeared many years later. The Major's daily adventures continued as before, just as funny with the same basic characters, and the Sunday features followed suit.

After Freyse's death in 1969, the *Boarding House* daily and Sunday strip was continued by other hands. Although the old Ahern-Freyse style was noticeably different, the fundamental characters of the strip continued as before: American institutions as familiar and comfortable as the Major's slippers and fez. Drawn by Les Carroll since 1971, the Sundays ended in March 1981 and the dailies came to a close in December 1984.

B.B.

OUR ERNIE (G.B.) *Our Ernie*, subtitled "Mrs. Entwhistle's Little Lad," was one of the funniest strips to appear in British weekly comics. It was created by a cartoonist named Holt for the first issue of *Knockout* (March 4, 1939), and the first adventure set the theme. Ernie, fishing for kippers near Blackpool Tower, was crunched up in the cogs of a crane. Clearly inspired by the famous ballad *Albert and the Lion*, long a part of Stanley Holloway's repertoire, *Our Ernie*'s caption writer took the adventures even closer with his versified libretti: Ma and Pa picked up their little son/All kinked and bent, but still in one/Said Ma, "I'm glad that you were saved/But I'm blowed if I like you per-

manent waved!" Pa Entwhistle says the line that became his regular last-panel catchphrase, "Daft, I call it!" Our Ernie responds with his classic "famous last words," "What's for tea, Ma?"

The strip established several "firsts" in comics: the first northern hero, the first comic use of an already-established radio gimmick, the repeated catch-phrase, and the first time a strip hero continually wound up in some incredible predicament.

After a few weeks, Hugh McNeill took over the strip and made it even zanier, particularly after he added a typical touch, a companion for Ernie—Charlie the Caterpillar. Charlie's corner comments added an extra level to the fun. When McNeill went to war, A. J. Kelly arrived to draw even wilder adventures. Kelly's untimely death did not affect *Ernie*, save in inspiration, for the strip continued under Reg Parlett, Denis Gifford, Fred Robinson, Frank Lazenby, and many other hands, until it disappeared in 1960.

D.G.

OUTCAULT, RICHARD FELTON (1863-1928) Richard Felton Outcault was born at the height of the Civil War on January 14, 1863, in Lancaster, Ohio, the son of well-to-do parents. Considered highly talented from early childhood, Outcault majored in art at McMicken University in Cincinnati, Ohio, then returned home to marry Mary Jane Martin on Christmas Day 1890. Moving to New York to pursue an art career, Outcault settled in Flushing, Long Island, and worked as a freelance illustrator, doing work initially for such publications as the *Electrical World*, but quickly discovered that his bent for humor gave him a market for the immediate sale of virtually every gag cartoon he drew and submitted to *Life* and *Judge*. As the *New York World* also provided a lucrative cartoon market, Outcault placed a few cartoons there and found an interest in some back-alley studies of Manhattan urchins he had been doing as a sideline. Initially named for various slum area streets and courts, the series quickly became known by its *Hogan's Alley* title. Once he was permanantly employed by the *World* in 1894, Outcault found increasing fame for the small, nightshirted figure of a bald child the artist usually placed among his juvenile figures. This latter figure became the "Yellow Kid"—so named by the public and later by William Randolph Hearst when he hired Outcault away from the *World*, although Outcault never adopted the name—and he soon starred as the central character of Outcault's slum series.

The hearty vulgarity of Outcault's *Hogan's Alley* kids charmed the readership of the *World* as much as it alarmed the self-appointed keepers of the big city's proprieties, and nothing seemed worse to the latter group than Hearst's upstart sensational paper, the *New York Journal*, which acquired Outcault's services in 1896. The combination of Hearst journalism and his widely flaunted *Yellow Kid* feature created an outpouring of acrimony from New York's elite establishment—an outpouring that had its effect on Outcault himself. Much as he relished the money the Kid was bringing, the notoriety of the legal squabble between the *World* and the *Journal* over the rights to the Kid was socially embarrassing to him, and as soon as he conveniently—and economically—could, Outcault left Hearst and introduced a new, more subdued character, *Poor Li'l Mose*, for the *New York Herald* in 1901. This new feature reflected Outcault's interest in black children as subjects of caricature—an interest carried to its extreme in a series of drawings he did at about the same time for *Judge* called *Shakespeare in Possumville*—but it failed to hold much appeal for the public, and in 1902 Outcault introduced his immensely popular *Buster Brown* to *Herald* readers.

This time the mixture of juvenile hell-raising and propriety was exactly right for the public palate. Although there were still angry noises from certain church and school groups about "bad examples," most people found the wealthy background of the young prankster, Buster, either familiar or something to which they aspired, and so not as frightening or repulsive as many had felt the *Hogan's Alley* locale was. Buster himself was an ordinary healthy boy of the times, exaggerated enough to make for hilarious reading in the Sunday papers (and Outcault never drew any daily continuity strips), and dressed in a manner that made him very attractive to parents, who garbed an entire generation of boys in "Buster Brown" clothing of all kinds.

Again lured by Hearst money, Outcault left the *Tribune* and returned to the *Journal* in 1905, continuing *Buster Brown* there. Because Outcault controlled the rights to his character, he was making more by this time from clothing and artifacts based on *Buster* than

from the strip itself. A wealthy man by 1910, the artist continued the Sunday *Buster* almost as a hobby, finally dropping it for good in 1920 (although reprints were circulated to many papers as late as 1926) in order to retire to pursue his basic love, painting. The Outcault Advertising Company of Chicago, which he formed to merchandise his Buster Brown figure, was also relinquished at this time to his son, Richard F. Jr., who became the firm's new president.

The author of several prose works on his characters, as well as of serious articles on cartoon art for various journals, and the compiler of a number of *Yellow Kid* and *Buster Brown* reprint volumes, Outcault enjoyed more than one major exhibit of his paintings, and was free to travel as well, a widely respected figure in American art. Taken unexpectedly ill in the summer of 1928 at his Flushing home, Outcault lingered for nearly ten weeks, suffering from a variety of ailments, but died on September 25, 1928, at the age of 65.

B.B.

OUTLAND (U.S.) Having abandoned *Bloom County* the preceding month, on September 3, 1989, Berke Breathed brought out *Outland*. As a Sunday-only distributed by the Washington Post Writers Group, it hadn't been planned as a sequel to the former strip, but it turned out that way anyhow.

The star of the piece was originally a little African-American girl named Ronald-Ann who sought solace from her bleak ghetto life in escapist dreams and ego-boosting fantasies. When asked to read her American history paper at school, for example, she averred that Columbus was "a black man named Nabutu Bubu . . . who built three ships from the African baobab tree." The former denizens of *Bloom County* started dropping in, however, beginning with Opus the penguin in search of his mother, followed by Bill the Cat, Steve Dallas, Milo Bloom, Oliver Wendell Jones, and all the others, displacing the hapless Ronald-Ann from her own strip.

The characters behaved pretty much as before, but at a hyperkinetic pace. Their tribulations ranged from the puzzling to the esoteric. Steve Dallas decided to write *The Bridges of Bloom County* (subtitled "A Romance for Men"), banging out at his typewriter the opening sentences of chapter one: "Francesco . . . gazed upon the barren dust of his farm, his marriage, and his life. Suddenly, a pickup stopped before him. The door opened and out stepped [pause] three stewardesses." ("Six," whispered Opus, who was sitting at his elbow.) In other vignettes, Milo uncovered the skeletons in his closet (unfortunately they kept asking for Michael Jackson or the President); and troopers from the Information Highway Patrol came to arrest precocious hacker Oliver Wendell Jones for making "an illegal left turn into the White House international memo network."

In an extended narrative Steve turned into "the lawyer lost in time," meeting Calamity Jane in the Old West, filing a claim for a caveman in 10,000 B.C., visiting the site of the Hindenburg dirigible disaster, and dropping in on an underground bunker in 1945 Berlin ("I'm a victim too," Hitler whined). These arcane references, coupled with compositions that grew more and more abstract, disconcerted a great number of readers, and newspapers started cancelling the strip left and right. Breathed bowed to the inevitable and in

R. F. Outcault.

January 1995 announced he was dropping *Outland*; the last installment appeared on March 26 of that year.

M.H.

OUT OF THE SILENCE (Australia) Based on a novel of the same name by Erle Cox (1873-1950), *Out of the Silence* appeared as a daily strip in the *Melbourne Argus* from August 4 to December 21, 1934, and was drawn by "Hix" (Reg Hicks). It was the first Australian adventure strip of any consequence and followed the earlier comic strip format of no speech balloons and typeset text below each panel. As much of the original novel was based on lengthy dialogues and static situations, this format allowed the strip to remain basically true to the theme. By contemporary standards, the artwork, though stiff and unpolished, was adequate.

Silence told the story of a huge sphere discovered by Alan Dundas, buried on his property. The sphere contained records of the accumulated knowledge of a great civilization that had perished 27 million years ago. It also contained the body of the remarkably beautiful Earani—a veritable superwoman, placed in a state of suspended animation and committed to remaking the world in the image of her own civilization. The story follows the attempts of Dr. Richard Barry to forestall the plans of Earani and the infatuated Dundas for world domination.

Cox originally wrote *Silence* between 1913 and 1916 but was unable to find a publisher upon its completion. As a part-time contributor to the *Argus*, Cox submitted the story to that paper, which published it in weekly episodes between August and October 1919. The following six years saw a steady stream of inquiries from both Australia and overseas and, in 1925, the book was published by Edward A. Vidler of Melbourne. The same year a British edition was published by John Hamilton Ltd. of London and in 1928 an American edition was brought out by Rae D. Henkle Co. of New York. Both French and Russian translations have been reported and further Australian editions were published by Robertson & Mullens of Melbourne in 1932 and 1947. Over the past half century, *Silence* has come to be regarded as a science-fiction classic.

While *Silence* was the first adventure strip per se, the first adventure strip using original material and speech balloons was *The Adventures of Larry Steele* (1937-40) by Reg Hicks. Despite the trail-blazing performance of *Silence*, Australia has produced very few strips of the science-fiction genre. Only a handful (*Space Patrol, Silver Starr, Captain Power*) would qualify. No doubt, the space devoted to overseas strips in the Australian press (*Flash Gordon, Buck Rogers, Brick Bradford, Twin Earths, Jeff Hawke*, and others) has deterred local growth in this area.

J.R.

OUT OUR WAY (U.S.) At once one of the richest sources of memorable strip characters and the most individually structured of daily strips, J. R. Williams's *Out Our Way* first appeared in NEA Syndicate distribution on November 22, 1921, in a one-panel format. Eye-catching from the outset, with its homely realism of style and content and invested with an almost unfailing wit and originality of concept, *Out Our Way* quickly began to develop a series of characters who recurred at irregular intervals of a few days each in panel episodes of their own. Each of these series within a strip carried its own running title, and before long,

"Out Our Way," J. R. Williams. © NEA Service.

narrative continuity between these individual series episodes was added. (In one such 1924 narrative with a Western setting, Williams presented the first realistically dead bodies ever seen in a comic strip.) So sharply perceived and individualized were the Williams characters and narratives that none of his episodic shuffling confused his enthusiastic and growing public in the least.

Among the early series with the *Out Our Way* title were, "The Crossing Watchman," "Why Mothers Get Gray" (the panel that introduced the Willits family), "Heroes Are Made, Not Born" (with the Worry Wart), "Elf Dakin," "Wash Funk," and others. Other series featured a number of characters within their framework, but carried no running titles as such; among these were the cowboy group, which covered a broad range of memorable individuals, all interrelated, over its three-decade-plus run, including Smoky, Spuds, Cotton, Wes, Chuck, the School Marm, Soda, Jiggin' Jack (a horse), and others; and the machine shop set, sometimes run under the recurrent title, "Bull of the Woods," referring to the shop foreman, in which many characters figure, instantly recognizable by face and manner but largely unnamed.

A Sunday page titled *Out Our Way* but largely based on the Willits family of the "Why Mothers Get Gray" series, was released by NEA in the early 1920s. Aside from keeping an eye on the story line, Williams had little to do with the weekly page, and most of the continuity was drawn by Neg Cochran, who also continued drawing the Willits panel series after Williams died in 1957, running these between selected Williams reprints for several years. Paul Gringle carried on the Sunday strip for a time, and was later replaced on it by Ed Sullivan. The feature was discontinued in 1977.

A major part of the American experience for those who grew up with it, Williams's *Out Our Way* daily panel was one of the richest sources of popular lore and authentic records of how a wide variety of Americans lived, looked, felt, and thought from the turn of the century to the 1950s. A good cross-section of Williams's work is found in a fine series of volumes published by Charles Scribner's Sons between 1943 and 1947, under such titles as *The Bull of the Woods*, *Kids Out Our Way*, and *Cowboys Out Our Way*. A permanent collection of his daily work is needed.

B.B.

OVERGARD, WILLIAM THOMAS (1926-1990) American artist born in Los Angeles on April 30, 1926. William Overgard grew up and attended public schools in Santa Monica, California. He graduated from high school and joined the U.S. Navy in 1944; he served for two years and saw action at Okinawa. After discharge from the service he attended Santa Monica City College, where he took art and art history courses.

His big push toward the comics started when he was 12 years old and wrote a fan letter to Milton Caniff. This began a longtime relationship during which Caniff became young Overgard's mentor and teacher. Even in the service Overgard would send strips and samples of his work to Caniff and receive tips and encouragement in return; Caniff advised Overgard to seek a profession in cartooning.

After the war, Caniff introduced his "pupil" around the industry. Overgard went to New York and joined Lev Gleason comic publishers under editor Charlie Biro. He worked on the *Boy* and *Daredevil* titles and wrote and drew *Black Diamond* Western comics. He soon moved to Western Publishing (Dell) and composed complete books of *Jungle Jim*, *Ben Bowie*, and others. During this time Overgard ghosted Caniff's *Steve Canyon* on occasion and wrote and drew two *Steve Canyon* comic books, as well as *Crime Buster* comics from 1950-53.

Also during this period—into the Wertham era—Overgard was constantly submitting strips to syndicates, particularly Publishers and United Features. *Gay Honor*, about a crusading woman lawyer, was one of many ill-fated efforts. Finally, early in 1952, Harold Anderson of Publishers Newspaper Syndicate contacted Overgard about a problem with *Steve Roper*: The foreground figure man had quit and Elmer Woggon's cartoony backgrounds were out of character with the adventure theme that had overtaken what used to be *Big Chief Wahoo*.

Overgard was engaged (Milton Caniff advised acceptance of the offer) and his first strips appeared in April of 1952.

Overgard's slick art, combined with writer Allen Saunders's maturing story-adventure script, brought *Steve Roper* new popularity. It picked up papers and soon became one of the leading story strips. Overgard

used the camera extensively and often posed himself as the model to achieve the realism he sought (and succeeded in capturing).

In later years Overgard spent several years living in Mexico and wrote a novel, *Pieces of a Hero*, a satirical adventure bought by 20th Century Fox. Other fiction efforts included a sequel, *Once More the Hero*, and a paperback, *Moonlight Surveillance*. Pop art master Roy Lichtenstein lifted an Overgard panel for his famous "I Can See Into the Room." Overgard left *Steve Roper* in 1982 to create *Rudy*, a gag strip about a talking gorilla, but it lasted only a little over a year. He died May 25, 1990, in Stony Point, New York.

R.M.

OVER THE HEDGE (U.S.) When suburban sprawl hits the border of the wilderness, some critters retreat further into the woods; others, like *Over the Hedge*'s R. J. the raccoon and Verne the turtle, adapt. While the animals have lost the theoretical purity of nature, they have become the most consumer-driven, junk-food-crazed creatures of any syndicated comic strip.

Over the Hedge began international distribution by United Feature Syndicate on June 12, 1995, and was aggressively marketed. It successfully filled the spot left vacant in many papers when *Calvin and Hobbes* ended syndication. *Over the Hedge* was created and is written by Michael Fry and drawn by T. Lewis, who met because they shared the same artist's representative in Houston, Texas. Fry also writes and draws the panel *Committed* for United Feature, about being married with children, that began syndication in 1994. *Committed* has been described as "*Family Circus* meets *The Far Side*."

Fry's offbeat sense of humor has developed over the years as he has had several strips almost, but not quite, make it. *Scotty* was a popular local comic strip published by the Houston Press from 1984 until 1991. His first syndicated strip, *Cheeverwood*, was distributed by the Washington Post Writers Group from 1985 to 1987. Then King Features distributed *When I Was Short*, which he did with Guy Vasilovich from 1989 to 1992. Fry has also written for the *Mickey Mouse* syndicated comic strip for King Features and the Walt Disney Company. His collaborator on *Over the Hedge*, Lewis, a fellow Texan, had been one of the cartoonists drawing *Mickey Mouse*. Lewis is also an illustrator of children's books, with over 15 published.

Fry and Lewis first worked on a strip idea they were unable to sell called *The Secret Life of Pigs*, which had a rural setting. Pigs were turned into a turtle and a raccoon, and the setting changed to suburbia, and *Over the*

"Over the Hedge," Michael Fry and T. Lewis. © United Feature Syndicate.

Hedge was born. It clicked with the syndicate and editors of major U.S. newspapers.

R. J. (alias Fur Boy, the Masked Malcontent, or the Racoonerator) and his philosophical pal Verne (alias Mr. Sensitive or the Terribly Taciturn Terrapin) bear a resemblance to Pogo and his fellow critters only in that they are funny animals. While social commentary abounds, *Over the Hedge* does not have political commentary. Also, R. J. and Verne, because of their constant contact with humans, make Pogo and friends look like hicks from the Okefenokee Swamp.

R. J. and Verne have taken a liking to watching a big-screen television through the living room window of their neighbors, Norene and Nathan Furkin, and eating the garbage that the Furkins carefully cover. But what's a trash can with a lid on it to a critter crazed for a junk food sugar rush.

"Nathan, I'm kind of shy about this with the curtains open," complained Norene in their darkened bedroom in one strip. "Norene, this is the last house on the block," answered Nate. "Nobody's out there except a few fuzzy critters, and they've got their own problems." The final panel showed 11 animals on wooden bleachers watching the couple, with R. J. complaining to Verne, "The popcorn's stale again." In a later strip, Norene became pregnant, and the "Boys in the Wood" monitored the pregnancy with the same curiosity that the act of conception engendered.

R. J. is smitten with Dolly, a pampered pooch whom Verne notes is "domesticated, spoiled," and, after she trips over her own ears, "highly inbred." However, Luby, the lady raccoon with long eyelashes and a polkadot bow, thinks R. J. is neat, even if he does have to be approached with "tongs." Verne the turtle has a girlfriend of sorts in a fellow terrapin, Velma.

Over the Hedge definitely is humor with a late 1990s edge. The critters not only love watching *The X-Files* on television, they'd probably qualify to be the subject of an investigation. It will only get funnier with the addition of Norene and Nate's baby.

Lewis's artwork has a contemporary look and does not copy the funny animal style of Walt Kelly or others. As the strip is new, expect the characters to change as time goes by. *Over the Hedge* features the bad boys of the animal world, and it would appear they are just getting warmed up for a long and successful syndicated run.

B.C.

OZARK IKE (U.S.) A baseball strip, the first of its kind to achieve success and one of the few sports strips to survive, *Ozark Ike* was sold to King Features Syndicate by sports cartoonist Ray Gotto. The first strip appeared in November 1945.

The hero was Ike, a lanky left fielder for the Bugs baseball team. He was something of a hick, and most

"Ozark Ike," Ray Gotto. © King Features Syndicate.

certainly a bad baseball player. His girlfriend, a blonde beauty with a Veronica Lake hairstyle, was named Dinah. Bubba Bean was the second banana of the strip; like Ike, he was tall, thin and ignorant. J. P. Moran, a harried and bristling "fat cat," was owner of the team.

Gotto's drawing style, unlike many strip artists and certainly unlike many sports cartoonists, was precisely mannered and almost mechanically rendered. Shading was meticulously laid in with careful lines, and the impression of overbearing stylization was just saved by Gotto's grasp of anatomy, composition, and action.

Unfortunately, a baseball strip, even a good one, would expect to have a rough opening season and *Ozark Ike* was no exception. But Gotto's effort managed to become a moderate success for King; its art stood out on the comic page, and the humor, though seldom outstanding, was stronger than the continuities. What caused Gotto to leave the strip in 1954 was a contractual disagreement with Stephen Slesinger, the so-called "producer" of the strip; he was, in fact, a kind of agent and acted in a similar capacity with other strips, notably *Red Ryder*.

The strip was enough of a success for King to find another artist (Bill Lignante) to continue it; it failed after a couple of years (in 1959), as did Gotto's rival effort for General Features, *Cotton Woods*, another sports strip but in a straighter vein.

R.M.

PAI, ANANT (1931-   ) Anant Pai was born September 17, 1931, in Karkala, Karnataka, India. Although his college degrees were in chemistry, physics, and chemical technology, Pai developed a lifelong passion for publishing, comics, and literary activities. From 1954 to 1967 he worked successively as an editor and publisher of a magazine, freelance writer, publishing house representative, partner in a book export/import company, and junior executive in the Times of India Books Division. While at the latter, he helped conceptualize one of India's first comics, *Inkrajal*, which led to his 1967 launch of the very successful *Amar Chitra Katha* ("Immortal Picture Stories") series of educational comics.

Pai said the inspiration for this venture came while listening to Indian children spout knowledge about Western civilization but remain mute about their own culture. He set out to remedy this shortcoming, offering to do a set of comic books, each devoted to a person or event in Indian history, religion, and mythology. He finally sold the idea to India Book House, which, during the next 24 years, brought out a total of 436 different titles. Pai conceptualized all of the books and wrote many of the scripts.

Amar Chitra Katha was both a financial and education success. By the 1990s more than 79 million copies of the English-language edition were sold, and more in a number of other language editions worldwide. The books impressed government officials, who allowed federal funds to be used to purchase them for school use, and overall, helped comics gain a moderate rate of respectability in India.

Additionally, Pai started one of India's first comics and cartoons syndicates, Rang Rekha Features, in 1969, and the monthly children's magazine *Tinkle* in 1980; he has also authored novels in Hindi and Kannada, and four volumes on personality development.

J.A.L.

PALACIO, LINO (1904-198?) An Argentine cartoonist born in Buenos Aires in 1904, Lino Palacio, a graduate of the School of Architecture, taught drawing for many years and held a variety of municipal positions in the city of Buenos Aires. He initiated his career as a caricaturist under the pseudonym "Flax," and he was for a long time cover designer of the children's magazine *Billiken*. His most famous comic creations included *Ramona* and *Doña Tremebunda*, both about opinionated women; *Don Fulgencio*, his first popular success (1935); *Tripudio*; and, most famous of all, *Avivato* (1946), which inspired a movie of the same name and gave birth to a magazine, also titled *Avivato*.

All the Palacio strips were carried on, after their creator tired of them, by anonymous cartoonists working in a style imitative of their master, who died in the late 1980s.

L.G.

PANDA (Netherlands) *Panda* is one of the many successful creations of Marten Toonder, sometimes called the Dutch Walt Disney because of the large number of funny comics and cartoons produced by his studio. *Panda* was created in 1946 and, as the name suggests, is a strip about a cute little panda bear. The strip appears in a number of Dutch newspapers, all of which are subscribers of GPD, a press service that distributes the comic feature. *Panda* is also exported to a number of foreign newspapers and magazines, and two versions of the feature are in existence: the more traditionally Dutch version of a strip with narrative below the pictures, and the more international format of the story told in captions and speech balloons. More than 120 adventures with lengths between 40 and 100 strips have appeared since the strip was created.

Panda is a kind of morality play in which innocence forever wins out over a crooked trickster. Little Panda, of course, is the innocent. His antagonist is the sly fox Joris Goedbloed (George Goodfellow, in English versions) who, from the very first episode that has Panda picnicking under a tree, has tried to outwit Panda, but he inevitably fails. Panda's motto is *"Ik moet nu zorgen dat ik vooruit kom in de wereld"* ("I must strive to get ahead in the world"). Thus, money and rewards play an important role in Panda, his honesty even helping him to become a millionaire. A somewhat static figure, Panda does not go into action by himself; he usually has to be forced to go into action by Goedbloed, who spends his fantasies and energy on get-rich-quick schemes. When success seems within reach, Panda waits in the wings to straighten things out and preserve the status quo. Nevertheless, Panda never turns Goedbloed over to the authorities as he probably has a secret, romantic admiration for the gentleman rogue.

Panda is a character readers identify with since he gets involved in the stories the same way they do, by watching the goings-on. By proving that innocence cannot be corrupted, *Panda* provides the reader with a vehicle that mirrors—and tests—his morals.

W.F.

PANHANDLE PETE (U.S.) An early and often hilarious strip by George McManus, *Panhandle Pete* (which began in the *New York World* in April 1904 and ended there late in 1910) was one of the major Sunday page pioneers in extending narrative over many weeks. Initially a weekly gag page (or half-page) about a very grubby and tattered tramp with a pot belly and an unshaven chin, Panhandle Pete had turned by 1905 to world exploration in long continued sequences, attempting to reach the south pole—not once, but twice; on the second time finding and coming back with the "pole" itself—conquering cannibal kingdoms, making rocket and balloon ascensions, etc., etc. Aided by a thin bum named Cecil and a fat one who remains nameless (as well as by a pugnacious goat called Bill),

"Panhandle Pete," George McManus.

"Pansy Potter," Blackaller. © D. C. Thomson.

Pete swindles and connives his way from port to port, even taking over an entire African kingdom by fraud. (McManus's native blacks probably represent the extreme of comic page racism: he represents them as being hatched from eggs!)

Pete's vocabulary has an independent fascination: he speaks of vazzes (vases), "J. Pinpoint Morgan," and so on, while his fat tramp buddy smokes what must be the most remarkable (and smelly) pipe on record: it is in the shape of a small wood-burning kitchen stove, and he belches endless quantities of smoke. The goat, Bill, is as personable as the three humans, and frequently makes comments on the action in spoken balloons (although he is not humanized, and never converses directly with the others).

McManus's stunning comic draftsmanship is as sharply in evidence here as in any of his work, but he has a good deal more to work with, in terms of exotic settings, strange animals, etc., than before or later (except for the fantastic *Nibbsy the Newsboy* and *Spareribs and Gravy*—the latter being a re-creation of *Panhandle Pete* in 1911, again featuring traveling tramps in strange parts of the world). It is a strange, funny, and gorgeous strip, well worth collecting in a single memorable volume.

B.B.

PANSY POTTER (G.B.) *Pansy Potter the Strong Man's Daughter* made its debut in the Christmas number of *Beano*, 1938. "Welcome to the *Beano*, Pansy," said a caricature of the editor of that weekly comic in her first six-panel adventure, but he was soon saying "Ow! Leggo!" (just like one of his comic characters), when the daughter of the World's Strongest Man shook his hand.

Pansy was created by Hugh McNeill, but her corkscrew curls and Popeye arms have been drawn by many cartoonists since, the best being Blackaller, who adopted an unusual (for *Beano*) "animated cartoon" style. Pansy, whose name was changed by a last-minute editorial decision from the original *Biff Bang Bella*, really got cracking once war was declared: her

favorite pastime was sinking Hitler's U-Boats—by hand!

She moved into two-color printing in 1942 and over to the back page on April 21, 1945. She was reduced to six panels again on page two from June 15, 1946, then dropped after a paper cut reduced the size of the comic on January 10, 1948. However, she returned to the fray with renewed strength on August 13, 1949, when *Pansy Potter in Wonderland* was a serial strip that filled the entire back page, in full color. This became a complete weekly episode, and ran until February 6, 1954, after which, displaced by *Dennis the Menace*, she retired. However, a good Strong Man's Daughter is hard to keep down, and publisher D.C. Thomson revived her for their new comic, *Sparky*, on January 30, 1965. She ended her career in the late 1980s.

D.G.

PANTERA BIONDA (Italy) In April 1948 there appeared in newsstands all over Italy the first issue of the fortnightly collection "La Jungla" ("Jungle") published by Casa Editrice ARC. The flagship of the series was *Pantera Bionda* ("The Blonde Panther"), about a well-endowed jungle-woman, which introduced a not unwelcome touch of sex into the world of Italian comics, until then rather straitlaced. With an eye toward the male public, the publisher thought that a female Tarzan might do nicely. While there had been a few instances of similar characters in American comic books (Sheena, Camilla), this was an absolute novelty in Italy.

With scripts by Gian Giacomo Delmasso and drawings by Enzo Magni (who signed "Ingam"), the blonde heroine swung into a 16-page king-size comic book priced at 30 liras. Pantera Bionda lived in Borneo, fought against cruel and treacherous Japanese soldiers, and had only two friends: the serene Lotus Leaf, an old Chinese woman, and her pet chimpanzee, Tao. She also had a boyfriend in the person of an American explorer named Fred, who was to play second fiddle for a long time.

The scantily clad heroine soon attracted the ire of the prude and the righteous, who accused the publishers of pornography. In order not to disturb the supposedly innocent minds of their youthful readers (and to continue to publish in the process) the artists had to lengthen the heroine's hemline, and cover her too revealing breasts. In spite of *Pantera Bionda*'s enormous

"Pantera Bionda," Gian Giacomo Dalmasso and Enzo Magni. © SEAT.

success (100,000 copies of each issue were reportedly sold—a record for the Italian market), the publisher grew tired of the many lawsuits and seizures brought on by the enraged pillars of the community and decided to stop publication after two years and devote himself exclusively to educational comics; thus was born *Il Piccolo Centauro* ("The Little Centaur").

G.B.

PARKER, BRANT (1920-   ) Brant Parker was an American artist born in Los Angeles on August 26, 1920. Parker attended public schools in Los Angeles, as well as the Frank Wiggins Trade School and the Otis Art Institute—which provided the closest, he has said, to cartooning instruction that he could get.

Ultimately he joined the Walt Disney Studio and, after the mandatory training in the animation school, went straight to the animation department. He aspired to the story department but was assigned to "in between" animation, working on miscellaneous shorts before entering the Navy in late 1942.

After his discharge in 1945, Parker worked for Disney another year and a half ("Make Mine Music" was a major credit) and then moved East to settle with his new bride, Mary Lou, in her hometown of Endicott, New York. He got a job drawing political cartoons and staff art for the *Binghamton Press*. After another hitch in the Navy, Parker returned to work for IBM in the Binghamton area. He rose from technical illustration to advertising and promotion, being transferred to the greater Washington, D.C., area in the process.

While still in Endicott, cartoonist Parker judged an art show that included work by a local high school student named Johnny Hart. A friendship began that manifested itself in the early 1960s in a phone call by

Hart (then successful with *BC*) to Parker concerning a new strip.

The strip, ultimately, was *The Wizard of Id*, as classic a strip as *BC* or any other in comic history. Parker and Hart sold the strip to the executives of the Herald Tribune Syndicate in a conference in a New York City hotel and, with an initial list of about 50 papers, launched *Wizard* on Nov. 9, 1964.

Parker's *Wizard* has remained consistently outstanding, his deceptively loose drawing style one of the medium's most painstakingly executed and the gags first-class lunacy (written in equal parts by Parker and Hart).

Appreciation of *The Wizard of Id* has been accorded by the National Cartoonists Society, which awarded it the Best Humor Strip award, LUCA 8, and other organizations. On behalf of NCS and USO, Parker has made several tours of Army hospitals and bases.

Parker, incidentally, must have one of the most unlikely influences on anyone's future career in cartooning: Jack Webb, the producer and star of the television detective series *Dragnet*. Webb was student body president at Parker's high school and cartoonist for the school newspaper. Impressed by the ability to draw, the thrill of publication, and the recognition received, Parker was inspired to become a cartoonist.

Parker's consistent quality and exacting personal standards for his strip make him one of today's most notable professionals and one of the comic art form's greatest exponents.

Brant Parker, in association with artist Bill Rechin and writer Don Wilder, created *Crock* in 1975. A newspaper strip starring Vermin P. Crock, the heartless commander of a hapless French Foreign Legion troop, it spoofs such old-time movies as *Beau Geste* and *Outpost in Morocco*. Parker also continues to draw *The Wizard of Id*, for which he received a Reuben Award in 1984.

R.M.

PATORUZÚ (Argentina) Patoruzú is a Pampa Indian who made his first appearance in 1928 as a secondary character in Dante Quinterno's humor strip, *Don Julian de Monte Pío* (started in 1926 in the daily newspaper *La Razón*). In 1931 Patoruzú gave his name to a new strip,

"Patoruzito," Dante Quinterno. © Dante Quinterno.

597

"Patoruzú," Dante Quinterno. © Dante Quinterno.

"Patsy," Mel Graff. © AP Newsfeatures.

also by Quinterno. From *La Razón, Patoruzú* passed to *El Mundo* in 1935, the year that also saw the birth of Quinterno's publishing empire patterned after the American syndicate system, an enterprise without precedent in the Spanish-speaking countries. From that time *Patoruzú* not only appeared as a daily strip but as a weekly color page as well, published in *Mundo Argentina* and in the comic weekly to which it gave its name in 1936. On October 11, 1946, *Patoruzú* also appeared in Quinterno's second comic magazine, *Patoruzito*, with scripts by Mirco Repetto. In the United States *Patoruzú* was published by the New York newspaper *P.M.*, starting in August 1941.

Patoruzú represents the myth of the good Indian confronted by civilization. Endowed with Herculean strength and an elemental, but practical, mind, he is the most outstanding member of a family of Patagon people, of the Tehuelche tribe. Patoruzú discovers Buenos Aires in the course of his wanderings, a place so different from his native land, where he meets his cousin Isidoro, who has already been corrupted by the big city. Other family members include the little Patoruzito and Upa, Patoruzú's brother, as guileless as he is big. Like Astérix and other heroes, Patoruzú gets help from a magic source, in this case a flute given him by the chief of a North American tribe. The strip ended its long run on April 30, 1977.

In 1942 Dante Quinterno produced a *Patoruzú* animated cartoon in which he used a new chromatic system named "Alex-color," developed by Connio Santini and Rosiano.

L.G.

PATSY (U.S.) Started by Mel Graff in 1934, *The Adventures of Patsy* (simply called *Patsy* by most newspapers carrying the strip) had a checkered career fairly typical of most comic features distributed by Associated Press.

Conceived at first as a little-girl fantasy strip (a kind of modern-dress *Alice in Wonderland*) *Patsy* took place in

the fairy-tale lands of Odd Bodkins and King Silhouette, where the little heroine tangled with witches, giants, and monsters from whom she was often rescued by the Phantom Magician (who turned out to be her uncle Phil Cardigan). In mid-1935 Patsy and her guardian were back in the real world, and in December 1936 arrived in Hollywood where Patsy got a role in the movies.

Mel Graff's graphic treatment of *Patsy* was at first sketchy and uncertain. In 1936 he came under the influence of his AP colleague Noel Sickles and his style firmed up, becoming more airy and impressionistic. Graff was a very slow worker, however, and always had trouble making deadlines; in 1939 he hired the out-of-work Sickles to ghost for him. This was to be the high point of Patsy's career, which came to an end in 1940 when Graff was hired to do the *X-9* strip.

Upon Graff's departure, the strip was taken over by Charles Raab, who did a creditable job before leaving in 1943 to create the ill-starred *Foreign Correspondent*. Raab was succeeded by George Storm (of *Bobby Thatcher* fame) who lasted only until 1945; then came Richard Hall (who took Patsy back to the stage and screen); followed in 1946 by Bill Dyer, who drew *Patsy* in a caricatural style until the demise of the strip in the early 1950s.

Like most other AP features, *Patsy* suffered from the indecisiveness of its editors, who could not quite make up their minds whether it should be a fantasy tale, a little-girl story, or a straight adventure strip; accordingly, it did not succeed in any of these genres. The strip is still fondly remembered today, chiefly because of the contributions of Graff, Raab, and the uncredited Sickles.

M.H.

PATTERSON, RUSSELL (1894-1977) American cartoonist and illustrator Russell Patterson was born December 26, 1894, in Omaha, Nebraska. Patterson's father, a railroad lawyer, took his family to Newfoundland soon after the boy was born, then to Toronto and later to Montreal where Patterson was educated at St. Patrick's School. After one year of studies at McGill University, Patterson started his cartooning career with the weekly *Standard* (he was fired after a few weeks), then went to the French daily *La Patrie* where he originated his first comic strip, *Pierre et Pierrette*. In 1914

Patterson tried to join the Canadian Army but was turned down; so he went to study at the Chicago Art Institute, working meanwhile as a designer for Carson, Scott, Pirie, then as a decorator for Marshall Field.

After four years of interior decorating, Patterson became bored and left for France. From 1920 to 1925 he stayed in Paris where he studied under the aging Impressionist master Claude Monet and painted oils (mostly landscapes). Back in Chicago after his Parisian fling, Patterson embarked on a career in illustration, where he practically created the flapper. His popular success prompted him to go to New York where he worked for all the important magazines: *Redbook, Harper's Bazaar, Cosmopolitan, College Humor,* the old *Life,* and *American Magazine.* He also designed costumes for the Ziegfeld Follies and for George White's Scandals. When the Depression signaled the end of the flapper era, Patterson moved to Hollywood where he designed movie sets and costumes.

In 1951 Patterson again tried his hand at a comic strip, the stylish *Mamie* for United Feature Syndicate. *Mamie* featured some of Patterson's most striking designs and compositions (as well as a bevy of fashionably dressed females), but the public was not receptive to the artist's slightly dated elegance, and the strip folded in 1956. He died in Brigantine, New Jersey, in 1977; a retrospective of his works was organized by the Delaware Art Museum in June of that year.

As Stephen Becker noted in 1959: "He [Patterson] is not primarily a comic artist at all; but he is a great illustrator, and his style has been imitated by more currently successful comic artists that would like to admit it." Russell Patterson was the recipient of many awards over the years, including the Academy of Design Gold Medal and the silver plaque for best cartoonist in advertising and illustration (1957). He was one of the founders of the National Cartoonists Society and served as its president from 1952 to 1953.

M.H.

PAUL TEMPLE (G.B.) The daily strip *Paul Temple* began in the *London Evening News* on November 19, 1951, and ran a 20-year span to May 1, 1971. The hero, however, a crime novelist turned private detective, was created many years earlier by the playwright Francis Durbridge. Temple first appeared in a six-part radio serial called *Send For Paul Temple,* broadcast by the B.B.C. in 1938. Hugh Morton played Temple, and the serial accumulated a record amount of fan mail. Naturally, other serials followed: *Paul Temple and the Front Page Men; Paul Temple Intervenes,* and so on, and the character was brought to the cinema in four Paul Temple films made during the 1940s.

Durbridge wrote the screenplays from his radio plays and also adapted his first serial into novel form. The character's continuing popularity on radio and successful transfer to television prompted Julian Phipps, the Associated Newspapers strip editor, to develop a strip version. Francis Durbridge wrote the original continuity, retaining all the regular characters: Paul, his wife Steve, and Sir Graham Forbes of Scotland Yard.

The original artist was Alfred Sindall, who left the strip in 1954 to create a more adventurous one, *Tug Transom. Temple* was taken over by Bill Bailey, but eventually settled down with John McNamara, who drew it until the end. It was McNamara who had to change Paul's likeness to that of his television persona, Francis Matthews.

Reprints of the strip were published in pocket-size comic books, *Paul Temple Library,* the first issue being *The Magpie Mystery.*

D.G.

PAYASO (Philippines) *Payaso* ("The Clown") is a comic book novel written and illustrated by Noly Panaligan, one of the most respected names in Philippine comics. It appeared in *Tagalog Klasiks* during 1953. The novel is about the adventures and escapades of Ariel, the impish and talented young clown.

Ariel becomes the ward of a palace after he saves a young princess, Flordelisa, from the clutches of a band of soldiers who tried to abduct her. He is groomed to become the future court jester of the king. His training is supervised by Gino, the current court entertainer. At the beginning, Gino resents the young upstart but eventually becomes fond of the young rascal, realizing that he is worthy of becoming his eventual replacement. Amidst the laughter and the social carryings-on in the palace, treachery is brewing, and it is up to the young Ariel to prevent any harm from befalling the pretty princess.

"Payaso," Noly Panaligan. © Tagalog Klasiks.

"Paul Temple," John McNamara. © Evening News.

One of the villains in the story is Kasan, who continuously tries to kidnap the princess. His attempts are always thwarted by the child-clown who happens to be at the right place at the opportune moment. The constant battle of wits between the older and seasoned warrior against the youthful and clever Ariel provides an entertaining and humorous aspect of the novel. Kasan, raging with fury, invariably becomes a victim of one of Ariel's shrewd maneuvers with hilarious results. But it takes more than a bag of tricks for Payaso to sustain himself from the dangers and intrigues of the royal court.

This serialized novel is set in Europe during the days of heraldic pageantry and knighthood. This particular series became the reference source for many young, aspiring Filipino artists who wanted to do some research on medieval architecture, costumes, weapons, and designs.

Payaso is considered the best work of Noly Panaligan, who has done a tremendous amount of work for the Philippine comic book industry. He is also well-known for his commercial and motion picture work. The 1950s is considered the Golden Age of Philippine comic art, and one of the persons most responsible for the high quality of the art produced then is Panaligan.

O.J.

PAYNE, CHARLES M. (1873-1964) An American artist, Charles M. Payne was born in Queenstown, Pennsylvania, in 1873. Payne was seven when his father died and the family moved to his grandmother's farm. In 1894 Payne hung around the offices of the *Pittsburgh Post*, suggesting cartoon ideas, and two years later he was offered a job on the art staff. He became a popular personality in that city and the trademark of his cartoons was a little raccoon—adopted later by Billy DeBeck when he drew editorial cartoons in Pittsburgh.

The little mascot became a regular in Payne's first comic strip, a Sunday feature called *Coon Hollow Folks*. Soon his other comics, such as *Bear Creek Folks, Scary William*, and *Yennie Yonson*, drawn for papers in Pittsburgh and Philadelphia, were picked up by the early boilerplate syndicates. When national popularity and a steady income were assured, Payne gave up his editorial cartoons in Pittsburgh and moved to Hollywood, California, with his family. From there he sent *Honeybunch's Hubby*, a thrice-weekly early married strip, to the *New York World*.

While on a prospecting trip in Death Valley, he sent a new feature idea to the *World*, and it soon caught the fancy of New York and the nation. He gave up life in the West and miscellaneous freelance jobs to draw the new hit, *S'Matter, Pop?* The year was 1910, and the wildly loose and very funny adventures of Pop, Willyum, Desperate Ambrose, and others were to continue for 30 happy years in the *World* (until 1917), and on and off via the Bell Syndicate. The revived *Honeybunch's Hubby* shared Sunday slots as the top strip and occasionally the major Sunday page.

After the demise of *S'Matter, Pop?*, Payne attempted to develop new comics, including *G.I. Daddy*, a hillbilly strip similar to his earliest comics, and a high-schooler strip with the latest slang—all efforts to no avail. Payne gradually grew poorer and dropped from the public eye. But around Christmastime 1962, an item appeared in the New York papers about a poor old man in a dingy apartment building who was mugged by three assailants—his jaw broken in four places: the attackers escaped with less than a dollar in change.

The man was Charlie Payne, and the tragedy was all the greater because of the life the octogenarian was leading in spite of his poverty. He was always active, lively, and full of humor, a ladies' man to the end and an agile dancer. The late Vernon Greene had been drawing Payne out of his seclusion and bringing him to meetings of the National Cartoonists Society, where he became a great favorite. The vicious assault broke his pride and spirit worse than the injured parts of his body, and "Popsy" Payne ("the girls away back in 1923 always called me that," he wrote to this writer) died soon thereafter.

If Payne was never quite a major figure in comics, he was certainly one of the most unique and individualistic. His style was consistent throughout his career and, like Fontaine Fox, he took only casual notice of the strict comic strip conventions of his times.

His pages were decorative statements taken in the whole; panels would drop, circles would replace them, figures would stand outside of panel lines, horizon lines would disappear, colors would be used boldly. If the figures were sketchy, the shading was seemingly careless—broad, free brush dabs.

But there was a homely quality, a friendly, informal humor and a familiarity to his work that could never be denied. There was a touch of Sterrett in his incidental props, and the dialogue, especially Desperate Ambrose's, was involved, stagey, flowery, and full of glorious malaprops and pretensions.

Payne's work was always a very personal statement—of his humor and his own unique sense of composition and design. His comics are delightful little glimpses into the nonsense world of scheming kids, indulgent fathers, and light fancy.

R.M.

PAYO, EL (Mexico) With the descriptive subtitle "A Man Against the World," *El Payo* started in 1966 as a weekly pocket-size comic book published by Editorial Senda. The scripts were by Guillermo Vigil and the artwork was supplied by Fausto Buendía, Jr., in a style similar to that of Angel-José Mora, although not of equal quality. Buendía was later succeeded by a string of other staff artists.

El Payo and his girl companion, Lupita, live in the Mexican town of Vilmayo, although the hero's adventurous existence leads him to the most distant places. In any locale in which he chances to be, El Payo encounters adventure as well as passionate women, in a skillful blend of violence and sex, in the best tradition of this type of public-oriented publication.

El Payo has inspired three motion pictures: *El Payo* (1971), *El Fantasma de Mina Prieta* (1973), and *Los Caciques de San Crispín* (1973).

L.G.

PAZIENZA, ANDREA (1956-1988) An Italian cartoonist and illustrator, Pazienza was born in S. Menaio (Foggia). After graduating from art school, Pazienza attended university for some years and was active as a painter. Pazienza drew cartoons and short comic strips for the satirical graphic magazine *Il male*. In 1978 he cofounded, along with Filippo Scozzari, Stefano Tamburini, Massimo Mattioli, and Tanino Liberatore the lampoon magazine *Cannibale*, to which Pazienza contributed cartoons and comic strips.

"El Payo," Guillermo Vigil. © Editorial Senda.

In 1976 he collaborated again with Filippo Scozzari to produce comic strips for the magazine *AlterLinus*, using the art name/art mark "Traumfabrik." From 1977 to 1981 he wrote and drew (in his own name) the series *Le straordinarie avventure di Penthotal* for *Alter Alter*. In this strip and his next, *Zanardi*, Pazienza depicted

the anxieties of an Italian juvenile protester of the late 1970s. His subject matter came from his own experiences; his drawing style hovered between realism and caricature.

In 1980, Pazienza cofounded the magazine *Frigidaire* with Scozzari, Tamburini, Mattioli, and Liberatore. Among Pazienza's other contributions appeared the stories *Zanardi* (1983), *Alter Alter* (1987), and *Pompeo* (1985), the moving drama of a young drug addict.

Throughout his career, Pazienza contributed to a variety of other magazines as well, including *Frizzer, Tango, Zut,* and *Glamour*. Additionally, he produced artwork for disk covers, publishing houses, a film poster (for Fellini's *La città delle donne*, 1979), and an advertising campaign. In 1988 Pazienza disappeared suddenly. Many of his works have been reprinted in book form by several publishers.

G.C.C.

PEANUTS (U.S.) The most shining example of the American success story in the comic strip field began inauspiciously in 1950 when a timid young cartoonist with the unlikely name of Charles Monroe Schulz started making the round of comic syndicates with a new feature which he wanted to call "Li'l Folks." After being turned down by a half-dozen syndicates, Schulz's brainchild was finally accepted by United Feature Syndicate editors who rechristened the strip *Peanuts*. Schulz resented the syndicate-imposed title (and still does) but went along with the change. On October 2, 1950, *Peanuts* made its debut as a daily strip.

Building slowly from an initial list of seven newspapers, *Peanuts* was carried by 35 papers in October 1951, and by 45 papers in October 1952 (by which time a Sunday page had been added, starting on January 6, 1952). As Schulz himself stated: "It took a long time to develop . . . in fact the next twenty years saw a basic evolution of the strip." Be it as it may, *Peanuts* was not long in hitting its stride, and by the early 1960s its success had already become phenomenal, and continued to grow until, as John Tebbel noted in a 1969 article,

Andrea Pazienza, "Finzioni." © Milano Libri Edizione.

"Peanuts," Charles Schulz. © United Feature Syndicate.

"the total income from the strip, including that of its twenty-one licensed subsidiaries, has been estimated at $50,000,000 a year." Today *Peanuts* is probably the most successful comic strip of all time: the *Peanuts* reprint books (handled by no fewer than seven different publishers) cover two full columns of *Contemporary Authors*; there has been (at last count) 16 *Peanuts* cartoons produced for CBS-TV, as well as two feature-length animated films for National General Pictures; a musical comedy adaptation, *You're a Good Man, Charlie Brown*, arrived in 1967 (and has since been seen all around the world); and the strip has been exegesized at length in evangelist Robert Short's two books, *The Gospel According to Peanuts* (1965) and *The Parables of Peanuts* (1968).

Yet the theme of *Peanuts* is the great American unsuccess story. The strip's meek hero, Charlie Brown, has proved himself so far unable to kick a football, fly a kite, or win a baseball game, to name a few of his more conspicuous failings. Charlie Brown's chief tormentor is a scowling, sneering child-bitch named Lucy van Pelt. Linus, Lucy's brother, is a precocious, fragile intellectual who goes to pieces without his security blanket. Schroeder, whose only passion is to play Beethoven on his toy piano, the rough but generous Peppermint Patty, the dirty Pigpen, Franklin, the bespectacled black boy (a relative newcomer to the strip) and a few others, complete the human cast of *Peanuts* (in which no adult is ever seen).

Of course Snoopy, Charlie Brown's beagle, occupies a place of his own in the strip; he is (if only in fantasy) the total antithesis to Charlie Brown: a great writer, great athlete, great lover, the owner of the most palatial doghouse in the world, as well as being the most celebrated World War I ace pilot in all history ("Some day, I'll get you, Red Baron!"). In 1969 NASA picked Snoopy as the name for the Lunar Excursion Module on the *Apollo 10* flight to the moon, a fitting tribute to the venturesome beagle.

These children who reason and act like adults, the situations in which comedy is but a thin veil thrown over underlying sadness, the cruelty hidden under laughter, all this endows *Peanuts* with a bittersweet quality and a subtle ambiguity which are often disconcerting. There is in *Peanuts* a cry of despair almost Kirkegaardian in its accent, and thoroughly modern in its pretense.

In 1997, after almost 50 years of existence, *Peanuts* still ranks among the five top newspaper strips in America and is distributed in more than 70 countries, a remarkable record. The feature and his creator have mellowed in the last two decades, but only to an extent. The most telling evidence of this "softening" came on March 30, 1993, when Charlie Brown was finally allowed to score a home run (the pitcher later confessed he had actually tossed him a grapefruit). Like the Lord, Schulz giveth, and he taketh away.

M.H.

PECOS BILL (Italy) The school of Italian comic strip artists that formed in Mondadori and Vecchi's magazines in the mid-1930s reached a very high level of proficiency in graphic excellence as well as in storytelling ability. Few features were produced but they were of high artistic value and could hold their own against the comics imported from the United States. After World War II, when the number of magazines grew, the increased demand for material led to a decline in quality. The only creation worthy of the prewar Italian production was *Pecos Bill*.

Pecos Bill was written by Guido Martina and drawn by Raffaele Paparella and Pier Lorenzo De Vita, with the assistance of Dino Battaglia, Leone Cimpellin, Gino D'Antonio, and others. The feature appeared in the *Albi d'Oro* comic books published by Arnoldo Mondadori from 1949 to 1955. The story opens at a cowboy campfire with the participants telling of the legendary exploits of Pecos Bill. Then the action moves to Pecos

"Pecos Bill," Piero Gamba. © Edizioni Alpe.

Bill himself, an athletic horseman with parted blond hair and traditional dress made of a blue shirt, leather armbands, leather jacket, neckerchief, and red pants. The hero does not carry a gun or a rifle; his only weapon is the lariat, which he uses with masterful versatility. Mounted on his black horse, Turbine ("Whirlpool"), whose help is often welcome, Pecos Bill roams the West, ever ready to do battle with rebel Indians or white outlaws, to defend the oppressed, and to right every conceivable wrong. His sweetheart, a blonde girl named Sue, welcomes him back after each adventure. Pecos Bill's heart, however, is throbbing for a more aggressive and dynamic woman: the former outlaw Calamity Jane, whom our hero had been able to reform. Together they fight against all odds in a bond made of mutual respect and admiration.

In 1956 there was a new, short-lived version of *Pecos Bill* drawn by Piero Gamba for Edizioni Alpe. In 1960 the old episodes were reissued, followed and continued by a third series (this time for Torelli) done by a number of artists, among whom were Armando Bonato and Cimpellin (1964-1966). An attempt to revive the series with new episodes only lasted from 1978 to 1980.

G.B.

PEDRITO EL DRITO (Italy) An amusing parody of the Western genre, *Pedrito El Drito* has been recounting the tragic-comic vicissitudes of its title hero ever since it first appeared in the pages of the comic weekly *Rocky Rider* in 1948. Born as a strip, the saga of Pedrito developed into a gag page (published by the weekly *Albo dell'Intrepido*) and then back into a continuity strip in the weekly *Il Monello*. In these three comic books (all published by Universo) *Pedrito* has managed to last for over 25 years: it was the last series to appear in *Rocky Rider* and, when this publication folded, it went to *Il Monello* where it remained until the weekly replaced all of its humor features with adventure strips (1972). Since then, *Pedrito* has been featured weekly on the back cover of *Albo dell'Intrepido*, a publication which has already passed the 1,500-issue mark.

Pedrito, the sheriff of Tapioca City, is an inveterate drinker and a chronic gambler. His vices are scarcely

toned down by the admonitions—reinforced by a few strokes of the familiar rolling pin—of his wife, Paquita, who vainly tries to bring her husband back to the straight-and-narrow. The good sheriff, whose work does not seem to bother him unduly, spends most of his time in fights with Paquita and in elaborate schemes designed to elude her and get him to the town saloon.

This series (more than slightly reminiscent of *Bringing Up Father*) is the creation of the prolific cartoonist Antonio Terenghi, who is also the author of many other comic features, including *Piccola Eva* ("Little Eva"), *Tarzanetto* and *Poldino* (which is published in France by Sagédition). It ended its ample career in 1975.

G.B.

PEDROCCHI, FEDERICO (1907-1945) Federico Pedrocchi was an Italian journalist and writer born 1907 in Buenos Aires, Argentina, of Italian parents. In 1912 Pedrocchi was brought back to Italy by his parents. His father died a few years later and Pedrocchi had to go to work as soon as possible, drawing during his free time.

In 1930, after a short stint in advertising, he started writing short novels, which he also illustrated, did book covers, and contributed, both as writer and cartoonist, to a number of magazines such as *Domenica del Corriere, Corriere dei Piccoli, Jumbo,* and *Tempo.* He made his comic strip debut in 1935 with a colonial story, *I Due Tamburini* ("The Two Drummer-boys"), for Mondadori. This was followed by a number of other contributions by Pedrocchi, and in 1939 he became editor for all of Mondadori's children's magazines, a position that he was to hold until 1942, when he was inducted into the army.

Pedrocchi's "Mondadori years" were his most productive; there he wrote the continuities for some of the most remarkable among Italian strips: *Kit Carson*, a Western strip about the legendary explorer and Indian fighter; *La Compagnia dei Sette* ("The Company of Seven") about a gang of high-spirited adolescents; *Virus, il Mago della Foresta Morta* ("Virus, the Mage of the Dead Forest"), one of the more successful forays into science fantasy; *Zorro della Metropoli* ("Zorro of the Metropolis"), *Gino e Gianni,* and others.

Discharged at the end of 1943, Pedrocchi became editor of the Carroccio publishing house, writing four novels for them based on his own comic strip narratives. At the same time he kept his ties with Mondadori and continued his career as a comic strip writer. In January 1945 Pedrocchi was killed when the train in which he was riding was strafed by English planes.

Federico Pedrocchi made a sterling contribution to Italian comics in the difficult period of the late 1930s and early 1940s. Helped by a remarkable group of artists whom he was able to assemble around him (Rino Albertarelli, Cesare Avai, Giovanni Scolari, and Walter Molino, among others) he was the leading figure in what has been termed "the Italian comic strip renaissance."

M.H.

PEKKA PUUPÄÄ (Finland) *Pekka Puupää* ("Peter Blockhead"), the famous Finnish comic strip, was created in 1925 by the Finnish cartoonist Ola Fogelberg (1894-1952), who was also known by his pseudonym "Fogeli," and was launched in the cooperative maga-

"Pekka Puupää," Ola Fogelberg. © Kuluttajain Lehti.

zine *Kuluttajain lehti* ("Consumers' paper"). Fogelberg made cartoons, illustrated gags, magazine illustrations, book illustrations, and calendars and worked as illustrator and publicity manager of a big Helsinki cooperative from 1918 to 1945. It was therefore no surprise that he should also try doing a comic strip for the cooperative's *Kuluttajain lehti*. Besides, he had already done another comic strip during the winter months of 1917 to 1918, before the Finnish civil war. This had been a strongly allegorical satire on the political life of the time, entitled *Janne Ankkanen* ("Jimmy Duck"). *Janne Ankkanen* was written by the famous Finnish satirist Jalmari Finne and was published in *Suomen Kuvalehti*, a big pictorial.

As in *Janne Ankkanen*, there was a decidedly ideological commitment in the *Pekka Puupää* comic strip, appearing in a consumers' paper propagating cooperative and leftist ideas. However, the comic strip also exposed human weaknesses in general. *Pekka Puupää* is drawn in a relatively simple, cartoony style, with text and dialogue printed below the pictures.

In 1945 Fogelberg turned to freelance work and started publishing his *Pekka Puupää* series in book form. With these annually published books, the series reached its peak of popularity, selling about 70,000 copies per year.

Soon after Fogelberg's death in 1952, a film based on the *Pekka Puupää* comic strip was produced by a big Finnish movie mogul, T. J. Särkkä. Over the next decade, a total of 13 films was produced. The films were mainly aimed at juvenile audiences. They are counted among the most popular Finnish films ever made. As happens so often, the movie version eclipsed the artistically subtle original. Nevertheless, the tradition of *Pekka Puupää* annuals was carried on after Fogelberg's death by his daughter, Toto Fogelberg-Kaila.

W.F.

PELLOS, RENÉ (1900-   ) A French cartoonist and illustrator born in 1900 near Lyons, René Pellos never received any formal art education, although he remem-

bers drawing from the age of five and filling his notebooks with sketches and caricatures. After dropping out of school, Pellos held all kinds of jobs—advertising artist, lithographer, book designer, stage decorator, and pianist (in 1919-1920). In the 1920s Pellos's career stabilized when he became sports cartoonist for the important Paris daily *L'Intransigeant*, while contributing cartoons and illustrations to other newspapers, doing sports panels for *Le Miroir des Sports*, and drawing covers for *Match* magazine.

Pellos's comic strip career started inauspiciously in 1935 with *Riri, Gogo et Lolo*, a kid strip that even its creator prefers to forget. Then came the dazzling *Futuropolis* (1937), a tale of anticipation in which Pellos displayed all his talents as an artist and designer. In quick succession there followed *Jean-Jacques Ardent* (a sports strip turned war strip at the outbreak of World War II), *Monsieur Petipon* (a humor strip not without merit), *Moustique* (a kid strip), and *Electropolis* (Pellos's second attempt at science fiction, unfortunately interrupted by the German invasion in June 1940).

During the German occupation, Pellos, while working as a sports cartoonist and illustrator and continuing some of his series (notably *Monsieur Petipon*), took

René Pellos, "Atomas." © Mon Journal.

an active part in the French Resistance. In 1944, following France's liberation, he resumed his professional career with contributions to such publications as *Record, Sporting,* and *Le Petit Echo de la Mode* (a woman's magazine). In 1946 he came back to the comic strip with *Durga-Râni* (on a script by Jean Sylvere), a kind of secondhand *Futuropolis* with a muscular young heroine instead of the obligatory male hero. In 1948 another science fiction strip, *Atomas* (on the well-worn theme of the power-mad scientist) followed. In the meantime Pellos had met Georges Offenstadt, who suggested that the cartoonist revive Forton's classic comic strip, *Les Pieds-Nickelés.* At first reluctant, Pellos finally accepted the offer, and his new version of the strip appeared in 1948.

Since then Pellos has devoted his career almost exclusively to *Les Pieds-Nickelés* (with an occasional foray into magazine or book illustration). A genuine artist who has excelled in all facets of his profession, he is especially noted for the innovations (and the breath of fresh air) which he brought to the anemic French comic strip of the prewar years. Since the death of Alain Saint-Ogan in 1974, René Pellos has been cast (somewhat diffidently) into the role of the grand old man of French comic art. In 1981 he left *Les Pieds-Nickelés* and went into retirement, although he continued to turn out an occasional drawing and give a number of interviews to the press.

M.H.

PENG GUOLIANG (1940-   ) As many others, Peng, from his childhood, liked art and especially cartoon art. But he was assigned to work as a photogra-

pher in a publishing house in Beijing at the beginning of his career. From 1979 to date Peng has worked as an art editor for *Young Children Pictorial,* a monthly journal published by the Chinese Children and Juvenile Publisher, in Beijing.

Among other comic strips for young children, Peng's *Little Dog Guaiguai* is one of the most popular strips that has been carried by *Young Children Pictorial* and other similar journals since 1986. Each story is narrated in about 30 color drawings in a two-page spread. The hero of each story, Little Dog Guaiguai (*guaiguai* in Chinese means "obedience") is a clever dog but does not always prove to be obedient. The disobedient dog, however, learns his lesson at the end of the story, which is intended to be of educative value to the young readers. For example, the little dog dislikes washing his head, as many children do in reality. After the little dog goes through all the troubles caused by being dirty, he learns that not washing his head is no good.

Little Dog Guaiguai was adapted into a 120-program series by a Beijing television station in the early 1990s, after ten years of being broadcast every month. These 120 stories in more than 6,000 drawings were also published in five volumes by Beijing Normal University Press in 1996.

In addition, Peng has created many other comic strips for children, including *Little Taotao, Little Pals, Little White Rabbit and Big Grey Wolf, Doggy Officer, Good Friends, Small Fox with Big Feet,* and others. Among them, *Doggy Officer* is an officer dressed in ancient-time uniform; the strip functions as a metaphor of life today.

H.Y.L.L.

Peng Guoliang, "The Little Dog Guaiguai." © *Peng Guoliang.*

PENGUIN, THE (Canada) Not to be confused with the villain of the same name in Batman and Detective Comics in the United States, the Canadian crimefighter and counterspy known as the Penguin made his debut in 1943 in issue number 15 of *Wow Comics*, one of six titles launched by Bell Features and Publishing Co., Toronto, after a wartime embargo wiped U.S. comic books off Canadian newsstands. The first issue of *Wow* (September 1941) appeared in full color; issues 2 to 8 in two colors, and thereafter in black and white with full-color covers.

Created by Adrian Dingle, later one of Canada's foremost painters, *The Penguin* featured a debonair crimefighter who wore a birdlike mask, white tie, and tails. And, like the majority of Bells's adventure strips, it was serialized. One of Dingle's gimmicks was to conceal the Penguin's real identify from the reader, never showing his face. Another break from comic-hero tradition was Dingle's readiness to have the Penguin unmasked by a criminal or ally. In Wow number 16, for example, Lugar, the fiendish master spy, unmasks the captive Penguin who says, "Those who peer under the mask don't live long." Eventually, of course, his warning comes true. In *Wow* number 18 the Penguin meets a good-natured American named Simon Snurge who accidentally learns his identity and then helps him break up a ring of gasoline ration coupon counterfeiters.

When Bell converted to full-color printing at the war's end to counteract the reappearance of U.S. comic books, Dingle continued the feature under the title, *The Blue Raven*, presumably because Bell was planning to try and crack the U.S. market with his color product and foresaw a conflict with National Periodical Publications over its right to the Penguin name. *The Blue Raven*'s flight was short-lived, however, and ended in the disintegration of the Canadian comic book industry in the face of U.S. competition.

P.H.

PENSION RADICELLE, LA (France) Eugène Gire is one of the unsung heroes of the French humor strip. He was one of the first to transplant the crazy humor of the Marx brothers to France, and he honed the lowly pun to a fine point of accuracy long before René Goscinny was cutting his teeth as an office boy at *Mad* magazine. As one of the pillars of the comic weekly *Vaillant*, he contributed innumerable series to the publication, from *R. Hudi Junior* to *Kam et Rah, les Terribles*. His masterpiece (if such it can be called) remains, however, *La Pension Radicelle* ("The Radicelle Boarding-House"), which unfolded its merry compendium of absurdities in July 1947.

In the boarding-house run by the big-hearted and elderly Mrs. Radicelle, a joyous band of youngsters led by the high-spirited, devilishly inventive Saturnin, spreads good-natured mischief in the region. When the kids run out of pranks to play on their neighbors, they elect to live in a deserted village, which they turn into a kind of pranksters' paradise. Then they leave for an African island (the resemblance with the Katzenjammers is evident) only to come back to their village.

La Pension Radicelle was a funny, nonsensical strip. Had Gire made up his mind whether he wanted it to be a chronicle of weekly gags or to turn it into a tale of humorous adventure, the feature would have probably gone on forever, so inexhaustible was the author's imagination. As it turned out, *La Pension Radicelle* ended its long career in *Vaillant* (now called *Pif*) on February 23, 1968.

M.H.

PEPITO (Italy) The protagonists of the rollickingly funny strip *Pepito*, while not well-known in their own country, are very popular abroad. Pepito, Ventoinpoppa, Hernandez De La Banane, Admiral Debath O'Lavoir, and the pirate Schiacciasassi were all created by the prolific cartoonist Luciano Bottaro in 1951. Carlo Chendi writes the scripts for this series which has been published in France since 1954, first as a fortnightly, then as a king-size monthly, by Sagédition. The French publishers have also issued several annuals, one-shots and hardbound volumes of *Pepito*. In Germany the strip has been published by Kauka Verlag since 1972. Under the name *Corchito*, it has also been translated into Spanish and Portuguese in several

"Pepito," Luciano Bottaro. © Edizioni Alpe.

Latin American countries. In Italy, on the other hand, after being initially published by Edizioni Alpe, it went out with hardly a murmur.

As happens quite often in the comics, the main protagonist of the strip is not the title character but a sidekick who had become popular with the readers. In this case it is Hernandez De La Banane, the governor, who appeared in the first episode of *Pepito*, but only on the sidelines. He later acquired his full personality as a petty colonial tyrant: two-faced, cheating, conniving, and deceitful, but ingratiating nonetheless. He is surrounded by a colorful entourage of wizards and soothsayers, admirals and inventors, noble ladies and witches. "His Ventripotence," as his subjects call him, pressures the people with all kinds of imaginative taxes, which he usually pockets. When a shortage is discovered by some zealous auditor, the governor arranges to have his ship scuttled by a crew of accommodating pirates.

Pepito and his corsairs, on the other hand, fight against the Spanish Crown and try to right the injustices committed by the governor.

The *Pepito* strip, on the strength of its popularity abroad, finally came back to Italy in paperback form published by Editrice Cenisio (1975). More than 40 years after its inception it is still going strong in Italy and abroad, especially in France where it is being reprinted over and over again.

G.B.

PERERA, CAMILLUS (1945?-   ) "Camillusge" is the prefatory signature to the titles of various Sri Lankan strips created and drawn by Camillus Perera and published in periodicals of his corporation, Camillus Publications. There are at least 15 major characters and eight periodicals, two of the latter, *Sathsiri* and *Rasika*, devoted entirely to comics.

Perera's strips are among the longest surviving and most popular in Sri Lanka; *Camillusge Don Sethan* dates to May 1, 1966, and *Camillusge Gajaman Samaga Sathsiri* to August 1972. These strips appeared in scattered comics papers (for example, *Gajaman* debuted in the country's first comics paper *Sathuta* and switched to *Sittara* and then *Sathsiri*, both Camillus papers) before Perera pulled them together under one corporate structure.

Three special magazines done by Perera in 1984 to 1985 formed the basis for Camillus Publications. In April 1984 Perera did *Camillusge Gajaman*, full of cartoons about the Sri Lankan New Year, followed by *Camillusge Samayan* and *Camillusge Gajaman 2* in December 1985. Sales of 200,000 to 300,000 prompted Perera to form the company.

Camillus comics take on a number of genres, such as love and romance (the most popular), historical fiction, jungle adventure, and humor. A typical issue of *Sathsiri* or *Rasika* consists of 16 pages with one story per page. Fourteen stories are done by almost as many different freelance artists; the fifteenth is the humor strip by Perera. Almost all stories emanate from Perera who commissions freelance artists to draw them; most are serialized, with some running for years.

As comics papers faced stiff competition from television and video in the 1990s, Perera was seeking other avenues, particularly animation.

J.A.L

"Le Père Ladébauche," Albéric Bourgeois. © La Presse.

PÈRE LADÉBAUCHE, LE (Canada) The character of Père Ladébauche (which could be translated as "Pop Debauchery") was created in 1879 by the prolific newspaperman, cartoonist, and writer Hector Bertelot. On March 5, 1904, this picturesque figure was adapted to the Sunday comic page by J. Charlebois for the newspaper *La Presse*. But it was only with the arrival of Albéric Bourgeois, who took over *Le Père Ladébauche* on February 11, 1905, that the feature really took off.

Père Ladébauche was a colorful rogue: bald, bewhiskered, with a twinkle in his eye, he had a fondness for liquor, gambling, and a pretty skirt. His adventures took place at first in the restricted locale of the province of Quebec, but he soon launched his ne'er-do-well career around the globe, which he circled several times, always coming back to Montreal to brag about his world-wise experiences. When he took over *Le Père Ladébauche*, Bourgeois was already in control of his drawing style: his line was elegant and humorous, his characters portrayed with a deft hand. Although he owed some of his techniques to the early American cartoonists (notably Richard Outcault and Charles Schulz from whom he borrowed his graphic treatment of children) Bourgeois was much his own man, and his style is highly individual. Thanks to his talent, *Le Père Ladébauche* became the best-known Canadian feature of the time, and it fended off the assaults of more famous (and cheaper) American imports for more than 50 years. The only survivor of the entire comic strip line of *La Presse* in 1910, *Le Père Ladébauche* was to pursue its long career until 1957, when Bourgeois retired from active life.

Le Père Ladébauche is indisputably the most important Canadian comic strip in the French language. After years of obscurity, it is now being studied by young

French-Canadian cartoonists conscious of their artistic heritage.

M.H.

PERISHERS, THE (G.B.) Maisie, Marlon, and Baby Grumpling were the original kids called *The Perishers*, a strip dreamed up by Bill Herbert, strip editor of the *Daily Mirror*, for the northern edition. It replaced *Hylda Baker's Diary*, a failure to adapt into strip form the popular radio comedienne. Artist Dennis Collins, then signing himself "Kol," was retained; writer Denis Gifford was replaced by Ben Witham.

The strip started on February 10, 1958, a shadow of the *Daily Sketch*'s popular *Peanuts*. Herbert brought in a new writer, advertising artist Maurice Dodd, and moved Witham to caption for Jack Greenall's panel, *Useless Eustace*. Dodd revived the absent Wellin'ton, the kid in a deerstalker who lives in a drainpipe, and fitted him out with Boot, a great big lovable lion of an Olde English Sheepdog. Then came Plain Jane, Fiscal Yere (B. H. Calcutta, failed), Tatty Oldbit, a beetle, a delinquent caterpillar, a Teutonic tortoise, assorted crabs and other scuttling things which "festoon the bottom of the strip like barnacles on a barge" (Dodd).

In July 1962 *The Perishers* moved to larger premises, a solo position out of the gallery where the rest of the *Mirror* strips lived. Their panels grew larger in size, upwards: the first day the little denizens solved the problem by taking to the air on stilts! They crossed the border to the Scottish edition of the *Mirror* in 1966, and currently appear in full color in that part of the world. Rod McKuen took them to the United States and published a hardback, *Old Boot's Private Papers* (1970), and

"The Perishers," Dennis Collins. © Daily Mirror Ltd.

regular paperback reprints began in 1962, the sixteenth arriving in 1974 together with an anthology, *The Perishers Omnibus*.

After Collins retired, Maurice Dodd took over the drawing chores but eventually found the daily grind too much of an imposition. Currently the strip is illustrated by Bill Mevin, a former children's comic artist with a number of television cartoon characters to his credit. *The Perishers* have also been animated into a successful television series.

D.G.

PERONI, CARLO (1929-   ) Carlo Peroni is an Italian cartoonist born on November 24, 1929, in Senigallia. After his art school studies, Peroni first devoted himself to the restoration of old paintings, then to frescoes and mural paintings in churches. This did not pay well, however, and he moved to all kinds of odd jobs— clerk, mechanic, warehouse guard, barrel-maker, songwriter—before going on to stage design. From there the step to comics was an easy one. In 1948 he moved to Milan and began contributing to *Vispa Teresa* magazine as an editor and artist. At the same time he ghosted for several comic artists, setting the pattern for his very personal and funny style.

In 1949 Peroni started working for the Catholic magazine *L'Aspirante* where he created *Lillo, Lallo e Lello*. Moving to Rome in 1952 he continued his collaboration with Catholic magazines, especially *Il Giornalino*, where he published centerspreads, illustrations, and comic strips, among which Brick is the most notable (1954). Brick was a puppetlike creature who often lived wild adventures in the company of movie stars (Frank Sinatra and Claudio Villa) or comic strip heroes (Dan Dare or Superman).

In 1959, in the pages of the pocket-size comic book *Capitan Walter*, Peroni produced a number of short-lived comic creations: *Grama Gramelloni, Gambalesta* ("Rubberlegs"), *Veneziano Telegtammi*; of longer duration, more than 100 episodes, was his comic saga, *Gervasio*, later continued in *Jolly*. After a stint as a layout man and a television graphic artist, Peroni went back to the comics in 1961, trying his hand at adventure with such features as *Sand e Zeos* and *Gorin e Obi*. Both were produced for the Communist Party weekly, *Il Pionere*, as was his zany *Gigetto, Pirata Picoletto* ("Gigoletto, the Diminutive Pirate").

More comic creation followed from Peroni's prolific pen: *Ping e Pong* (1961); *Teddy Sprin* (a Western parody, 1963); *Zio Boris* a pastiche of horror movies written by Alfredo Castelli; and *Van Helsing*, about a screwball vampire, on texts by Castelli and Baratelli (both in 1969); *Lumak* (1971), from which a book, *Mondo Lumace*, was produced; and in 1973, *Gianconiglio* ("John Rabbit"), a very successful strip which now absorbs all his time. Among his latter creations mention should be made of *Spugna* (1976) and *Gipsy* (1984). He is also among the staff that draws the *Sherlock Holmes* comic stories and the Hanna-Barbera characters.

Carlo Peroni has also enjoyed a successful career as an animator, working on such series as *Calimero, Ferrarella, Gatto Silvestro* ("Sylvester," the cat created by Warner Bros. studios), *Braccobaldo, Coccobill*, and others.

G.B.

PERROTT, REG (1916?-1948?) A British cartoonist born in Charlton, London, Reg Perrott joined the Morley Adams and Henry Fidler Agency as a staff artist in 1934, contributing strips and illustrations to the newspaper features and comic sections syndicated by that concern. At first he drew humorous strips: *Benny & Buster* in the *South Wales Echo, Bobbie & Bertie Bruin* in the *Scottish Daily Express, The Imps* in the *Yorkshire Evening News* (all 1933). In 1934 he continued this style with *Buster & Bones* (Y.E.N.), *A Hair Raising Voyage* (S.W.E.), and *Roly & Poly*, a daily strip in the *London Evening Star*. During that year he suddenly switched styles with a dramatic picture serial called *Luck of the Legion* for the *Bristol Evening World*.

It was the birth of a new talent, and Perrott rapidly rose to the forefront of British adventure artists with his succeeding series for the same newspaper: *The Archer Highwayman* (1934) and *Targa the Tiger Man, Land of the Lost People*, and *Code of the Northland* (1935). In 1935 he left Adams & Fidler to freelance for the Amalgamated Press. Whirling Round the World on the back page of *Joker* visualized a voyage in a new design of autogyro. *Wheels of Fortune* (March 3, 1935) on the back of *Jolly* featured young Bob Dean as the driver of Lord Tom's new racing car, the Red Flash. The Young Explorers (October 17, 1936) brought thrills aboard the school ship *Sea Foam* to *Puck*.

A new opportunity arose when Walt Disney Productions launched *Mickey Mouse Weekly* in 1936. Perrott contributed a tremendous historical serial, *Road to Rome*, then went into full color for the first time with a Western, *White Cloud*. He followed this with the superb color serial, *Sons of the Sword*, and a complete story for the *Mickey Mouse Holiday Special* called *Secret of the Manor*.

Perrott began 1937 with another Western, *Golden Arrow*. *Puck* presented this strip as if it were a film; it was the first time this children's weekly had broken with tradition. Instead of captions in type beneath the pictures, Perrott lettered captions and balloons within the panels of the strip. He also varied the size and shape of his panels as required by the situation. Another 1937 departure was his serial *Golden Eagle*, a two-color (black and orange) saga of Ace Eagle and his experimental aircraft, on the back of *Golden* (October 23, 1937). The title was later changed to *Kings of the Air*. The year ended with *Crusader's Christmas*, another complete strip for *Mickey Mouse Holiday Special*.

In 1938 Perrott was back in *Mickey Mouse Weekly* with another flying serial, *Wings of Fortune*, and he did another complete strip, *Rescuer's Reward*, for the *Holiday Special*. His best strip began on October 8, 1938, in the first issue of *Happy Days*. In full-color gravure, this historical saga was called *Song of the Sword*, and in it he used long cinemascopic panels for battle scenes. His last major work was the Western serial *Red Rider* in *Jolly*, another two-tone (red and black) job (March 18, 1939).

Perrott enlisted in the Royal Air Force Regiment in 1939. Discharged, he was made art editor of *Mickey Mouse* (by now a fortnightly). In 1944 he drew a small comic serial, *Sir Roger de Coverlet*, followed by *White King of Arabia* (1945). Replaced when Basil Reynolds returned, he freelanced *Spaceship to the Moon* to a one-shot comic, *Look & Laugh* (1948?), and illustrated the book, *King Harold's Son* (1946). His early death robbed British comics of perhaps their best adventure artist.

D.G.

PERRY (Germany) Perry is the comic book version of *Perry Rhodan*, the most successful science fiction hero to come out of postwar Germany. Perry Rhodan, the practically immortal Terran Overlord, first started in the comic realm with *Perry Rhodan im Bild* ("Perry Rhodan in Pictures") in 1968. Twenty-seven issues later, in 1970, the title of the book was changed to *Perry*, the numbering starting once again from 1. Whereas *Perry Rhodan im Bild* had stayed fairly close to the original novels, *Perry* started a new line of stories that made use of a somewhat streamlined cast of characters. This change was made so that the comic book would be more appealing to readers not yet initiated by the novels.

Since No. 37, *Perry* is being written by Dirk Hess. From the very beginning, the artwork was provided by the Studio Giolitti. Some of the earlier issues were by German-born artist Kurt Caesar, who occasionally worked for the Giolitti shop in Rome, Italy. With *Perry* No. 37, a change was made to make the book more visually stimulating. Giorgio Gambiotti, another artist from the Giolitti stable, had devised a new style that was inspired by pop art and Marvel Comics. The futuristic flavor was further enhanced by doing away with most of the women's wear. Rectangular and square

"Perry," Studio Giolitti. © Moewing Verlag.

"Peter Piltdown," Mal Eaton. © Herald-Tribune Syndicate.

panels were given up for full-page compositions with interlocking pieces. This was toned down in time to make the stories less puzzling. The new style showed a strong penchant toward the art of John Buscema. Thus, cameo appearances of The Thing and the Silver Surfer or of the changeling computer from one *Star Trek* episode may have been meant as inside jokes.

To be sure, *Perry* doesn't exactly come as a revelation to either comics or science fiction fans. Yet, besides giving glimpses of shapely females accompanying the hero through space, *Perry* is keeping the sci-fi format alive in Germany and, thanks to the new style initiated with No. 37, foreign language reprints in France, Italy, and Israel have been made possible.

The *Perry* comic book did not remain the only spin-off of the Perry Rhodan novels. In 1967 to 1968 Rhodan was put on film—a fact much deplored by disgruntled fans—and, for some years thereafter, some of the Rhodan space operas have been marketed as stereo dramas on long-playing record albums.

In its heyday, *Perry* made a comic strip guest appearance in *Bravo*, a weekly magazine for the teenage movie, television, and pop music fans. Early in 1975, however, the *Perry* comic book ceased publication with No. 129, a victim of ever-increasing production costs. Due to a sales method of regional distribution and redistribution, that last issue did not go on sale in some parts of Germany until late in the summer of 1975.

W.F.

PETER PILTDOWN (U.S.) Leading caricaturist Mal Eaton introduced his unique stone-age comic strip *Peter Piltdown* to the *New York Herald-Tribune* Sunday section on August 4, 1935. Each week his group of motley urchins created havoc and slapstick adventure with their mischievous pranks in the tradition of *Buster Brown* and *The Katzenjammer Kids*.

Peter was an artful figure supported by more developed innocents and meddlers, such as Charlie Cro-

Magnon, Oofty, and the guiltless girl Inna-Minnie. The situations Eaton created were usually manic and full of hilarious slapstick. Minus a handful of parental appearances, the strip's sole adult, bearded hermit Mr. Shadrack, stumbled into the feature in 1940, adding a classic personality and perfect comic foil to the cast. Ever spouting tall tales of fictitious valor, he was often the victim of capers prompted by the unruly imps or any of the limitless species of animals that populated their primeval world. Kiltie the scottie, Bolivar the octopus, Artie the dinosaur, and other members of the menagerie shared equal importance with their human companions and paved the way for the eclectic cast of Johnny Hart's *B.C.* some years later. In 1940 he also added Pookie, a carrot-top simpleton whose naive charm made her another target and the strip's most endearing figure. By 1943 the prehistoric aura was diluted with less frequent sightings of dinos, while contemporary dress replaced animal skins.

Eaton's drawing style was loose and physical, capturing well the activity in fluid simplicity and the varying environs in rich textures. On December 15, 1946, the strip ceased, replaced for a short time with *Pookie*, a daily-sized Sunday filler. In the early 1950s it reappeared as *Rocky Stoneaxe* within the comics section of *Boy's Life* magazine, retitled after its only new character. There the feature appeared monthly until finally disappearing in 1973, and it is forgotten today. Eaton's strip should be recalled for its consistent humor and unique treatment of classic comic formulas.

The strip's name was clearly inspired by the "Piltdown Man," the skeleton of a purported prehistoric man discovered near Piltdown in England. The "discovery" was exposed as a hoax in the 1950s, but it held credibility for a long time: as late as the 1970s it led Australian cartoonist Donald Langmead to create *Piltdown—the Almost Human*, which ran from 1973 into the 1980s.

B.J.

PETER RABBIT (U.S.) Harrison Cady's adaptation to the Sunday comic page format of Thornton W. Burgess's children's animal narratives, *Peter Rabbit*, began in the *New York Tribune* on August 15, 1920. Cady, the noted illustrator of the highly popular Burgess books, was the effective scripter of the comic strip, but soon departed sharply from the story and character lines of the Burgess works, within a few months after beginning the strip. Domesticating Burgess's bachelor hero of many stories, Cady made Peter Rabbit a cozily married bunny with two twin boys, either or both of whom responded to the name "Petey," while the Cady-created Mrs. Rabbit was named "Hepsy." Cady also quickly abandoned the many Burgess characters and introduced such regular figures of his own as Old Mr. Bear and Mr. (or "Professor") Possum.

Leaning heavily on wild, rambunctious slapstick rather than on the mildly poetic subtleties of the Burgess books, Cady swiftly shaped a strip which generally pleased the 6-to-10-year-olds at whom it was aimed over the 30-plus years of its existence. Never carried in a large number of papers, and reprinted only infrequently in comic books between 1937 and 1950, *Peter Rabbit* was essentially an institution of the *New York Herald-Tribune* until Cady retired on July 25, 1948. After the few remaining Cady Sunday pages were run, Vincent Fago took the strip over with disastrous effects (a worse artist would be hard to imagine in any context), and it was omitted from even the *Herald-Tribune*'s pages after a few years in 1956.

B.B.

PETE THE TRAMP (U.S.) In the late 1920s C. D. Russell had created the character of a seedy, weather-beaten tramp who appeared in a series of gag cartoons in the magazine *Judge*. Hearst, always looking for new talent, spotted Russell's tramp cartoons and had him signed up by King Features Syndicate. Russell's creation *Pete the Tramp* appeared for the first time as a Sunday feature on January 10, 1932. (There briefly was a *Pete* daily strip as well, starting in February 1934 and lasting till June 1937.)

Pete and his yellow mutt, Boy (who later had his own strip titled *Pete's Pup*), roam the streets and parks of the city in search of food, shelter, and companionship, most often rebuffed, sometimes beaten up, but never disheartened. In the sad little tramp's breast hope springs eternal, and he concocts the wildest

"Pete the Tramp," C. D. Russell. © King Features Syndicate.

schemes to mooch a meal or swipe a fat cigar. There is more than a bit of pathos in Pete's small triumphs, and in the bitter years of the Depression the humor must have rung as true as it did funny.

Pete's only support is the cook Linda who often bakes a pie or prepares a meal for the little tramp; and his nemesis is O'Leary, the fat cop who delights in waking up poor Pete and rousting him off his park bench with a blow of his nightstick. Later Pete was also to acquire an adopted infant as sad-looking as himself.

After the 1940s *Pete*'s tramp humor began to wane, and the gags often seemed repetitive and forced. *Pete the Tramp* finally folded on December 12, 1963, shortly after the creator's death.

M.H.

PFEUFER, CARL (1910-1980) Carl Pfeufer is an American comic strip and comic book artist born September 29, 1910, in Mexico City. In 1913 the Pfeufer family moved to New York where the young Carl grew up and went to high school, majoring in commercial art. After graduation he went on to Cooper Union, studying freehand drawing (he won first prize three different times), to the National Academy of Design (where he unsuccessfully competed for the Prix de Rome), and to the Grand Central Art School. Toward the end of the 1920s Carl Pfeufer started work with the McFadden publications doing layouts, spot illustrations, and editorial cartoons.

In the mid-1930s Pfeufer was working as a staff artist for the *Brooklyn Eagle* when he created with writer Bob Moore a Sunday comic page comprised of two features: *Don Dixon and the Hidden Empire*, a science fiction strip, and *Tad of the Tanbark*, a jungle story (both started on October 6, 1935). In December 1936 Pfeufer took over *Gordon, Soldier of Fortune* from John Hales. All three features were initially distributed by the *Eagle* itself, but were later farmed out to the Watkins Syndicate. *Tad* folded in 1940; *Gordon* and *Don Dixon* lasted a while longer, until July 1941.

Like so many other unemployed comic strip artists, Pfeufer turned to comic book work, at first for Marvel (*The Human Torch*, *Submariner*) then (from 1943) for Fawcett, where he enjoyed an enduring career. His credits there include *Ibis the Invincible*, *Commando Yank*, *Don Winslow*, and a host of Western titles (*Hopalong Cassidy*, *Ken Maynard*, *Tom Mix*, and *Gabby Hayes*). In 1955, following Fawcett's wholesale discontinuance of their comic book line, he shifted to Charlton, working on many of their titles, notably *Charlie Chan*. (In the meantime Pfeufer had tried his hand at newspaper strips again with such short-lived creations as *Bantam Prince* for the *Herald-Tribune* and *Chisholm Kid* for the *Pittsburgh Courier*.) From Charlton he went to Dell, working on many television comic titles, and in the 1960s he quit comic book work altogether.

Making his home in Texas, Pfeufer devoted the last years of his life to turning out paintings and sculptures for galleries around the world. He died in 1980, and his passing went more or less unnoticed.

M.H.

PHANTOM, THE (U.S.) 1—In the wake of *Mandrake*'s success Lee Falk brought out another adventure strip for King Features, *The Phantom*. First appearing as a daily strip on February 17, 1936 (with a Sunday page added in May 1939), the feature was originally drawn

"The Phantom," Lee Falk and Ray Moore. © King Features Syndicate.

by Ray Moore. Moore, however, suffered a grave injury in 1942, and his assistant Wilson McCoy took over gradually. From 1947 to 1961 (the date of his death) McCoy alone assured the drawing of *The Phantom,* which then passed for a few months into the hands of Bill Lignante. Sy Barry took over in 1962 and is still drawing the feature today.

A mysterious, hooded figure of justice, the Phantom carries on a long tradition of crime fighting begun in the 16th century and passed on from father to son. He is, therefore, not just a man but a legend, "the ghost-who-walks," believed to be invincible and immortal. Like all legendary figures he has his symbol—"the sign of the skull"—whose simple mention instills fear in the heart of the most callous criminal. In his fight against crime, the Phantom is assisted by Guran, the crafty leader of the dreaded Bandar pygmies and by Devil, his faithful gray wolf. But the Phantom is also human: a great part of his time is spent in the pursuit of his fiancee, Diana Palmer.

After the war the Phantom changed his base of operations from the Bengal region of India to a mythical country, part African, part Asian. He was also a naturalized American under the name of Kit Walker (in the earlier episodes he was English, the 20th descendant of Sir Christopher Standish) and now had a whole organization, "the Jungle Patrol," working for him. The Phantom and Diana finally were married, after many a mishap and contretemps, in December 1977, and in the spring of 1979 twins were born to the happy couple: Heloise and Kit, Jr., thus ensuring that the legend of the ghost-who-walks would go on for at least another generation.

Skillfully playing on this aura of myth and mystery, Lee Falk has been able to raise *The Phantom* above the customary level of the adventure tale into the realms of the fable and the parable.

Ever since its beginning, *The Phantom* has been among the half-dozen or so top adventure strips. It is especially popular overseas and is being translated and read in some 60 countries. There have been countless imitations of the character in the United States and

abroad. *The Phantom* was adapted to the screen in 1943, and a series of paperback novels (purportedly written by Lee Falk) are now being published by Avon. A theatrical movie version of *The Phantom,* starring Billy Zane, was released in 1996.

M.H.

2—Despite its great success in the syndicated newspaper field, *The Phantom* feature has had a less successful and generally nondescript career in comic books. Its first half dozen appearances came between 1939 and 1949 in David McKay Publishing's *Feature Books,* which were simply reprints of *The Phantom* comic strip in comic book format.

And while the feature's second series—less than a dozen stories in *Harvey Hits* and *Harvey Comics Hits* between 1951 and 1960—did utilize new material, the stories and artwork left much to be desired.

The latest Phantom comic book series began in November 1962; Gold Key comics published 17 issues before abandoning the title. Not wishing to see their character lose the comic book market, however, King Features began publishing the book beginning with number 18 (September 1966). And while the King version was considered the best of the comic book lot—it featured art by Wallace Wood, Jeff Jones, Al Williamson, and also *Flash Gordon* back-up stories in many issues—the company gave up the ghost with the 28th issue in December 1967. In February 1969, Charlton Comics purchased the comic book rights from King and resumed publication of *The Phantom.* And although the Charlton series used material by artists like Steve Ditko and Jim Aparo, not everyone was happy. "Lee Falk was complaining about how we were handling his creation," editor George Wildman was quoted as saying, and Charlton began using translations of Spanish and Italian *Phantom* stories in June 1974. There were a few short-lived attempts at reviving the character in the late 1980s and early 1990s.

J.B.

PHANTOM LADY (U.S.) 1—*Phantom Lady* was a minor back-up feature, which made its first appearance in Quality's *Police* number 1 for August 1941. Created by artist A. Peddy, Phantom Lady was really Sandra Knight, daughter of a U.S. senator. Her adventures were pedestrian at best, but her greatest asset was her costume: a revealing halter and tight, short pants. The character never merited any considerable financial or artistic attention, but the Quality version is best remembered for a one-liner uttered during comic books' high-pitched patriotic days. "America comes first," explained Phantom Lady, "even before Dad." *Phantom Lady* appeared in *Police* through the 23rd issue (October 1943).

2—When Fox decided to return to comic publishing, they immediately exhumed the Blue Beetle—in a way. He rarely appeared on the cover—he narrated crime stories on the inside while a long-legged girl in underwear adorned the cover. When Fox acquired the rights to *Phantom Lady*, much the same thing happened. She would appear on the cover—breasts jutting seductively forward, just barely covered by her tight halter—and then simply narrate crime stories on the inside.

And while this reincarnation lasted only between August 1947 and April 1949, one of the worst of the covers eventually appeared in Dr. Fredric Wertham's *Seduction of the Innocent*, a 1953 attack on comic books, The *Phantom Lady* cover (April 1948) showed a large-breasted, scantily clad Sandra Knight tied to a wooden post; Wertham claimed it represented "sexual stimulation by combining 'headlights' with the sadist's dream of tying up a woman." Whether he overreacted or not, the cover has come to be regarded as an example of the seamier aspects of comic book publishing.

3—A third *Phantom Lady* feature, published by Ajax, appeared briefly between December 1954 and June 1955. A more reasonable anatomy and a less-revealing costume were used in this four-issue series, however.

J.B.

PHILÉMON (France) *Philémon* was created in 1965 by Fred (pseudonym of Othon Aristides) for the French comic weekly *Pilote*. The first two episodes (dating back respectively to 1965 and 1966) were not yet clearly defined, hovering between parodic adventure and satirical fantasy, with Fred not quite making up his mind about which way he wanted to go. With the third sequence, however, "Le Naufragé du 'A'" ("The Stranded Man of 'A'"), Fred finally hit his stride, making *Philémon* into one of the most exciting comic strip creations in recent times.

With *Philémon*, we squarely step over the fine line between science fiction and fantasy. Philémon, Fred's stringy farm-boy hero, accidentally crosses into a parallel world, landing on one or another of the letters of the words "Atlantic Ocean" in the mythical Sea of Maps. Along with the old well-digger Barthélémy, the stranded man of the title whom he meets there, he runs into countless perils, which include sinking into a mirage, fighting a deadly grand piano, and having to answer a Sphinxlike riddle asked by a giant mousetrap. After overcoming all the dangers of "A," Philémon and Barthélémy succeed in getting back to the everyday world; but they will try and try again to rejoin the fantasy world they have known, made each time more inaccessible.

The stories of *Philémon* are always imaginative and fresh, with unpredictable turns and twists, and Fred's universe is full of weird creatures, magical landscapes, and surreal vistas, reminiscent of *Krazy Kat*. In the

"Philémon," Fred (Othon Aristides). © Editions Dargaud.

1980s Fred started parallel careers as scriptwriter for television and children's book illustrator and publisher; as a result, new *Philémon* adventures have become few and far between.

One of the high points of the modern European comic strip, *Philémon* has been translated in several languages, and all its episodes reprinted in hardbound form by Editions Dargaud.

M.H.

PHIL HARDY (U.S.) The first 100-percent, all-out, concentrated adventure comic strip, and one of the best, was George Storm's sadly short-lived *Phil Hardy*, which began distribution by the Bell Syndicate on November 2, 1925. Nominally scripted by the byline-credited "Edwin Alger, Jr." (Jay Jerome Williams), *Phil Hardy*, dealing with a boy adventurer of 15, was overwhelmingly infused with artist Storm's stunning stylistic pace, narrative visualization, and prolongation of suspense and violence at every opportunity. (Williams's own normal, dull narration is best perceived in its correct perspective in his later *Bound To Win*, or *Ben Webster's Career*, one of the tritest, flattest strips ever published.) Filled with brutally dispatched corpses and a swashbuckling atmosphere of derring-do within the first few weeks of continuity, *Phil Hardy* presented at full-length what such other early adventure epics as *Wash Tubbs* and *Little Orphan Annie* could then only hint at.

Unfortunately, this rapid and uncompromising strip (derived from such rousing boys' adventure fiction as *Treasure Island* and *Tom Cringle's Log*) was too sharp and sudden an innovation for editors and many readers, and both its distribution and thematic influence were minimal at the time. As a result, *Phil Hardy* lasted barely 11 months, to be replaced by the much milder and more conservative narrative strip, *Bound To Win*, which Williams—initially using Storm's art—undertook for the same syndicate. Storm, however, departed shortly to begin his own highly successful adventure strip, *Bobby Thatcher*, for McClure. With its initial rousing cast of characters from Phil himself to old Jason Royle, the gun-wielding ship's cook, through such rough customers as Ghost Hansen, Baldy Scott, and Captain Eli Bent, *Phil Hardy* was strong stuff for its time, although the syndicate warily slackened its forceful pace several months before the strip closed on September 29, 1926. Brief and memorable, the landmark, *Phil Hardy*, should be reprinted complete in a compact volume.

B.B.

PHOEBE ZEIT-GEIST (U.S.) An American attempt at duplicating *Barbarella*'s *succès de scandale*, *Phoebe Zeit-Geist* appeared for the first time in 1966 in the pages of *Evergreen Review* as a comic feature written by Michael O'Donoghue and drawn by Frank Springer.

Phoebe Zeit-Geist, the lovely 24-year-old heroine, is drugged and abducted during a party in Antwerp; she is then to know a series of ordeals comparable only to those suffered by Sade's Justine: she is violated (a number of times), whipped, branded, suspended from a flying helicopter, raped by a giant iguana, and so on. The authors were evidently trying for satire and social criticism (with references to Vietnam, the Congo, the race problem), but their approach was ham-handed and far from the mark. Springer's drawings were adequate but did not quite fit the point of the story. The whole enterprise was singularly lacking in conviction and looked like the put-on that it indeed was.

Phoebe Zeit-Geist was reprinted (in both hardbound and paperback forms) by Grove Press, the publishers of *Evergreen*.

M.H.

PICCOLO SCERIFFO, IL (Italy) Just after World War II the regular comic book was replaced by a so-called "strip book" of five inches by four inches in size. This product allowed for greater sales because it could be sold very cheaply. From the 10 lire which it cost at the beginning, it went up to 12, then 15, and stayed at 20 lire for several years. The later increase in page number and in price (which reached 50 lire) led to its disappearance in the early 1960s. However, during its 15 years on the market the "strip book" made the fortune of several publishers, chief among them Tristano Torelli who, after the success of *Sciuscia*, issued *Il Piccolo Sceriffo* ("The Little Sheriff") in 1950 with illustrations by Dino Zuffi.

Kit, the son of Sheriff Hodgkin, took the place of his father who had been killed by outlaws. With the help of his sister, Lizzie, his fat sidekick, Piggie, and his girlfriend, the beautiful Flossie, he fought for more than 20 years to bring law and order to the Wild West. His enemies were sometimes a ruthless band of criminals, sometimes Indian rebels. Kit's youth—he was 16—won him the loyalty of young readers who identified with him. The lively and buoyant character of the hero made up for any holes in the plots—of which there were many—as well as for the mediocrity of Zuffi's draftsmanship.

Once the strip book closed down, the adventures of the little sheriff—which were by then called *Il Nuovo Sceriffo* ("The New Sheriff"), since the hero had grown up in the meantime—were published first in pocket book format and then in a giant comic book. Over the years there have been reprints of the series in the original as well as book formats.

The strip's writer, Giana Angissola, authored a novel based on the little sheriff's adventures in 1951, with illustrations by Ferdinando Tacconi. A movie was also produced in 1950.

G.B.

PICHARD, GEORGES (1920-   ) The dean of French erotic cartoonists, Georges Pichard was born January 17, 1920, in Paris. Following studies at the School of Applied Arts, he embarked on a traditional advertising career, later setting up his own ad agency in 1946. After contributing a number of cartoons to the humor magazine *LeRire*, in 1956 he signed his first comic strip for the very staid girl's weekly *La Semaine de Suzette*; a conventional teenage girl tale titled *Miss Mimi*, it in no way foreshadowed his creations to come, although his knack at drawing pretty girls was already in evidence.

In 1964 he met Jacques Lob, who was to become his most constant scriptwriter. After turning out a number of superhero parodies (*Tenebrax*, *Submerman*, etc.), the duo came up in 1967 with their first overtly erotic creation, *Blanche Epiphanie*. A spoof of turn-of-the-century dime novels, the feature was notable for showing the well-endowed heroine in various states of distress and undress. Pichard followed in the same vein in 1970 with *Paulette* (on a script by fellow cartoonist Georges Wolinski), detailing the progress of a voluptuous redhead who went through all sorts of harrowing ordeals, of which rape was the least objectionable. He later sounded much the same theme with *Caroline Choléra* (1976), but perhaps due to the fact it was written by a woman—Danie Dubos—it provided an interesting twist to the proceedings. Caroline experienced the whole gamut of kinky sex out of sheer feminine curiosity.

Pichard crowned his already notorious career with *Marie-Gabrielle* (1977-1981), in which he pulled out all stops in a horrendous tale of a buxom, dark-haired beauty subjected to every conceivable form of torture and torment—in full color and minute detail. Perhaps as a take on one of the Marquis de Sade's most famous anthology pieces—wherein Justine and her companions are victimized by an order of monks—he had his Marie-Gabrielle and her cellmates tormented by nuns who kept piously reciting the catalog of tortures visited upon Christian saints and martyrs all the while meting out the most barbarous treatment to their helpless charges.

Like most of his colleagues in the same line of work, he also illustrated in the 1990s a number of classics of erotic literature, notably Guillaume Apollinaire's *Memoirs of a Don Juan* and the *Kama-Sutra*. In a related but somewhat more acceptable vein he has produced a highly intriguing version of the *Odyssey*, *Ulysses* (in 1968, with Lob), an entirely uncanonical adaptation of *Carmen* (1981), as well as a tongue-in-cheek tale of evolution gone mad, *Bornéo Joe* (with Dubos, 1982-1983). In addition Pichard has turned out countless book and magazine illustrations, humor cartoons, and lithographs in his 40-plus-year career.

M.H.

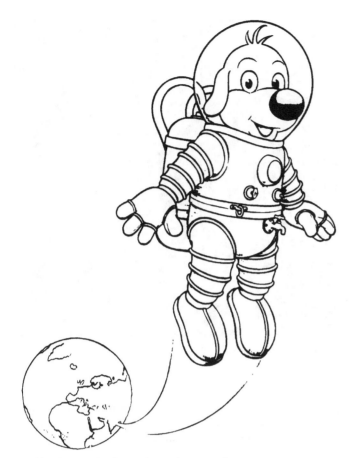

"Pif le Chien," Claude Arnal. © Editions Vaillant.

was appearing (which became *Le Journal de Pif*, later changed to *Pif-Gadget*).

Due to age and illness (he died in 1982), Arnal left more and more of the drawing to other hands in the 1970s, notably those of Roger Mas and Giorgio Cavazzano. In 1992, after more than four decades, *Pif* was scuttled along with the weekly that bore its name, but the strip can still be seen in reprints.

M.H.

PINCHON, JOSEPH PORPHYRE (1871-1953) Joseph Porphyre Pinchon was a French cartoonist, illustrator, and painter born in Paris in 1871. After graduating from the School of Fine Arts, devoted himself to painting and illustrating. Around the turn of the century he became an illustrator for the various magazines published by Gauthier-Languereau. In 1905 in the girl's weekly *La Semaine de Suzette* Pinchon illustrated a filler story written by one of the publishers, Maurice Languereau, under the pseudonym "Caumery." The story was "Bécassine" and it proved an immediate hit. For the rest of his life Pinchon devoted the best of his talent to the drawing of further adventures of the little Breton maid nicknamed Bécassine.

In addition to *Bécassine* Pinchon contributed a number of other picture-stories (none of them could be called comic strips in the strict sense): *La Vie des Hommes Illustres* ("The Lives of Famous Men"), *La Famille Amulette* and *Patatras* (inspired by *Gasoline Alley*) in the 1920s and 1930s; and *La Vie des Grands Fauves* ("The Life of the Big Cats") in the weekly *Fanfan la Tulipe* from 1941 to 1943.

Pinchon never stopped painting and he was for a long time the president of the National Society of Fine Arts. He died in 1953.

M.H.

PINKERTON, JR. *see* Radio Patrol.

PINKY RANKIN (U.S.) In 1942 the editors of the *Daily Worker*, the newspaper of the Communist Party U.S.A., decided to create their own comic strip hero who would compete with the bourgeois representatives of the commercially syndicated adventure strips. The result was *Pinky Rankin* drawn by Dick Floyd and scripted by the paper's staff writers. (The *Daily Worker* did have another home-grown product, *Lefty Louie*, but its hero was judged too tame for the purpose.)

Pinky was a proletarian hero who took part in the struggle against the Nazis as an underground fighter in the occupied countries of Europe. When he was not busy blowing up bridges, derailing trains, and killing off lines upon lines of advancing German storm troopers with witheringly accurate machine-gun fire, he could be counted on to deliver stern lectures on the role played by American Communist workers in the struggle against fascism, and on the necessity for a second front. The strip was one of the most brutal of the war years, and graphically depicted scenes of torture, rape, and slaughter perpetrated by the German soldiers who were portrayed as sadistic brutes and sexual degenerates. The end of the war in Europe and the onset of the Cold War contributed to the decline of *Pinky Rankin* and its subsequent demise occurred around 1948.

Dick Floyd's graphic style, while never very distinguished, was adequate. The texts, however, were far-fetched, even by the standards of the time, and cannot

detail. For years, the French Communist Party newspaper *L'Humanité* had been running *Felix the Cat* (one of the editors' personal favorites) when, after the start of the Cold War, the Party hierarchy decided that the King Features strip was too glaring an example of American enterprise to be tolerated any longer in the pages of their official publication. Accordingly, they turned to Claude Arnal (José Cabrero Arnal) who was then doing the successful *Placide et Muzo* animal strip for the communist-financed comic weekly *Vaillant*; and in 1950 *Pif le Chien* was thus launched on its long career.

Pif was a rather cheerful mutt, with a perpetual grin and an oversize nose (hence his name), in the humanized tradition of Walt Disney's animals. His adventures were pedestrian and a far cry from the inspired tribulations of Felix. The outside world might at times frustrate or infuriate him, but it was never heartless or cruel. Pif's main adversary was the cat Hercule, whom he loved to outwit at every turn. The drawing was latter-day Disney and a bit cloying in its slavish imitation of the master's style.

Whether Pif was popular with the readers of *L'Humanité* remains a well-kept secret; at any rate in 1952 he went on to *Vaillant* where he was given an entire page in which to pursue his harmless pranks. In 1955 the overworked Arnal (he was also doing the *Placide et Muzo* feature for *Vaillant*, and another animal strip, *Roudoudou*, for the magazine of the same name) relinquished *Pif* to René Mas, who was in turn succeeded in 1970 by Louis Cance, without significant improvement in either drawing or story line.

Pif le Chien has been so popular that it added a spin-off in 1964: *Pifou* (Pifou is Pif's pup) by René Mas; and in 1965 it gave its name to the newspaper in which it

"Pinky Rankin," Dick Floyd. © Daily Worker.

"Les Pionniers de l'Espérance," Roger Lécureux and Raymond Poïvet. © Editions Vaillant.

be taken today without a large dose of salt. *Pinky Rankin* is included here as an oddity rather than for any outstanding qualities of its own. It also serves to illustrate the point that, for philosophical reasons, it is very difficult to create a credible hero of the Left (a problem which Chinese comics have had to grapple with ever since Mao Tse-Tung's accession to power).

M.H.

PIONNIERS DE L'ESPÉRANCE, LES (France) *Les Pionniers de l'Espérance* ("The Pioneers of the Hope"), written by Roger Léureux and drawn by Raymond Poïvet, first appeared in the French comic weekly *Vaillant* on December 14, 1945.

The *Hope* is a spaceship whose crew is made up of men and women of different nationalities: Professor Wright, an English naturalist; Maud, the American woman doctor; Tsin-Lu, a Chinese woman chemist; Tom (later called Tangha), a filmmaker from Martinique; Rodion, a Russian physicist; and Robert, a French engineer and the designer of the vehicle.

Since 1945, when they embarked on their first interplanetary expedition, the pioneers of the Hope have lived through an incalculable number of adventures, some of them in outer space, some of them right here on the planet Earth. The first episode, which took place on the alien planet "Radias," was clearly inspired by Alex Raymond's *Flash Gordon*, but the strip later acquired its own distinctive look and flavor.

In the 1950s Léureux and Poïvet introduced their readers to all kinds of different universes, some natural, some artificial, peopled by menlike creatures, by machines, and even by crystallike thinking molecules; they also refined their themes away from conventional space-opera and into the more sophisticated patterns of classical science fiction. It ended its run as a weekly feature in 1973, but a number of independent stories appeared in the late 1970s and early 1980s.

Les Pionniers de l'Espérance has always been highly imaginative in conception and execution; where it is weakest is in the creation of memorable characters (even the protagonists blur after a while), but remains nonetheless one of the best and most popular of the European science fiction strips.

M.H.

PIPPO (Italy) *Pippo*, which first appeared in the Catholic magazine *Il Vittorioso* in 1940, is probably Benito Jacovitti's most famous comic creation.

At first Pippo was only an emblematic figure, dispensing to the readers the moral advice and beliefs of the editors. He was a good boy, always ready to help his neighbors whenever his assistance was needed. He was born during the war years and his first adventures pictured him fighting the British. Then he gradually went on to satirize the Fascist government; in his latter exploits Pippo was politically nonaligned.

Jacovitti has thrust Pippo into the most desperate predicaments in the most remote places: in the American West, Africa, India, or in some imaginary kingdom. Pippo's sworn enemy is Zagar, the symbol of evil, always attired in black tights, in what seems to have been a spoof of *Diabolik* many years ahead of its time! After a period of time Pippo has acquired two comic allies, Pertica and Palla, and a normal dog (at least insofar as any man or beast can be called normal in Jacovitti's weird world) named Tom. Pertica ("Bean Pole") is a lanky and absentminded fellow who always gets in trouble because of his gullibility; on the other hand Palla ("Ball") is chubby, astute, and spunky. They both play as foils to Pippo.

It is impossible to get bored with the adventures of Pippo and his friends (the "three P's" as they are affectionately called), not only because of the very funny satire but also for the outlandish situations in which the heroes find themselves—from 16th-century France to ancient Rome, from Cleopatra's Egypt to the America of today. They now live mostly in reprints of their old adventures.

G.B.

PIP, SQUEAK AND WILFRED (G.B.) The most famous and popular children's strip in British newspa-

"Pip, Squeak and Wilfred," A. B. Payne. © Daily Mirror Ltd.

pers, *Pip* (a dog), *Squeak* (a penguin), and *Wilfred* (a rabbit) began quietly. On Monday, May 12, 1919, the *Daily Mirror* launched their postwar revival of their prewar children's corner, *The Children's Mirror*. It was edited and written by journalist Bertram Lamb, who called himself "Uncle Dick," and in his first "letter" he introduced his pets, Pip and Squeak. They were so named in honor of Lamb's former Army batman, who had been nicknamed "Pipsqueak." A small illustration drawn by A. B. Payne, a Welsh cartoonist who worked on the children's comics, accompanied the text.

There was an immediately favorable response, and by the end of the month the single panel had become a four-panel strip. The following year Pip and Squeak found a baby bunny and christened it Wilfred (February 7, 1920). The trio was complete. Wilfred, who could say only "Gug" (because he was a baby) and "Nunc" (meaning "uncle"), stole everyone's heart, and ultimately (on January 3, 1927) the Wilfredian League of Gugnuncs was inaugurated, with badges, songs (The Gugnunc's Chortle), and a climactic rally of 87,000 members in the Royal Albert Hall (April 14, 1928).

Payne's daily strip had expanded to six panels a day, with an edition in *Sunday Pictorial*. All this in turn expanded into a pull-out weekly comic supplement to the *Mirror* called *Pip & Squeak* (October 15, 1921, reducing to a single page by 1925), and another supplement, *Children's Own Sunday Pictorial* (August 6, 1933, reducing during 1934).

The first reprint of the strips was published as a book in November 1920, and Pip and Squeak Annual appeared every Christmas from 1923 to 1939. This was supplemented by Wilfred's Annual from 1924 to 1938 and Uncle Dick's Annual (1930). Lancelot Speed ani-

mated a series of cartoon films called *The Wonderful Adventures of Pip, Squeak and Wilfred* for Astra National Films in 1922.

Payne introduced a supporting cast of fascinating characters: Auntie, the shaggy old penguin who had not learned to talk English ("Oomsk! Oogle!"); Peter, the Dalmatian pup; Stanley, the baby penguin; Wttzoffski, the anarchist, and his pup, Pop ski. The strip was concluded on June 14, 1940, and revived on January 18, 1947, again drawn by veteran Payne. This time the strip was published weekly, on Saturdays.

After Payne's retirement the characters were revamped and given a modern look by Hugh McClelland, who dressed the hitherto naked animals in dungarees and skirts. Despite a revival of *Pip, Squeak and Wilfred Annual* (1953-1955), the "new" characters did not really catch on. They were discontinued on March 9, 1955, transferred to the weekly newspaper for children, *Junior Mirror*, and then dropped. But old Gugnuncs still greet each other with their secret password: "Ick-ick! Pah-boo!"

D.G.

PISTOL JIM (Spain) The Western strip *Pistol Jim* was created in the first issue (October 1945) of the comic magazine *Gran Chicos* by Carlos Freixas. The feature had an eventful career in the course of its five episodes, which were published not only in the aforementioned magazine, but also in the weekly, *El Coyote*, in the comic book collection "Mosquitó," and in the Argentine publication, *Aventuras*.

Pistol Jim was a hero always attired in black (not unlike Hopalong Cassidy) and always wearing his emblem, a six-shooter, on his chest. The weapon sym-

"Pistol Jim," Carlos Freixas. © Carlos Freixas.

bolized the hero's spirit of justice, which often led him to uphold the law by means of a quick draw. In the course of his cleaning out the West, Pistol Jim was assisted in his labors by the freckle-faced Nick, a jujitsu expert and the Spanish idea of American boyhood as pictured in countless Hollywood movies. In addition to his task of policing the West, Pistol Jim also had the delicate duty of choosing between the love of his childhood sweetheart—the rich ranch owner Nelly Cayo—and the seductions of the alluring saloon singer, Belle Smith. *Pistol Jim*'s scripts were simple and straightforward, but Carlos Freixas (son of the master, Emilio Freixas) displayed an elegance of line and an energy that made the strip more than a simple recital of fist and gun fights.

L.G.

PITCH AND TOSS (G.B.) *Pitch and Toss*, subtitled *The Nautical Nuts*, was cast in the classic mold of all British comic double acts: fat and thin, tall and short. They were first sighted in *Lot-O-Fun* on April 3, 1920, where Joe Hardman drew them upsetting their punt at the Boat Race. But it was a false start, and after an early retirement they were reenlisted by the editor of *Funny Wonder*, who gave them to Don Newhouse to draw. Newhouse passed them on to his young assistant, Roy Wilson, and the result, with its brand-new subtitle, *Our Saucy Shipwrecked Mariners*, floated onto page five of *Funny Wonder* number 449, dated October 28, 1922. They anchored in this weekly for 22 years. After much drifting on their raft, they hove to on the back page as a full 12-panel strip. There they shipped aboard the good ship *Saucy Sal*, and proceeded to make life miserable for the skipper, Cap'n Codseye (who labeled his cabin "No admish without permish"), not to mention Clarence the Cookie and the noble owner, Lord Topnoddy.

In the 1930s came another move, which proved out their enormous popularity: they up-anchored for the front page of *Funny Wonder*, where Bertie Brown's strip of *Charlie Chaplin* had reigned supreme since 1915. Charlie continued on an inside page, while *Pitch and Toss* grew stronger and stronger. Wilson added two newcomers to the crew, Pengy the Penguin and Occy the Octopus, and from April 26, 1941, color was added, a two-tone effect in red and black. The merry mariners were finally pensioned off in 1944, and Wilson replaced them with a soldier, *Private Billy Muggins*.

D.G.

PITT, STANLEY JOHN (1925-   ) Born at Rozelle, N.S.W., Australia, in 1925 the son of a plasterer, Stanley Pitt became attracted to drawing when he was a young boy. Educated at the Marist Brothers, he was

Stanley Pitt, "Flash Gordon." © King Features Syndicate.

constantly in trouble for drawing instead of pursuing his studies. By the time he left school in 1940, he had fallen under the spell of Alex Raymond, through the Flash Gordon pages appearing in the *Sydney Sunday Sun*. Raymond's sense of the heroic and romantic, coupled with his proportions, anatomy, and crisp, fine line left an indelible impression on Pitt—and all his future artistic efforts were directed at emulating Raymond's efforts. While working as a milkman in 1942, he sold his first comic to *Consolidated Press: Anthony Fury*.

In 1943, he began to sell four-page comics to Frank Johnson Publications, which allowed him to rub shoulders with such artists as Cecil "Unk" White Rhys Williams, Carl Lyon, and Emile Mercier. This was invaluable experience as Stanley Pitt was never to take a formal art lesson in his life. In 1945, he began producing comic strip advertisements for Colgate-Palmolive, which lead to being placed under contract by *Associated Newspapers Ltd.* to produce a science fiction adventure strip. The resultant *Silver Starr in the Flameworld* appeared in the *Sunday Sun* in November 1946 replacing *Flash Gordon*. The following two years saw Pitt set a new standard in realistic-style comic art, and *Silver Starr* became a household name. Due to a dispute about the printed size of the strip, Pitt left the paper and the last *Silver Starr* appeared on November 14, 1948.

Almost immediately, Pitt was approached by the *Sunday Herald*, for whom he created another Sunday color strip, *Captain Power*. Dissatisfied with the story line (provided by a journalist) and his salary, Pitt left the paper in late 1949 and returned to the comic book field. With the assistance of his brother, Reginald, Paul Wheelahan, and Frank and Jimmy Ashley, he produced 32 issues of *Yarmak Comics* for Young's Merchandising. In the early 1950s, with his brother, he attempted to get two strips, *Lemmy Caution* and *Mr. Midnight*, syndicated in the United States. When these attempts failed he joined the *Cleveland Press* in 1956 to produce new *Silver Starr* comics and, when the comic industry folded, to produce covers for Western paperbacks.

The magnificent artwork on his unpublished strip, *Gully Foyle*, became legendary in the late 1960s. Samples of this work were responsible for Pitt being asked to produce comics for *National Periodical Publications* and *Western Publishing* as well as ghosting an 11-week sequence of *Secret Agent Corrigan* in 1969, and a further four weeks in 1972. Because of his detailed style and perfectionist approach, Stanley Pitt has not been a prolific producer of comic art—yet, combining dedication with integrity, he has become recognized as a leading illustrator of science fiction, and the finest comic artist in the classic tradition that Australia ever produced.

J.R.

PLACID ET MUZO (France) *Placid et Muzo* (the names of the characters can be broadly translated as "Placid and Mug") started in issue 56 of the comic weekly *Vaillant* (as *Muzo et Placide*) on May 16, 1946. Its creator was the Spanish cartoonist Claude Arnal (pseudonym of José Cabrero Arnal).

The story relates the rather innocuous adventures of two animal friends, Placid the slow-witted bear and Muzo the sly fox. They frolic and gambol amid pasteboard scenery and cardboard animal caricatures. Arnal's drawings are an obvious imitation of the Disney style, just as his animal characters are directly derived from countless cartoons turned out by the Disney studio. Indeed, *Placid et Muzo* is so inane in its story line and sugary in its psychology that it may well be called a "sillier symphony." As it was, however, it met with fair success among *Vaillant*'s young readers, who made up the bulk of its audience and was promi-

nently featured on the first page of the magazine until it was later dethroned by the author's next and equally bland creation, *Pif le Chien*. (It should be noted that the scenarios of the first few years were written by Jean Ollivier, who often used doggerel verse—thus accenting the resemblance with Disney's *Silly Symphonies*.)

In 1958 *Placid et Muzo* passed into the hands of cartoonist Nicolaou and is ploddingly pursuing its career toward the 30-year mark. Still in the hands of Nicolaou it has now passed the half-century milepost.

M.H.

PLASTIC MAN (U.S.) Created by humor artist and writer Jack Cole in August 1941, *Plastic Man* made his first appearance in Quality Comics' *Police* number 1. An unabashed parody of all the existing superhero strips, the feature handled crime fighting with tongue-perennially-in-cheek, allowing "Plas" and Woozy Winks, his maladroit assistant who was added in *Police* number 13, a full range of zany antics, outrageous situations, and offbeat villains.

Plastic Man wasn't your run-of-the-mill superhero, either. He eschewed the almost mandatory cape and cowl, opting instead for sunglasses and a red jumpsuit. Even Woozy was strangely attired, always wearing the same straw hat, polka-dot shirt, and green trousers in all his appearances. The team also had origins which were less than superhero pristine: Plastic Man was once a petty crook named Eel O'Brien, who gained his stretching power after being thrown into a vat of acid; Woozy, on the other hand, was well-known as a notorious jail breaker who went straight only after Plastic Man allowed him to become his partner. In short, the pair were two characters who didn't fit the mold, and that made their adventures refreshingly different from the glut of deadly serious crimefighters prevalent in the 1940s.

Plastic Man was handled by creator Cole with tremendous verve and style, always striking a wholesome balance between antic slapstick and sophisticated humor. From the strip's inception, Cole knew *Plastic Man* wouldn't follow in the steps of *Batman*, *Superman*,

"Placid et Muzo," Claude Arnal. © Editions Vaillant.

"Plastic Man," Jack Cole. © Comic Magazines.

and the like. The strip was to be played strictly for laughs, and Cole's judicious mixture of "bigfoot" and realistic artwork made the feature one of the best ever to appear in comic books. Novel villains like sad-faced Sadly Sadly and beautiful temptresses like the Figure allowed Plastic Man to assume outrageous shapes to combat evil. At times he was a lightning bolt, or a steamroller, or a glider, or a bull's-eye, or dozens of other objects, all allowing Cole to exploit every possible satiric angle.

Plastic Man also appeared in his own magazine as well as in 102 issues of *Police*. *The Plastic Man* comic book began as a one-shot in 1943 and continued until November 1956. Unable to handle the story load by himself, Cole had some outstanding artistic help, including Bernie Krigstein, Lou Fine, and Chuck Cuidera; after Cole left the strip in 1950, Russ Heath took over as the main artist. Novelist Mickey Spillane also scripted several of the character's tales in the mid-1940s.

National Periodicals produced a second series of Plastic Man adventures, albeit without Woozy Winks, starting in December 1966. A greatly inferior version, however, it lasted only ten issues and ceased publication in June 1968. A revival was attempted from 1976 to 1977, and a *Plastic Man* miniseries appeared in 1988 to 1989.

J.B.

PLAUEN, E. O. *see Ohser, Erich.*

POGO (U.S.) In 1943 Walt Kelly, fresh out of the Disney studios, imagined the adventures of a little boy living in the (Okefenokee) swamp in company of an alligator. *Bumbazine and Albert the Alligator* first appeared in issue number 1 of Animal Comics. In subsequent years the little boy Bumbazine faded out of the strip, which was rechristened *Albert and Pogo* (Pogo was Albert's opossum friend). Unfortunately the *Albert and Pogo* comic books lasted but a few issues.

A few years later (1948) Kelly transferred his creation to the *New York Star* of which he was art editor, under the title *Pogo*—but the *Star* folded in January 1949. Undaunted, Kelly persuaded the Hall Syndicate to distribute (and the *New York Post* to run) the strip which soon became a success.

In the loose social structure of the Okefenokee swamp, where everybody and anybody tries to impose their idiosyncrasies, there throbs a teeming population composed of all animal (and social) classes: worms, insects, birds, reptiles, herbivores, and carnivores cohabit in more or less peaceful harmony, in pursuit of their variegated goals. Dr. Howland Owl, his head surmounted by a wizard's cap, indulges in obscure and crack-brained experiments; P. T. Bridgeport the bear tries to promote his mind-boggling schemes; Beauregard, the retired bloodhound, epitome of war veterans everywhere, never tires of relating his former exploits; Churchy-la-Femme the turtle pokes his beak into everyone else's business, while Porky the porcupine vainly attempts to keep his from everyone else. (Politi-

"Pogo," Walt Kelly. © Walt Kelly.

cal figures—under animal guise—make their appearance from time to time in the swamp; one could recognize the late Senator McCarthy, Castro, Khrushchev, etc., but this is a minor, if overplayed, aspect of the strip.)

Pogo the little opossum, sagacious, modest, tolerant and generous, and Albert the alligator, anarchistic, nihilistic, egotistic, and vain, dominate this little world. With his wild flights of fancy, his sudden impulses, his unbridled imagination, Albert is the perfect incarnation of the poet whom Plato wanted to run out of the city. It is Pogo's role in the strip to reestablish the order and harmony of the society, which Albert does his best to disturb.

The privileged relationship between Albert and Pogo has been analyzed in detail by critics and researchers. Reuel Denny has compared Pogo to Socrates confronting Albert the Sophist. Some psychologists such as Kenneth Fearing have seen in Pogo and Albert the symbolic representations of the Ego and the Id. Whatever interpretation one chooses to give it, *Pogo* is undeniably the most self-analytical and self-reflective strip in the whole history of the comics—of which Walt Kelly gave the following definition in a famous 1959 *Pogo* page: "A comic strip is like a dream . . . a tissue of paper reveries . . . it gloms, an' glimmers its way through unreality, fancy an' fantasy."

In the 1960s Walt Kelly became increasingly ill and left more and more of the drawing to others; since his death in 1973 the strip has been taken over by his widow, Selby, and his son, Stephen, with the help of several assistants.

Simon and Schuster have published close to a score of *Pogo* books in hardcover, as well as a remarkable anthology, *Ten Ever-Lovin' Blue-Eyed Years with Pogo*, compiled by the artist himself. A Pogo animated cartoon was shown on television in 1969.

Pogo was discontinued on July 20, 1975. Almost a decade and a half later, an attempt was made to bring the strip back to life. Written by Larry Doyle and drawn by Neal Sternecky, a new version started appearing on January 8, 1989, under the title *Walt Kelly's Pogo*. In February 1991 Doyle left the strip and Sternecky carried on alone for about a year; he was replaced by two of Kelly's children in March 1992, but they only managed to carry the strip into 1993, when it ended.

M.H.

POÏVET, RAYMOND (1910-   ) A French comic strip artist born in Paris, Raymond Poïvet made a brief passage at the School of Beaux-Arts in Paris. After this Raymond Poïvet served his apprenticeship with several French artists and sculptors. In the 1930s he designed a number of war monuments but also executed the decoration for several Paris nightclubs, and made a name for himself as a decorator and designer.

Poïvet started on his comic strip career in 1941 with a rather fanciful adaptation of Daniel Defoe's *Robinson Crusoe*. This was followed by a number of pseudo-historical comic strips such as *Christophe Cofomb* ("Christopher Columbus"), *Marion Delorme*, *La Reine Margot* ("Queen Margot"), and other regrettable (albeit entertaining) distortions of historical figures.

In 1945 Poïvet, in collaboration with Roger Lécureux, created *Les Pionniers de l'Espérance* ("The Pioneers of the Hope"), his masterpiece and a trailblazer in the field of graphic science fiction. Poïvet was later to pro-

duce two other science fiction strips, *Marc Reynes* (1946) and *Mark Trent* (1959), but both were short-lived.

Poïvet has over the years contributed a number of other comic creations: *P'tit Gus* ("Li'l Gus"), a comic strip mixing fantasy with realism; *Colonel X*, a tale of French resistance during the German occupation; *Minouche*, about the adventures of a teenage girl; and *Guy Lebleu*, a mystery-adventure series, none of them very successful.

Upon leaving *Les Pionniers* in 1973, he created *Tiriel*, a tale of heroic fantasy that ran until 1983. In addition to contributing a number of comic strips to a variety of publishers, he also illustrated several didactic works on French history, science, the Bible, and so on. His most notable works in this cultural context have been his adaptations of famous operas such as *The Magic Flute* and *Faust*. He is now semiretired.

Raymond Poïvet's style has been compared to Alex Raymond's although it probably comes closer to Austin Briggs's. After years of relative obscurity, Poïvet has finally been recognized as one of the foremost French comic artists of the last quarter century.

M.H.

POLLY AND HER PALS (U.S.) Cliff Sterrett's 40-year-long masterpiece of comic narrative and innovative graphic art called *Polly and Her Pals*, which began daily on December 4, 1912, and Sunday on December 28, 1913, is perhaps the most remarkable example of artistic legerdemain in the history of the comic strip.

Polly and Her Pals was foreshadowed by a 1911 strip (run as a Sunday feature by some papers) called *For This We Have Daughters?*, which Sterrett drew for the New York Telegram and Herald Co. and in which the basic four characters (a soundly middle-age father and mother called Maw and Paw, a ubiquitous family cat, and a college-age daughter named Molly) were ringers in manner and appearance for the *Polly and Her Pals* cast to come. It is difficult, in fact, to tell from the published strips (titles and copyrights aside) at what point *Daughters* ends and *Positive Polly* (the first title of the classic strip Sterrett was hired by Hearst to draw for his National News Company) begins.

Positive Polly first appeared in the *New York Evening Journal*. The cumbersome title was dropped within six weeks, however, and replaced by the familiar *Polly and Her Pals* on January 13, 1913. (The Hearst Sunday page, launched a year later, was originally titled *Here, Gentlemen, Is Polly!*, then retitled *Polly!* for a time, then simply *Polly*, which remained the Sunday title until November 7, 1925, when the *Polly and Her Pals* title of the daily strip was finally adopted by the Sunday page.)

The title in all its variations was misleading from the outset, since Sterrett always focused the primary attention of the strip on the activities of Maw and Paw (Samuel and Susie) Perkins, and on the hilarious comic menage which surrounded them in the Perkins home, rather than on the distinctly minor theme of Polly and her collegiate suitors. The Dickensian household figures included Paw's scapegrace nephew, Asher Earl Perkins; the family butler, Neewah; a malignant brat named Angel and her doting mother, Maw's Cousin Carrie; a scrawny cat who is Paw's constant shadow, named Kitty; and many others who moved on and off the Perkins scene over the years. Polly herself was

"Polly and Her Pals," Cliff Sterrett. © King Features Syndicate.

chiefly occupied with her constant string of boyfriends, foreshadowing such later comic heroines as Blondie (before her marriage, of course) and John Held's Margy.

Sterrett began to introduce graphic and thematic fantasy into his strip as early as 1918, gradually increasing the level of pictorial strangeness and novelty (with frequent heady incorporation of elements of cubism, surrealism, and even Dadaism) through the 1920s and well into the 1930s, then relaxing these elements in the later, closing years of the strip. Sterrett himself stopped drawing the daily *Polly* on March 9, 1935, after which it was ghosted by Paul Fung and others. He continued with the Sunday page, however, until his retirement in 1958, the last Sunday page appearing on June 15 of that year.

Curiously, only very minor reprint volumes based on Polly have been published: a Saalfield-Big-Little-Book style title in 1934, and a coloring book reprint of some of the 1935 daily strips constituting the total. No film or stage adaptations of the strip were even undertaken.

Polly and Her Pals, in terms of narrative and graphic wit and inventiveness, as well as inspired characterization and a rich sense of comedy, is one of the most memorable works of comic art yet created.

B.B.

PONCHO LIBERTAS (France) *Poncho Libertas* appeared in the very first issue (November 20, 1944) of the comic magazine *Coq Hardi*, the creation of cartoonist Le Rallic and the magazine's editor, Marijac (pseudonym of Jacques Dumas).

Poncho Libertas was a horse-opera of a different color: it took place in Mexico and glorified the exploits of a daring band of rebels led by the dashing Poncho Libertas. The hero's persona owed as much to the French Resistance fighters of World War II as to Pancho Villa, on whose legend he was obviously based. The plots were tight and filled with hair-raising exploits, breathless horse rides, and villainy and heroism a-plenty. Le Rallic's stiff style was more than offset by his brilliant depiction of horses and the limitless Mexican vistas.

Poncho Libertas ended its run on December 30, 1948. Some of its episodes have been reprinted in fan publications.

M.H.

POP (G.B.) The first classic in British newspaper strips, Pop was created by John Millar Watt, who signed with the occasional cryptic initials J. M., for the *Daily Sketch*. *Pop* first appeared on Friday, May 20, 1921, under the title *"Reggie Breaks it Gently."* Pop, the rotund paterfamilias, "something in the city" with his waistcoat, his top hat, his striped trousers, was at first both mustachioed and pince-nez'd, the bald, put-upon papa henpecked by wife and family: a middle-class variant of *Bringing Up Father*, the American strip which was, curiously enough, currently running in the same newspaper. However, Pop always rose above the daily drag with a snappy retort, a verbal crack that Watt echoed in his printed caption, a sort of secondary wisecrack. To the verbal pranks Watt added a visual twist, often using his fourth and last panel as a silent comment or

"Pop," J. Millar Watt. © Associated Newspapers Ltd.

punctuation mark. Another visual gimmick he originated was to set his complete strip against a single continuing landscape or setting, divided into equal portions by the borders of his panels, while his figures carried action along from frame to frame.

The cast of players included Pop's queen-size wife Mag, daughters Phoebe (elder) and Moreen (schoolgirl), son Johnny (schoolboy) and baby Babs. Pop's principal opponent was the Colonel, tall and distinguished. During the war years Pop was reduced from four to three panels, and apparently enlisted in every known branch of the services! An extra strip was added for the *Illustrated Sunday Herald* in 1924, and a special feature on his 25th anniversary was run in the *Daily Graphic* (his newspaper was suffering a temporary name change), including tributes from Sir Alfred Munnings, Chic Young, David Low, and Strube. On Watt's retirement the strip was taken over by Gordon Hogg, who signed himself "Gog." The strip was finished on January 23, 1960, after it failed to survive a reduction to a single gag panel.

Pop was one of the few British strips syndicated in the United States (by Bell Features), and appeared each year in *Pop Annual* (originally a hardback), in 24 editions between 1924 and 1949.

D.G.

POPEYE *see* Thimble Theater.

PORKY PIG (U.S.) Porky Pig made its comic book debut in *Looney Tunes* and *Merrie Melodies* number 1 published by Western Publishing Company in 1941. This was some six years after the character first appeared in animated cartoons produced by Leon Schlesinger for Warner Brothers Studios. The rotund, stuttering pig first appeared in "I Haven't Got a Hat," a musical cartoon emulating the Hal Roach "Our Gang" comedies of the day. The film, directed by Friz Freleng, and based on an idea by Bob Clampett, launched a successful series of films, two of which—"Porky's Duck Hunt" and "Porky's Hare Hunt," introduced the characters who soon evolved into Daffy Duck and Bugs Bunny. *The Porky Pig* cartoons were made until the late 1960s, their directors including Frank Tashlin, Fred ("Tex") Avery, Norman McCabe, Ub Iwerks, Bob Clampett, Chuck Jones, Art Davis, and Robert McKimson.

Like the other Warner Brothers cartoons, the *Porky Pig* films made their character very much in demand for merchandising items such as books, records, toys, and, of course, comic books. After his initial appearance in *Looney Tunes*, Porky returned in every issue thereafter until the book was dropped in 1962. It resumed in 1975 with Porky in guest-star status. The earlier *Porky Pig* stories were by Chase Craig and Roger Armstrong, among others, although, like the other early W.B. stories, they carried the byline of Leon Schlesinger (who was neither a writer nor an artist). In 1943, the first comic devoted exclusively to *Porky Pig* was issued, a special in the Dell Four Color series (number 16). Twenty-five specials followed until the first regular issue of *Porky Pig*, number 25, was issued in November of 1952. After issue number 81, the book suspended publication and resumed in 1965 under Western Publishing's Gold Key banner with a new numbering system. *Porky Pig* also turned up in issues of *March of Comics*, *Golden Comics Digest* and in guest-starring roles, the character has appeared in the comics featuring

other Warner Brothers characters and vice versa. The series ended in July 1984.

Most *Porky Pig* stories deal with coping with life in a suburban setting. The crises that confront Porky range from romantic spats with his girlfriend, Petunia (created for the cartoons by Frank Tashlin), to adventure stories that find Porky and his ward, Cicero, in grave peril. Scripts have been supplied by many writers including Lloyd Turner, Vic Lockman, Don Christensen, Bob Ogle, Tom Packer, Don Glut, and Mark Evanier. *Porky Pig* artists have included Phil De Lara, John Carey, and Lee Holley.

In addition, Porky, Petunia, and Cicero were made regulars in the *Bugs Bunny* newspaper strip (NEA) almost from its inception in 1942.

M.E.

POSITIVE POLLY *see* Polly and Her Pals.

POTTS, THE (Australia) Originally entitled *You and Me*, *The Potts* was created by Stan Cross for *Smith's Weekly* in 1919. The main characters were Pott and Whalesteeth and, initially, the strip was political, commenting on bread-and-butter issues that affected the average citizen. With the introduction of Mrs. Pott, the strip assumed something of a domestic flavor even though the humor was based on frank, uninhibited low comedy. Constant bickering, cursing, and marital squabbling typified the humor of this strip until Stan Cross left the paper in late 1939. The strip passed into the hands of Jim Russell, who recast the tone of the strip but retained the general flavor of domestic cat-and-dog fights. In the process of altering the strip, the name was changed to *Mr. & Mrs. Potts*.

When *Smith's Weekly* ceased publication on October 28, 1950, the strip was accepted by the *Herald and Weekly Times Limited*, for syndication in all Australian states. Because the adult-male humor of *Smith's* was not acceptable to the more respectable, conservative daily newspapers, the basis of the strip's humor had to be toned-down considerably. Pott, the former star, became almost a "straight man"; Mrs. Pott received most of the punchlines and the name of the strip was changed to *The Potts*.

For 30 years, the Potts had no children—when Russell decided to give the strip a new dimension by suddenly materializing a daughter, Ann; son-in-law, Herb; and grandchildren, Mike and Bunty. In the quest for respectability, a new character was added in the form

"The Potts," Jim Russell. © The Herald and Weekly Times Ltd.

of Uncle Dick; a genteel scrounger who became an increasingly important contributor to the strip's humor and who shares top billing with *The Potts* in the Sunday page. With Uncle Dick gradually eliminating the original character, Whalesteeth, the strip assumed the mantle of a conventional domestic strip.

By 1958, *The Potts* had become an international strip appearing in 35 U.S. dailies as well as New Zealand, Turkey, Canada, Finland, and Ceylon, with an estimated daily circulation of 15 million.

Australia's first newspaper strip, *The Potts* has become something of an institution, having been blessed with consistently good art; a reasonably high level of humor (not always typically Australian), and an ability to adapt to topicality. The latter is assisted by many strips being drawn on location of major events such as the Coronation, Olympic Games, and so forth, and involving *The Potts* family in these events. As of 1996 Russell had been drawing the strip (now called *The Potts and Uncle Dick*) for 56 years, arguably a world record.

J.R.

POWERHOUSE PEPPER (U.S.) When artist and writer Basil Wolverton decided to create comic book humor features, he joined the Timely group and introduced *Powerhouse Pepper* in *Joker* number 1 in April 1942. Powerhouse himself was possessed of tremendous physical strength, and in that sense, was a superhero of sorts. On the other hand, he was also cast as something less than a mental giant. Early in the feature's history, Powerhouse had a somewhat belligerent attitude, but this soon disappeared. In fact, if it's at all possible to define his character, Powerhouse could only be described as "lovable," replete with the clichéd "heart of gold." He never had a steady job, although he was often cast as a cowboy or prizefighter.

Wolverton invented a unique—and as yet uncopied—textual device: beginning with the strip's third appearance, all the characters in *Powerhouse Pepper* spoke in rhymes and alliteration. This technique became so popular, Wolverton eventually used it on all his other humor strips, too. But it was always best handled in *Powerhouse Pepper*, perhaps the quintessential usage coming in *Joker* number 9 when Powerhouse is rejected for Army service because no helmet would fit him:

Pepper: "You mean I'm in, doc, old sock?"
Doctor: "No, you're out, sprout, because it's hopeless to hang a helmet on a head like yours!"
Pepper: "Isn't my bean clean?"
Doctor: "It's too lean, if you know what I mean! See? A helmet teeters down over your cheaters, and there's no way to clap a strap under your map!"
Pepper: "Fap! I must look like a sap!"

It went on continuously in all Powerhouse stories, rarely appearing strained or tiresome. Wolverton occasionally would leave a rhyme incomplete or dangle a string of alliterations, but, more often than not, Powerhouse would simply exclaim: "Madam! Don't tan your man with that pan!", the woman would refrain: "Out of my road, toad!", and Wolverton would move on.

Artistically, the strip was totally without precedent, although Wolverton would occasionally borrow a technique from Elzie Segar. The strip featured tight line work, fine detailing, and elaborate shading. Wolverton populated the strip with outrageously exaggerated

"Powerhouse Pepper," Basil Wolverton. © Basil Wolverton.

anatomy and cluttered backgrounds with off-beat sight gags. It was not uncommon for him to draw signs like "Fighters: don't mope on the rope" and "Don't pile in this aisle" into the background of a prize-fighting scene.

Powerhouse Pepper appeared in *Joker* through issue 31 (April 1942 to Spring 1948), five issues of *Powerhouse Pepper* (1943 to November 1948), five issues of *Gay*, and nine issues of *Tessie the Typist*.

J.B.

PRAN KUMAR SHARMA (1938-) Pran Kumar Sharma (Pran) was born on August 15, 1938, in Kasur (now Pakistan). With the partition of the subcontinent in 1917, he crossed over to India with his family, settling in Madya Pradesh. He earned a university masters in political science and studied fine arts as a nonresident student at the J.J. School of Art, Bombay.

His career began in 1960 on an Urdu newspaper in Delhi, *Milap* ("Togetherness") where he did a comic strip and a front-page pocket cartoon. At the time, Indian newspapers used American and European syndicated strips exclusively, so that Pran's strip, *Daabu*, the adventures of a teenage boy and a science professor, was unique. Pran takes credit for not only doing the first Indian comic strip, but also for starting the comics syndicate, as *Daabu* appeared in three other periodicals besides *Milap*. As newspapers and magazines called for other characters, Pran created them. In 1969, he started *Chacha Chaudhary*, the story of a wise and simple man, who with his hefty alien sidekick, Sabu, solves people's problems without the use of superman powers or miracles. Used originally in the humor magazine, *Lodpot* ("Laugh"), *Chacha Chaudhary* went on to become the most popular and longest lasting of comics personalities in India. The second most popular Pran title among the more than 295 comic books he has done is *Shrimatiji*, a humorous strip built around a middle-age housewife; others are *Billoo, Pinki and Uncle Sulemani, Raman and Bhagat Ji,* and *Daabu and Dangerous Capsoul*.

Pran works with three assistants in a studio in his home, drawing daily strips that he self-syndicates through Pran's Features to 20 newspapers and magazines throughout India. Later, the strips are compiled into books produced and sold by Diamond Comics in seven language editions. Pran estimates the readership of his comics at more than 10 million and believes his success results from doing straight and simple humor based on a number of gags.

J.A.L.

PRATT, HUGO (1927-1995) Hugo Pratt was an Italian comic strip artist and illustrator born near Rimini on June 15, 1927. As a child Pratt acquired a taste for travel as he moved along with his parents, first to Venice, then to Ethiopia (when it became an Italian colony) before coming back to Venice in 1942, after Italy's defeat in Africa.

In 1945, while attending the Venice Academy of Fine Arts, he created, in collaboration with Mario Faustinelli and Alberto Ungaro, *Asso di Picche* ("Ace of Spades") about a hooded justice fighter in the best comic book tradition; this was followed in 1946 by *Junglemen*. Opportunities for a burgeoning cartoonist in postwar Italy weren't good, however, and in 1950 Pratt accepted an invitation to work in Argentina, first for the publisher Cesare Civita, then for Editorial Abril in Buenos Aires, and later for Hector G. Oesterheld, editor of Editorial Front era. It was there that he created some of his most important strips: *Sgt. Kirk* (1953), a Western in the new, revisionist mode; *Ernie Pike* (1956), the story of a war correspondent (inspired by the real-life Ernie Pyle); *Anna della Jungla* (1959), about a young girl in darkest Africa; *Wheeling*, an adventure tale set in colonial America, and many others.

For a while during his South American period Pratt went to San Paulo, Brazil, and taught at the Escuela Panamericana de Arte. He returned to Argentina in 1959, then resumed his peripatetic career, working in London in 1964 for the *Daily Mirror* and the *Sunday Pictorial*, and for Fleetways Publications, went briefly back to Argentina where he edited the magazine *Mister X*. In 1965 he settled back in Italy, working for the *Corriere dei Piccolo* in Milan, then in 1967 for the newly created monthly *Sgt. Kirk* to which, in addition to the title strip, he contributed *Capitan Cormorand*, a pirate story, *Luck Star O'Hara*, a detective strip, and foremost, *Una Ballata del Mare Salato* ("A ballad of the Salty Sea"), a brooding tale of the South Seas worthy of Conrad or London. When *Sgt. Kirk* folded in 1970, Hugo Pratt created *Corto Maltese* (based on one of the characters in *Ballata*) for the French comic weekly *Pif*. In 1973 he went over to the Belgian *Tintin*, where he created *Les Scorpions du Désert*, a war story set in North Africa; and continued the adventures of Corto Maltese.

At first an obvious imitator of Milton Caniff, Pratt in the 1960s and 1970s evolved his own striking style, at once more calligraphic and less documentary than Caniffs. Not as boldly innovative as his equally celebrated compatriot Guido Crepax, Hugo Pratt is also less esoteric, which accounts for his greater popularity—a popularity which has made him the best-known European cartoonist of the last decade.

In addition to pursuing the *Corto Maltese* cycle, bringing the adventurer up to the mid-1920s, Pratt also created a number of independent comic strip series in the last 20 years of his life. Most notable were *Cato Zulu* (1984), a tale of the colonial wars in South Africa; *West of Eden*, an adventure set in the wilds of East Africa; and especially *Jesuit Joe*, subtitled "The Man of the Far North" (1978-1984). He also wrote the scripts for two outstanding graphic novels illustrated by Milo Manara, *Indian Summer* (1983) and *The Gaucho* (1991).

In addition he found time to write several prose novels as well as a book of memoirs. He was working on a new episode of *Corto Maltese* when he died of cancer at his home near Lausanne, Switzerland, on August 20, 1995.

M.H.

PRENTICE, JOHN (1920-   ) An American artist born in Whitney, Texas, on October 17, 1920, John Franklin Prentice moved with his family to a variety of small towns in Texas during his boyhood as they followed work on oil fields. He obtained his early education in public schools, followed immediately (1940) by six years with the Navy during World War II.

Prentice was exposed to major illustrators and comic strip artists for the first time during his years in the Navy; although he had followed the works of Raymond, Caniff, and Crane as a boy, he now discovered the magazine work of Al Parker, Austin Briggs, Peter Helck, Harold von Schmidt, and Noel Sickles. He enrolled at the Art Institute of Pittsburgh in 1946 and left after 10 months to handle layout and design work with Industrial Publications of Hazleton, Pennsylvania, for the same amount of time.

In New York in late 1947, Prentice succeeded in breaking into the popular art field, handling advertising and magazine illustration before entering the comic book market. His work in comic books included *Buckskin Benson* for Hillman, *House of Mystery* and other titles for National; and work for the Simon & Kirby and Ziff-Davis studios. Most of his work was penciling and inking.

On September 6, 1956, Alex Raymond was killed in an auto crash. It was suggested to Prentice by veteran inker and background man Philip (Tex) Blaisdel to apply for the job of continuing Raymond's *Rip Kirby*. Unbelievably enough, Raymond drew only ten days in advance of publication so King Features Syndicate was desperate for an artist.

Prentice competed with a host of other straight artists and on the basis of one sample strip and his portfolio of illustrative work (Alex Raymond had been an early influence of his), he got the awesome nod to fill the shoes of one of the art's greatest visual masters.

Prentice, by all accounts, succeeded well. The taut story line continued—Fred Dickinson doing the continuity—and the artwork was so close to Raymond's that King Features challenged editors to discern when Raymond stopped and Prentice began. In fact, *Rip Kirby* picked up papers after Raymond's death, an unusual occurrence with any strip.

John Prentice's art has remained in Raymond's slick *Kirby* style, with only subtle stylistic changes. He employs a variety of cinematic angles and cross hatches which, respectively, lend a rich maturity and visual excitement to the comic strip. His style remains one of the smoothest and least tacky of the story strips, a genre increasingly taken over by formula art, fashion-drawing clichés, and unimaginative uniformity.

To the regret of both Prentice and fans, the recent paper crunch has led to strictures in *Rip Kirby* and all other strips. He has met the challenge with more close-ups and less rendering. Prentice has employed, at various times, some of the most talented assistants in the business, which, under his direction, has kept the quality of *Kirby* high: Al McWilliams, Al Williamson, Frank Bolle, Angelo Torres, and Gray Morrow.

Rip Kirby by John Prentice was voted three times the Best Story Strip by the National Cartoonists Society.

R.M.

PRICE, CYRIL (1905-1970) Cyril Gwyn Price, who drew under the several pen names of "Gwynne," "Kim," and "Spike," was one of the few Welsh cartoonists to work in Great Britain, and perhaps the only one to rise to national success in both children's comics and adult newspapers.

Price was born in Penrhiwfer, Glamorgan, Wales, in a coal miner's cottage on February 8, 1905. The family moved to Abertridwr where he was educated at the village school. Showing early signs of artistic aptitude, Price was encouraged by his headmaster and won a place at the Caerphilly County School, then the equivalent of a modern grammar school. The poverty of his family, however, forced him to go to work at the age of 14, and he was sent down Windsor Colliery. Here he lost the tip of one finger, which luckily had no effect on his artistic ability. After ten years down the pit, the closing of many Welsh coal mines caused widespread unemployment, and Price was forced to leave his homeland in search of work.

Price went to the city of Bristol, and while there began to accompany his uncle, a well-known amateur athlete, to various athletic meetings. His uncle introduced Price to several newspaper reporters and, encouraged by them, he began to submit caricatures of local athletes to the newspapers, all of which had special sporting editions published every Saturday. These were published and as his cuttings mounted, the newly confident Price approached the largest paper in the area, the *Bristol Evening World*, with some specimen cartoons. His talent was immediately recognized and the paper's publisher, the large national company of Northcliffe Newspapers, signed him on.

The *Evening World*, one of the first newspapers in the country to introduce a colored comic supplement for children, was a perfect venue for Price and an ideal place in which to develop the cartooning side of his talent. From 1932 he drew *Junior and Happy*, then *Smash and Grab* (1933), *Fitz and Startz* (1934) as well as the large front-page cartoons for the comic.

In 1934 Price tried his hand at drawing strips for the London comic publisher, Amalgamated Press, and drew *Chimp and the Imp* for *Joker* and *Private Potts* for *Chips*. By 1935 he was drawing *Komedy Kids* in *Butterfly*, *Tomato Khan* for *Comic Cuts*, and *Susie Snaffle* for *Joker*. His success, with a style clearly inspired by the A.P.'s top cartoonist, Roy Wilson, caused his abandonment of the provinces and a move to London, where a regular flow of work from A.P. kept him fully employed.

Price's politics were, as with many with his background, left-wing and during the 1940s he supported Russia and the communists by art-editing a series of children's comic-style one-shots for the Junior Press. At the same time he ran the harmless *Screwy Scrapbook with Pop Cornish*, a joke page for *Knockout Comic* (1943).

In 1948 he joined the *Daily Graphic* (later *Daily Sketch*) to draw their daily children's corner. This was *The Whiskers Club*, the first postwar return to prewar-style children's corners, and featured *Whisk the Squirrel* and his animal pals. Later becoming a strip, this

series, which ran for some years, revealed Price's wondrous ability for depicting humanized animals. The best strips were published every Christmas in a delightful run of children's annuals and were signed "Gwynne," the first of Price's pen names. The Whiskers eventually wound up in the weekly *T.V. Comic* (1957), where Price had found a second home drawing television favorites like Tusker and Tikky and Coco the Clown. At the same time he was drawing a newspaper strip for the *Daily Sketch* featuring a "silent" character called Harry. This one was signed Kim, another pen name.

By 1970 he was back with Fleetway Publications, the successor to the Amalgamated Press, drawing *Georgie's Germs* for *Pow* and *The Spooks of St. Luke's* for *Thunder*. He died of a heart attack on September 17, 1970, at age 65.

D.G.

PRINCE ERRANT (U.S.) H. C. (Cornell) Greening, a longtime cartoonist for *Judge* magazine and an early Sunday supplement comic strip artist, created *Prince Errant* for the *New York Herald* in 1912.

Greening was a versatile artist whose style ranged from crude exaggeration in the late 1880s to restrained starkness in the 1920s. But granting that, *Prince Errant* was still a remarkable work—both in relation to his other work and intrinsically.

First, it was one of the first strips to have its time frame in another age (F. M. Howarth did a strip for Hearst also based in medieval times—*A Lad and His Lass*); it ran without balloons; and artistically was several cuts above other comics (and even Greening's other work).

The Prince was a young lad whose adventures and misadventures were gently humorous. *Prince Errant* always ran a full page and the continuity underneath the panels gave the strip a respectable narrative air that befitted its artistic maturity. The strip was definitely in a class with *Little Nemo*, Peter Newell's *Polly Sleepyhead*, Palmer Cox's *Brownies* and Lyonel Feininger's pages—all comic pages wherein artistic quality and sophistication of story line combined to transcend the level of the average color comic.

Greening gave up the doings of the luckless Prince, after a short stint in 1914. Perhaps he could not sustain the high level demanded by *Prince Errant*; *Percy the Mechanical Man—Brains He Has Nix*, and other Greening creations ran concurrently. Perhaps *Errant* suffered by comparison with a strip it followed, *Little Nemo*. In any event, Greening's notable work should be remembered at least because the tale of a medieval prince in such a format obviously—if unknowingly—presaged *Prince Valiant* by a generation.

R.M.

PRINCE VALIANT (U.S.) *Prince Valiant* was created by Harold Foster for King Features Syndicate on February 13, 1937. As early as 1934 Foster had proposed the idea to United Feature Syndicate (his then current employer) which had turned him down—to their everlasting regret, presumably.

Carefully plotted and laid out far ahead of time, the scenario of *Prince Valiant* is not a collection of unrelated episodes arbitrarily woven around the central character, but an organic whole reflecting the vicissitudes and joys of the hero's life as well as the (legendary) times and society around him—which is the strip's greatest

FORTUNATELY THE BATTLE HAS TURNED, AND THE SAXONS ARE MORE INTENT ON ESCAPE. SO EDWIN IS SAVED, BUT AT THE COST OF LEAVING A GAP IN THE LINES.

"WE WON! WE WON!" CRIES EDWIN GLEEFULLY, BUT AT THE SIGHT OF VAL'S SET FACE, HIS SMILE FADES.

"YOU CAUSED A GAP TO BE LEFT IN OUR LINE, THROUGH WHICH MOST OF THE ENEMY ESCAPED TO THEIR SHIPS, TO RAID OUR LAND ONCE MORE!" AND VAL ADDS CRUELLY,— "RECKLESSNESS WILL WIN APPLAUSE ON THE TOURNAMENT FIELD; IT IS A HINDRANCE IN BATTLE."

"Prince Valiant," Harold Foster. © King Features Syndicate.

narrative achievement. The action however, moves slowly, due partly to Foster's rather weighty text, partly to the static composition of his pictures (a fault most apparent in the last two decades).

The son of the exiled king of Thule, Valiant attaches himself as squire to Sir Gawain before becoming a full-fledged knight of King Arthur's Round Table. Brave and sometimes reckless, he will fight for the glory of the king and for his own renown against the Saxons and the Huns who have come to invade Britain. He will roam the globe, all across Europe and to the Holy Land, and as far away as the jungles of Africa and the forests of the New World in search of glory or in pursuit of Princess Aleta, "queen of the Misty Isles" whom he will finally marry in 1946, and who will give him four children. Having thus become a *pater familias* Valiant will gradually fade out of the strip which has become of late the playground of his elder son, Arn.

Prince Valiant is clearly in the tradition of the novels of chivalry, and only unthinking critics can talk of Foster's historical authenticity and accuracy: his is the Europe of legend and folklore and not the Europe of historians (this in no way detracts from Foster's formidable achievements as an interpreter and chronicler of medieval lore). *Prince Valiant* is awesome as a work of illustration and fiction, but lacks rhythm and pacing, and thus fails to be a trailblazer of the same magnitude as Foster's earlier *Tarzan*.

In 1971 Foster relinquished the drawing of the Sunday page (there never was a *Prince Valiant* daily strip) to John Cullen Murphy—which only accelerated the feature's steady decline of the last decades. In the more than 20 years of his tenure, Murphy has turned *Prince Valiant* into a family affair, with his son, Cullen Murphy, writing the scripts and his daughter, Meg Nash, doing the lettering and coloring.

A series of seven novels faithfully adapted from *Prince Valiant* and illustrated with a profusion of drawings from the strip have been published by Hastings House, and there were also a number of *Prince Valiant* comic books. In 1953 noted movie director Henry Hathaway adapted *Prince Valiant* to the screen with Robert Wagner in the title role and Janet Leigh as Aleta.

M.H.

PRINCIPE AZZURRO, IL (Italy) It is a common tradition to call "Principe Azzuro" (literally "Blue Prince," although better rendered as "Prince Charming") the future husband for whom every young girl prays. He was usually portrayed as a long-haired, blue-eyed blond knight with a regal bearing. Nowadays this figure is not as common, but it was everywhere evident in the 1930s. Therefore, the publishers speculated, a comic strip featuring such a hero would appeal to women who until then had spurned the comic magazines.

Principe Azzuro was introduced on April 9, 1938, in the pages of *L'Intrepido*, the comic magazine published by the brothers Del Duca. The strip, signed "Tredi" (Domenico Del Duca who wrote the text and Antonio Salemme for the art), told of the adventures of Selim, "handsome as the sun." In the very first page Selim saved the life of Bubi, Princess Aurora's greyhound, and love instantly blossomed between the two young people. It was a stormy and much-contraried love whose incidents kept thousands of young girls breathless. A trio of evil characters—Princess Orchidea (Orchid) seeking revenge on Selim, who had scorned her; Raja Karval, Aurora's father who wanted the Blue Prince out of the way for reasons of state; and "Milord," his scheming and hateful English counselor—stood in the way of the lovers.

The feature, which lasted until the suspension of *L'Intrepido* during the war in 1943, is the most outrageous example of a production concocted by greedy publishers in order to cash in on the-less-educated strata of the population. It is also important because it was at the origin of a new kind of publication: the photonovel weekly, with the start in 1948 of *Grand Hotel*, now an illustrated magazine, but at the beginning made up only of comic stories in the soap opera genre.

G.B.

PRIVATE BREGER   *see Mr. Breger.*

PROCOPIO (Italy)   Short, stubby, and bald, Procopio is one character who did not rely on his looks to win over his readers. Yet he has been immensely successful and draws a lot of fan mail. *Procopio* was created by the talented cartoonist Lino Landolfi and first appeared in the Catholic weekly *Il Vittorioso* in 1951, passing recently into the pages of *Il Giornalino* (1974).

In fact there is not one Procopio but a multitude of Procopios!—indeed as many as the ancestors of our "Procopio," a dumb but gentle American cop who tells of the adventures of his ancestors to please his grandchildren; or who relives in his nightmares some of their most perilous encounters. In the scores of stories so far published, "Procopio" has assumed many guises: a caveman; a knight of the Middle Ages; a seventh-century Scot; an opponent of Cardinal de Richelieu; or a pioneer of the American West.

Procopio has been drawn in a bold, personal style by Landolfi, in a break from the traditional "big foot" school of cartooning. While it is drawn in a grotesque line, *Procopio* is also filled with minute, realistically rendered technical details, which are hard to find even in straight adventure strips. *Procopio* often poked fun at the adventure heroes' ethos, as in a devastatingly funny "metaphysical" spoof of the popular Ace of Spades entitled "Procopio and the Ace Poker."

For years *Procopio* has been produced as a continuity strip, never as a comic book; yet it was so successful that it won a radio contest in 1958—eliminating in the process scores of other characters from the movies, comics, and literature. This led to a short-lived series of animated cartoons for television, as well as to a best-selling record (1959). Landolfi's death in 1988 brought the character to an end.

G.B.

PROFESSEUR NIMBUS, LE (France)   One of the innumerable heirs to the tradition of the absentminded professor, Nimbus appeared in 1934 in a daily newspaper strip called *Les Aventures du Professeur Nimbus* ("The Adventures of Professor Nimbus"). His creator was French cartoonist André Daix.

Nimbus was a middle-aged, sad-faced little man: he was entirely bald except for one hair growing over his pate in the form of a question mark, which made him look like a wizened version of Carl Anderson's *Henry;* like *Henry, Nimbus* was a pantomime strip. At the beginning the titular hero justified his professorial status by coming up with the most outlandish contraptions designed to solve the problems of gravity or perpetual motion. Later on, however, he could be found in various guises (as an explorer, a navy captain, a magician, etc.) and in the most exotic climes, from Africa to the North Pole.

After the hiatus caused by World War II the strip made its reappearance in the late 1940s under the shortened title *Le Professeur Nimbus*, signed by Darthel (this might have been a pseudonym). Darthel's style was a faithful imitation of that of his predecessor, but the formula had by then worn thin, and Nimbus's increasing irrelevance to modern problems led to the gradual disappearance of the strip in the late 1960s (it now runs only in a few provincial newspapers). There was a resurgence of sorts after Robert Velter had taken over the character in 1973; when he quit in 1977 he was replaced by Michel Lefort and in 1981 by Pierre LeGoff, who brought the series to an unlamented close in 1991. During all that time the strip kept carrying the signature "J. Darthel" (except at the very end when LeGoff was finally allowed to sign his own name).

Le Professeur Nimbus is not a very original or artistic creation; it owes its importance to the fact that it was the very first French daily newspaper strip. As a novelty it thus enjoyed a fair success in the 1930s, being reprinted several times in book form, and even inspiring a few animated cartoons.

M.H.

PROFESSOR PI (Netherlands)   *Professor Pi*, the work of Dutch artist Bob van der Born, debuted in the newspaper *Het Parool* on January 2, 1955, and for more than a decade enthralled readers with its insight, wit, and unbounded imagination.

Bob van der Born, born October 30, 1927, in Amsterdam, Netherlands, received his formal art training at the Kunstnijverheidschool (School of Arts and Crafts) department of art teachers. When Van der Born started doing his *Professor Pi* in 1955, the business end of the deal was handled by the Swan Features Syndicate, founded by Mr. De Zwaan, who undertook this project after leaving his managerial position at the Marten Toonder Studios in 1953; this makes him one more person of the Netherlands comics scene to have been associated at one time or other with the seemingly omnipresent Mart en Toonder who, because of his many humorous strips and animated cartoon studios, is sometimes called the Netherlands's own Walt Disney.

Professor Pi originally started out as a pantomime gag strip that usually had three pictures per strip. The star of the strip was an almost run-of-the-mill egghead professor stereotype. But in time the strip's individual pictures merged into one oblong illustration, thus straddling the narrow line between cartoon and comic strip. The feature, nevertheless, belongs more in the realm of the comic strip, as each episode narrates a story that must be "read" from left to right with a sweep of the eyes if one is to understand the point of the episodes. In a way *Professor Pi* makes perfect use of the split-panel technique dividing one large background into several segments, with the action partitioned by the segments. *Professor Pi*, one is tempted to say, uses the split-panel technique without the seams showing (for example, the professor's meeting another explorer, read from left to right, first informs us that we are witnessing an explorer's hike, next we learn that the professor is walking through a vast expanse of even terrain and, finally, that he is meeting another explorer

"Le Professeur Nimbus," André Daix. © Opera Mundi.

"Professor Pi," Bob van der Born. © Swan Features.

hacking away at imaginary jungles). *Professor Pi*, with modernistic style, bizarre gags, and enjoyable wit, has also been made available in the more lasting form of book reprints.

W.F.

PROTHEROE, GLYN (1906-   ) Welsh cartoonist Glyn Protheroe, who frequently signed his artwork "Glynne," was born in Swansea on July 3, 1906. He studied art under Walter Fuller from 1923 to 1926, thereafter coming to London to live. He worked in a commercial art studio in Southampton Row and later moved to a different one in Shaftesbury Avenue. Full of amusing ideas, he was successful in contributing gag cartoons to many popular magazines of the period, including *The Leader*, *The Sporting News*, and *The Sports Post*. He was helpful to younger aspiring cartoonists, and gave a helping hand to many, including George Chatterton, who would be forever grateful.

Glyn's hobby was to breed canaries and study and draw wild birds, and this brought him F.Z.S. (Fellow of the Zoological Society) after his name and eventually the editorship of a bird fanciers' magazine, *In Your Aviary*. However, it is his comic work that interests us, and this began during the war when the barrow-boy turned publisher, Gerald G. Swan, launched his chain of comic books, the first in Britain. From his home in Mount Pleasant, Swansea, whither Protheroe had returned to avoid the London Blitz, he submitted an adventure strip entitled *Jakun of the Jungle*. This was immediately published in Swan's *War Comics* (1942). Glyn followed through with *Castle of Terror* (*Topical Funnies*), and then he got lucky with several series for Swan's rival, A. Soloway and his group of four irregular comic books. He ran several series beginning with *Scoop Smithy*, a reporter (*Comic Capers*), 1943. Then came *The Man from the Past* (*All Star*), a Western, *The Kansas Kid* (*Comic Adventures*), *Richard Venner, M.D.*, an unusual theme for those days (*Comic Capers*), *Dude Dawson* (*All Fun*), plus many comic pages.

In those wartime days of paper shortages, the independent publishers issued many one-shot eight-pagers, and Glyn drew five complete comics in this format for Philipp Marx (P.M. Productions) through 1944 to 1945: *Merry Comics*, *Midget*, *Bantam*, *Mighty*, and *Monster*. He also drew some paperbacks, pictorial pocketbooks of facts and puzzles. His clean, perhaps repetitive style, easily understood by young readers, did not suit the major publishers, however, and early postwar he left comics to concentrate on his bird illustrations.

D.G.

Salvador Pruneda, "Don Catarino." © Salvador Pruneda.

PRUNEDA, SALVADOR (1895-198?) A Mexican cartoonist born November 3, 1895, in Veracruz, Salvador Pruneda is the son of noted painter Alvaro Pruneda. Salvador Pruneda took part in the Mexican revolution, alongside his father and his two brothers, Alvaro and Ernesto.

Pruneda's first cartoons were published in the magazine *El Jacobino* as early as 1907. He then worked in most countries of the American continent, including the United States. In 1921 *El Heraldo de Mexico* asked him to come up with the idea for a daily strip: the result was the hilarious *Don Catarino*, which Pruneda created on texts by Fernández Benedicto. The strip passed later to *El Demócrata* and from there went to *El Nacional*.

Salvador Pruneda is a founder of the National Union of Newspaper Editors, the Association of Press Photographers, the Mexican Press Club, and the Workers' Union of *El Nacional*. He has written three books: *Estampas* ("Etchings"), *Huellas* ("Traces"), and *La Caricatura como Arma Politica* ("Caricature as a Political Weapon"). He is also the recipient of numerous awards and honors, both for his cartooning work and for his civic and professional contributions. He died in the late 1980s. (His son Alvaro was also a cartoonist.)

M.H.

PUSSYCAT PRINCESS (U.S.) Grace G. Drayton (she drew under her married name of Wiedersheim before her second marriage) drew perhaps the most "cutesy"

"The Pussycat Princess," Ruth Carroll. © King Features Syndicate.

of all the children's cartoon features, including Rose O'Neill (*The Kewpies*) and Bertha Corbett (*Sunbonnet Babies*). She was certainly the most active female cartoonist involved in children's comics, followed closely by Fanny Y. Cory.

Drayton created the Campbell Soup Kids (continued in advertising a generation later by the young Dik Browne) and drew a Sunday page in the early 1910s, *Dolly Dimples and Bobby Bounce*. Eventually this kid comic was picked up by Hearst and run with coloring pictures as a top-strip feature.

The Pussycat Princess was picked up when *Dolly* was retired. The first appearance of the Sunday-only comic was on March 10, 1935, with art by Drayton and text by Ed Anthony, an editor and executive with Crowell-Collier Publishers. Soon after the start of the strip, Ruth Carroll took over the art.

The strip, described by Waugh as cuddly, was casted by kittens—the Princess herself, different ladies in waiting, knights, and, strangely, everyday contemporary cats with contemporary problems and concerns. Puns on anything feline were abundant.

The Pussycat Princess was last run on July 13, 1947—something less than a cat-astrophe; few papers outside the Hearst chain ever carried the strip, and Hearst's own papers went through a decline themselves during this decade.

R.M.

PUTZKER, RONALD (1962-   ) Ronald Alfred Alexander Putzker was born September 13, 1962, in Wiener Neustadt, Austria. He grew up in the Tyrol. He drew his first comic books at age 5 and sold them to his grandmother. He started going to high school in Innsbruck but dropped out after five years, started a six-year stint as rock musician while also becoming an apprentice cook at the suggestion of his father, a surveying engineer and official. Putzker never got his diploma but moved to Vienna instead where he started taking courses at a graphic designer school. Finally he

tried his hand at studying to become a bookseller. At the time he discovered the comics store of Heinz Pollischansky, who also was a publisher of comic books and collector of original art.

Upon seeing an album by Milo Manara his childhood interest in comics was reawakened. He produced a 46-page photo comic entitled *Linda Denim*. It was later published under the new title of *Eva Sedlitzky* in a comics fanzine. This led to a job as bookseller in the comic store of comics fanzine publisher Wolfgang Alber. Putzker soon started to do the graphic design for the fanzine, then at the suggestion of the late Markus Tschernegg, a devoted Austrian comics fan, translator and journalist, started drawing comics. Putzker created *Inspektor Burnadz*, the name allegedly a combination of Burenwurst, a Viennese fast-food sausage, and an Austrianized transcription of the word "nuts," as in "being nuts."

The first album had a print run of some 35 copies, which he gave away as Christmas presents. This got Wolfgang Alber to suggest he start drawing comics for his fanzine *Comic Forum* in 1984. Thus Putzker's career as comic artist got underway. His work was published in Alber's *Comic Forum* and in German fanzines. At the time the coincidence of a stuffed-up drain got Putzker to meet writer Erich Nussbaumer who then started writing scenarios for Putzker.

The incredible happened. Offers started coming in. Another series, *Aglaya*, was conceived for publication in album form in 1987 in Germany. This series was followed by *Anna Stein* in 1989, also in Germany. Then, finally, Putzker achieved the realization of a dream: working on a newspaper strip, *Kolumbus*. This strip, published in 1991 to 1992, was conceived for publication in the weekly Austrian newspaper *Die ganze Woche* but with the idea of making it into a 52-page comic album afterward. Now foreign publishers started showing interest in his work.

From that time on the indomitable Alfred Putzker has continued to produce comic stories and albums

Ronald Putzker, "Inspektor Burnadz." © Ronald Putzker.

together with writer Erich Nussbaumer or, alternatively, with Günter Brödl. He is also busy working as illustrator for the Austrian newspapers. Putzker's comic style, although influenced by Milo Manara, is usually looser than Manara's, and instead of hatching he uses solid blacks. Putzker's career may seem unorthodox.

But then who said there was an orthodox way of becoming a comic artist in Austria?

W.F.

QUADRATINO (Italy) In a short period, 1908-11, *Il Corriere dei Piccoli* became the most successful Italian publication for children with the highest circulation among weekly magazines; it was recommended by educators and read in every middle-class Italian home. This success was due, in no small measure, to the generous amount of good illustrations published in the magazine. In turn, the *Corriere*'s style was established by two of the great Italian masters of illustration: Attilio Mussino and Antonio Rubino, who filled the pages of the *Corriere* with the adventures of scores of characters they had created. These artists each created a comic feature that they are often associated with; *Bilbolbul* was created by Mussino, *Quadratino* ("Little Square Head"), which first appeared in 1910, is Rubino's most unforgettable creation.

Quadratino owed his name to the shape of his head, which was a perfect square. He was a relative of Scientific Knowledge; Geometry was his mother, Mathematics his grandmother, and Algebra was his aunt. Quadratino, however, was not too happy with his stern relatives, and he played pranks any time he could. As a result he very often got his head out of shape, and his relatives, with perfect, rational, and scientific formulas, had to return his head to its normal form.

This symbolic conflict between science (or reason) and fantasy (or just normal childhood) was most often solved in favor of the age-old traditional lifeview, but Rubino sometimes managed to make it clear that he disagreed with this tradition-bound method of educating children. The strip ended in the 1940s.

A selection of *Quadratino* episodes was anthologized by Garzanti in their collection, *The Golden Age of the Comics*.

G.B.

QUINCY (U.S.) In 1970 King Features Syndicate, prompted by the growing success of Morrie Turner's *Wee Pals*, decided to produce an "integrated" strip of its own. Jamaica-born cartoonist Ted Shearer was promptly contacted, and on June 17, 1970, *Quincy* made its debut.

Again, as in *Wee Pals*, readers were confronted with a lively and lovable bunch of youngsters. Some were black, like Quincy himself, the bright-eyed enterprising title character; his sloppy kid brother, Li'l Bo; and his flirtatious and self-assertive girlfriend, Viola; others were white, like the ravenous Nickles, Quincy's best friend (a twist on the old-line disclaimer: "some of my best friends are"). Over the tightly knit little group (whose doings were quite sedate by modern, or any other, standards) hovered the kindly presence of Granny Dixon, sandwich-maker, pants-mender, and ego-booster extraordinare.

There was great topicality in *Quincy*, and much hip talk, but the ethnic humor sounded forced somehow, as if Shearer did not quite believe in the goings-on. The drawing was competent, but no more, and the kids' fires seemed, for the most part, to have been banked. All in all, this King Features contribution to interracial understanding was—like so many other "do good" efforts in the fields of art, literature, cinema, or the comics—more an embarrassment than a help.

Since 1976, however, there has been a reappraisal of the strip and its place in newspaper comics history (or at least in black newspaper comics history). In *100 Years of American Newspaper Comics*, Bill Crouch wrote, "*Quincy* is blessed with artwork of strong design and a creative use of zip tone." Whatever the strip's charms, Shearer's creation started faltering in the late 1970s and it was discontinued by the syndicate in 1986. A *Quincy* paperback was released by Bantam Books in 1972.

M.H.

QUINO *see* Lavado, Joaquin.

"Quincy," Ted Shearer. © King Features Syndicate.

RAAB, FRITZ (1925-   ) Fritz Raab, German journalist and writer, was born April 2, 1925, the son of a pediatrician in Siegen. Raab's high school education was interrupted when he was drafted into the Luftwaffe, the German air force, from 1943 to 1945. He returned to secondary school for his final exams after the war. He then became an editor from 1948 to 1949, and then finally a freelance journalist and author.

Raab has written some 200 radio plays for the educational programs of the North and West German radio authorities, NDR and WDR. He has also authored 50 radio plays, 20 scripts for television dramas, and eight novels for children. In 1959 he created the popular comic strip *Taró*, published in the weekly illustrated magazine *stern* ("star") from June 13, 1959, to March 3, 1968. Raab was fascinated by the comic medium ever since he had first seen "genuine" comics as a private in occupied France. Therefore, he was delighted to be offered the chance to create a comic strip of his own. He worked much in the vein of Karl May, the prolific German adventure novelist, unknowingly using the same method of carefully researching geographic and ethnographic data for his stories.

Taró is the story of a highly educated Latin American Indian working as an inspector in the Indian Protection Agency in the Mato Grosso area. The exoticism of the locale and the characters, paired with an unending number of plot twists and the very graphic art of F. W. Richter-Johnsen made for an extraordinary comic strip. Raab usually wrote four episodes at a time, much in the form of a movie script. He handed them over to the editors of *stern*, who in turn handed them to artist Richter-Johnsen. The writer and the artist of *Taró* only met four times during the nine years that the strip lasted. *Taró* was canceled because of a reduction of *stern*'s children's supplement, *sternchen* to just two pages of the magazine itself. In a way, the comic strip was saved the disgrace of being disproved by atrocities of the Indian Protective Agency of Brazil that were headlined 17 days after the strip ended. Nevertheless, *Taró* will be remembered for its careful writing and art that created mood and atmosphere, strong characters and fascinating stories. Raab's work is also positive proof that adventure and excessive violence in comics need not be synonymous. When *Taró* ended, Raab returned to writing novels, some of which were made into movies for television.

W.F.

RABOY, EMANUEL (1914-1967) Emanuel Raboy was an American comic book and comic strip artist born April 9, 1914, in New York City. After attending government-funded drawing classes, "Mac" Raboy became a work-project artist and several of his wood engravings from this era remain in the permanent collection of New York's Metropolitan Museum. He entered the comic book field in 1940 as an artist for the Harry "A" Chesler shop and quickly began producing

well-drawn material for Fawcett features like *Mr. Scarlett* (1941), *Ibis* (1942), and *Bulletman* (1941-1942). But his biggest opportunity came when Fawcett editor Ed Herron created *Captain Marvel, Jr.*, and recognizing Raboy's talents from his previous Fawcett superhero work, assigned him to visualize the strip.

Heavily influenced by the outstanding *Flash Gordon* work of Alex Raymond, Raboy created *Captain Marvel, Jr.* in its image. His figures were lithe and majestic, tightly rendered and classically posed. Like Raymond, Raboy avoided the heavy use of blacks and all of his work on *Captain Marvel, Jr.* was bright and exciting. The anatomy and draftsmanship was always perfect. Another outstanding point of his two-year term on the feature—which soon outgrew its origins in *Master Comics* and expanded into its own book—was his superlative cover work. Unlike most of his colleagues, Raboy did not draw his covers "twice-up" (or double the size of the printed page). Instead, he opted for a size almost as small as the printed cover. The result was a static, poster-type illustration, an almost serene still-life rendering, completely different from the hectic, active covers gracing most contemporary superhero books.

Raboy left *Captain Marvel, Jr.* in 1944 to draw the adventures of Spark Publications' *The Green Lama*, a pulp-hero-turned-comic-book-superhero. The strip became a minor classic, but it never sold enough. After the book folded in early 1946, Raboy spent most of 1946 and 1947 as a commercial artist.

He returned to the comic art field in the spring of 1948, however, when King Features signed him as the new artist on his idol's old strip, *Flash Gordon*. Producing the strip's Sunday pages, Raboy made a creditable showing on the feature, but the highlight of his comic art career remained his short-lived but brilliant period as the definitive artist on *Captain Marvel, Jr.* He continued illustrating *Flash Gordon* until his death in December 1967.

J.B.

RADILOVIĆ, JULIO (1928-   ) The first Yugoslav cartoonist to have his work syndicated throughout the world by Strip Art Features (and thus published in France, Germany, Spain, Brazil, the United States, and other countries), Julio Radilović, like many Yugoslav cartoonists, is equally competent with both realistic and humor comics. His mastery of details can be seen in each of his drawings. Radilović was born in Maribor, on September 25, 1928. When he started to read, his uncle sent him American papers regularly. It was his first contact with comics and Radilović liked them. However, cartooning soon became more than a hobby for Radilović and therefore he never finished secondary school. His brother worked at the Studio for Animated Films in Zagreb and helped him to find his first job on a comic strip in 1952.

In 1956 Radilović met noted scriptwriter Zvonimir Furtinger and they realized a dozen episodes of the comic strip *Izumi i otkrića* for the German publisher, Rolf Kauka. In the same year Radilović and Furtinger started the production of one of the longest historical strips in Yugoslavia. The strip had more than 160 pages, was titled *Kroz minula stoljeca* ("Through the Past Centuries") and was published by *Plavi Vjesnik*. The strip was discontinued in the spring of 1959 when Radilović became ill. A Yugoslav motion picture became very popular in the early 1960s and Radilović produced four episodes of *Kapetan Leši*, using the movie characters in the strip. In the spring of 1962, after he read Edgar Wallace's novel, *Sanders of Africa*, Radilović got an idea for a strip and together with Furtinger realized three episodes of *The African Adventures for Plavi Vjesnik*. Their other realistic and humor comics were also very popular, especially the Western series, but their most popular comic strip remains *Herlock Sholmes*.

Radilović is a master of color and has produced cover pictures and illustrations for many publications, including a complete set of Tarzan books. Since the late 1970s he has worked mainly for foreign publishers, notably turning out *Jaimie McPheters* for the British market and *Die Partizanen* for the Dutch magazine *Eppo*.

E.R.

RADIO PATROL (U.S.) In 1933, responding to many requests from their readers, the editors of the *Boston Daily Record* assigned two of their staff people, Eddie Sullivan the night city editor and Charles Schmidt, to produce a detective strip with an urban setting. In August of the same year *Pinkerton Jr.*, written by Sullivan and drawn by Schmidt, made its appearance; its success was such that Joseph Connolly, editor of King Features Syndicate, decided to give it national distribution. A revamped version thus appeared under the title of *Radio Patrol* (and later *Sergeant Pat of the Radio Patrol*) starting as a daily strip on April 16, 1934, followed by a Sunday page on November 11 of the same year. (Like most strips of the 1930s, *Radio Patrol* had a top, *Public Enemies Through the Ages*;—a kind of "Who Was Who In Crime"—it didn't last long.)

The basic appeal of the strip was founded on a recent police innovation, the radio patrol car. In this case the car was occupied by two Irish cops, the red-haired, ruggedly handsome Pat and his elephantine partner Stutterin' Sam. In the course of their assignments, which included from time to time busting a gang of racketeers, infiltrating the ranks of truck hijackers, or putting the arm on safe-crackers, kidnappers, bank robbers, and assorted miscreants, Pat and Sam were often assisted by their young pal Pinky (the Pinkerton Jr. of the earlier version) and his faithful Irish setter named (what else?) Irish. The romantic interest was supplied by female police officer Molly Day, a beautiful slip of an Irish lass, and a sharp crime-solver in her own right.

In spite of hot competition from other police strips (*Dick Tracy* chief among them) *Radio Patrol* enjoyed honorable, if not spectacular popularity for over a decade. The postwar years, however, proved fatal to the feature's mix of ethnic corn and righteous pow, and *Radio Patrol* soon faded into oblivion (the Sunday page in October 1946, the daily strip in December 1950).

A *Radio Patrol* radio program was regularly broadcast in the 1930s, and in 1937 Ford Beebe and Clifton Smith directed a movie serial, with Grant Withers as Pat and Adrian Morris as Sam.

M.H.

RAHAN (France) Rahan (subtitled "the son of the grim ages") was started on February 24, 1969, in the comic weekly *Pif-Gadget*; the prolific Roger Lécureux was the scriptwriter, and André Chéret the illustrator.

Rahan is a caveman, a member of "those who walk erect" and roam the prehistoric world, going from tribe to tribe, never settling with any one group: it can be said that he was the first citizen of the world. In those faraway ages of ignorance and superstition, he keeps an open and searching mind and possesses uncanny powers of insight and observation: these lead him from one momentous discovery to another (such as fire and

"Radio Patrol," Charlie Schmidt and Ed Sullivan. © King Features Syndicate.

"Rahan," André Chéret. © Editions Vaillant.

the throwing spear). Ever generous, Rahan shares his discoveries with all of mankind. (Mankind does not always pay him back with kindness, however, and his fellow-men prove at times as much of a deadly threat as the savage beasts he has to fight to keep alive.)

If Rahan's adventures often recall Tarzan's, and Chéret's compositions sometimes resemble Hogarth's, the major merit of the strip lies in the evocation—at once naturalistic and fabulous—of these distant times. Lécureux's scenarios are imaginative and thoughtful, Chéret's line firm and assertive. After a slow start, Rahan now figures at the top of European adventure strips, and has been reprinted several times in book form.

The character also appeared in the pages of an eponymous magazine published irregularly between 1971 and 1984. Because of this added workload Chéret left many episodes to be drawn by other artists, Enrique Romero and Guido Zamperoni most notably. After Editions Vaillant ceased publication in 1992, *Rahan* went into very successful reprinting in chronological order. The series was also adapted to animated cartoons seen on television in 1987.

RAPELA, ENRIQUE (1911-1978) An Argentine cartoonist born in Mercedes in 1911, Enrique Rapela started his cartooning career in 1937 with a series of illustrations published in the magazine *El Tony*. His comic creations, for which he is best known, are all inspired by the folklore and the characters common to his native land; these include *Cirilo El Audaz* ("Cirilo the Bold"), a daily strip originated in 1940 in the newspaper *La Razón*, *El Huinca*, and *Fabián Leyes*.

Rapela is also famous for his series of illustrations for books depicting Argentine folklore and customs. He died on February 9, 1978.

L.G.

RASMUS KLUMP (Denmark) *Rasmus Klump* is a cute little teddy bear living in a world of fantasy especially designed for younger readers. *Rasmus Klump* is the very

successful creation of Danish artist Vilhelm Hansen, who originated the charming little tyke and his entourage in 1951 for syndication as a daily strip. Until 1959, captions were printed below the pictures. Since 1959 *Rasmus Klump* and friends have been talking in speech balloons and continue to do so in about 75 daily newspapers and magazines in Denmark, Sweden, Norway, Finland, Iceland, Holland, Belgium, France, Spain, Italy, Japan, Great Britain, Austria, Switzerland, Germany, Ghana, and South Africa. Thus far, more than 8,000 individual strips have been produced, also some 25 children's books which have been translated into 12 languages (including Japanese). After starting the feature on his own, Hansen has enlisted the help of his wife, Carla, in the production of the strip.

The title, *Rasmus Klump*, besides being the name of the strip's star, does not tell much about the strip itself, except maybe suggesting the strip's modern fairy tale contents, which are done in a style very close to children's book illustrations. (This is a fitting style, as the *Rasmus Klump* books are primarily aimed at a young readership.) The alliterative German title of the strip, *Petzi, Pelle, Pingo*, immediately suggests a strip with anthropomorphic animals—a little bear, a pelican, and a penguin. These three stars of *Rasmus Klump* are aided in their funny adventures by a large cast of other animals who play out stereotypes and roles.

Of the three main characters, the pelican is the most interesting. He is the wise bird, coming up with solutions for everything and always carrying around all kinds of tools in his pelican's beak, fitting them in the same way Mary Poppins fits all of her belongings into her carpet bag. What boy would not wish for pockets as large and magical as the pelican's beak to hold all of his treasures? It is the wish fulfillment capacity intrinsic to the *Rasmus Klump* strip that makes it such a success with children.

The feature, which is reprinted *ad infinitum* enjoys great popularity especially in Europe and in Japan. In the 1980s the adventures of Rasmus Klump and friends were also produced as animated cartoons for television.

W.F.

"Rasmus Klump" ("Petzi"), Vilhelm Hansen. © Vilhelm Hansen.

RAVIOLA, ROBERTO (1939-1996) Roberto Raviola is one of the most prolific and peculiar Italian cartoonists. Raviola signed his artwork with the pen name "Magnus" (the beginning of the Latin expression *Magnus pictor fecit*—"A great painter did it"). Born in Bologna July 31, 1939, Raviola started to draw the series *Kriminal* (1964), a negative hero, then *Satanik* (1965), a criminal heroine, and *Agent SSO18* (1965), an international spy, and finally *Gesebel* (1966), a science fiction heroine. Magnus's style, based on the very effective contrast between black and whites, helped to lend more fascination to these characters, a fact which, along with *Diabolik*, launched a new genre called "black comics." With the series *Maxmagnus* (1968) and *Alan Ford* (1969), Magnus showed his ability in comical and grotesque styles as well. All the previous series were written by Bunker (Luciano Secchi) and printed in black and white pocket-size book form by publisher Corno.

In 1975 Magnus divorced from Bunker and Corno but went on writing and drawing an impressive number of comics adventures inspired by two somehow different standards: the first is a kind of realistic storytelling with some grotesque graphic aspects; the sec-

Roberto Raviola, ''I Briganti.'' © Edizione l'Isola Trovata.

ond is a comical and humorous storytelling quite grotesque in style. Samples of the first genre are the series *Lo sconosciuto* ("The Unknown," 1975), which portrays the dramatic adventures of a former soldier of fortune who now fights alone and all over the world against crime, injustice, and political totalitarianism. *Lo sconosciuto* is moved by progressive ideals, and the setting of the adventures, though fictional, is well documented and marked by crude realism. The series *I briganti* ("Brigands," 1978), is a long saga inspired by a Chinese medieval novel that tells of a people's revolt against the authoritarian central government. The series *Milady* (1980) is a peculiar science fiction adventure where the heroine is engaged to do justice. And later on is *L'uomo che uccise Ernesto "Che" Guevara* ("The man who killed Ernesto Che Guevara"), a violent and detailed account of the death of the famous guerrilla.

Examples of the second genre are the series *La Compagnia dell Forca* ("The Gallows Company," 1978), which narrates the funny vicissitudes of a shabby company of mercenary troops wandering through medieval Europe and the Near East. The series *Necron* (1981, written by Ilaria Volpe) is a screwball comedy where a mad female doctor gives life to a monstrous human creature of whom eventually she loses control. *Le 110 pillole* ("110 Pills," 1988) and *Le femmine incantate* ("Enchanted women") are two long, polished stories of extreme graphic elegance inspired by Chinese erotic novels.

During the last years of his existence Magnus illustrated some books, wrote and drew some short stories, but mainly devoted himself to illustrating with extreme accuracy *La valle del terrore* ("The Valley of Terror"), a long adventure of the Italian Western hero Tex, written by Nizzi and printed after the author's death on February 5, 1996. Many comics stories by Magnus have been reprinted in book form. In spite of his great popularity and probably because of it, he did not enjoy a full critical appraisal, especially on the side of the comics criticism that confuses comic art with political engagement, seriousness, and incommunicability, and has thus completely misunderstood Magnus's work inspired, with reference to the different genres he has produced, by a great familiarity with Asian culture and art, a political anarchist attitude, and a real popular comic spirit.

G.C.C.

RAWHIDE KID (U.S.) The creation of writer and editor Stan Lee, the *Rawhide Kid* debuted in the comic book of the same name published by Atlas (later known as Marvel) in March 1955. Issue number 1, illustrated by Bob Brown with assistance from Joe Maneely, told the story of the young gunslinger whose reputation preceded him across the West. The Rawhide Kid boasted the fastest gun around and wielded a bullwhip, employing both with brutal results. The violence was tempered, however, with the second issue, the first under the Comics Code seal.

Within a year, the format was altered further with the Kid abandoning his bullwhip and buckskin costume to become a rancher. Randy Clayton, a young protégé from the first two issues, returned to the strip as "Kid Randy," whose relationship to the Rawhide Kid was never made clear. The two of them lived on a ranch near Shotgun City and their stories, drawn by Brown and Dick Ayers, dealt with cattle rustlers and outlaws disrupting the peace of the town. The ranch-owner format proved unsuccessful and the book folded with number 16, September 1957.

In 1960 the comic book was resurrected with Ayers inking the pencil art of Jack Kirby. The origin issue, number 17, introduced a different Rawhide Kid in the person of Johnny Bart. Johnny was an orphan adopted by Ben Bart, a retired Texas Ranger who taught Johnny his fast-gun skills. When Johnny reached 18, his mentor was gunned down by outlaws. Johnny avenged the death and set out to protect the West from similar terrorists. In subsequent issues, he encountered a variety of Western outlaws and early American super-villains. Following Kirby on the art chores were Jack Davis, Dick Ayers, and Jack Keller before Larry Lieber took up both scripting and penciling duties in 1964. Lieber continued on a regular basis in stories that found the Kid roaming the West, encountering gunslingers out to gain reputations by outdrawing the famous Rawhide Kid. Occasional art fill-ins were done by Ayers, Paul Reinman, and Werner Roth.

In October 1968, publication of *Mighty Marvel Western* began, a title reprinting stories of three Marvel Western strips: *Two Gun Kid*, *Kid Colt*, and *Rawhide Kid*. In 1970 reprints began appearing frequently in the *Rawhide Kid* comic book and, in 1973, edged out the new material completely. Stories of *Rawhide Kid* also appeared in two one-shot books: *Rawhide Kid Special*, 1971 and November 1973. *Rawhide Kid* ended in May 1979 but reappeared briefly in 1985.

M.E.

RAYMOND, ALEX (1909-1956) Alex Raymond was an American cartoonist and illustrator born October 2, 1909, in New Rochelle, New York. After studies at Iona Preparatory School in New Rochelle and at the Grand Central School of Art, Alexander Gillespie (Alex) Raymond served out his apprenticeship first with Russ West (creator of *Tillie the Toiler*), then with Lyman Young (*Tim Tyler's Luck*), from 1930 to 1933. In 1932 and 1933 he ghosted both the daily strip and the Sunday page of *Tim Tyler*.

Toward the end of 1933 Raymond was asked by King Features Syndicate to create a Sunday page made up of two features: *Flash Gordon* (a space strip) with *Jungle Jim* (an adventure strip) as its top piece. In addition Raymond was to draw the daily *Secret Agent X-9*, a police strip scripted by Dashiell Hammett. All three creations started publication in January 1934. By the end of 1935 the load was too much for Raymond, who abandoned the drawing of *X-9* to lavish all his care on his Sunday features. Under his pen they became world famous (especially *Flash Gordon*).

In May of 1944 Raymond relinquished *Flash Gordon* and *Jungle Jim* to his former assistant Austin Briggs and joined the U.S. Marine Corps. He was commissioned a captain and saw action in the Pacific aboard an aircraft carrier in the Gilbert Islands. Demobilized as a major in 1946, Alex Raymond created in March of that same year *Rip Kirby*, a daily police strip, which soon became another popular and critical success. Alex Raymond died at the top of his fame, on September 6, 1956, after a car accident near Westport, Connecticut.

Of all the comic strip creators, Alex Raymond unquestionably possessed the most versatile talent. His style—precise, clear, and incisive—was flexible enough to enable him to master every kind of strip at which he tried his hand. His influence on other cartoonists was considerable during his lifetime and did not diminish after his death.

One of the most celebrated comic artists of all time as the creator of four outstanding comic features (a feat unequaled to this day), Alex Raymond received many distinctions and awards during his lifetime for his work, both as a cartoonist and as a magazine illustrator. He also served as president of the National Cartoonists Society in 1950 and 1951.

M.H.

RAYMONDO O CANGACEIRO (Brazil) Unlike what could have been expected from a country of its size, Brazil never developed a national comic industry of any importance. The early comic newspapers such as the fabled *O Tico Tico* carried only American features. After World War II European and South American strips partially replaced the American production. Only in the 1950s did Brazil produce some worthy features of its own: one such strip was *Raymondo o Cangaceiro*, by José Lanzelotti.

The *cangaceiros* have always been a popular literary subject in Brazil. Bandits who roamed the *serta'* of Northeast Brazil in the first decades of the century, they have been glorified in the Brazilian media much as the Western desperadoes have been in the United States. They have inspired several novels and movies, including Lima Barreto's *O Cangaceiros*, which won a prize at the 1953 Cannes Festival. That same year also saw the first of Lanzelotti's series of comic books devoted to the adventures of Raymondo the Cangaceiro. As depicted in the strip, Raymondo is a bush Robin Hood who, with the assistance of his band of rebels, rights the wrongs committed against helpless *peones* by corrupt government officials and greedy landowners. Lanzelotti's graphic style was quite good, with many accurate details of Brazilian life, and the stories were entertaining, if loosely plotted.

Raymondo o Cangaceiro enjoyed fair success until the 1960s, when its subject became politically objectionable and it was discontinued.

M.H.

Giorgio Rebuffi, "Lo Sceriffo Fox." © Edizioni Alpe.

"Red Barry," Will Gould. © King Features Syndicate.

REBUFFI, GIORGIO (1928-) Giorgio Rebuffi, one of Italy's most famous cartoonists, was born November 6, 1928, in Milan. He began to draw while attending the university and created *Sceriffo Fox* in 1949 for Edizioni Alpe. This series met with great success and convinced Rebuffi to embark on a cartooning career. In 1950 he took over *Cucciolo e Beppe*, originally a strip about two little dogs, also for Alpe. Rebuffi changed the characters into human beings and gave the strip its contemporary graphic look.

Among Rebuffi's innumerable creations mention should be made of *Lupo Pugacioff* ("Pugacioff the Wolf," 1959), *Grifagno Sparagno* (1963), and *Professor Cerebrus* (1967). He also created the popular humor strip *Tiramolla* in 1952 in collaboration with script-writer Roberto Renzi. In recent times Rebuffi has been responsible for *Romeo Lancia* (1969), about a lackadaisical playboy, *Vita di un Commesso Viaggiatore* ("Life of a Traveling Salesman," also 1969), *Vita col Gatto* ("Life with the Cat," 1970), and *Esopo Minore* (1970), on which Rebuffi does everything, including the lettering. The last two are the pillars of the comic books published by Alpe, along with *Redipicche* and *Whisky & Gogo*.

In addition to his work for Edizioni Alpe, Rebuffi has also drawn *Donald Duck* and *Mickey Mouse* stories for Walt Disney Productions and produced two more strips: *I Dispettieri* ("The Spiteful Ones") for *Il Corriere dei Piccoli* in 1974, and *Volpone Dulcamara* ("Bittersweet the Fox") for Editrice Cenisio in 1975. From 1989-1992 he was one of the many cartoonists to draw the French series *Pif le Chien*.

Giorgio Rebuffi is one of the few Italian cartoonists who has been able to make a personal statement through his graphic and narrative undertakings. When he is not drawing or writing scripts, he snorkels and devours science fiction novels.

G.B.

RED BARRY (U.S.) *Red Barry* was one of a quartet of police strips fielded by King Features Syndicate against *Dick Tracy* in 1934; drawn and written by Will Gould (no kin to Chester Gould), it made its first appearance on March 19 as a daily strip, followed by a Sunday version a year later.

Will Gould made *Red Barry* into a disturbingly accurate synthesizing of a Warner Bros. gangster movie of the period. The atmosphere is dark and oppressive, the lighting violent and contrasted, the dialogues fast and tough. Red Barry himself physically resembles James Cagney, with his red hair and sullen expression. He is an "undercover man" for a big-city police force (the city is not named but the feel and backgrounds are unmistakably New York's), and his main beat seems to be Chinatown. He is alternately advised, cajoled, and scolded by his superior, Inspector Scott, loved by the blonde, wistful girl reporter Mississippi, and sometimes assisted by the street urchin Ouchy Mugouchy and his "terrific three," a juvenile trio straight out of the *Dead End Kids*.

Among the villains Red meets and subdues in these fast-paced tales of mystery and suspense, one can mention the mysterious "Monk," head of a gang of murderous thieves; the Eurasian adventuress "Flame," and Judge Jekyll, a former magistrate turned killer after going underground (this episode was obviously inspired by Judge Crater's real-life disappearance).

In 1938, frightened by readers' mail protesting *Red Barry*'s blackness and violence, King Features tried to change the format of the strip. It reappeared in 1940 as an eight-page comic book insert (after the fashion of Will Eisner's *The Spirit*) that never saw print.

Red Barry occupies an honorable position among detective strips, somewhere between *Dick Tracy* and *Secret Agent X-9*; it is regrettable that Will Gould was not allowed to develop the feature into what might have become one of the most exciting action strips of the era.

An ironic footnote should be added: the strip was adapted into a 1938 movie serial starring Buster Crabbe and featuring an unknown actor, Donald Barry, who henceforth was to be known under the screen name of "Red" Barry long after the original had become a memory.

M.H.

RED DETACHMENT OF WOMEN, THE (China) The story which inspired this Chinese comic book is among the most famous and best-known works of fiction in the People's Republic of China. First published as a short story by the noted author Liang Hsin, *The Red Detachment of Women* was soon adapted to the stage and later became a staple of the Peking Opera (a movie of the ballet was made in 1970). In 1966 the scriptwriter Sung Yu-chieh adapted the famous story to the medium of the comics, and Lin Tzu-shun did the artwork; the comic book faithfully follows the plot and

"The Red Detachment of Women," Sung Yu-chieh and Lin Tzu-shun.

century scrolls) and Western composition (there are even some interesting camera angles). The page layout, however, is monotonous, with each picture neatly enclosed within the same rectangular frame (obviously rhythm and pacing have been sacrificed to the needs of indoctrination). In spite of its orthodox line, the book was nonetheless attacked during the Cultural Revolution for "bourgeois tendencies" and "revisionism."

The Red Detachment of Women is a very popular comic book in China. In 1967 it was translated into English and circulated in Hong Kong (and probably other Far Asian countries as well). *The Red Detachment* also figures among the collection of Chinese comics published in the United States by Doubleday in 1973.

M.H.

action (even in the exact reproduction of colors) of the opera version.

The action takes place in 1930 on the island of Hainan. Wu Chiung-hua, a slave-woman in the household of the warlord Nan, succeeds in escaping and later joins the Red Army, setting up a detachment composed uniquely of young women like herself. Under Wu's leadership and the guidance of Hung, the political commissar attached to the outfit, the Red Detachment fights against land-owners, foreign capitalists, and other class enemies until they reach final victory.

The plot and narrative of the strip (written entirely in text underneath the pictures—there is no balloon, a rarity among Chinese comic books) are representative of the "socialist realism" prevalent in mainland China. If one discounts the political elements, however, *The Red Detachment* reads like a good adventure story: there is plenty of action; fights, escapes, and ambushes abound; the authors provide a good deal of suspense and even a slight hint of sex.

The intrigue is clear and competently handled, and the drawing style strikes a happy medium between traditional Chinese design (such as can be found in 19th-

REDEYE (U.S.) Gordon Bess started *Redeye* for King Features on September 11, 1967, as a daily and on September 17 as a Sunday strip.

Redeye is the somewhat eccentric sachem of a no less bizarre tribe of Indians living on the borderline of white "civilization" in a state of half-war, half-peace. Grouped around him are some of the most incompetent, befuddled, and outrageous braves ever to wear a feather headdress—always ready to run in the opposite direction when the sachem orders a charge, or to get drunk on smuggled firewater. Tanglefoot in particular is an albatross around the sachem's neck: not only can't he tell a herd of buffaloes from an oncoming train but his persistence in trying to marry Tawney, the sachem's lovely daughter, gives Redeye a special pain. (Nor are these the sachem's only trials: he is poisoned by his wife's cooking, badgered by his young son Pokey, outsmarted by the medicine man, and constantly thwarted in his dreams of military glory by his faint-hearted mustang Loco.)

In this gem of a comic strip Gordon Bess tellingly but unobtrusively commented on a number of topical subjects: conservation, the ecology, and the ethics of business, without the ham-handed approach of many other "relevant" strips. He made his point lightly and humorously, always leaving a laugh at the end. He also put his firsthand knowledge of the West (Bess lived in

"Redeye," Gordon Bess. © King Features Syndicate.

Idaho) to good use, and scenery, customs, and animals were depicted with a sure if satirical hand. He died in 1989, and the strip passed into the hands of Bill Yates for the writing and Mel Casson for the drawing.

Redeye is one of a few hilariously funny strips to come along in a long time and it is no doubt headed for a long career.

M.H.

REDIPICCHE (Italy) *Redipicche* ("King of Spades") appeared for the first time, and simultaneously in Italy and in France, in the spring of 1969 in the bimonthly magazine bearing its name. The idea for the characters was much older, however, and was concretely formulated, albeit in a less sophisticated form, as early as 1950.

Written and drawn by Luciano Bottaro, the series deals with the vicissitudes of Redipicche and the three other kings, each representing a suit in the traditional deck of cards: hearts, clubs, and diamonds. The biggest play is given to the antagonism between Redipicche, a petty tyrant who is choleric and inept, and Redicuori (King of Hearts), a peaceful and fun-loving monarch. Some other characters weave their schemes around the two protagonists, such as Barone Catapulta (Baron Catapult), the arms manufacturer, and the bloodthirsty Generale Falco (General Hawk).

Redipicche's aggressive disposition seems due to a variety of frustrations, including a liver ailment and a nagging mother-in-law. So he fights against his neighbors but finds the going rough, with such enemies as the witch Filippa; Filippone da Todi, the forest archer, and the Alchemist of Hearts, conjurer of terrible nightmares with which he plagues the hapless monarch.

Redipicche did not meet with overwhelming success at first, but it was picked up some years later by the established weekly *Corriere dei Piccoli* where it became extraordinarily popular with the younger readers. The surprised (but delighted) author then decided to play down the satirical aspects of the strip in favor of the fantasy elements already present in the original version. It has now become one of Bottaro's most popular

series, and from the mid-1970s on it has been published in France, Germany, Sweden, Mexico, and Brazil.

In complement to *Redipicche* in the *Corriere dei Piccoli*, Bottaro has been drawing *Il Paese delAlfabeto* ("Alphabet Land"). This series (written by Carlo Chendi) is a fantasy involving the letters of the alphabet and is bathed in an atmosphere not unlike that of the older strip.

G.B.

RED KNIGHT, THE (U.S.) Cartoonist Jack W. McGuire and scriptwriter John J. Welch (who had previously collaborated on an ill-starred adventure strip called *Slim and Tubby*) started *The Red Knight* for the Register and Tribune Syndicate in June 1940.

The Red Knight was the laboratory creation of Dr. Van Lear, who exclaimed at the end of his experiment: "Finished! My scientific masterpiece! A man who through chemical process will become all-powerful in body and mind!" Thus charged with the doctor's secret formula (which he called "Plus Power"), the Red Knight could perform all kinds of superhuman feats from tearing down buildings to turning invisible. The only hitch was that Plus Power wore off quite rapidly, and the Red Knight had to get back each time to be revitalized. Welch played on the conceit theme awhile, but not too successfully; the Knight's adventures, a pale echo of the Superman exploits, were not quite suspenseful or gripping enough to hold the reader. Even McGuire's excellent (if hurried) artwork could not save the feature, which folded in 1943.

The Red Knight was not a very remarkable strip—albeit pleasant in a mindless way—but it featured the first superhero especially created for the newspaper page and, as such, deserves mention.

M.H.

REDONDO, NESTOR (1928-1995) Filipino artist Nestor Redondo was born in Candon, Ilocos Sur, Philippines on May 4, 1928. After attending high school Redondo studied to be an architect. His elder brother

"Redipicche," Luciano Bottaro. © Bierreci.

"Red Ryder," Fred Harman. © NEA Service.

Virgilio, who is an artist and a novelist for the comics, influenced the younger Redondo to take up his trade. The older brother became the better writer while Nestor became a better artist. The two teamed together and became a formidable duo. Nestor first achieved success with a superheroine feature named *Darna* by Mars Ravelo, one the Philippine's foremost comic book novelists. In the 1950s it became apparent that Nestor was the most popular artist in the comics. He had a great influence on other artists and many tried to copy his style. Someone once described his drawings as "pleasing to the eye." His heroes were always rugged and handsome, while the heroines were always beautiful. On many occasions he received fan mail from girls requesting to meet the models he used for his heroes, but Nestor never used a model.

Like many artists of his time, Nestor Redondo was influenced by Alex Raymond and Harold Foster. But he was also influenced a great deal by American magazine illustrators such as Jon Whitcom, Albert Dorn, Robert Fawcett, Norman Rockwell, and Dean Corneal. Nestor would usually draw in the evening, far into the early hours of the morning. He used a Chinese brush and hardly ever a pen. On tight schedules he used assistants. When not drawing for the comics (which was rare), he dabbled in oil painting and was an avid chess player.

In the 1960s Redondo published his own comic book in the hope that he could produce the kind of high standard and quality-oriented comic he always dreamed of, but inflation and the high costs forced him to fold and go back to drawing for the other publishers. In the early 1970s one of the biggest comic book publishers, D.C. National, saw the potential that Nestor had to offer and they hired him. It was not long before his popularity soared to a level where the publishers gave him a book all his own. This was *Rima*; followed by *The Swamp Thing*. He was also commissioned to do a series in a giant-size comic book on the Bible. Until his death on December 31, 1995, Nestor Redondo had a studio where he trained and taught young, aspiring artists for the comics.

M.A.

RED RYDER (U.S.) Fred Harman's *Red Ryder* was first distributed as a Sunday feature by NEA Service on November 6, 1938; a daily version was added on March 27, 1939.

The action of *Red Ryder* takes place in the 1890s after the last of the Indian wars but before the advent of the automobile. Near the little town of Rimrock, Colorado, Red Ryder owns a ranch, which he manages with the help of his aunt, the Duchess. Ranch life is carefully and lovingly depicted by Harman, himself a rancher. But oftentimes Red must come to the help of old Sheriff Newt; he then puts on his boots and his beat-up Stetson and with the aid of Little Beaver, the Navajo orphan he has adopted, he rides into the wilderness, ranging far and wide, from the northern Rockies to Old Mexico, in pursuit of some stagecoach robbers or cattle rustlers.

Red Ryder's enemies have included (among the more notable) the sinister gambler and hired assassin Ace Hanlon, Banjo Bill the music-loving killer who would hide his gun in his instrument, Donna Ringo, the seductive head of a gang of train robbers, not to mention a gang of circus freaks operating out of a traveling tent show. Among other things, Red has also brought peace to ranchers and farmers, settled disputes between miners and cattlemen, and between whites and Indians, ridden shotgun on stagecoaches, and prospected for gold in the desert.

In 1960 Fred Harman left the comic strip field to devote himself to painting. *Red Ryder* lingered a while longer under the uninspired pen of Bob McLeod, before disappearing in the late 1960s.

The most popular of all Western strips, *Red Ryder* was adapted into comic books (among the contributing writers was Dick Calkins, of *Buck Rogers* fame) and to the screen (no fewer than 22 times!). It was also voted "favorite comic strip" by the Boys' Clubs of America. *Red Ryder* may also have been the first comic strip to achieve transatlantic cross-media recognition: in 1947 a play called *Les Aventures de Red Ryder* was staged in a theater in Brussels.

M.H.

RED SONJA (U.S.) "Know also, O prince, that in those selfsame days that Conan the Cimmerian did stalk the Hyborian kingdoms, one of the few swords worthy to cross with his was that of Red Sonja, warrior-woman out of majestic Hyrkania. Forced to flee her homeland because she spurned the advances of a king and slew him instead, she rode west across the Turanian Steppes and into the shadowed mists of legendri." So stated Robert E. Howard's *Nemedian Chronicles*. In 1972 the fiery-haired Sonja crossed into comic books, making a couple of appearances in Marvel's *Conan the Barbarian*. She later starred in *Marvel Features* before finally getting her own title toward the end of 1975.

Dubbed "the she-devil with a sword," the well-endowed heroine took up pillaging as her trade and crossed swords with Conan along with a myriad of other male opponents. Because of the double standard then prevailing in comic books, she was never allowed (unlike Conan) to enjoy triumphs in the bedroom as well as on the battlefield, on the convenient pretext of a vow of chastity. She came close at times to losing her virtue, but her otherwise scanty chain-mail bikini provided too great an obstacle to the awestruck males who came into bodily contact with her.

Red Sonja owed much of her initial success to the artistry of Frank Thorne, whose depiction of the fierce-tempered amazon remains the definitive one. Thorne uncannily captured her fiery sexiness as well as her more contemplative side. He also managed to re-create with a great measure of accuracy the landscapes, trappings, and flavor of the original Howard novels. On the other hand, Roy Thomas scripted the texts and dialogues in a flat, mindless variation on Howard's pseudo-archaic prose, his writing falling miles short of Thorne's excellence of drawing.

Thorne left Sonja in 1978 to create his own warrior heroine, Ghita of Alizzar. In the early 1980s Thomas departed in his turn, to be replaced by Tom de Falco, while Mary Wilshire assumed most of the artwork. The title steadily declined in the course of the decade and, despite high expectations, was not helped by the *Red Sonja* movie, with Brigitte Nielsen in the lead role, which was released in 1985: the comic book was canceled the next year.

M.H.

REGGIE (Philippines) Reggie is the pen name of a well-known, young Filipino artist. Along with Malaya, he is the most underground of underground artists. His biting and caustic political cartoons are vivid commentaries on the inequities and injustices of the social conditions in his homeland.

Some of his earliest works appeared in *Ang Bali tang Pilipino* (the "Filipino News") and in the literary publication, *Kapatid*. In 1971 he collaborated with the well-known Filipino poet Serafin Syquia, to do a humorous comic strip called *Flip*.

A highly accomplished etcher, Reggie captures and conveys the agony and suffering of the oppressed. He likens himself to Goya and Daumier—artists who portray the realities of the human condition. His graphic works are dramatic statements dealing with the brutalities and excesses of war, as well as historical documentations of the physiological and psychological manifestations caused by the painful, degrading, and humiliating experiences brought on by fear, poverty, ignorance, greed, hunger, and corruption.

Reggie, "The Demonyo Made Me Do It." © *Reggie.*

His most popular work is the comic book publication titled *The Demonyo* ("Devil") *Made Me Do It*. It is a satirical account of the colonialization of the Philippines by the Spaniards who used religion as their main tool for subjugating the populace. It also deals with the coming of the Americans and their relationship with the inhabitants. It was published by Pilipino Development Associates, Inc., in 1973.

Stylistically, Reggie's cartoons are deceptively simple but powerful in their visual impact. By means of allegory and personification he weaves a seemingly innocent tale that actually contains several levels of interpretations.

Reggie is the most respected of the younger Filipino artists, along with Ed Badajos, who did the unique *Filipino Food*, an innovative sequential visualization of the "now" generation.

A gifted painter, Reggie has won awards for his scenic paintings of the Philippines. Among his favorite subjects are the nipa huts that are still found in the provinces of Luzon, Mindanao, and the Visayan Islands.

O.J.

REG'LAR FELLERS (U.S.) *Reg'lar Fellers* began in the latter days of World War I as an adjunct feature to Gene Byrnes's popular *It's a Great Life If You Don't Weaken*. The title of the major comic strip became a slogan of the day and because of it, Byrnes gained a national reputation. These and other creations were the mainstays of the fledgling *New York Telegram* and its syndicate operation; a Sunday comic, *Wide Awake Willie*, was distributed into the 1920s by the parent company of Byrnes's paper, the *New York Herald*.

Shortly after its introduction *Reg'lar Fellers* became a sensation; Byrnes had a particular talent for portraying the world of kids. The *Herald* itself picked it up and the comic soon became one of the most popular in the nation. (*Wide Awake Willie* continued for a few years as a Sunday feature, but with virtually the same cast of kid characters.)

In the *Fellers* cast were Jimmie Dugan, Pudd'nhead and his little brother Pinhead, Aggie, Bump, various parents, Flynn the cop (who wears a Keystone Kop uniform), neighborhood adults like Heinbockle the Baker, and Bullseye the dog-a copy (or vice versa) of the dog from the *Our Gang* movies.

The Fellers' neighborhood was in the suburbs or residential outskirts of a city. They played in fields but also in lots. The Fellers were less conniving than Ad Carter's *Just Kids* (no doubt created by Hearst to answer Byrnes's success) and less than the philosopher-urchins of Percy Crosby; the Fellers' struggles with ontology never left the realms of boyhood perspectives. The kid life affectionately portrayed was, therefore, very real and sympathetic and, to many, the truest of the comics' many depictions of kid life.

The ups and downs of the feature illustrate the problems that often stem from the lack of syndicate ownership and management. Byrnes eventually left the *Herald-Tribune* and was handled by an early mentor, John Wheeler of the Bell Syndicate. But later he sought to distribute the comic himself, and it suffered the fate of such other ventures as *The Bungle Family*: uneven distribution, the loss of major markets, disappearance and resurfacing. The *Reg'lar Fellers* comic died in 1949.

During its decline, however, Byrnes kept it alive in different forms: a *Reg'lar Fellers* radio show replaced Jack Benny in the summer of 1941; a book, *Reg'lar Fellers in the Army*, was published during World War II with many propaganda photographs interspersed with some colored cartoons by Byrnes; and the title was lent to *Reg'lar Fellers Heroic Comics*, blood and guts stuff published by Famous Funnies during the war. Earlier, a series of hard- and softcover reprint books were published by Cupples and Leon. Hollywood filmed a series of six-reel comedies based on the characters.

Byrnes shared an innovation with his one-time Bell stablemates Fontaine Fox and Charlie Payne: Sunday pages were often composed in unorthodox, asymmetrical ways, dropping panel lines and employing circles instead of boxes.

For years Byrnes had two talented ghosts—"Tack" Knight, whose style was inalterably identical, and G. Burr Inwood, once among the funniest gag cartoonists on *Judge* and *Ballyhoo*.

R.M.

RÉGNIER, MICHEL (1931-   ) Belgian cartoonist, writer, and editor born May 5, 1931, at Ixelles, near Brussels. Michel Régnier was attracted to drawing and writing at an early age and he edited several school newspapers during his student days. After graduation from college, he became a copywriter for a rather tacky newspaper agency grandiosely named Internationale Presse. There he met other fledgling authors and cartoonists: Albert Uderzo, Jean-Michel Charlier, Eddy Paape, René Goscinny, and contributed innumerable stories and drawings to the agency comics, under his pen name of "Greg" (by which he is best known).

In 1960 Greg was given the opportunity to enlarge his public when he published his Western parody, *Rock Derby*, in the comic weekly *Tintin*. This was followed in 1963 by a re-creation of *Zig et Puce*, Alain Saint-Ogan's classic comic strip (also for *Tintin*), but the results were disappointing and Greg dropped the feature in the late 1960s. In 1963, however, (in the pages of the comic magazine *Pilote*) Greg's *Achille Talon* began, the hilarious tale of an egotistical petit-bourgeois, which met with instant success.

On January 1, 1966, Greg became *Tintin*'s editor and its driving force for over eight years. He changed *Tintin*'s rather staid formula, infused new blood into the magazine, and launched a whole raft of new features to which he very often contributed the scripts. Indeed it seemed at times that the whole publication was being written by Greg from cover to cover! Among the memorable series he created, let us mention: *Bernard Prince* (1966), an adventure strip, and *Comanche* (1971), a Western, both superbly drawn by Hermann; *Bruno Brazil* (1967), another adventure strip (which he signs "Louis Albert") drawn by William Vance; *Olivier Rameau* (1968), a fantasy strip illustrated by Dany (Daniel Henrotin); *Les Panthères*, a girl strip with Edouard Aidans as illustrator (1971); and *Go West!*, a humorous Western illustrated by the Swiss cartoonist Derib (Claude de Ribeaupierre).

Greg has also written the dialogues and/or scripts of many of the animated films produced by Belvision in Brussels, including those for *Tintin et le Temple du Soleil* and *Tintin et le Lac aux Requins*. In September 1974 Greg left *Tintin* after a contractual dispute and is now working for Editions Dargaud in Paris.

In 1983 Greg set up Dargaud International in the United States to promote and distribute Dargaud's comics production. The enterprise ended in failure after a few years, however, and he returned to France. Since that time he has written several crime novels and a number of telescripts in addition to his comics.

M.H.

REICHE, VOLKER (1944-   ) Volker Reiche, one of the new breed of comic artists in postwar Germany, was born May 31, 1944, in Belzig near Brandenburg but grew up in the area of Frankfurt am Main. He studied law but, despite his diploma, never followed a career in law as his love for drawing got in the way. For his first comic album, *Liebe* ("Love"), he had to become his own publisher in 1979 as German comic book publishers had no intention of publishing newcomers at the time.

From 1978 to 1981 Reiche worked sporadically for the satirical monthlies *pardon* and *Titanic* as well as for *Hinz und Kunz*. The latter was a magazine published on their own by aspiring comic artists. In the German language the names *Hinz* and *Kunz* used in conjunction are meant to signify just about anyone. Hence the magazine's pages were open to just about anyone and not only to established artists and writers. One of

Volker Reiche, "Willi Wiederhopf." © Volker Reiche.

Reiche's stories published there was titled *"In Biblis ist die H'lle los"* ("Hell broke loose in Biblis"). It depicted in comic strip form the protest movement against building a nuclear power plant near the town of Biblis and police reaction to the protests.

Reiche's early work in theme and art showed that he was obviously influenced by American underground comics. However, Reiche did not intend to become known as an underground artist only. He therefore developed a more commercial style. This end of his work was helped along by his love for the work of Carl Barks on *Donald Duck*. Once again, his efforts to draw *Donald Duck* were futile in Germany. However, the Dutch publishing group Oberon, which had permission to create their own Disney material, bought half a dozen of his stories right away and helped him with artistic suggestions.

Reiche created a comic character of his own in the early 1980s, *Willi Wiedehopf* ("Billy Hoopoe"). The first comic album of his series appeared in 1984. He also started drawing for animated cartoons for television. Then along came the chance of a lifetime. After a seven-year hiatus, the popular mascot of the television weekly *Hör zu* was to be revived in 1985. Reiche was asked to do the new series of *Mecki* comic strips for weekly publication in a strictly funny comic format. He took the character of Mecki and the group of characters added by Reinhold Escher and put them into a family situation comedy making good use of the story-telling hints he had gotten while doing *Donald Duck*. The cheerful stories that always are good for a chuckle or a hearty laugh have been published ever since. On the side, Volker Reiche has started painting oils.

W.F.

REID, KEN (1919-1987) *Fudge the Elf*, a long-running provincial newspaper strip for children, and *Jonah*, an even longer-running crazy page in *The Beano* comic, were perhaps two of the most famous series created by Kenneth Reid, a meticulous and wacky-minded cartoonist whose funny artwork appeared in some of Britain's best comics.

Reid was born in Salford on December 18, 1919, the son of a manufacturing chemist. Always an artist, at the age of nine he was confined to bed with a tubercular hip and whiled away his time with sketchbook and pencil. Eventually returning to school, he won a scholarship to the Salford Art School when be was 13 and in 1936 set up his own freelance art studio. His father helped him contact clients, including the art editor of the *Manchester Evening News*, who was contemplating beginning a daily feature for the children of his readers. Reid submitted some ideas and six weeks later was contracted to supply the daily adventures of *Fudge the Elf* as a serial of three pictures per day. From Fudge's first appearance on April 7, 1938, Reid wrote and drew 11 serials before he was called into the Royal Army Service Corps in 1940. In his three years of life Fudge had become so popular that Fudge Dolls were produced and several compilations of the strip were published as books by Hodder & Stoughton and the London University Press.

After the war Reid returned home and the *Evening News* restarted the strip. This time Fudge had a longer run: from 1946 to 1963, when Reid had an illness that stopped him working for a while. His first contact with children's comics came in 1952 when he contacted the editor of *Comic Cuts*, a weekly paper that had been published by the Amalgamated Press since 1890. The comic was seeking to modernize itself and introduced Reid's semianimated style with great hopes. He drew *Super Sam*, a Superman burlesque, and *Foxy*, an animated animal, followed in 1953 by Billy Boffin, a boy inventor. However the comic was destined to fold and when it did so in 1953, Reid's brother-in-law, the comic artist Bill Holroyd, introduced Reid's work to his own editor at *The Beano*.

Reid's first series for D. C. Thomson, the Scots publisher of *Beano*, was *Roger the Dodger*, about a naughty boy in the already classic mold of *Dennis the Menace*. He followed with *Grandpa*, a mischievous old man; *Little Angel Face*, a female version of *Roger*, and *Bing Bang Benny*, a kid cowboy (1956). In 1958 came the debut of Reid's first comic classic, *Jonah*. This cursed sailor had virtually only to look at a ship to sink it, and was greeted with cries of "It's 'im!" by terrified nauticals. The full-color back pages, designed for 12 pictures, often reached as many as 36 under Reid's crazy pen. Later characters included *Ali Haha* (*Dandy*, 1960) and *Jinx* (*Beano*),which was Reid's last for Thomson.

Reid now moved south to the higher-paid pages of Odhams Press, where his characters took a left turn into the macabre. *Frankie Stein*, frequently verging on the truly horrific, started in *Wham* (1964), followed by *Jasper the Grasper*, a mean old miser (1965), and *Queen of the Seas*, a revamped variation on *Jonah* for *Smash*. *Dare-a-Day Davy* (1967) was the star of *Pow*, Odham's third comic, but the company was bought by IPC, who also now owned the Amalgamated Press.

Reid's final switch, to the IPC Group, was crowned by his creation of *Faceache* for *Jet* (later *Buster*) in 1971, a boy who could pull any kind of face, man or beast! Later came *Hugh Fowler* and *Soccer Spook* for *Scorcher & Score*, a sporting comic (1972), *Creepy Creations*, a truly repulsive full-page cartoon series for the comedy horror comic *Shiver & Shake* (1973), and the similar *World Wide Weirdies* for *Whoopee* (1974). More macabre creations were seen in his *Martha's Monster Makeup*, in which a girl turned herself into monstrosities, in *Monster Fun* (1975).

Reid's final series was the science fictional funny *Robot Smith* in *Jackpot* (1979) He died on February 2, 1987, of a sudden stroke suffered while drawing his last comic page. Ken Reid's books include *The Adventures of Fudge the Elf* (1939), *Frolics with Fudge* (1941), *Fudge's Trip to the Moon* (1947), *Fudge and the Dragon* (1948), *Fudge in Toffee Town* (1950), *Fudge Turns Detective* (1951), *Adventures of Dilly Duckling* (1948), and *Fudge in Bubbleville* (1949).

D.G.

RÉMI, GEORGES (1907-1983) Georges Rémi was a Belgian cartoonist known as Hergé born May 22, 1907, near Brussels. Hergé (his pen name is the phonetic rendering in French of the initials of his name, R. G.) was raised in les Marolles, a working-class neighborhood of Brussels whose dialect was later to find its way into his writings.

Hergé's first contribution to comic art was *Totor de la Patrouille des Hannetons* ("Totor of the June Bug Patrol") for a boy-scout newspaper in 1926. In 1929, encouraged by Alain Saint-Ogan, he created his world-famous feature *Tintin* in the weekly supplement of the Belgian daily *Le Vingtième Siecle*. In 1930 the first Tintin book, *Tintin in the Land of the Soviets*, was published, followed in succession by 21 more books, the most notable being: *The Blue Lotus* (1936), *King Ottokar's Scepter* (1939), *The Crab with the Golden Claws* (1941), *The Secret of the Unicorn* (1943), *Prisoners of the Sun* (two tomes, 1948 and 1949), *Explorers on the Moon* (two tomes, 1953 and 1954), *The Calculus Affair* (1956), *The Red Sea Sharks* (1958).

Hergé is also the creator of a series of juvenile adventures, *Jo, Zette et Jocko*, and of *Quick et Flupke*, a gag strip depicting the tribulations of two Brussels street urchins. Also of note is a satirical animal strip in book form *Popol et Virginie ou Pays des Lapinos* ("Popol and Virginie in the Land of the Lapinos").

Hergé is the most famous of all European cartoonists. His influence has been immense; he has created around himself and his studio of collaborators a whole school of cartooning sometimes referred to as "the Brussels school," and has spearheaded the post-World War II renaissance of European comic art. He has received wide acclaim around the world as well as countless awards and distinctions.

Hergé published his twenty-third (and last) *Tintin* album, *Tintin and the Picaros*, in 1976. He died on March 3, 1983, after a long illness: the Tintin story he had been working on for more than two years—which would have taken his hero into the world of art counterfeiting—was left unfinished and, according to the creator's express wish, will never be completed.

M.H.

RENE *see* Lehner, René.

RENSIE, WILLIS *see* Eisner, Will.

REX BAXTER (Canada) Most of the adventure strips that appeared in the World War II era comic books known to collectors as "Canadian whites" differed in one major respect from their American counterparts: the Canadian strips were serialized. Perhaps the best example of all is *Rex Baxter*, a *Flash Gordon*-type feature created by artist Edmond Good for Bell's *Dime Comics*. The initial Baxter adventure, subtitled "The Island of Doom," began in the premiere issue of *Dime* in February 1942, and ran for a total of 13 episodes, each with a cliffhanger ending.

Baxter is introduced as an "adventurous young soldier of fortune returning aboard the *S.S. Luxor* to enjoy a well-earned rest from duty with the British army in northern Africa." A Nazi U-boat torpedoes the *Luxor*, and Baxter and a shipboard acquaintance, Gail Abbott, are set adrift. They land on a tropical island where they encounter two strange men aboard a flying metal sphere, Captain Zoltan and Tula, who take them underground to the lost cavern empire of Xalanta, the setting for a curious mixture of futuristic inventions and ancient buildings.

Shortly after their arrival, Riona, queen of Xalanta, is dethroned by her adviser, Lerzal, who sets himself up as dictator and, upon learning of the existence of the surface world, embarks on a plan to become master of that world by unleashing germ warfare. Rex, Gail, Queen Riona, and Zoltan escape to carry on the fight against Lerzal and—after a series of adventures in the cavern world of Xalanta, right prevails.

With issue number 14 of *Dime Comics*, Adrian Dingle took over the strip, Edmond Good having left to do the *Scorchy Smith* newspaper strip in the United States. Dingle introduced a new series called *Xalanta's Secret*, which took Rex and Gail to the South Pacific in search of Zoltan, their Xalantan friend who had been missing since the flying sphere bringing them back to the surface world crashed at sea and sank. A subsequent serialized adventure by Dingle was entitled *Rex Baxter, United Nations Counterspy*, a postwar story in which Baxter was assigned to track down Adolf Hitler, a quest taking him to the undersea kingdom of Mu. *Rex Baxter* did not survive the subsequent transition by Bell to full-color comics, although the *Dime Comics* title eventually became, for a brief period, a catchall for reprints of minor U.S. strips such as *Captain Jet Dixon of the Space Squadron, Rocketman,* and *Master Key*.

P.H.

REX MORGAN, M.D. (U.S.) Begun on May 10, 1948, *Rex Morgan, M.D.* was the brainchild of author Nicholas Dallis, a psychiatrist, and artists Frank Edgington, a background man, and Marvin Bradley. Dallis, who sold the strip to Publishers Syndicate in Chicago with the help of Allen Saunders, based *Morgan* on his own experiences in the medical profession.

The title character is the hero of the strip, about 40 years old, and a bachelor. The nurse at his office is June Gale, who is secretly in love with her boss; in return she receives appreciation and respect from Morgan. The third major character is Melissa (she has never been given a last name), an elderly cardiac patient. She comforts June, scolds Rex, and assumes the role of the matriarch of this "family." These are the only major characters.

Although the minor characters come and go like epidemics, which keeps the story line very fluid, most stories are related to the hero's profession, unlike the companion strip, *Judge Parker. Morgan* is one of the best examples of soap opera in strip form, relying as it does upon dramatic and tangled plots and strong characterization.

The artwork, which continues to be done by its original team, however, is merely competent and never exciting. It is more static than Dallis's other strips and too often appears mired in its own conventional stereotypes.

"Rex Morgan," Nicholas Dallis and Marvin Bradley. © *Field Newspaper Syndicate.*

Following Marvin Bradley's death in 1984, Tony DiPreta took over the drawing of *Rex Morgan*, and for a time spruced up the strip's tired look. When Dallis died in 1991, Woody Wilson took charge of the scripting. The new team imparted a more relaxed tone to *Rex Morgan*, even allowing the good doctor and his devoted nurse to marry on August 3, 1996.

R.M.

Basil Reynolds, "Skit and Skat." © Willbank Publications.

REYNOLDS, BASIL (1916-   ) British cartoonist and illustrator Basil Hope Reynolds was born on December 22, 1916, in Holloway, London. He was the beneficiary of a tremendous artistic heritage: His grandfather, Warwick Reynolds, drew cartoons for *Ally Sloper's Half Holiday*, and others, while his father, Sydney, drew a famous advertising poster for Nugget Boot Polish; his uncles Percy, a comic artist, Ernest, a political cartoonist, and Warwick, a boy's story illustrator and famous nature painter, shared an interest in art with Reynold's two elder brothers, who were also artists.

He was educated at Holloway County School, studied art at evening classes, and joined the Adams and Fidier Agency in 1933. Morley Adams, a designer of newspaper features, had convinced several newspapers of the viability of a weekly comic supplement and was producing complete comics, drawn mainly by staff artists. Reynolds joined Stanley White, Reg Perrott, Tony Speer, Wasdale Brown, and others and became possibly the youngest cartoonist with strips in national newspapers: *Our Silly Cinema* in the *South Wales Echo & Express* (1933) and *Septimus and his Space Ship* in the *Scottish Daily Express* (1934). He added a daily strip in 1935, *Billy the Baby Beetle* in the *Daily Sketch*, his first work in the Walt Disney style. When the Disney organization opened up in Britain with *Mickey Mouse Weekly* on February 8, 1936, Reynolds was on the staff, creating *Skit, Skat* and *the Captain* and writing and illustrating *Shuffled Symphonies*, a serial incorporating all the Disney characters.

After his war service Reynolds returned to *Mickey Mouse* as art editor, painting full-color covers, then drawing *Bongo* (1948), *Li'l Wolf and Danny the Lamb* (1949), *True Life Adventures* (1953), and others. He joined the staff of Amalgamated Press as art editor of *Jack and Jill, Playhour,* and *Tiny Tots,* color gravure weeklies for the nursery age. He drew *Peter Puppet* (1955) for *Playhour* and became the last editor of *Tiny Tots* (discontinued on January 24, 1959). He created *Bizzy Beaver* (1962) for Robin and took over *Nutty Noddle* from Hugh McNeill.

He returned to his favorite Disney characters for *Disneyland* (February 27, 1971), painting the cover spreads and drawing *O'Malley's Mystery Page* for *Goofy* (October 20, 1973). This puzzle feature started a new trend for him, and he currently specializes in devising puzzle books and games featuring Disney characters.

D.G.

RIC HOCHET (Belgium) *Ric Hochet* was created in March 1955 for the comic weekly *Tintin*, the product of the collaboration between cartoonist Tibet (Gilbert Gascard) and the scriptwriter André-Paul Duchateau.

Ric Hochet is a rather conventional police strip. The hero, Ric Hochet, is a young private detective, son of a retired police official, who gets involved in all kinds of mysteries, which he always manages to solve one step ahead of the police, as represented by the grumpy, middle-age Commissaire Bourdon.

Tibet's draftsmanship, terrible in the beginning, has steadily improved over the years, and is today adequate, and even agreeably refreshing. His compositions have also evolved from the simplistic, one-dimensional pattern of the strip's beginning, and are now well-conceived and expertly handled.

The greatest part of the credit should go, however, to A. P. Duchateau, who was already a noted author of detective fiction when he started on the strip. The action is suspenseful, the mysteries always enjoyable (in the great tradition of the writers of classic crime fic-

"Ric Hochet," Tibet (Gilbert Gascard) and A. P. Duchateau. © Editions du Lombard.

tion), and the characters entertaining and often offbeat. Duchateau has taken his hero into the worlds of finance, cinema, and espionage with the same attention to detail and the same concern for verisimilitude that have characterized his noncomic writings. These qualities have enabled *Ric Hochet* to become one of the most successful of contemporary European strips (in the past eight years, it has consistently classed first in the referendums organized among *Tintin*'s readers).

Since 1963, Ric Hochet's adventures have been reprinted in hardcover form by Editions du Lombard in Brussels. To mark the release of the fiftieth title in the series, in 1991 the publisher issued *Dossiers Ric Hochet*, retracing the history of the feature and adding an original tale.

M.H.

RICHTER-JOHNSEN, FRIEDRICH-WILHELM

(1912-   ) F. W. Richter-Johnsen, German painter, graphic and comic artist, was born April 23, 1912, in Leipzig. He grew up and went to public and secondary schools in Leipzig, finally studying philosophy at the university there, but soon giving that up for studies at the Academy of Graphic Arts and Printing Trade. He studied under H. A. Müeller and Tiemann, then continued his studies under Gulbransson in Munich, Germany, before returning to Leipzig for additional studies in wood engraving.

After World War II, Richter-Johnsen earned money as a railway worker and house painter before being able to freelance in art jobs like drawing portraits of American troops occupying Germany. This also brought first contact with American comic books, which he viewed with "amused dismay." Richter Johnsen soon moved on to stage painting and freelance editorial cartooning for *Weserkurier* and *Bremer Nachrichten* (both are Bremen newspapers). In 1954 he moved to Hamburg and started working for the Springer newspaper chain. This led to the creation of *Detektiv Schmidtchen* for *Bild*, a large circulation daily newspaper published by the Springer chain. *Detektiv Schmidtchen*, for the eight years of its run, may have been the only daily newspaper comic strip of German origin. The series was created and written by Frank Lynder, who wanted to raise a German comics emporium of Disney dimensions, a project that never materialized because of a lack of artists. When Lynder went on to other things, Friedrich-Wilhelm Richter Johnsen took over writing *Detektiv Schmidtchen*. The adventures of the kindly police commissioner who had a white mouse for a pet ended when *Bild* got a new editor-in-chief who disliked comic strips.

While working on *Detektiv Schmidtchen*, Richter-Johnsen was contacted by the editors of the weekly illustrated *stern*, who wanted him to do the art on a comic strip created and written by Fritz Raab. Thus *Taró* came into being, to fascinate readers from June 13, 1959, to March 3, 1968. This script ended when the children's supplement of *stern* became just two pages of the magazine. Besides painting, Richter-Johnsen has continued illustrating for newspapers and magazines. He has also used comic techniques in advertising campaigns for various companies. Earlier in his career he had done a large number of loose-leaf giveaway comic strips for a margarine company. These giveaways had a wide thematic range, giving Richter-Johnsen a chance to display his talents and techniques.

Richter-Johnsen does most of his illustrative work (and did all of *Taró* and *Detektiv Schmidtchen*) on textured illustration board, that allows for both solid blacks and grainy grays and helps prevent the somewhat mechanical look of acetate overlays. His work is rich in precision and realism as well as in mood. The action is relatively subdued, giving the strips an aura of calm.

While still working for newspapers and magazines, Richter-Johnsen has refrained from doing more comic work.

W.F.

RICK O'SHAY (U.S.) Stan Lynde's *Rick O'Shay* was created for the Chicago Tribune-New York News Syndicate; the Sunday page appeared on April 27, 1958, followed by a daily version on May 19 of the same year.

Rick O'Shay occupies a unique position midway between humor and adventure. The action takes place in the mythical ghost town of Conniption where, at one time or another, several colorful characters have chosen to take permanent refuge: first there was Deuces Wilde, the gambler who elected himself mayor of the town and appointed his likable partner Rick O'Shay as marshal. They were later joined by Hipshot Percussion, the gunslinger; Gaye Abandon, saloon singer and Rick's heartthrob; Basil Metabolism, M.D.; the Mexican cowpoke Manual Labor, and others. From time to time, Horse's Neck, the crafty chief of the neighboring Kyute Indians, and General DeBillity, the befuddled commandant of nearby Fort Chaos, also drop in.

All is not sweetness and light, however. Undesirable characters also drift into town and invariably try to take it over. Then Rick, Hipshot, and the other worthy citizens of Conniption have no other recourse than to shoot it out in the best tradition of the Old West (at first Lynde had placed the action in modern times, but in 1964 he shifted it to the 1890s).

When Lynde created *Rick O'Shay*, the popularity of the cowboy strip was already on the wane. Since the demise of the Lone Ranger in 1971, *Rick O'Shay* remains the only Western strip with any sizable following; it is also the most authentic since the early *Red Rider*. It is to Stan Lynde's credit that he continues his work with talent and integrity at a time when other cartoonists have either given up or turned to slapstick and caricature.

Unfortunately Lynde left in 1977 after a contractual dispute with his syndicate. Alfredo Alcala (artist) and Marion Dern (writer) carried the strip into 1981, when it was discontinued. In an ironic twist, Lynde later bought back the rights to *Rick O'Shay*, which he has been releasing with great success in high-quality paperbacks under his own imprint, Cottonwoods Graphics. In 1992 he even started turning out new Rick stories for an ever-growing public.

M.H.

RIP KIRBY (U.S.) *Rip Kirby* was created by Alex Raymond upon his return to civilian life, on an idea suggested by King Features editor Ward Greene. The first daily strip (there never was a Sunday version) appeared on March 4, 1946.

Kenneth Rexroth once wrote that all adventure stories can be reduced to two prototypes: the *Iliad* and the *Odyssey*. Alex Raymond, whose Flash Gordon was cer-

"Rick O'Shay," Stan Lynde. © Chicago Tribune-New York News Syndicate.

tainly the Achilles of the comic strip, wished to create its Ulysses with Rip Kirby. Kirby is a criminologist, a former Marine Corps major (like Raymond himself). He has none of Flash Gordon's driving fixations, but displays a worldly wisdom, a superior intellect, and a brilliant wit that were too often absent from Raymond's earlier creations. The whole atmosphere is changed, morally and spiritually, more relaxed, less action-ridden, as if Raymond had decided to poke gentle fun at everything Flash Gordon stood for.

Unrelenting, violent physical action is not the keynote in *Rip Kirby* (as it was in *Flash Gordon*). There is no paucity of fist- and gunfights, but Kirby does not rely primarily on his athletic prowess to solve the difficult cases handed to him. He wears glasses, smokes a pipe, plays chess, and can appreciate the complex harmonies of modern music as well as the aroma of a fine French brandy.

In his investigative methods Kirby often follows his hunches (or calculated guesses) based on solid criminological foundations, with a sprinkling of extralegal gambits, and a dash of violent action. He is, in short, a combination Philo Vance and Philip Marlowe. His assignments are usually vague: locate a missing wife, trace a fortune in stolen diamonds, stop a blackmailer, but the plot soon thickens and takes on flesh.

Around the hero there lurks a netherworld of two-bit hoodlums, blackmailers, gigolos, shyster lawyers, trigger men, and other seedy characters who are depicted with a high sense of realism as well as of drama. Whatever the dangers he faces, Rip Kirby can count on the unswerving loyalty of his majordomo Desmond, a reformed burglar who plays Watson to his master's Sherlock, and on the love of Honey Dorian, the blonde fashion model who is Rip's inamorata.

Alex Raymond made the strip famous from the start. Bold and striking, his style can also be gentle and soft,

"Rip Kirby," Alex Raymond. © King Features Syndicate.

even subdued, as he closely parallels the action. Away from the brilliant colors of the Sunday page, Raymond proved that he could be a master of the black-and-white technique as well.

After Raymond's accidental death in 1956, the strip passed into the hands of John Prentice, who proved worthy of the succession. Prentice's style has a clarity, vigor, and precision especially suitable to the requirements of the detective strip. Prentice is also a master of compositions made up of alternating masses, of elaborate chiaroscuros and daring visual effects. A good share of the credit for *Rip Kirby's* continuing success should also go to Fred Dickenson, who has been writing the continuity since 1952. In 1996 *Rip Kirby* celebrated its fiftieth anniversary with Prentice still drawing and now also writing the feature.

Rip Kirby had a comic book version in the 1940s and 1950s, but in spite of its popularity, was never adapted to the screen, although the unflappable, world-wise Rip should have been a natural for a television series.

M.H.

RITT, WILLIAM (1901-1972) An American newspaperman and writer born in Evansville, Indiana, on December 29, 1901, William Ritt grew up in Evansville and after graduation from high school worked on the staff of local newspapers. In 1930 he moved to Cleveland where he worked for the *Press*. In 1933 the Cleveland-based Central Press Association (later incorporated into King Features) asked him to create an adventure strip for distribution to the midwestern papers served by the association. In collaboration with Clarence Gray he produced *Brick Bradford*, which saw the light of print on August 21, 1933. Ritt's imagination, nurtured on mythology tales and Abraham Merritt's stories, and Gray's superior draftsmanship contributed to make *Brick* into an exciting tale of adventure and science fiction. In 1935 Ritt also wrote the short-lived companion strip to *Brick, The Time Top*.

Fired by the success of *Brick Bradford*, Ritt tried his hand at writing another action feature in the mid-1930s, *Chip Collins, Adventurer*, which did not last long. He then went back to writing the continuity for *Brick Bradford*, but left the strip in 1952 for reasons never made clear. Returning to his job on the *Cleveland Press*, Ritt did a number of articles and feature stories, and contributed a regular column to the paper, *You're Telling Me*. He also wrote short stories, as well as nonfiction, and contributed a chapter on the Kingsbury Run torso murders for a book on Cleveland murder cases. He died on September 20, 1972.

M.H.

ROBBINS, FRANK (1917-1994) Frank Robbins was an American artist born September 9, 1917, in Boston, Massachusetts. Robbins displayed amazing artistic qualities at an early age, won several art scholarships at nine, painted great murals for his high school at 13, and received a Rockefeller grant at 15. All this happened, however, in the midst of the depression years and Frank Robbins, moving along with his family to New York, had to look for work, foregoing a college education. This setback, painful as it may have felt at the time, did not prove altogether baneful. As Robbins later wryly remarked: "I can attribute my success today to two scraps of paper. My high school and college diplomas . . . or rather the lack of them! Without them, I went to work at fifteen . . . with them I might have accepted a job as a bank president and gone through life . . . a failure!"

After an apprenticeship as an errand boy in an advertising agency, Robbins was noticed by the well-known muralist Edward Trumbull, who was then working on the Radio City project, and Robbins drew the sketches for the murals of the NBC building. In 1935, having dropped out of the project because of poor health, Robbins did promotion and poster illustrations for RKO Pictures, painting in the meantime and winning a prize at the National Academy show that same year. In 1938 he flirted briefly with the comic book medium and, the following year, was asked by Associated Press to take over the *Scorchy Smith* daily strip which had been floundering ever since Sickles had departed from it in 1936.

Under Robbins's aegis the strip flourished, so much so that a Sunday page was added in the 1940s. King Features then took notice and asked Robbins to produce an aviation strip for them: it turned out to be *Johnny Hazard* (1944). The new strip met stiff competition in the changed atmosphere of the postwar years, and in the 1960s Robbins was forced to go back to comic books (while continuing his work on *Hazard*). He has worked almost exclusively for National, writing for such titles as *Batman, The Flash,* and *The Unknown Soldier,* and doing occasional artwork on *The Shadow*.

After *Johnny Hazard* ended in 1977, Robbins again went back to comic books, working for Marvel that time. There he labored briefly on such titles as *Captain America* and *Ghost Rider*. Discouraged by the cold reception his work was receiving from comic book readers, he quit comics altogether and retired to Mexico, where he took up full-time painting and sculpture. He died in San Miguel de Allende, Mexico, shortly before Christmas 1994.

Frank Robbins is an artist of almost awesome powers. In addition to his comic artwork, he has done illustrations for such publications as *Life, Look,* and the *Saturday Evening Post*. His paintings have been exhibited at the Corcoran Gallery, the Whitney Museum, and the Metropolitan Museum. The number of awards and distinctions he has received is staggering, but he never attained the fame that his undisputed talent should have brought him. Perhaps his very versatility is the cause of his undeserved obscurity; at any rate a reevaluation of Robbins's work seems to be now in order.

M.H.

ROBBINS, TRINA (1938-) An American cartoonist and writer, Trina Robbins was born in Brooklyn, New York, on August 17, 1938. After attending Cooper Union in New York City ("expelled after one year," she states), she moved to California, where she designed clothes for such rock stars as David Crosby, Donovan, Mama Cass, and Jim Morrison, and later went back to her first love—drawing comics. "Trina in 1966 gave up six years of marriage and Los Angeles to return to New York to do an underground strip for *The East Village Other*," Ronald Levitt Lanyi wrote in the *Journal of Popular Culture*. "This work was followed by strips for the comics tabloids *Gothic Blimp Works* (New York) and *Yellow Dog* (San Francisco)." These and other creations established Robbins as the preeminent woman cartoonist on the underground scene in the late 1960s and the 1970s.

Trina Robbins and Chris Browne, "Crystal Sett." © Robbins and Browne.

Among the many comic books Robbins contributed to, mention should be made of the underground *After Schock*, *Girl Fight Comics*, and *San Francisco Comic Book*. For mainstream publishers she illustrated and/or wrote *Meet Misty* (Marvel, 1986), *Wonder Woman* (DC, 1986), *Barbie* (Marvel, 1990-1993), and *The Little Mermaid* (Marvel/Disney, 1994-1995). She is the author of *The Silver Metal Lover*, a graphic novel originally published by Crown in 1985. She also edited the first all-women comic book, *It Ain't Me Babe*, in 1970, and she later established, along with other female cartoonists, the longer lasting *Wimmen's Comix*. In addition she has been a frequent contributor of cartoons and illustrations to magazines as diverse as *Playboy*, *National Lampoon*, *High Times*, and *Heavy Metal*.

Starting in the mid-1980s Robbins evidenced a knack for study and research into neglected areas of the comics field. In 1985 she coauthored (with Cat Yronwode) *Women and the Comics*, a book about the lives and works of women cartoonists. This she later updated and expanded into *A Century of Women Cartoonists* (1993), and in 1996 she published the self-explanatory *The Great Superheroines*. For her endeavors in and out of comics, Robbins has received many distinctions, from the Inkpot Award for Excellence in Comic Art to the NOW Outstanding Feminist Activist Award.

M.H.

ROBERTO ALCAZAR Y PEDRÍN (Spain) *Roberto Alcazar y Pedrín* was created, in the form of a weekly comic book, by cartoonist Eduardo Vaño. Juan B. Puerto was the first scriptwriter of the series (it is currently being written by Tortajada).

In the first episode titled "The Air Pirates," Roberto Alcazar is a newspaperman who is sailing to Buenos Aires aboard the liner *Neptunia*. He has been assigned to watch over the five fabulous "Gypsy" diamonds. It

"Roberto Alcazar," Eduardo Vaño. © Editorial Valenciana.

"Robin Hood and Company," C. R. Snelgrove. © Toronto Telegram.

is during this crossing that he meets the stowaway, Pedrín, a Portuguese ragamuffin of about 14 who becomes his inseparable companion in adventure.

In the course of their adventurous and action-packed career, Roberto Alcazar and Pedrín have helped put away innumerable malefactors. In return the "fearless Spanish adventurer" and his "little pal" (as they are dubbed) have received countless citations from the authorities, as well as large quantities of reward money which they have either given to poor children or deposited in the boy's savings account "for when he is grown up." It is likely, however, that Pedrín, like Peter Pan and Joselito before him, will never grow to be 15. The series ended in the mid-1980s when its publisher went out of business. It still can be seen in reprints, however.

L.G.

ROBIN HOOD AND COMPANY (Canada) Of all the heroes of lore and legend none has had a more diversified career in comic strips than the outlaw of Sherwood Forest. Robin's adventures have been pictorialized not only in England, but also in the United States (at least twice), France, Italy, and Spain, and probably in other countries as well. In 1935 one of the more entertaining versions, *Robin Hood and Company*, made its appearance in the comics page of the *Toronto Telegram*, written by Ted McCall and drawn by *Telegram* staff artist Charles R. Snelgrove.

The Robin of the strip was true to the character of legend: brave, cocky, and fleet-footed, he was always on the side of the weak and the oppressed, laughing when cornered, generous when triumphant. Around him gathered the gallant band of merrymen whose names have become famous through countless retellings: Little John, Friar Tuck, Scarlett, and others. Robin's adventures did not follow the exploits ascribed to him by legend (as the later Robin Hood movie version was to do) but were original stories. Thus we could find the outlaw fighting robber barons such as the dreaded Red Roger, helping restore King Richard to his throne, defeating the Norsemen who had come to invade England, and even being taken to North Africa by Barbaresque slave traders.

Robin Hood and Company was one of the few epics to last for any length of time in the comic strips. This was primarily due to McCall's deft writing, inventive plots, and earthy humor. (Snelgrove's drawing was ade-

quate—and probably better than that of any other Canadian comic strip artist of the period—but certainly not outstanding.) The strip (which disappeared in the mid-1940s) enjoyed a good deal of success in Canada and in Europe (it doesn't seem to have appeared anywhere in the United States).

M.H.

ROBINSON (Germany) *Robinson* is one of a number of long-running and often underrated comics to come out of Germany. Robinson seems to be only a distant relative of the Robinson Crusoe of literature, who has lived his adventures in a series of 222 comic books published between December 1953 and May 1964. Robinson did emerge from the same mold, however, sailing the seven seas on his trusty ship, *Sturmvogel* ("Storm Bird"), and accompanied by Xury, a native boy sporting a huge turban. The shipwreck in the first issue of the *Robinson* comic book is not much more than a token recognition of the character's literary origins, which serve as a starting point for high adventure.

The comic book started out as a full-color comic book, slightly smaller than the standard comic book format, but for most of its run it was reproduced very cheaply in black and white on newsprint. Despite the seemingly substandard appearance, the *Robinson* strip, usually filling a bit more than half of each comic book and continued in the best of serial traditions, is endowed with remarkably good writing. The plots are very imaginative and make use of a number of subplots, one of them centering around the Portuguese girl, Gracia, accompanying Robinson on many of his voyages. There also is the confrontation of the Christian and Islamic religions as the backdrop for some of the action and as characterization of protagonist and/or antagonist. This is handled in the best tradition of the novels of Karl May.

Yet another surprise is the exceptionally good art of most of the books. Credit for this goes to Helmut Nickel, who has elected to stay anonymous and has since abandoned comics for another career. The

"*Robinson*," Helmut Nickel. © Druck-u. Verlagsanstalt.

anatomy of Nickel's figures is perfect, and the artist has a knack for adding a cartoony touch to some of the characters, thus providing the comic relief that so often is the frosting of the cake in adventure stories. The first 125 issues of *Robinson* were reprinted in a 32-volume book series in 1979-1980. During the initial run of the comic book the material from issue 126 on was all reprints. While *Robinson* had been initiated by artist Willi Kohlhoff, it was turned into a Nickel creation upon his taking over as artist and writer.

W.F.

ROBINSON, FRED (1912-198?) British cartoonist Fred Robinson was born in Walthamstow, London, October 20, 1912. He left school at 14 to become office junior at Cambridge University Press, studying art in the evenings at Bolt Court Art College. His first art job was in the studio of Sir Joseph Causton & Sons advertising agency. In 1930 he joined the studio of C. Arthur Pearson publishing company, illustrating *Pearson's Weekly*, and others. His first joke cartoons were published in *The Scout*.

After four years with Pearson, Robinson joined the Amalgamated Press, contributing strips on a retainer. In 1934 he took over Terry Wakefield's *Quackie the Duck* for *Tiny Tots*, and this area of cartooning—simple comedy for the nursery-age group—became his specialty, despite occasional forays into slapstick. His first original characters, *Ambrose and Al*, two monkeys based on Laurel and Hardy, appeared in *Butterfly* (1935). His first color work was the full-page serial *Crasy Castle* in *Happy Days* (October 8, 1938), the pioneering gravure comic.

During the war Robinson took over *Our Ernie* and created his best-remembered characters, *It's the Gremlins* (1943), based on the famous Royal Air Force myth. When Amalgamated Press took over *Sun* and *Comet* in 1949, he did much work on them and was made that company's first art editor on the new gravure comic *Jack and Jill* (February 27, 1954). In 1966 he joined Polystyle Publications to paint full-color strips of television characters: *Sooty and Sweep* (1967) in *Playland* and *Chigley and Trumpton* (1973) in *Pippin*. This excellent artwork is only excelled by his color pages in these comics' annuals.

His strips include: *Pecky the Penguin* (1935); *Star Struck Sam* (1936); *Bruno Lionel* and *Percy Thggins* (1937); *Andy Benjamin* and *Chick* (1938); *King Toot* (1939); *The Kitties* (1940); *Scoop* (1949); *Dotty and Scotty* (1951); *Flipper the Skipper* (1954); *Peter Puppet* (1957); *Noah's Ark* (1958); and *Musical Box* (1966). He died in the 1980s.

D.G.

ROBINSON, JERRY (1922-   ) Jerry Robinson is an American comic book and comic strip artist, writer, and critic born in New York in 1922. In 1939, at 17, Bob Kane hired him as an art assistant on the newly created *Batman* strip Kane was doing for National Comics. In reality, even though he was officially Kane's assistant, he was a better artist, and his material was easily recognizable. It was usually better detailed, more imaginatively designed, and better crafted than the work Kane was producing.

Robinson assumed the complete *Batman* art assignment in 1941 when Kane moved on to other features. And although Robinson was the major artist on the strip until well into the late 1940s—not only was he drawing *Batman* stories, he was also drawing the covers for *Batman* and *Detective* and *Alfred*, Batman's butler, the back-up feature—he never received bylines. In fact, Kane's byline was the only one to appear on the feature until well into the 1960s.

Besides the anatomical improvement and drafting crispness Robinson lent to the strip, he was instrumental in the creation of two of *Batman's* major supporting characters. Together with writer Bill Finger, Robinson injected both Robin, the Wonder Boy, Batman's ward, and the Joker, Batman's arch-villain, into the feature in 1940. The Joker was probably the paramount Robinson creation: sardonic, absolutely insane, and possessing green hair, ruby lips, and a white face. The Joker became the greatest villain in the comics and eventually got a book of his own (1974).

Robinson also did considerable work for other strips during his comic book career, which extended through 1963. He worked on *Green Hornet* (Harvey, 1942-1943), *Atoman* (Spark, 1944), *Fighting Yank* and *Black Terror* (with Mort Meskin, for Nedor from 1946-1949), *The Vigilante* and *Johnny Quick* (again with Meskin, for National from 1946-1949), *Lassie, Bat Masterson, Rocky and Bullwinkle*, and *Nancy Parker* (for Western, 1957-1963). Over the years he also drew and wrote for Timely (1950-1955) and Prize (1946-1949).

In 1955 Robinson turned to the newspaper strip with *Jet Scott*, for the New York Herald-Tribune Syndicate, which lasted four years even though it was only a mediocre science fiction feature. In 1963 Robinson began his *still life* daily panel for the NewsTribune Syndicate. In addition he also does *Flubs and Fluffs*—a Sunday strip for the *Daily News*, which illustrates children's bloppers—and *Caricatures by Robinson*, a weekly feature which takes off on people in the news.

In the 1970s Robinson created *Life with Robinson*, a satirical panel feature that he syndicated himself. This eventually led to the establishment of the Cartoonists and Writers Syndicate, which is now distributing the work of more than twoscore cartoonists worldwide. The success of his syndicate paradoxically forced the overworked Robinson to abandon *Life with Robinson* in 1996.

Robinson has also been active as a book author and illustrator and has over 30 books to his credit. In 1974 G. P. Putnam published his *The Comics: An Illustrated History of Comic Strip Art*. Robinson is also a former president of the National Cartoonists Society (1967-1969).

J.B.

ROBOT IMPERIUM (Germany) This comic about a Robot Empire is the first European comic ever to be produced entirely on a computer (an Atari 520). It was the creation of Michael Götze who had started publishing comics in fanzines in 1973 and finally moved on to a professional career with seven *The Flintstones* albums for a German publisher in 1974. In 1976 he was taken on by another publisher for whom he drew all kinds of action and funny comics. Apart from his mass production stuff, Götze also started his own series *Voltfeder, ufo*, and *Commander Mantell* beginning in 1979. Götze's *Vorg* was a barbarian along *Conan* lines.

In 1984 Götze's previous comics were put aside for an idea he was obsessed with: creating comics with the help of a computer. First he took a course in computer programming, then it took him some two years to program his computer, translating his designs of machines and landscapes into his computer. The most complicated thing to program was the human anatomy with some 20,000 single points. Finally, in 1986, the result of his efforts—which combined computerized artwork as well as artwork drawn with the help of a mouse and computer "colored" with shades of gray—was presented at the Frankfurt Book Fair: the first volume of *Robot Imperium*. It was fascinating to look at, even to read. A number of European publishers immediately grabbed at the novelty production; and Götze followed up this herculean effort by a second volume, which had the added dimension of computer coloring.

While interest in Götze's robot empire was high, the effort invested was a bit much for one person to handle since the artist continued producing mass-market comics like the *Masters of the Universe* series and doing covers for German editions of Marvel comics.

W.F.

ROBOT SANTŌHEI (Japan) *Robot Santōhei* ("Private Robot") was created in 1952 by Koremitsu Maetani. It appeared first in comic book form (six books were released in all) and then made its reappearance in the June 1958 issue of *Shōnen Kurabu*.

Santōhei was a funny little robot created by the scientist Dr. Toppi. At the end of the Pacific war Santōhei joined the army where he soon became one of the worst goofs this side of Beetle Bailey. Artist Maetani had been a soldier during the war and hated the experience, vowing never to make war again. His sentiments were reflected in the misadventures of his creation (officially, at least, the army represented in the strip was not the Japanese Army). Nevertheless *Robot Santōhei* represented the common soldier in the grip of an idiotic and unfeeling organization, and leveled many barbed criticisms against the military.

Santōhei was an imperfect robot in that he had feelings (these had been instilled in him by an angel, not Dr. Toppi) just like a human being. *Robot Santōhei* was not just a service comedy (like *Beetle Bailey*), it was also a satire on war, and the artist quite freely expressed his bitter views on war and militarism.

Robot Santōhei made its final bow in the December 1962 issue of *Shōnen Kurabu*.

H.K.

"Rob the Rover," Walter Booth. © Amalgamated Press.

ROB THE ROVER (G.B.) The first dramatic serial strip in British comic history, *Rob the Rover* came floating in from the sea on May 15, 1920, 23 years before *Garth* did the same thing. Rob was found by grizzled old Dan the Fisherman, who became his close companion and father-figure during a search for identity that lasted for 20 years. When the weekly comic paper *Puck* folded suddenly during the war (May 11, 1940), Rob roved over to *Sunbeam*, but unhappily that comic, too, folded two weeks later (May 25, 1940), leaving Rob stranded in mid-rove.

Rob was created and drawn by Walter Booth, hitherto a "comic" man, with occasional adventures done by Vincent Daniel when Booth was busy launching other serials. The style of the strip was very much British traditional, with storybook-type illustrations over seven-line typeset captions. Later strips were printed in black and red, but English readers never saw Rob in full colors. This privilege was reserved for the Danes, who had Rob's rovings reprinted in full color in one of their magazines.

"The picture story of a Brave Boy who was All Alone in the World" (the regular subtitle) took Rob to fight an octopus on a desert island (1921), with a film company to the North Pole (1922), to a Lost City in the jungle (1930), to the Valley of the Lost Kings (1931), to an underwater temple (1932), to save an Indian Rajah's jewels (1933), to the mysterious Veiled Lady (1935), and, especially, on a trip aboard Professor Seymour's secret submarplane, the *Flying Fish* (1936). In his last adventure Rob saved his girl chum, Joan, from the Leopard Men.

D.G.

ROB-VEL *see* Velter, Robert.

ROCKY RIDER (Italy) *Rocky Rider* first appeared in 1951 and, like *Forza John* before it, it originated as a free comic book insert offered by *L'Intrepido* to its readers. It had the added advantage of being partly in color and having more pages than similar publications regularly sold on newsstands.

Rocky Rider (the name is clearly inspired by Harman's Red Ryder) is a sheriff who lives in a somewhat unrealistic West. He is very fast with his gun and his lariat and, true to tradition, he stands ever ready to fight for law and justice. His adventures involve him with rum-runners plotting to spur an uprising by selling liquor to the Indians, or with swindlers trying to con gullible prospectors out of their gold. Rocky Rider is a friend to cowboys and Indians alike, and he is determined to see that both obey the law. In compliance with the editorial policy of *L'Intrepido*, romantic and soap opera elements are always present in the story line. For this reason the handsome sheriff spends a good portion of his time looking for kidnapped or runaway children. The strip also never loses an opportunity to offer the reader a few tears wedged in between gunfights.

In his struggle for the triumph of justice Rocky Rider is helped by the brawny trapper Moses and by a freckle-faced boy named Golia ("Goliath").

In 1953 *Rocky Rider* was transferred to the pages of *Il Monello*. The strip has been written by a variety of authors; Alfredo Castelli has been writing many of the scripts in recent times. In the early 1960s it was drawn by the talented Mario Uggeri, who was later replaced by Loredano Ugolini. The strip ended in the late 1960s but there has been a number of reprints since then.

G.B.

ROD CRAIG (Australia) Created by Syd Miller for the *Melbourne Herald*, the strip first appeared in November 1946 and ran daily until November 1955. In a country with a built-in aversion to using local adventure strips to compete with imported strips, *Rod Craig* set a standard in art, story line, and longevity that proved Australian continuity strips could be a viable proposition. As well as appearing in a number of Australian papers, the strip was syndicated in Jamaica, Paris, and Buenos Aires—and became the first Australian adventure strip to be adapted to radio.

Originally intended to follow Craig's adventures as a charter boat owner servicing the Pacific Islands, the story line soon became centered on the Australian mainland and took on the general theme of a detective strip. *Rod Craig* was an excellent example of comic strips that reflect the thoughts and attitudes of a particular era. The postwar preoccupations with large black-market operations, Nazi war criminals cloaked by a veneer of respectability, secret political organizations, gun-running, and so forth, can all be found in the strip. Because Miller was greatly influenced by current trends and events, Rod Craig was constantly on the move and—with some stories as short as six weeks—it was obvious that certain plots were finalized quickly to allow the strip to be diverted in the direction of Miller's latest inspiration. The strip's topicality was assisted by the emphasis placed on melodrama and suspense.

Although Rod Craig was the nominal hero of the strip, his rather conservative, stereotyped personality was overshadowed by the myriad of supporting characters who vied for space in the strip. There was Geelong, a gentle giant and former circus strongman

"Rod Craig," Syd Miller. © The Herald and Weekly Times Ltd.

who stayed on and replaced Cal Rourke as Craig's Man Friday; the curvaceous Lacey, stage assistant to the crooked nightclub owner, Cherub Bim, and later Geelong's girlfriend; Indigo, the scarred-face former R.A.A.F. Squadron Leader, pilot of the remarkable "Stingray" aircraft and employed by Head, the crippled dwarf of the One-World Government organization—to mention but a few of the colorful characters that contributed to the advancement of the strip. Perhaps the most constant of these characters was Carlina, the female villain. She first appeared in October 1947, and continued to cross Craig's path over the years—always chasing easy money. Initially presented as a willowy, thin-lipped, hard-faced woman, she blossomed with the passing years into a well-proportioned, attractive lady. Even more attractive was Anna (first called Leeanna), Craig's blonde girlfriend, who made her debut in the first story as the White Goddess. Most of the women in the strip were wide-eyed, well-fleshed beauties who reflected Norman Linday's influence on Miller.

The strip abounded in the use of Australian towns, cities, and locales and these, along with a good proportion of colloquial expressions, assisted in giving the strip a distinct Australian flavor. Miller used many different styles in illustrating the strip—delicate fine line, intricate hatching, stark black spotting, drybrushing, halftones—with each style calculated to assist the mood.

Rod Craig was concluded because of Miller's wish to attempt another type of strip. It is a tribute to Syd Miller's skill and versatility that he was immediately able to follow *Rod Craig* with a daily humor strip, *Us Girls*, which ran until 1957 when Miller left the field of comic art.

J.R.

RODRIGUEZ, EMILIO D. (1937-   ) In the Philippines, where many of the finest comic illustrators and cartoonists are self-taught, Emilio Rodriguez holds the distinction of being one of the few individuals who received a full range of academic education in the field of art.

Born on October 15, 1937, in Sorsogon, Rodriguez finished high school as the valedictorian at the Sorsogon School of Arts and Trades, and later attended the University of the Philippines, receiving the degree of Bachelor of Fine Arts (cum laude). He also studied at the Cranbrook Academy of Art, Michigan, as a

Fullbright/Smith Mundt scholar, and obtained a masters degree in fine arts. He taught at the University of the Philippines College of Fine Arts and Architecture.

Apart from Federico Javinal, "Emile" Rodriguez is the foremost exponent of the Francisco Coching style of comic illustration. This style is characterized by bold strokes, exuberant and dynamic action scenes, effective use of dramatic angles, good composition and design, and, foremost, the ability to make one scene flow smoothly into another. The rendering is loose but controlled and accurate.

Not satisfied with just emulating the works of Coching, Emile Rodriguez developed his own individual artistic approach. His work is distinguished by his imaginative use of negative space. When a script calls for a classical approach to the subject matter, his work is a joy to behold. His highly decorative rendering and flourishes are done in good taste, just enough that the panels are not overdone or crowded. And when the story requires a simple but effective style, he readily adjusts to the conditions and makes his work come to the point. He excels in calligraphy; his comic book logos are among the most beautiful in the field.

He has worked with many well-known writers in the Philippines, among them are Virgilio Redondo, Nemesio Caravana, and Angel Ad Santos. He illustrated the popular graphic novel *Carlomagno* for *Liwayway*, did short stories for Ace Publications, and biblical adaptations for *Kenkoy Komiks*.

In 1963 Rodriguez collaborated with Gemma Cruz, the former Miss International beauty queen, to produce the prize-winning children's book, *Makisig, The Little Hero of Mactan*. The book deals with the invasion of a Malayan province in the Visayan Islands. The invaders fail due to the heroic exploits of a child who is able to warn the great *Datu* ("Chief") Lapu-Lapu, the first Asian to repel European intrusion.

Emile Rodriguez was one of the first Filipino artists to work for American comics when he illustrated short stories for Treasure Chest comics.

O.J.

ROLAND EAGLE (Italy) After World War II the comic weekly *L'Intrepido* changed its editorial policy. New comic features were created and, while they did not temper the sentimentality that was *L'Intrepido*'s trademark, they gave more play to action, adventure, and even eroticism (without allowing them to get out of hand). This process (still continued to this day) is best represented in *Bufalo Bill* and *Roland Eagle*, both created by Carlo Cossio in 1951.

In *Roland Eagle* in particular the erotic element is very strong in the figure of Jasmine, the savage girl turned into a civilized woman for love. Unlike most other comic strip heroines, whose main functions seem to be getting into some kind of trouble so that the hero can rescue them, Jasmine can take care of herself and fights with the courage of a lioness. Raised by the members of a Dayak tribe, she is actually the daughter of a Malay princess and a white man. Her mysterious origins have always fascinated the readers who like to speculate on who her father might be.

Roland Eagle, on the other hand, is an uncomplicated young man, skipper of the schooner *Eagle of the Seven Seas*. His adventures are filled with Malay princes and princesses (Jasmine is only one of them), slave-traders and mad scientists who want to rule the world. The action takes place in modern times (one of the

early episodes involved him and his boat in a secret mission against the Japanese) and it is full of storms, shipwrecks, and other catastrophes. Around Roland are his boss, Machete, who takes care of him like a father, Lady Barbara, and her sweet daughter, Lili, whose life Roland saved, and many others.

Cossio was later succeeded by Ferdinando Corbella on the strip, which lasted into the 1960s.

G.B.

ROMANO IL LEGIONARIO (Italy) After only one year of publication, the Catholic weekly *Il Vittorioso* paid its dues to the Fascist regime with the creation of one of the most jingoistic and propagandistic comic features ever produced in Italy: *Romano il Legionario*, written and drawn by the German-Italian Kurt Caesar (under the pen name "Cesare Avai") in 1938.

In the first months of his adventures, Romano, piloting his Fiat CR 32 fighter, fought against the "Reds" during the Spanish Civil War. Then, after Franco's victory, he came back to Italy and resumed his duties as a civilian pilot. Not for long however: hours after he had heard Mussolini's voice on the radio announcing to the Italian people that Italy was at war against France and England, Romano left his humdrum job—and his new bride, Isa, a Red Cross nurse—to offer his services to the fatherland. Romano fought in all of Italy's battles—in Africa, in Greece, in Russia—until the fateful day when Italy was knocked out of the war and nothing was left to legionaries like him but to fade into the shadows.

If on one hand *Romano* was excellent for the quality of its images and the wonderful technical rendering of the realities of combat, on the other hand it was pitifully shortsighted as to Italy's actual potentialities and oppressively blinded by its own propaganda, which Romano compulsively spouted in his balloons and which Caesar further reinforced in his captions.

The technical details were originally conceived and laid out with an almost photographic precision. The characters, however, owed much to Alex Raymond, whom Caesar faithfully and almost slavishly copied. Romano, in particular, is very close in conception and make-up to Flash Gordon: they share a common moral

"Romano il Legionario," Kurt Caesar. © Nerbini.

affinity, and are similarly endowed with the qualities of courage, loyalty, and duty, and possess the ability of rising to every occasion to an exceptional degree.

G.B.

ROMITA, JOHN (1930-   ) American comic book artist born January 24, 1930, in Brooklyn, New York. After studies at the School of Industrial Arts and the Phoenix School, Romita spent a year in commercial art and then began drawing all types of stories for Stan Lee's Atlas group in 1949. Concentrating mainly on horror and romance stories—the romance titles were particularly terrible, he once said, because he "had never drawn a girl before"—he also had a short stint on the short-lived, 1954 *Captain America* revival. He also drew several war, crime, and Western features, most notably the *Western Kid* strip.

When Atlas faltered in 1957, Romita was unceremoniously released in the middle of a Western story. Turning to National, he was rejected by the superhero and Western departments, and refused to even try the war group because he said editor Bob Kanigher "ate" artists "and spit them out for breakfast." He eventually drifted into the romance department; he spent eight anonymous years there, never signing his work, even though he penciled and inked at least six stories a month and all the romance covers. And although his work was consistently the most dynamic in the romance field, it was ignored.

Consequently, when National's romance line faltered in 1965, Romita was dismissed and had to return to Lee, who was then riding herd on Marvel's increasingly popular superhero group. He began by inking the *Avengers*, then moved to penciling *Daredevil*, before gaining Marvel's most important feature, *Spider-Man*. Original illustrator Steve Ditko, whose intriguing presentations had garnered considerable admiration, left the strip after a dispute with Lee, and Romita was handed the assignment in September 1966.

In complete contrast to Ditko's individual handling of the feature, Romita brought *Spider-Man* in line with the rest of Marvel's handsomely illustrated titles: Ditko's homely women gave way to Romita's voluptuous girl-next-door types; Ditko's "everyman" Peter Parker yielded to Romita's smashingly dashing Parker; and the overall appearance of the strip went from "common man" to "superheroic." Whereas Ditko's *Spider-Man* was populated by everyday people, Romita's *Spider-Man* was populated by noble-bearing and majestic-looking characters. Under Romita's and Lee's guidance, the character became the quintessential antihero of the late 1960s and early 1970s.

Romita began easing off *Spider-Man* in 1971 to assume greater responsibility for Marvel's artistic direction, and was appointed art director in October 1972. When the *Spider-Man* newspaper strip started syndication in 1977, Romita was entrusted with the artwork. He drew the feature with his customary artistic flair and dynamic line until 1982, when he was promoted to an executive position at Marvel. His son, John Romita, Jr., is also a talented comic book artist.

J.B.

ROOM AND BOARD (U.S.) In the late 1920s, a minor cartoonist named Sals Bostwick was hired by King Features to draw a daily panel series to compete with NEA's successful *Our Boarding House* by Gene Ahern. Named *Room and Board*, the panel ran obscurely in a few Hearst papers, failed to catch on with general readers (drawn in a nondescript style vaguely similar to Frank Willard's, the strip had no memorable characters to attract attention), and was dropped in due time. But Hearst did not give up. By 1935, he solved the competitive problem by hiring Ahern himself to draw a revived *Room and Board* for King Features. Peopled with all-new characters created by Ahern, the new daily and Sunday strip was very similar in cast, narrative, and format to his famous *Our Boarding House* (which was adeptly continued by Bill Freyse for NEA).

The feature character, a fat braggart whose wife runs a boarding house to bring in the bread, is named Judge Homer Augustus Puffle (he is, of course, as much a judge as Major Hoople was an Army officer). His wife, Nora, takes care of a 12-year-old nephew (named Duncan in this case), and the same Greek chorus of bachelor boarders (Snoff, Steve, etc.) comments on the Judge's bumbling gambits for fame and fortune. There is no equivalent of Jake Hoople in *Room and Board*, but the Judge is plagued by the recurrent appearances of a Two-Gun Terry, a mildly dangerous lunatic who fancies himself a lawman of the Old West and shoots up the boarding house on occasion. A maid named Delia is another minor variation from the *Our Boarding House* format.

Physically, Judge Puffle simply reverses Major Hoople (except in the vast belly). Puffle's nose is small, his mustache is less pronounced, his chin is normally proportioned—in sum, he is a much less striking comic figure. His background seems to be more southern than the Major's: his speech, especially in placating his tyrannical wife, is somewhat more flowery. But the differences are minor; essentially Judge Puffle and *Room and Board* are duplicates of Ahern's earlier inventions, so that fans of one at the time could "double their pleasure, double their fun" with both, by reading Ahern's King Features imitation of *Our Boarding House* together with Bill Freyse's exact continuation of the original feature for NEA—at least until *Room and Board* ceased publication with Ahern's death in 1960.

B.B.

ROSCHER, FRANZ (1928-   ) German cartoonist and graphic designer, born May 26, 1928, in Aussig, in the then German Sudeten, Franz Roscher went to school and high school there. While in school, his artistic talent was discovered and encouraged by an understanding teacher.

Wanting to pursue a career in the arts, Franz Roscher took the qualifying examinations at the Academy of Arts in Prague after leaving high school. He had already been accepted by the Academy's standards when World War II ended and his family fled west to Southern Germany. There he found work painting and drawing for a club entertaining Americans only.

More or less self-educated in the graphic arts, he also started working as a decorator and doing posters before attending the Blochauer school of graphics in order to further his means of artistic expression.

While working for U.S. troops, Franz Roscher also got to know American comic books and was thoroughly impressed and influenced by them. This experience gave him a penchant for the comics medium. He kept his fondness of comics, carrying it over into his advertising work by using the comics format whenever possible.

"Rose Is Rose," Pat Brady. © United Feature Syndicate.

He then got several chances to put his fondness of comics to the test by actually doing comic book work for several German publishers. In the 1960s this culminated in his two-year appointment as studio head of Rolf Kauka productions. This position involved watching over artistic continuity in the *Fix und Foxi* comic book according to the style of the book by Walter Neugebauer. The style influenced Roscher's later freelance comic book work for other publishers.

Roscher created *Plop*, a multicolored troll, that was featured in *Max und Molli* before being awarded its own comic book which folded after about a year. Then Roscher created *Michel*, a daily comic strip published by the Munich newspaper *tz* from September 1968 to December 1969. The antics of Michel, a German Mr. Average, ended after the newspaper had a change of editor-in-chief. The clear, well-rounded style of Franz Roscher has since been used largely in his advertising work (sometimes in the form of comic strips) while plans for new comics led to Roscher's starting to create comic strips for Catholic children's and youths' publications for which he is also doing numerous illustrations.

W.F.

ROSE IS ROSE (U.S.) The huge success of *Rose Is Rose* by Pat Brady proves there will always be a place in American syndicated cartooning for upbeat family strips full of love, humor, fantasy, and imaginative artwork. *Rose Is Rose* began syndication by United Feature Syndicate in 1984 with 30 newspapers subscribing. It now is way over 400 newspapers and growing. However, cartoonist Brady has seen the downside of syndication. His first syndicated comic strip *Graves, Inc.* lasted only three years and dwindled to a scant 12 subscribers.

In a warm mix of fantasy and reality, *Rose Is Rose* presents the just regular-folks Gumbo family. Rose is proud to be a stay-at-home mom. She and husband, Jimbo, a decent Neanderthal type who works as a handyman, still have white-hot heat between them. Their son, Pasquale, began in the strip only being able to gurgle baby talk, which Rose had to interpret: now he's in kindergarten. Other characters include Pasquale's infant cousin, Clem, a neighbor, Mimi, and an engaging cut-yet-cagey kitten, Peekaboo. Pasquale's ever-present guardian angel, who changes size and demeanor at any perceived threat to his charge, features in many dailies and Sundays. Cartoonist Brady claims that daydreaming is an important part of his thought process in developing gags and short continuities for *Rose Is Rose*. Hence everybody from Rose to the kitten has out-of-body daydream sequences.

It's implied by Pasquale's guardian angel that he'll grow up to be an astronaut. Jimbo dreams of traveling with a Shaolin priest and Kung Fu master. Rose's alter ego wants to ride a big Harley motorcycle through Paris wearing her jacket, miniskirt, and cycle hat all of black leather. Her regular eyeglasses become cool, dark glasses. She sports a rose tattoo (what else?) on her thigh. The sweet, sexy Rose has become in her own fantasy one of the hottest women in all syndicated comics. Cartoonist Brady claims he has no political agenda. His goal seems to be to present the upbeat side of love, marriage, and raising children. Not that *Rose Is Rose* is lacking its pensive moments.

At a time in syndicated cartooning when good drawing is less important than good writing, *Rose Is Rose* displays both. Pat Brady's treatment of artistic perspective is innovative and extraordinary in today's comics, especially in his Sunday pages where he is one of the few cartoonists to make full use of the color palette. On Sundays, Brady's drawings are ones that readers seek out to see what he's tried next. In one, a colorful kaleidoscope shows in the intricate design first the Gumbo house, then trees, then Pasquale, then his face, and finally the snowflake that lands on his nose.

Love rules in *Rose Is Rose*. Although Brady denies the characters are autobiographical, he tends to favor dressing in the baseball cap, plaid shirt, and jeans that are Jimbo's uniform. Several newspaper stories have also noted that Rose is physically very similar to his wife, showing that brunettes with glasses can have lots of fun.

A classic *Rose Is Rose* gag has Rose telling Jimbo, "I found an old leftover kiss that I never used. Do you want it?" When he responds in the affirmative, she puts a Louisiana-liplock on him that literally has his hair standing straight up, his shirt all rumpled. Jimbo sputters, "It tasted fresh!" Assuming a modest pose, Rose answers, "I think my sweetness acts as a preservative!"

Sure it's cute and lovey-dovey, but *Rose Is Rose* is a beautifully crafted strip that readers look for, and it ultimately does its job of entertaining and selling newspapers.

B.C.

ROSIE'S BEAU (U.S.) A Sunday strip of long duration by George McManus, *Rosie's Beau* first appeared as a full-color page in the Hearst weekly comic sections on October 29, 1916, where it replaced the short-lived McManus Sunday feature, *The Whole Blooming Family*. Running for a little over a year and a half, *Rosie's Beau* was replaced in its turn by *Bringing Up Father* on April 14, 1918. It then dropped from sight until it was resurrected by McManus as a companion page-topper to the *Bringing Up Father* Sunday strip on June 13, 1926,

"Rosie's Beau," George McManus. © King Features Syndicate.

where it supplanted a minor gag strip called *Good Morning, Boss* and ran for almost two decades.

Rosie was a typically lovely young girl of the comic pages, courted by a typically foolish and ardent young office-worker of the funnies named—in this case—Archie (or Archibald, as Rosie often calls him). Archie, based physically on McManus, was fat and double-chinned, but shone as a Paladin in armor to his beloved Rosie. The two lovers, much to the disgust of Rosie's father (who is later, in the 1920s, Archie's boss as well), continually exchange the soppiest possible *mots d'amour*. Surprisingly, McManus managed to get enormous comic strip mileage out of this seemingly limited and cloying subject, keeping the little Sunday strip fresh and amusing until November 12, 1944, when he finally replaced it with a new strip called *Snookums*. Archie was in the army at the time (amusingly, he was turned down for the army in World War I), but no nearer marriage with Rosie.

No book collection of *Rosie's Beau* was published; it had only brief comic book reprinting in the late 1930s, and there was no film or radio adaptation.

B.B.

ROSINSKI, GRZEGORZ (1941-   ) Belgian cartoonist and illustrator Grzegorz Rosinski was born in Stalowa Wola, in southeastern Poland, on August 3, 1941. Rosinski was first exposed to Western-style comics as a child reading *Vaillant*, a French Communist children's weekly that was widely distributed in Poland. He drew his first comic strip for his high school newspaper. After studies at the Warsaw School of Fine Arts, from which he graduated in 1967, he devoted himself to drawing and writing comics as his life occupation.

From the late 1960s to the mid-1970s he turned out a great number of comic books, mostly adventure and mystery stories, along with several epic and science fiction strips for the Warsaw magazine *Relax*. The excellence of his drawings attracted the attention of the editors of the Belgian magazine *Tintin*; and in 1976 Rosinski was invited to Brussels. In that year his long professional involvement with Editions du Lombard (publishers of *Tintin* magazine) began. He contributed a few short comic stories for *Tintin*, as well as a fantasy strip for the rival publication *Spirou* (on that occasion he used the alias "Rosek" and greatly simplified his sophisticated graphic style).

In 1977, on scripts by Jean Van Hamme, he started in *Tintin* what was to turn into his masterwork, *Thorgal, Fils des Etoiles* ("Thorgal, Son of the Stars"). A sweeping tale of heroic fantasy, it has majestically unfolded over 30 episodes to date. Endowed with super- and extra-sensory powers, Thorgal had been adopted by a band of Vikings who found him lying unconscious on the ocean shore and gave him the name of Aegirson, son of Aegir, the sea god. In adventures that took him over the seas and into unknown lands, Thorgal is not without resemblance to Prince Valiant. Furthermore, Rosinski's graphic style, in its meticulous renderings and compositions, has undoubtedly been inspired by Harold Foster's. Be that as it may, *Thorgal* is withal a gripping historical saga and a masterly tale of sword-and-sorcery.

In addition to his long-term commitment to *Thorgal*, Rosinski has found the time to turn out several other comic book series, the most notable being *Hans*, a postnuclear war tale scripted by André-Paul Duchateau, which he illustrated from its outset in 1980.

M.H.

Really Gentlemen if you gaze on me in this manner you will put me quite to the blush?

Thomas Rowlandson, "A Lump of Innocence."

ROWLANDSON, THOMAS (1756-1827) English cartoonist and engraver born July 1756 in the Old Jewry, London. Thomas Rowlandson attended Dr. Barrow's Academy in Soho and distinguished himself by the caricatures he made of his fellow-students and school teachers. In 1772 he went to Paris at the invitation of his Uncle Thomas's French widow. There he made rapid advances in the study of the human figure (so one of his biographers tells us, perhaps with unconscious humor) and upon his return to London he registered at the Royal Academy to which he had been admitted before his visit to Paris.

In 1775 Rowlandson exhibited at the Academy with a number of allegorical scenes. From 1778 to 1781 he devoted himself to painting portraits, several of which were also exhibited at the Academy. Rowlandson was veering away from serious art to caricature, and his first cartoons began appearing in 1784, among them "An Italian Family," "Vauxhall," and "The Serpentine River." During this time Rowlandson was supported by his aunt's liberalities and when the lady died in 1788 she left him several thousand pounds besides other valuable property. Rowlandson was now free to indulge his penchants for women and gambling, losing not only his legacy but sinking further and further into debt; this situation left him no alternative but to turn back to drawing, which he called "my only left resource." He was a prolific worker and frequently produced two finished cartoons a day. *The Miseries of Life, The Comforts of Bath, The Cries of London* were among

the remarkable cartoon series which he then produced (they were later collected into books). But Rowlandson's most celebrated creations were produced under the prodding (and with the generous assistance) of his long-time friend, the book and print-seller Ackermann. *The Tour of Dr. Syntax in Search of the Picturesque* (with accompanying text in verse by William Combe) appeared first in Ackermann's *Poetical Magazine* in 1809, was reprinted in book form in 1812, and was followed by two more *Tours of Dr. Syntax* books (*In Search of Consolation*, 1820; *In Search of a Wife*, 1821).

Rowlandson's narrative sequences (especially *The Tours of Dr. Syntax*) provide a direct link between the 18th-century picture story and the modern comic strip (they only lack dialectic motion to qualify as full-fledged comic strips). Along with his contemporary, James Gillray, Rowlandson also pioneered in the use of the balloon as a dramatic device. Thomas Rowlandson died in 1827.

M.H.

ROY, YVES *see* Hildago, Francisco.

ROY TIGER (Germany) *Roy Tiger*, a creation of the editorial staff of Bastei Verlag, came into being in collaboration with a group of Spanish artists including Esteban Maroto, Carlos Gimenez, L. Garcia, A. Usero, Lopez Ramón, et al. By and large this ensured a high standard of illustration for this comic series taking place in the exotic jungles of India. However, as so often happens, Bastei Verlag did not fully realize the art potential of the series and ruined some of the books by heavy-handed "improvement" drawing of the same kind that had helped wreck the style of Arturo del Castillo's Western, *Kendall*, Joseph Gillain's *Jerry Spring*, or Raymond Poïvet's *Les pionniers de l'Espérance*. The exotic flair of *Roy Tiger* nevertheless escaped destruction and allowed for its publication in 79 issues in a period of some two years.

Roy Tiger first saw print on April 15, 1968, in *Lasso*, number 63. *Lasso*, a Western comic book featuring *Kendall* at the time, should have been the most unlikely title in which to try out a series taking place in India. Nevertheless, it was done. In fact, the Wild West had to turn over four more complete issues to mysterious India before *Roy Tiger* was allowed to continue on its own as a biweekly comic book. For awhile the book was even stepped up to weekly status. The series ended in June 1970 after a reshuffling of the Bastei comic lineup. It may also have ended because Spanish artists involved in the production of *Roy Tiger* moved on to other projects.

Spanish readers had a chance to follow some of the *Roy Tiger* material in *Trinca*. At the time *Roy Tiger* was published, Bastei Verlag sold their comics nationwide at the same date of sale. The books not sold by the time the next issue rolled around were then returned to be bound in volumes for later sales. Since then Bastei's system of distribution has changed in order to reduce the number of leftover books. This was achieved by selling according to the six Nielsen areas of Germany, six regions defined by infrastructure as separate marketing areas. What is not sold in one Nielsen area is collected for shipment to the next and so forth.

Roy Tiger, while the book lasted, told the story of Roy Tiger, the sandy-haired son of a Caucasian doctor; Khamar, an Indian of the Kalong tribe; Paki, the orphaned Kashmiri native boy; and their animal friends, Shumba the python, Sheeta the black panther, and Shimmy the monkey. Occasionally they were also aided by an elephant named Lahani. Between them they saved the Indian subcontinent from some major catastrophes and helped put their share of criminals behind bars. Roy Tiger's parents rarely entered the scene, making the comic strip ideal wish-fulfillment for the young readership for whom the feature was intended.

W.F.

RUBINO, ANTONIO (1880-1964) Italian cartoonist born 1880 in Sanremo. Antonio Rubino started his career as an advertising artist and book illustrator; in 1907 he entered the field of children's illustrations with contributions to the *Girnalino della Domenica*. In 1908 he became one of the most important contributors to the newly created *Corriere dei Piccoli*: it was Rubino who dreamed up the idea of replacing the speech balloons in the Italian version of such famous American comic strips as "Fortunello" (*Happy Hooligan*), "La Checca," (*And Her Name Was Maud*), "Bibi e Bibo" (*The Katzenjammer Kids*), and "Arcibaldo e Petronilla" (*Bringing Up Father*) by captions in verse (this was to become the hallmark of the Italian comics).

In addition to his editorial duties, Rubino created a myriad of different titles for the *Corriere*, most of them only ephemeral features that appeared and disappeared from the pages of the magazine without any seeming regularity or pattern. In the course of his long tenure (1908-1927) it is possible to distinguish a few creations which proved longer-lasting or more noteworthy than the others: *Quadratino* ("Little Squarehead," 1910), *Pino e Pina* (a kid strip, also 1910), *Lola e Lalla* (1913), the hilarious and long-lasting saga of *Il Collegio 1a Delizia* ("The Delight Boarding-School," 1913), *Italino e Kartoffel Otto* (the Italian comic strip's contribution to World War I, 1915), *Pierino e il Burattino* ("Peter and the Puppet," 1921), *Rosaspina* (1922), *Pippotto ed il Ca prone Barbacucco* ("Big Joe and Barbacucco the Billy-Goat," 1924), *Lionello e Nerone* (1926).

During World War I Rubino also contributed to the army magazine *La Tradotta* for which he created a host of memorable characters like Corporal C. Piglio, always ready with advice, the handsome hero Muscolo Mattia, Apollo Mari the troublemaker, along with the grotesque figures of the rulers Cecco Beppe, Guglielmone, and Carletto.

In 1927 Rubino was invited to contribute to the Fascist Youth's magazine *Il Balilla*: during the short time he worked for that publication his most notable contribution was a pictorialization of Aesop's fables. In 1931 he started his long collaboration with the publisher Mondadori, becoming in 1934 the editor of the comic weekly *Topolino*, in whose pages he used speech balloons for the first time (he always maintained that captions were educationally superior to balloons in stories for children). In 1942 *Rubino* added to his activities that of animator, producing *Il Paese dei Ranocchi* ("The Land of the Frogs") which won the award in the animated cartoon category in that year's Venice Biennial.

After the war, Rubino devoted himself to painting, but when he was called back to the *Corriere dei Piccoli* he could not resist one last fling at comics. His stories no longer appealed to the public, however, and he retired in 1959.

Antonio Rubino's style was a combination of geometric design and floral pattern, with a sinuous line akin to Art Nouveau. He was also a master of color and must be regarded as the chief architect of *Corriere dei Piccoli*'s success during the two decades of his tenure. Then, in the 1930s, the American comics established themselves and Rubino's conceptions became more and more obsolete. Antonio Rubino died at Sanremo on July 1, 1964.

G.B.

RUDI (Germany) Rudi, a very human dog, is the main comic hero of a number of comic albums produced by writer/artist Peter Puck, a native of Heidenheim where he was born July 23, 1960. The name Peter Puck, incidentally, is not a pseudonym. Puck studied history of art and literature and is a self-educated comic artist whose style was strongly influenced by that of Carl Barks's.

Rudi was first published in May 1985 in the Stuttgart magazine *Stuttgart live* and later on continued in the Stuttgart magazine *lift*. The full-page strips published there have been collected in a number of comic albums since 1987 and have gone through numerous printings. The stories that straightforward Rudi and his anarchic friend Fred get involved in are social satires of life in Germany with all kinds of people and happenings straight from everyday life. As a Stuttgart newspaper once put it: "Rudi is a better guide through German subculture and youth culture than the most alternative city guide. . . ."

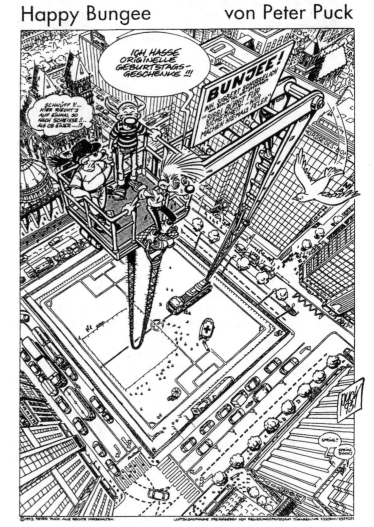

"*Rudi,*" Peter Puck. © Peter Puck.

Puck depicts his world in realistic backdrops filled with cartoon characters. In fact, Puck may be one of the funny-animal artists with the most realistic background drawings. Puck's material has become so popular in Germany that he was nominated twice for best German comic artist at the Erlangen Comic Salon. In 1994 his large format originals were also presented in an exhibit at the Erlangen Salon.

Puck gave up his academic studies to devote himself entirely to creating comics and to produce advertising using funny comic elements. While his artwork certainly is one of the reasons for the success of *Rudi*, the writing is at least as important. While sometimes speech balloons are filled with lots of dialogue they only appear text-heavy. Actually, dialogue is as much a necessary tool as is the artwork for Puck to create his aura of visual and verbal verisimilitude necessary to make for a functional and witty satire.

W.F.

RUFUS *see* Flook.

RUGGLES (G.B.) John Ruggles and family (wife Gladys, teenage daughter Maisie, young son Herbert, and the mother-in-law) were the first working-class family in British newspaper strips. A step down the social scale from city gent *Pop*, they reflected the readers of the *Daily Mirror* and quickly caught on. The first strip appeared on March 11, 1935, signed "Blik" (Steve Dowling on art, Frank Dowling on script), and was a simple gag strip. Domestic jokes were the routine until continuity was introduced during 1937. Interest immediately increased and caught 74 percent of the readership in the first Mirror strip poll. This rose slightly by 2½ percent in 1946, but dwindled to 51 percent in 1949, a year after the strip had taken an unprecedented turn.

For years the serial ran as a soap opera tinged with humor; Ruggles in bowler and raincoat rising above domestic troubles and unlikely romantic entangle-

ments with glamorous Greta, while Maisie had married boyfriend Julian Balham and borne a child, and Herbert had taken up with teenaged Elsie Watson, a fellow architecture student. Suddenly, in 1948, Ruggles turned to face his readers and said, "Look out for us on page two. We're taking a trip to Margate on the *Royal Eagle* and we're going to see if you're aboard!" For the first time a cartoon hero stepped into reality—or vice versa—and the real life Mrs. Pearson and family found themselves featured in a strip! Although Ruggles's "meet the people" was a new idea, and certainly worked for a while, the actual readership appreciation fell, and the strip was killed on August 3, 1957. The last writer was Ian Gammidge, while the artist remained Steve Dowling.

D.G.

RUPERT (G.B.) Rupert is an endearing little bear cub in his checked trousers, jumper, and scarf, who lives in Nutwood with Mummy and Daddy. (If not the original Three Bears, then certainly the originals as far as British newspaper strips go.) Not strictly a strip, *Rupert*'s panels have never exceeded two per day (for some years reduced to one), with his story carried in text or verse beneath, but he has also appeared in strip form in the *Daily Express Children's Own* (May 20, 1933), a pull-out comic, and is currently reprinted in strip form and in full color in *Pippin* (1974), a weekly nursery comic. The panels also take on strip form in the annual reprints in color, *Rupert Annual* (1945-   ).

With successful children's strips running in the *Daily Mirror* and *Daily News*, R. D. Blumenfeld, editor of the *Daily Express*, asked his night news editor to look for something similar. Herbert Tourtel told his wife, Mary, no mean artist and writer, and within days she had come up with *The Little Lost Bear*. It commenced on Monday, November 8, 1920, ran its course, and was replaced by a different story. But readers wrote in demanding more adventures of Rupert Bear, and so Mary obliged with a sequel. Soon other stories were dropped altogether, and by the 1930s Rupert had a full-blown club, The Rupert League, and regular reprints in book form.

"Ruggles," Steve Dowling. © Daily Mirror Ltd.

"Rupert," Alfred Bestall. © Beaverbrook Newspapers Ltd.

Rupert's regular playmates include Bill Badger, Algy Pug, and Edward Trunk the elephant, and his adventures always have a fairy-tale touch of fantasy, landing him safely home in Nutwood. Mary Tourtel retired in 1935 when her eyesight failed after drawing 105 stories. She died in Canterbury in March 1948, aged 74. The strip was taken over by Alfred Bestall, illustrator and *Punch* cartoonist. His first story, *Rupert and the Smugglers*, commenced June 28, 1935. After 30 years he too retired, and Alex Cubie took over the drawing, while Frederick Chaplain, a former comic editor from Amalgamated Press, took on the writing. Rupert celebrated his fiftieth anniversary (1970) by expanding his activities. He was turned into a puppet film series for television—and also appeared pornographically in the underground paper *Oz!*

In 1984 pop stars Paul and Linda McCartney financed a fully animated cartoon film, *Rupert and the Frog Song*. The film was produced, directed, and animated by Geoff Dunbar, but plans to expand it into a feature collapsed, and the film was released as a short.

D.G.

RUSSELL, CLARENCE D. (1895-1963) Clarence Russell was an American cartoonist born in 1895 in Buffalo, New York. C. D. Russell studied at the Chicago Art Institute and, after freelancing cartoons to magazines around the country, he came to New York City in 1915. When World War I rolled around he enlisted in the Marines, became sports editor of *The Leatherneck*, the Corps' publication, and was sent overseas with the American Expeditionary Force.

Back in the United States in 1920, Russell worked for different New York newspapers, notably the *Evening Mail* and the *Evening Post*. At the same time he contributed regularly to *Judge* (legend has it that the editors of *Judge* had him signed under exclusivity in 1927 to keep him out of *Life*). Around that time Russell developed the character of a peppery little tramp who appeared with increasing frequency in the pages of *Judge*. Eventually the cartoonist was contacted by King Features Syndicate and drew the little tramp into a new comic strip, *Pete the Tramp*, which first appeared in January 1932.

For the rest of his life Russell stayed with King, contributing a number of other strip creations as companion pieces to *Pete*. *The Tucker Twins* (a pale imitation of the Katzies) and *Pete's Pup* were not remarkable either in style or content; *Shorty*, about a shrimpish bum even seedier than Pete, did have some merit but basically it was only more of the same. In 1946 Russell helped form the National Cartoonists Society of which he became the first secretary. He died of cancer at Kings Bridge Veterans Hospital in the Bronx on October 22, 1963, and *Pete the Tramp* died with him.

The possessor of a very remarkable graphic talent, C. D. Russell never knew how to develop his potential to the fullest. Fresh and imaginative when it came out in the 1930s, *Pete* soon floundered on the shoals of irrelevance and repetitiveness. With all its shortcomings, however, it remains the only work for which Russell deserves to be remembered.

M.H.

RUSSELL, JAMES NEWTON (1909-   ) Australian cartoonist born at Campsie, N.S.W., Australia, in 1909, the son of a council plumber, who was killed in an accident when Russell was six years old. On completing school at Lewisham Christian Brothers, in 1924, he became a copy boy on the *Sydney Daily Guardian* and soon transferred to *Smith's Weekly*. With no prospects of advancement and because his drawing ability had not reached the standard required for publication, Russell drifted into a series of jobs in leather and steel factories and worked as a junior in the office of Sydney Stadium, where he also became a preliminary boxer for a brief period. During this time he improved his drawing skills by sketching notable boxers, which were published in the Sydney papers. In 1926, the head artist of Fox Films offered to tutor Russell in the fundamentals of art if he paid $200 and worked for two years without pay. Russell accepted the offer and by the time he left Fox Films he had become a capable artist.

He joined the *Sydney Evening News* in 1928 and became the youngest political cartoonist in Australia. When the paper folded in 1931, Russell became a sports caricaturist with the *Referee* and soon transferred back to his original paper, *Smith's Weekly*. Here he was to spend almost two decades in handling single-block cartoons as well as strips. When Stan Cross left *Smith's* to join the *Melbourne Herald*, in 1940, Jim Russell not only inherited the strips *Smith's Vaudevillians* and *You and Me* but also took over the position as art editor. He altered the tone of *You and Me* and changed the name to *Mr. & Mrs. Pott*. During the war years, Russell was responsible for two satirical strips, *Adolf, Hermann* and *Musso* and *Schmit der Sphy*, which not only delighted his readers but were rumored to have put Russell on a blacklist, if the Allies lost the war.

In 1950, when *Smith's* folded, Russell was able to sell a further modified version of *Mr. & Mrs. Pott* (retitled *The Potts*) to the *Herald & Weekly Times Ltd.* for national and, eventually, worldwide syndication. While influenced by artists of *The Bulletin* and *Smith's Weekly* schools, Russell developed a slick caricature technique that is closer in origin to the U.S. style of humorous cartooning than any particular Australian style. His international rather than national approach to both art and humor would appear to be the basis of the wide acceptance of *The Potts*, rather than any unique qualities inherent in the strip.

Jim Russell is a writer, tennis administrator, radio and TV personality, publisher of dancing and music magazines, President of the White City Club, Sydney, and finds time to run two travel agencies. In his biographical entry for the 1996 *National Cartoonists Society Album* he also lists himself as the NCS representative for Australia.

J.R.

RUSTY RILEY (U.S.) Frank Godwin's last creation, *Rusty Riley* saw the light of print as a daily strip on January 26, 1948, and was followed by a Sunday version on June 27 of the same year. The feature was distributed by King Features Syndicate, and Rod Reed wrote the daily continuity, while the Sunday page was authored by Frank Godwin's brother Harold.

In the first episode, Rusty, a bright, attractive lad of about 14, flees in the company of his fox terrier Flip, the orphanage where he had been confined since the accidental death of his parents. In the course of his wanderings he comes upon the estate of Mr. Miles, a wealthy race-horse owner, where he works as a stable boy, and later as a jockey, bringing his trusted horse, Bright Blaze, to victory in the Kentucky Derby.

"Rusty Riley," Frank Godwin. © King Features Syndicate.

The horse-racing scenes alternate with stories of detection in which Rusty and Patti Miles, Mr. Miles's teenage daughter, often foil the plots of robbers or racetrack fixers. Slowly romance blooms between the two young people, but this aspect of the strip was cut short by the sudden disappearance of Rusty Riley in the summer of 1959, a few weeks before its creator's own death.

Rusty Riley is a work of old age (Godwin was 60 when he started it), but it carries with it the luminescence of youth, a youth certainly romanticized and idealized, but as vital and vibrant as Godwin's art. The trite story line is irrelevant; Rusty Riley was always purely an artist's strip, and it should be enjoyed as such by all those who appreciate elegance of line, artistry of execution, and sheer graphic excellence.

M.H.

RYAN, TOM K. (1926-   ) American cartoonist born June 6, 1926, in Anderson, Indiana. Tom K. (T. K.) Ryan grew up in small Indiana towns, and later studied at Notre Dame University and the University of Cincinnati. Ryan, who always wanted to become a cartoonist, started his career as a commercial artist (he designed the football helmet emblems of the Green Bay Packers and the New York Giants). He was bored, however, and started reading Western literature. ("It was kind of an escape for me as well as a hobby," he was later to confide.) In turn, his reading led him back to cartooning and he decided to try a new "hip" idea, which would combine, in his words, "the Old West with a hip approach."

T. K. Ryan's brainchild, *Tumbleweeds*, was thus launched in September 1965. Distributed by the small Lew Little Syndicate, it was later picked up by the Register and Tribune Syndicate (and eventually by King Features Syndicate). Today *Tumbleweeds* is carried by more than 300 newspapers around the country. Originally Ryan had intended *Tumbleweeds* to be a gag strip, but later he went more and more deeply into continuity, keeping a sharp eye on the 30-odd characters in the cast.

Ryan's style is simple, even basic, harking back to the caricatural line and slapstick situation of the early comic strip artists. His humor is pointed, but never offensive, and though he keeps his dialogue up to date, it is still literate. T. K. Ryan, a somewhat shy artist who never joined a professional society and seldom appears in public, lives and works in Muncie, Indiana. His dedication to *Tumbleweeds* is total, and it shows in the high narrative and graphic quality of the strip. In one of the rare interviews that he granted (to Beth Slocum of the *Milwaukee Journal*), Ryan expounded his artistic philosophy in simple terms: "I believe strips should be relevant and attuned to modern times and language, but not message oriented." In the case of *Tumbleweeds*, of course, the medium itself is the message.

The growing success of his strip in the 1970s persuaded Ryan to join the National Cartoonists Society. Still shunning the limelight, he devotes the greatest part of his time turning out *Tumbleweeds*, now in its fourth decade. His recognizable line and brand of humor have inspired many later cartoonists, including Jim Davis, who was his studio assistant from 1969 to 1978, prior to creating *Garfield*.

M.H.

SABAKU NO MAŌ (Japan) *Sabaku no Maō* ("The Devil of the Desert") was created by Tetsuji Fukushima for the comic monthly *Bōkenō* where it first appeared in April 1949. (*Bōkenō* is now the only monthly comic magazine for boys left, as all the others—*Shōnen, Mangaō, Bokura,* etc.—having gone out of existence.) Earlier in 1949, in the first issue of *Bōkenō,* Fukushima created *Daiya Majin* ("Diamond Devil") which served as the prologue and the springboard for *Sabaku no Maō.*

Inspired by the legend of Aladdin and the magic lamp, *Sabaku no Maō* featured the adventures of a genie and his enterprising young master, Boppu. Sabaku had sprung out of an incense burner when Boppu had inadvertently let it burn out: he wore a scarlet cape, a huge sword, a white turban, and long boots. This costume occurred to Fukushima while he was reading an issue of the *National Geographic* magazine about an old African regal ceremony. Sabaku unquestionably obeyed the orders of the master of the lamp, as he was invincible: no weapon known to man, whether arrow, spear, gun, or cannon, could bring him down. Thanks to the large ruby embedded in his turban (the Hikōseki, or "flying stone") he could fly through the air.

Sabaku no Maō soon became one of the more successful boys' strips. The highlight of each story was Sabaku's obligatory battle scene with armies mounted against him. Fukushima's dynamic composition and arrangement of glittering colors led the readers into a fantastic and enchanting story world. *Sabaku no Maō*'s last appearance was in the February 1956 issue of *Bōkenō.*

H.K.

SADHÚ (Spain) A jungle strip created by Emilio Freixas on scripts by José Canellas Casals, *Sadhú* started in issue 326 of the comic weekly *Chicos* (November 1, 1944). The first episode was titled "The Tiger of Sambar" and was followed by "The Seven Altars of Sapta Mata," published in *Chico*'s 1948 annual. Many years later, after Freixas's temporary retirement from the comic field, this feature helped him make a comeback. Again written by Canellas, this new version of *Sadhú* appeared in the first issue of the magazine *Chito* (October 1, 1974). It lasted only a few years.

Sadhú is a grown-up Mowgli: like Kipling's hero he is a friend of animals. He also has a certain resemblance to Bomba, the jungle boy. Freixas's mastery in the rendition of animals, along with his exotic and baroque backgrounds, help him to re-create accurately the locale and atmosphere in which his hero finds himself.

L.G.

SAD SACK, THE (U.S.) The creation of ex-Disney animator and striker George Baker, *The Sad Sack* debuted in the pages of *Yank* magazine, the army weekly, in 1942. He was, according to Baker, an aver-

age soldier, steeped in psychological, if not actual, reality and reflected the soldiers' state of mind: resigned, tired, helpless, and beaten.

The Sack, a classic variant of the Little Man, became one of the most popular characters to come out of the war, surpassing *Yank*'s other star, Private Breger (G.I. Joe). The *Sack* cartoons were always in strip form and in pantomime. He saw action, during his over three and a half years with *Yank*, in every theater of the war and on every front.

The Sack's tormentors were many usually master sergeants, but often, a la Happy Hooligan, Charlie Chaplin, Robert Benchley, and others in the tradition, his troubles were simply a natural function of his existence in the harsh world around him. The world seemed to conspire against the Sack: He never got the girl, regulations foiled his sincerest efforts, superiors inevitably took advantage of him. In keeping with the elements of the classic comic figure, he was designed to reflect the frustrations of the common man but at the same time became something for the common man to look down on. *The Sad Sack* was enormously popular.

He was too popular to die with the armistice. The ever-alert John Wheeler, near the war's end, arranged for the republication of the best of the *Sack* strips in stateside papers through his Bell Syndicate. After the war the Sack lived on in a Sunday page distributed by Bell; it debuted on May 5, 1946. But in civvies the Sack was a fish out of water. That and Bell's traditionally poor promotion and sales caused *The Sad Sack* Sunday page to dwindle to nothing. It was discontinued in the early 1950s.

Elsewhere, however, back in uniform, the Sack happily suffered his persecutions. The original cast of the

"The Sad Sack," George Baker. © George Baker.

Sack, a growling Sarge and ever-changing faces, was beefed up to include the General, the K-9 Muttssy, the ugly WAC Sadie Sack, and others in the pages of a wide range of titles for Harvey. Many artists have worked on these books, most recently Joe Dennett, but Baker continued to draw all the covers until his death in May 1975.

Merchandising was also heavy, with many Sad Sack ash trays, pieces of jewelry, glasses, and other items. He also came to life on the screen when Jerry Lewis played the title role.

Baker had one of the great comic drawing styles. His Disney training stood him in good stead, although there were no traces of the cutesy, animator style that was popular in the postwar years. There was a great deal of movement, expression, and very basic humor in the drawings. Baker varied the angles in his panels; the view was always slightly from above and employed the classic comic strip conventions: beads of sweat, symbols of pain and consternation, clouds of dust. Pot bellies were everywhere, every pant leg bagged absurdly at the knee, the feet were the biggest since Zim, and, all in all, *The Sad Sack's* adventures were presented in a most agreeable, old, slapstick style.

R.M.

SAGA DE XAM (France) Spurred on by the heady praise heaped on two of his previous ventures, *Barbarella* and *Jodelle*, the indefatigable Eric Losfeld released in 1967 yet another comic strip novel, *Saga de Xam*, written by Jean Rollin and illustrated by Nicolas Devil.

Saga is a beautiful young woman from Xam, a distant planet of our galaxy. Xam, inhabited exclusively by women, is threatened with a terrible alien invasion. Not used to violence and war, the inhabitants of Xam send Saga to learn the ways of evil and destruction from the people of earth. Saga then starts on a space and time odyssey which takes her to the Middle Ages, in among the Vikings, to ancient Egypt, China, and the United States. Upon her return to Xam she will have the opportunity to apply her newly acquired knowledge. . . .

Saga has been highly praised by some, yet, to most, it remains a sophomoric exercise, dull and derivative, a sterile attempt at being original at all costs, without regard to the niceties of good storytelling and accomplished draftsmanship.

M.H.

SAINT-OGAN, ALAIN (1895-1974) Saint-Ogan was a French cartoonist, journalist, and writer born in Colombes, near Paris, on August 7, 1895. His father was a newspaper editor, and the son decided very early in life to become a press illustrator. He studied at l'Ecole Nationale des Arts Decoratifs in Paris and had his first drawings published in 1913. He enlisted during World War I and was sent to the Balkans. After the war he resumed his career as a cartoonist and newspaperman. In 1925 he created his first comic strip, *Zig et Puce*, about two venturesome youngsters, for the French weekly *Dimanche Illustré*. The series met with instant success and was followed by a number of other comic features: *Mitou et Toti* (more kids, brother and sister this time; 1932), *Prosper l'Ours* ("Prosper the Bear") in 1933; *Monsieur Poche* (1934), a gag strip about a fat and stuffy French bourgeois; and *Touitoui* (an elf) also in 1934.

Alain Saint-Ogan.

At the same time Saint-Ogan wrote and drew for a number of newspapers and magazines. In 1941 he became editor of the children's weekly *Benjamin* (where he created *Trac et Boum*, yet more kids) and he was also active in the Resistance. From 1950 to 1958 he was cohost of a radio show and later became a television producer. Saint-Ogan has also illustrated a number of books and was the author of several novels and two books of memoirs. He toned down his activities in the 1960s. Alain Saint-Ogan died on June 23, 1974, of circulatory trouble.

Alain Saint-Ogan is widely regarded as the artist who gave fresh impetus to the French strip in the 1920s and 1930s. His greatest merit was to introduce the art deco look (of which he is one of the foremost representatives) to the comic strip. He has influenced countless numbers of European cartoonists (including Hergé, who owes his cartooning start to Saint-Ogan). Saint-Ogan was the recipient of a number of awards and distinctions. In 1967 he became the first cartoonist to have a medal coined in his effigy by the French Mint, and a retrospective exhibition of his works was organized by the Bibliotheque Nationale in 1971.

M.H.

SAITŌ, TAKAO (1936-) Japanese comic book artist born in Osaka on November 3, 1936, Takao Saitō wanted to be an illustrator; he studied toward that goal during his high school years. One day, however, he discovered by chance the work of Osamu Tezuka (particularly *Shin Takarajima*, "The New Treasure Island") and there and then made up his mind to become a comic strip artist.

In 1954 Saitō produced his first comic strip, *Kūki Danshaku* ("Baron Kuki"), which strongly showed Tezuka's influence. Later he drew many more comic strips for Kage, one of the most important and durable of the *kashibonya yō manga* (comic book companies that did not distribute through dealers but circulated their publications through rental libraries) as well as for Machi and Deka.

Takao Saitō.

Among his most successful comic strips are: *Taifu Goro* (a detective strip, 1960); *Bugei Kikou* (a samurai story, 1962); his 007 series (which he adapted from the Ian Fleming novels for the monthly *Boy's Life Magazine* in 1965); *Muyōnosuke* (the story of a one-eyed professional prize-fighter in the Edo era) for the weekly *Shōnen* magazine; and *Golgo 13*, about a professional killer, for the bimonthly *Big Comic*. After ending *Golgo*

13 in 1994 after a record-breaking run of 25 years, he went on to produce a number of shorter works.

Saitō's art style, at first very simple and even caricatural, grew more realistic with time. Saitō is widely regarded as the artist who gave fresh impetus to the Japanese comic strip in the 1960s. His work, which has influenced a whole new generation of Japanese cartoonists (Takeshi Kanda, Yuzuro Saitō, Fumiyasu Ishikawa, Saburō Takemoto, to name a few), is representative of contemporary Japanese comic art, with its emphasis on speed, thrills, and sex.

H.K.

SALINAS, JOSÉ LUIS (1908-1985) Argentinean cartoonist and illustrator born in Buenos Aires on February 11, 1908, Salinas broke into illustration in 1929 without the benefit of formal art studies. He worked for such magazines as *El Tony* and *Paginas de Columba* in his native country before embarking on a career as a designer and advertising illustrator for the Exitus agency.

His first contribution to the comics was *Hernán el Corsario* (''Hernán the Privateer''), a sea adventure story set in the 1600s, which he wrote and drew for the magazine *Patoruzu* from 1936 to 1938, and again from 1940 to 1946. It was on this strip that Salinas honed his skills as a master craftsman and graphic storyteller. In the same period he also adapted a number of famous novels, such as Jules Verne's *Michel Strogoff* and Alexandre Dumas's *The Three Musketeers*, into comic strips for the magazine *El Hógar*.

By the end of the 1940s his fame had spread far beyond his native Argentina, and he went to the United States in search of more lucrative employment than he could find in his country. His contacts with

José Luis Salinas, ''Hernán el Corsario.'' © *José Luis Salinas.*

King Features proved fruitful, and in 1951 *The Cisco Kid*, a Western based on an O. Henry story and starring a flamboyant Mexican righter of wrongs, debuted in American newspapers: drawn by Salinas on texts by Rod Reed, it lasted until 1968 and received much critical acclaim. The artist, who in the meantime had settled in the States with his family, then returned to Argentina.

He kept up his contacts with King, however, and in 1973 made a comeback with *Gunner*, a detective strip set in the milieu of professional sports. In 1975 he abruptly left the strip and abandoned comics for good. He died in Buenos Aires on January 10, 1985, having devoted the last years of his life to illustration again and to painting.

Called by Franco Fossati "a superlative artist of the comics," Salinas, more than any of his contemporaries, helped develop the style and look of Argentine comics in the last half-century. His son, Alberto Salinas, is also a renowned cartoonist.

M.H.

SALLY FORTH (U.S.) King Features Syndicate touts *Sally Forth* as "every working mother's story" and has carved out a niche of more than 600 subscribers for this comic strip about a woman who juggles marriage, a child, and a full-time job outside the home. In 1995 *Sally Forth* took a quantum leap in popularity expanding its subscriber base by 25 percent. Part of the reason is that *Sally Forth* delivers an audience to newspapers desperate to reach two-income families. Women in particular like *Sally Forth*; the strip is often published in the "Style" (a.k.a. women's) section of newspapers just as Universal Press Syndicate's *Cathy* is.

With more than 70 percent of all women who have school-age children working outside the home, Sally's trials and tribulations have a ready audience. Editors publish *Sally Forth* because they know she reflects the lifestyle of most married women, albeit not all are in middle management like Sally.

Sally Forth was originally developed by Field Syndicate and debuted January 4, 1982. Since then Field has been absorbed by King Features. Just signed "Howard," many readers have been surprised to discover their beloved Sally was created by a man, Minneapolis attorney Greg Howard. A partner in a law firm with more than nine years of litigation experience, he left that career to become a cartoonist. Greg Howard has always considered writing his strength. He

himself has called his artwork "crude" and has struggled to improve to "mediocre."

Although Howard's poor drawing style did keep *Sally Forth* out of a number of newspapers initially, it was the concept of the script and the writing that sold it, not pretty art. The same might be said of Universal Press's *Cathy*.

Sally puts up with a demanding boss, Ralph, and a husband whom she often gets to help her with "women's work" around the house. Sally is not a wimp, but her ever-so-politically-correct husband is, in the opinion of many male readers. When asked by Sally, who is running late, to iron her blouse for her, Ted raises his arms and shouts, "Yes! 1,000 husbanding points!" When she changes her mind, he whines, "Rats. That would have been enough points to last me a whole month."

Sally and Ted Forth's eight-year-old daughter, Hillary, rounds out this nuclear family. With Hillary the challenges of raising a precocious, upscale child are ever present. She's also expert at dropping lines such as, "I'll ask Dad. It's probably men's work anyway." When Sally jumps to fix her bicycle, Hillary notes to herself and the reader, "A friend of mine taught me that trick for getting fast action."

Because of cartoonist Howard's limited drawing ability the action of *Sally Forth* was until 1991 limited to Sally's office and the kitchen, living room, and bedroom at the Forth's home. At the office, the strip has the same type of corporate culture satire that's a proven success in *Dilbert*. When the new voice mail system is installed, Sally comments, "Nothing that comes with a 78-page manual is going to make my life easier."

In November 1991 *Sally Forth* and Greg Howard experienced the "artwork incident." Recognizing his own limits as an artist and successful enough to hire an assistant, Howard changed the drawing style of the strip. Specifically, he brought in Craig MacIntosh, editorial cartoonist for *The Minneapolis Star* and cocreator with Steve Sack of the kids' comic strip *Professor Doodle's* for Tribune Media Services. MacIntosh was to draw and Howard would write. It proved to be a disaster with *Sally Forth* fans. Suddenly Sally was too thin and curvy. The characters' faces were too angular. The stiffness of Howard's drawings, which readers interpreted as calm, was gone. All hell broke loose. More than 1,000 irate fans called up King Features, and that was just the beginning. Recognizing his mistake,

"Sally Forth," Craig MacIntosh and Greg Howard. © King Features Syndicate.

"Sam's Strip," Jerry Dumas. © King Features Syndicate.

Howard worked with MacIntosh to only slightly modify the original drawing style. However, MacIntosh's skill as an artist has permitted *Sally Forth* to improve as a strip. (With all the publicity the strip picked up 40 new subscribers.)

As *Sally Forth* continues to gain popularity, it's an anomaly that Greg Howard's *Sally Forth* isn't cartooning's first *Sally Forth*. Blonde, buxom, given to wearing little or nothing, Wallace Wood's *Sally Forth* was first published and copyrighted in the late 1960s in the independent civilian-owned *Overseas Weekly* newspaper, sold at military bases in Europe and Asia.

Wood's *Sally Forth* was the antithesis of Howard's. She started as an "R-rated" *MAD* magazine-style parody and ended her career in porno comics that Wood drew shortly prior to committing suicide in 1981.

Wood himself reprinted his *Overseas Weekly Sally* stories between 1976 and 1978. When Field Syndicate launched Greg Howard's *Sally Forth* in 1982, one of Wood's publishers wrote Steve Jehorak, then president of Field to inform him of the double Sallys. He received no response. Naughty *Sally Forth* reprints are still readily available at comic conventions. Her existence, which predates Greg Howard's *Sally Forth*, will remain in cartoon history just one more twist of life for modern working mom Sally to handle with grace, wit, and humor.

B.C.

SAM AND SILO   *see* Sam's Strip.

SAM'S STRIP (U.S.)   This short-lived burst of brilliance was the comic fan's comic strip. *Sam's Strip* starred Sam (no last name) and his assistant (who never had any name) and a cast of thousands. The supporting players were great comic strip characters of the past.

The genre of the strip was the biggest prop; forms and conventions were discussed matter-of-factly; characters longed for days off; panels became the literal stage as backgrounds would be erased; old-time figures such as Happy Hooligan and Krazy Kat would reminisce about the old days; comic strip character conventions were periodically held.

Mort Walker conceived the idea with Jerry Dumas; both were comic fans since childhood, the former did the lettering, the latter the drawing, and both men cooked up the ideas.

In the context of the forms of the comic strip, *Sam's Strip* was surreal and high camp. Beginning in early

October 1961, it died in June of 1963 with 48 papers after peaking at 60 papers and never graduating to a Sunday page.

A collection of *Sam* strips was published privately by Mort Walker in 1968. In 1977 the strip came back in a new incarnation as *Sam and Silo*. Sam and his sidekick (now bestowed the name of Silo) are now the entire constabulary of a small town and find themselves confronted, in a series of mildly humorous gags, with petty crooks and an ornery citizenry, not to mention the feckless town fathers. Turned out by Jerry Dumas, the feature now only appears daily (the Sunday version was discontinued in 1995).

R.M.

SANDMAN (U.S.)   *Sandman* was created by artist Bert Christman and writer Gardner Fox and made its first appearance in National's *Adventure* number 40 in July 1939. The original Sandman dressed inconsequentially in superheroic terms. He wore a simple, snap-brimmed hat, a green suit and cloak, a yellow gas mask, and a gas gun. In civilian life, he was playboy Wesley Dodds, and many of the adventures centered around the caprices of his girlfriend, Diane Belmont. Most of the early stories also cast the character as an outcast wanted by the police. His only real method of attacking criminals, however, was his somewhat dubious sleep-inducing ability.

This *Sandman* format didn't last too long, despite the best efforts of artists like Gill Fox and Craig Flessel. So, beginning in December 1949 with *Adventure* number 69, a new Sandman was born. Created by the already well-known team of Jack Kirby and Joe Simon, this Sandman sported a yellow and purple supersuit and cowl. Simon and Kirby even added a young sidekick, Sandy Hawkins. And although he never became a major hero, *Sandman* lasted until *Adventure* number 102 in February 1946. He also made appearances in *World's Finest, All-Star,* and *World's Fair.*

When the superhero boom of the 1960s brought about a general revival, the original *Sandman* was rejuvenated as part of the Justice Society. And although he was never awarded a strip of his own, he was an interesting character in the Justice League/Justice Society format. When Jack Kirby and Joe Simon were again working for National, they created a one-shot entitled *Sandman* number 1. Published in January 1974, but drawn in early 1973, this *Sandman* was still another rendition, resembling neither the Green Hornet-ish Sandman of 1939 or the first Simon and Kirby Sandman.

DC brought back the character in 1989 in a new version scripted by Neil Gaiman, who provided a number of well-crafted story lines and original situations to the title, as well as bringing forth some imaginative supporting characters, such as Death (an angelic-looking young girl). The excellence of the writing attracted many talented artists to *Sandman*, including Sam Kieth, Kelley Jones, Clive Barker, Chales Vess, and Todd McFarlane. It received consistently good notices and even inspired a spin-off, *Sandman Mystery Theatre*, in 1993. Two years later Gaiman decided it was time for him to move on to different things, and he retired from the series.

J.B.

SANDY HIGHFLIER   see Airship Man, The.

SAN MAO (China)   San Mao is a teenage boy known to adults and children in China from 1947 up to today. *San Mao* ("Three Hair") first appeared in Shanghai, where he was living in the streets. The boy is an orphan with a soft heart, always willing to help others in trouble, although his own life is full of misfortune. His good intentions are often rewarded by others, especially the rich. To make a living, San Mao has tried baby-sitting, polishing shoes, apprenticing in a printing shop, and performing in a circus; he has even tried to sell himself. With a bitter humor, readers often shared in San Mao's sufferings in every story: In one strip San Mao was sleeping in a street covered by some newspapers, which caught fire when a cigarette butt was thrown from a car ("The cover caught fire"). In another, San Mao and his friend were hungry and freezing in the streets while a rich-family boy, the same age as San Mao, was eating ice cream, sweating from sitting in an overheated room ("Two worlds"). Hungrily, San Mao ate bark peeled off a tree. He was beaten and chased away by a policeman who was protecting the trees along the street ("Eating tree bark is forbidden").

Usually by means of a four-panel cartoon, San Mao's life was told successively in Shanghai's *Da Gong* newspaper every day in the late 1940s. People, especially children, in Shanghai eagerly waited to see *San Mao*'s next episode of fortune and misfortune. Some children sent money, clothing, and shoes, and often wrote letters to Zhang Leping, the cartoonist who drew *San Mao*, expressing their concern for and desire to help San Mao. This imaginary San Mao was so popular that one family in Shanghai even named their seven children Da Mao ("Big Hair"), Er Mao ("Two Hair"), and so on, until the last child, called Qi Mao ("Seven Hair"). When San Mao suffered from hunger and cold in the strip, these children tried to save food and offer their sweaters to San Mao via the newspaper editorials. When San Mao was beaten by his boss because he broke a glass bottle, Wu Mao ("Five Hair") in this family immediately found a bottle and wanted to "pay it to the boss of San Mao" in order to spare San Mao from being further punished.

The *San Mao Liu Lang Ji* ("San Mao the Homeless") collection has been republished since 1959 with more than 16 million copies sold up to 1990. In another collection, *San Mao Can Jun* ("San Mao Joined the Army"), which was first published in 1947 and repub-

lished in 1990, the cartoonist described the misfortunes of San Mao when he became an underage soldier. In all of the stories, which lasted into the 1950s and 1960s, the title hero never grew older.

Zhang Leping (1910-1992), known as "Father of San Mao," was born in a poor family whose father was a teacher in a village school. As a child Zhang began to draw by first helping his mother who was trying to make extra money to support the family of six by doing tailoring and embroidery. Zhang learned his art from copying and cutting the paper designs. He learned drawing in elementary school, but at 15 he had to quit school and work in various jobs: as an apprentice in a lumber company, in a printing shop of an advertising company, and in a studio making calendars. Some of the stories of *San Mao* were based upon Zhang's own teenage life. After the People's Republic of China was founded Zhang continued to create children's cartoons, and most of them were carried on the children's pictorial series *Xiao Peng You* ("Little Friends") since 1956. All of them emphasized teaching children good behavior and helping needy people, of which a collection of 72 cartoons created in the 1950s and 1960s was published by the Children Publishing House, entitled *Wo Men de Gu Shi* ("Our Stories") in 1990.

One of Zhang's storytelling characteristics was that most cartoons were told by drawings without words except a title, which made them easier to be understood by almost everyone, especially young children. *San Mao* has been popular through generations not only in mainland China but also in Taiwan. A well-known woman writer in Taiwan named Chen Ping wrote a letter in August 1988 to Zhang in Shanghai. She stated that she read *San Mao* when she was three years old. Because she liked it so much, she used "San Mao" as her pen name when she became a famous writer. In 1989, she came to mainland China and handed to Zhang the *San Mao the Homeless* book reprinted in Taiwan. Since then she called Zhang "father" (until she committed suicide in Taiwan in the early 1990s).

H.Y.L.L.

SANTOS, JESSE F. (1928-   )   As far back as he can remember Jesse Santos has always been drawing. When he was 10 years old, the Filipino cartoonist, born June 24, 1928, in Teresa, Rizal, did a mural that was placed in front of the town church. At the age of 15 he embarked in the field of professional art. He did portraits of American GIs and Japanese soldiers who occupied his hometown. Filipino guerilla fighters also sought out his services to draw and embellish *antingantings* (talismans) on their clothing.

While working as a sidewalk portrait artist he was discovered by Tony Velasquez, the well-known cartoonist. In 1946 Santos illustrated his first comic book feature, *Kidlat* ("Lightning"), for *Halaklak*, the first comic book to be published in the Philippines. When Pilipino Komiks appeared on the scene Santos teamed up with Damy Velasquez to do *DI 13*, which became the most famous detective strip ever to appear in the country. This series continued until the 1960s when Santos left for greener pastures. The strip was so popular that offshoots appeared, such as *DI Jr*, which Santos also illustrated. The best cartoonist in the country, Larry Alcala, did a series called *13½*, which was a spoof on *DI 13* and on Santos. *DI 13* was also made into a movie.

Santos attended the University of Santo Tomas but quit when his services as an artist became more in demand. He was the chief artist for *Paraluman* magazine, staff contributor for Gold Star publishing company, and a permanent staff contributor for Liwayway, Ace Publications, Graphic Arts Inc., and G. Miranda & Sons Publishing Co.

Despite a hectic schedule doing magazine and book illustrations, covers, movie ads, and portraits, he somehow found time to collaborate with Mars Ravelo, Pablo Gomez, Greg Igna De Dios, Mauro Cabuhat, and Larry Tuazon to produce many comic book serials such as *Inspirasiyon* ("Inspiration"), *Boksingera* ("The Girl Boxer"), *Dambanang Putik* ("Altar of Mud"), *ROTC, Paula, Tomador,* and *Dar Aguila.*

For many years Santos served as a member of the board of the Society of Philippine Illustrators and Cartoonists (SPIC) and was elected vice president several times. In 1965 he won a SPIC award for his published works. He is also a member of the National Press Club of the Philippines.

Santos came to the United States in 1969. In 1970 he started to work for Western Publications doing the book illustrations for *Davy Crockett.* Currently he has been doing the art chores for Gold Key's *Brother of the Spears, Dagar, Dr. Spektor,* and *Tragg.* He also worked for *Mystery Digest* and *Red Circle Comics.*

He has contributed artwork for literary publications such as *Kapatid* and the Pilipino-American anthology *Liwanag* ("Light"). His paintings have been exhibited by the Society of Western Artists, and he has won the best of show award. His fine art paintings have been exhibited at international art shows, galleries, universities, museums, and in private collections. He is a senior advisor of the Philippine Comic Archives and a member of the Philippine Science-Fantasy Society. In the 1980s he worked on *Mystery Digest,* a pocket-size anthology of weird tales; he has devoted his efforts of late to painting murals and drawing record covers.

Santos's works in the comics have a lifelike quality to them. This is due to his many years experience in the portraiture field. He excels in utilizing cartoon techniques such as exaggerations and distortions and in using them effectively in a realistic manner.

O.J.

SANTOS, MALANG (1928-   ) A Filipino cartoonist and painter born in Manila on January 20, 1928, Malang, as he is most widely known, joined the *Manila Chronicle* as a staff artist in 1947. He created a captionless character called Kosme the Cop, which the *Chronicle* carried daily. His was the first and only local strip to appear along with the well-known American strips. At an early point in his career, Malang was sued by the Manila police department for one of his prize-winning cartoons satirizing the practice of bribery among the members of Manila's finest. After several months Malang retired Kosme from the force and the strip has been known since then as *Kosme the Cop (Retired).* Malang also created a cartoon character, Chain Gang Charlie, and a third one, Belzeebub, was featured in *Pageant* magazine. However, it is Kosme the Cop (Retired), the henpecked husband with an endless stock of ways-out, with which Malang is most associated.

Malang also became very popular for his ads depicting barrio scenes, which he did for a well-known cola drink. Soon there was a great demand for his illustra-

tions by the advertising agencies in the country. Using tempera, a medium he has mastered as a commercial artist, as well as colored ink, his paintings are owned by the former First Lady of the Philippines and by prominent publishers in the United States. He has been commissioned to do murals as well.

From a lowly cartoonist in 1947 to one of the highest paid painters in the country, Malang's success has encouraged other artists similarly employed (working in newspapers or ad agencies) to raise their art to a serious plateau.

M.A.

SAPPO (U.S.) E. C. Segar's fourth comic strip, the satiric science-fantasy work called *Sappo,* began as a daily strip named *The Five-Fifteen* in Hearst's *New York American* on December 24, 1920. Initially, the six small panels of each episode told a simple daily gag about a resident of suburban Despaire named John Sappo, emphasizing his tribulations in riding the 5:15 a.m. Funkville-City train to his office job, and occasionally involving his wife, Myrtle. By February 24, 1923, when the strip's name was changed to *Sappo the Commuter* in the *American,* and simply to *Sappo,* in other Hearst papers, long continuity had become a mainstay, with a story about Sappo's twin brother, Jim, being the most amusing of this period.

The Sunday *Sappo* began on February 28, 1926, about a year after the daily strip had folded on February 17, 1925. The revived *Sappo* returned to the early gag format for a time, then resumed continuity on March 18, 1928, with Sappo and Myrtle taking up oil painting in bitter rivalry. Once Segar got his narrative gears in action, *Sappo* became hilariously gripping, and before long Segar had introduced a series of ingenious and hugely comic devices invented by Sappo.

These inventions became the keynote of *Sappo* from 1930 on. And after May 8, 1932, when the arrival of Professor O. G. Wottasnoozle added the strip's greatest character to its limited cast (the Professor taking up residence with the Sappos), no limits of any kind were set on the imaginative range of the *Sappo* narrative; and Segar's dauntless characters traveled more than once to the outermost reaches of the solar system, probed the recesses of the most minute particles, and casually but satirically toyed with invisibility, robotics, hypnosis, and hyperpilosity.

Sappo reached its imaginative peak between the enlargement of the strip to its final, full size of three rows of panels on August 16, 1931, and its close with Segar's death on September 18, 1938. (Its continuation by inferior hands, such as those of Bela Zaboly and Bud Sagendorf, is hardly worthy of comment.) Surprisingly little has been reprinted since the strip appeared as one small book, *Sappo,* in 1935, and ran for a time in the reprint magazine, *King Comics,* in the 1930s. One of the most continually amusing and absorbing comic strips ever created, *Sappo* needs to be reprinted in full for the fresh appreciation of a new generation of readers.

B.B.

SASUKE (Japan) Created by Sanpei Shirato, *Sasuke* made its first appearance in the September 1961 issue of the monthly *Shōnen.* Sasuke was a boy-*ninja* (a peculiar caste of Japanese warriors, almost raised to superhuman status through the mastery of their secret art called *ninjutsu*), the son of the great ninja, Ōzaru. The strip detailed the process of Sasuke's growing up under

"Sasuke," Sanpei Shirato. © Shōnen.

the guidance of his father, who intended that his son become a great ninja. Sasuke mastered the ninjutsu but also learned many other things as well, such as the importance of life and the severity of the ninja code.

Going out into the world Sasuke met with a host of troubles and had to fight many enemies: some were rival ninjas such as Hanzō Hattori, the chieftain of the ninja warriors of the Tokugawa shogunate, and his daughter, who was responsible for the murder of Sasuke's mother. Others were swordsmen and brigands trying to thwart Sasuke's progress. When the hero was in a tight situation, he was indirectly helped by his father, but his feats of arms were his own. Part one of this long saga ended with the death of Sasuke's father, Ōzaru, along with Ōzaru's new wife and daughter, in an ambush set by Hattori.

Part two spelled more trouble for Sasuke and his baby brother, Kozaru. Fights, intrigues, and treachery abounded, with Sasuke getting out of every trap set for him. Kozaru, however, was not so lucky: he was killed in a riot. The strip ended with Sasuke roaming the fields in a mad search for his brother's body.

Gōseki Kojima assisted Shirato on some parts of *Sasuke*, which ended in March 1966. The strip has inspired a series of animated cartoons, and in 1968 the weekly *Shōnen* Sunday started reprinting the old episodes of *Sasuke* in their entirety.

H.K.

SATONAKA, MACHIKO (1947-   ) Born January 24, 1947, in Osaka, Machiko Satonaka knew by the seventh grade that she wanted be a manga artist. She wasted no time in fulfilling that dream. By age 16, whe made her debut with *Pia no Shōzo* ("A Portrait of Pia"), for which she was awarded the Kodansha prize for new artists. A year later she dropped out of high school, moved to Tokyo, and launched a professional career that made her, by age 30, one of the most popular and best comics creators for young girls and women.

Satonaka's stories concentrate on romance and melodrama, although she has dabbled in other genres. She explained, "I wanted to do everything, children's kindergarten, romance, crime stories for high school students, female adult, historical, and classical themes." Many of her works take novel twists, incorporating social commentary themes such as the Nazi persecution of Jews, the Vietnam War, and racial discrimination. In *Watashi no Joni* ("My Johnny"), published in 1968, she portrayed love in a southern U.S. town between a white woman and a black man.

The amount of work Satonaka puts out is prodigious. While still "young and healthy" she did eight titles simultaneously, a number of which were major works stretching to more than a thousand pages each. Since the 1980s she has been doing two series monthly for *Kodansha* and one monthly for *Shogakan*, a total of 150 pages. Some of her series, averaging 40 to 60 pages each, have lasted for a year, one for more than a decade.

Among her early titles were *Lady Ann* (1969), *Manayome Sensei* ("Teacher Bride," 1971), *Ashta Kagayaku* ("Shining Tomorrow," 1972), and *Hime Ga Yuka* ("Hime Goes Forth," 1973). The latter two won her the 1974 Kodansha Shuppan Bunka award (children). In recent years, Satonaka has catered primarily to young male readers with *Pandora, Akiko,* and *Atom's Daughter,* all of which provide advice on how to deal with women.

Besides setting high standards for *shōjo* (comics for young girls) and lending skilled draftmanship to all her works, Satonaka has been the spearhead behind movements to protect and advance manga generally. She has organized campaigns to block manga censorship, to exchange cartoonists internationally for the enhancement of global understanding, and to protest against Disney for lifting parts of Osamu Tezuka's *The Jungle Emperor* in the making of *Lion King.*

J.A.L.

SATURNO CONTRO LA TERRA (Italy) In 1934 American adventure strips started appearing in the more popular Italian comic weeklies, such as *L'Audace* and *L'Avventuroso*: among them *Flash Gordon* became the most successful feature of the genre. Several Italian publishers then sought to emulate *Flash*'s formula; among the more successful attempts was *Saturno Contro la Terra* ("Saturn Against the Earth") conceived by Cesare Zavattini (later Federico Fellini's most constant

"Saturno Contro la Terra," Giovanni Scolari. © Mondadori.

screenwriter) and written by Federico Pedrocchi. On December 31, 1937, the strip appeared in the pages of *I Tre Porcellini*, and then moved to the more widely circulated *Topolino*, where it remained until 1943 and where it was revived from 1945 to 1946.

The artwork of *Saturno* was entrusted to Giovanni Scolari, who was a master of background and technical details: his weapons and machines were especially well-rendered. Scolari's line, however, left something to be desired, and while *Saturno* tried to emulate *Flash Gordon* in spirit, it came closer to *Buck Rogers* in realization. This long saga told of the adventures of Rebo, the terrible chief of the Saturnians, and of his burning dream to conquer earth and the whole solar system. Rebo was opposed by the 80-year-old Italian inventor, Marcus, and his youthful son-in-law, Ciro, in the classical combination of brain and brawn. The strip was complete with old-time unabashed nationalism: for instance, the meeting of all the powers of earth took place in the Po valley. Aside from political restrictions, however, *Saturno* displayed a good deal of character and suspense, and it gave a few novel twists to the hackneyed plot.

One of the most highly entertaining of the science-fiction strips, *Saturno Contro la Terra* has been widely translated abroad: in the United States it appeared (with color added) in the ephemeral Future Comics of the 1940s. Several episodes of *Saturno Contro la Terra* were also reprinted by Milano Libri in 1969.

G.B.

SAUNDERS, ALLEN (1899-1986) An American comic strip writer born in Indiana on March 24, 1899, Allen Saunders learned to draw by taking the Landon correspondence course and attending classes at the Chicago Academy of Fine Arts. He graduated from Wabash College in 1920 and taught French there for the next seven years. At the same time he freelanced as both a cartoonist for humor publications and a detective story writer for pulp magazines. He even acted in stock for one season.

In 1927 Saunders quit teaching and joined the *Toledo News-Bee* as a reporter and cartoonist. He became its drama critic a few years later. In 1936, in collaboration with Elmer Woggon for the drawing, Saunders produced a comic strip about a hard-blowing medicine man, *The Great Gusto* (later changed to *Big Chief Wahoo*, later still to *Steve Roper*) for Publishers Syndicate. At about the same time Saunders also created a humor panel, *Miserable Moments*, which he both wrote and drew, but this attempt was short-lived.

In 1940, when Martha Orr announced her decision to quit *Apple Mary*, which she had created in 1932, the syndicate called upon Saunders to take up the continuity while female cartoonist Dale Connor assumed the drawing. (The strip, retitled *Mary Worth's Family*, was signed Dale Allen until 1942 when Ken Ernst took over the drawing and the strip's name was further shortened to *Mary Worth*). A third strip bearing Allen Saunders' byline appeared in 1968, *Dateline: Danger*, an adventure strip drawn by Al McWilliams. In addition to being a writer, Saunders is also editor at Publishers-Hall Syndicate. He served as chairman of the Newspaper Comics Council in 1958. Saunders stopped writing for comics in 1979, when he officially retired, but he kept an eye on his features, now being scripted by his son John. He also wrote his memoirs (published only in excerpts in fan magazines) and continued to participate in various promotional activities. He died in Maumee, Ohio, on January 28, 1986.

Next to Lee Falk, Allen Saunders is probably the best-known as well as the most dramatically gifted of comic strip writers. His scripts are sophisticated and his dialogues literate without being stuffy.

M.H.

SAZAE-SAN (Japan) *Sazae-san* was created by female cartoonist Machiko Hasegawa. Machiko Hasegawa conceived the characters of the strip while she was vacationing at the seaside resort of Momoji: she then gave all the characters names related to the sea. Thus there was Sazae herself (*Sazae* means "propeller"); her father, Namihei ("wave"); her mother, Fune ("boat"); her younger brother, Katsuo ("bonito fish"); and her younger sister, Wakame ("seaweed"). The family name was Isono ("beach"), and thus Namihei Isono meant waves rolling on the beach. Hasegawa carried this idea further by having Sazae marry Masuo Fugata ("trout") by whom she had a son, Tarao ("codfish").

Sazae-san first appeared in May 1946 in the Fukunichi evening newspaper. Toward the end of 1949 it transferred to the Asahi evening paper. *Sazae-san* was the top newspaper strip of the postwar years and a perfect example of the kind of domestic strip pioneered by *Blondie* in the United States. Sazae-san was a cheerful, simple, carefree housewife, married to a working man of limited means. The Fugatas lived with Sazae's parents and had only mild adventures. In the beginning Sazae was tall and graceful, but after her marriage she became smaller and dumpy.

Sazae-san was one of the longest-running newspaper strips in Japan; it was discontinued in 1975 but was revived the next year and lasted up to the time of Hasegawa's death in 1992. Sazae herself was the most famous strip character for young and old alike. The feature was reprinted in book form a number of times (it was a million-seller), and has inspired a television series, a series of animated cartoons, as well as a stage play.

H.K.

SCARTH (G.B.) Readers of the renovated *Sun*, a new tabloid version of the former companion newspaper to the *Daily Mirror* under the control of Australian magnate, Rupert Murdoch, saw a near-naked blonde passing out in the path of a speeding auto. This was their first glimpse of Scarth, a cross between Jane and Garth:

"Scarth," Luis Roca. © The Sun.

a science-fiction stripper! They would see more of her in the future: she became the first full frontal nude female in British newspaper strips.

Scarth not only lost her flimsy G-string, she also lost her long tresses. A brain transplant, which revived her from her death on the superway, also gave her the cute crewcut that remained her trademark for the rest of her life. Set 200 years in the future, the first episode appeared on November 17, 1969; the last exactly three years later. She was finally killed, not by another accident, but by an incoming newspaper executive who disliked the permissive tone of the strip. It had introduced a hermaphrodite, Rudolf Quince, a bearded lady married to an army captain. Despite its demise, the strip continues in world syndication, although it has lost its subtitle: *Scarth A.D.2170*.

Scarth was created by Les Lilley, a scriptwriter whose work includes *Better or Worse*, which was later retitled *Jack and Jill*, and then *Bonnie*. The artist was Luis Roca, a resident of Barcelona whose decorative art had previously graced many romantic comic books for girls. Roca is no longer working in newspaper strips, but Lilley is currently scripting other strips.

D.G.

SCHAFFENBERGER, KURT (1920-   ) Kurt Schaffenberger is an American comic book artist born in Germany on December 15, 1920. His family moved to America in 1927, and Schaffenberger eventually attended the Pratt Institute in Brooklyn, New York. Joining the Jack Binder shop in 1942, he produced strips for many publishers, including work on *Captain Marvel, Bulletman, Fighting Yank, Captain America,* and many others. He was inducted into the army in 1943, and, on his return to comic books in 1945, produced material on a freelance basis for Fawcett, publishers of the Marvel Family.

Although C. C. Beck was the recognized star and chief artist on the Marvel Family, Schaffenberger's work also gained considerable respect. While Beck championed the more cartoony illustrations, Schaffenberger's work was heavily influenced by Alex Raymond and Hal Foster and always leaned to realism and straight adventure.

When Fawcett discontinued their comic book line in 1953, Schaffenberger did work for Timely and others before drifting into commercial artwork. He returned as the artist for National's newly created *Lois Lane* feature in 1958; his 11-year stint and his clean, uncluttered renditions made him the feature's definitive artist. While he was producing material for *Lois Lane*, he also created a horde of commercial comic strips for Custom Comics, and under the pen name of "Lou Wahl," invented the *Nemesis* and *Magic Man* features for ACG comic.

When National revived the Marvel Family in 1972, Schaffenberger was slated for only spot duty but took over the bulk of the work when C. C. Beck resigned over a jurisdictional dispute. From that time on he worked on virtually every DC title until the early 1990s. He now occasionally draws comics for advertising.

J.B.

SCHEUER, CHRIS (1952-   ) An Austrian comic artist born in 1952 in Graz, Chris Scheuer stems from an artistically inclined family. With one grandmother a sculptor, the other one a jazz pianist, one grandfather a sculptor, and his father a restorer of paintings, it seems only natural that Chris Scheuer should become interested in art. He discovered comics in the 1970s and liked their way of telling stories in a combination of words and pictures.

He popped into view as a comic artist in 1982 when a first collection of comic short stories was published in Austria; some of his stories were published in *Schwermetall*, the German version of *Heavy Metal*. He teamed up with the late Markus Tschernegg, computer specialist, comic fan extraordinaire, and writer, for a comic feature that was published in *Comic Forum*, the Austrian comics fanzine and center for a line of comic publications. But their plan for a comic album to be published in Germany did not work out. Instead, Scheuer's first comic album, *Sheshiva*, was published in 1983 in Austria. Scheuer's career went ahead at dizzying speed with the 1984 Max und Moritz Award at the Erlangen Comics Salon as best German-language artist.

While this award did not entice German publishers to dare produce an album by Scheuer right away, he was asked by Dargaud to work for *Charlie Mensuel*, and later on for *Pilote* and *Charlie*. The first story he did for them with a scenario by French writer Rodolphe was *Marie Jade*. Scheuer then moved to Hamburg for four years to cooperate with writer Wolfgang Mendl on an album for Carlsen Verlag, *Sir Ballantime* (1990), and to create a large number of comics and illustrations for advertising. While in Hamburg, Scheuer also worked out storyboards for television ads, drew posters and magazine advertisements, and worked under contract to create posters for the Hamburg Opera. For some time Scheuer collaborated with Matthias Schultheiss and colored René Lehner's *Bill Body* strips. Scheuer has a very distinctive style with very distinctive, well-endowed girls. They pop up in various European countries, including his native Austria to which he has since returned to continue producing comics, paintings, and portfolios of his work.

W.F.

SCHMIDT, MANFRED (1913-   ) German cartoonist, journalist, and writer born in Bad Harzburg on April 15, 1913, Schmidt grew up in Bremen where he also went to school. While most of his high school teachers praised the joy and beauty of fighting and dying for home and fatherland, an art teacher who had returned from the battlefields of World War I, a convinced pacifist, opened his class's eyes with his description of the sordid mess that war inevitably is. Thus Schmidt no longer put heroic images on paper and started cartooning. At the age of 14 the newspaper *Bremer Nachrichten* published the first cartoon he had sent in.

After his final exams he had to choose between the careers of art teacher, musician, pastor, dentist, or movie director. He decided to go into the motion picture business. Starting from the bottom, he had to lug around the heavy gear at minimal wages, so he returned to drawing. However, he had to forget about his career for four years of fighting in World War II. He lived through several retreats at various fronts. While the troops retreated from Russia he drew cartoons for *Panzer Voran!* ("Forward, Tanks!"), a soldiers' newspaper that kept its title during a retreat of over one thousand miles.

Returning to civilian life and cartooning, Schmidt got hold of a *Superman* comic book and immensely dis-

Chris Scheuer, a page from an adventure graphic novel. © Chris Scheuer.

liked it. He decided to do a satire of the superhero by creating Nick Knatterton, a cross between *Superman*, *Dick Tracy*, and *Sherlock Holmes*. In the autumn of 1950 the first episode of *Nick Knatterton* appeared in the German weekly illustrated paper *Quick*. It met with unprecedented success. Schmidt's simplistic, yet effective style is one of many individual styles that could be termed to be in the German tradition of cartooning.

After killing off the *Knatterton* strip, Schmidt wrote a great many articles and humorous books, aptly illustrated with cartoons. He also wrote and produced

several travel features and animated cartoon advertisements for television.

With his animation studio Schmidt was himself "forced" into producing *Nick Knatterton* as an animated cartoon program that first ran as a continued feature to loosen up advertising time blocks for *Westdeutscher Rundfunk*. The feature was picked up by other stations, with some splicing them together and broadcasting them as complete stories. These cartoons are now also available on videocassette. As Schmidt produced the films himself, they are true to the original comic strip

"Les Schtroumpfs," Peyo (Pierre Culliford). © Editions Dupuis.

spoof in contents and in artwork. The narration is supplied by Schmidt himself, giving the films an additional sarcastic note.

Despite Schmidt's aversion to regular comics he was lured into hosting a 13-episode half-hour program about the history and the genres of comics scripted by Wolfgang J. Fuchs and Reinhold Reitberger in 1976. While he strayed from the scripts to inject some of his criticism of comics in the narration, sometimes in an ironically entertaining way, the series nevertheless managed to be quite informative and presented original animation of some comic strips that up to then had not had their own television show.

W.F.

SCHTROUMPFS, LES (Belgium)

Peyo's *Les Schtroumpfs* evolved as a spin-off from his earlier comic strip creation, *Johan et Pirlouit*. In 1957 Johan and his companion Pirlouit came upon the fabulous country of the Schtroumpf little people who were so friendly and endearing that they soon received a strip of their own in the pages of the weekly magazine *Spirou* (1960).

The Schtroumpfs are a race of gentle, civilized, and utterly charming elves whose ingenuity triumphs over all the mishaps that often befall their sleepy village. Identical in appearance and costume, but each with his own personality, the Schtroumpfs form a microcosm of society under the wise and enlightened guidance of the Grand Schtroumpf. The strip is drenched in a poetic atmosphere directly derived from European folklore, and its landscapes are often reminiscent of *Little Nemo*'s fairy-tale settings. Peyo's style, subdued and simple as are his stories, is never too cute and mannered, despite the temptations of the genre.

Peyo (Pierre Culliford) has been throwing his little people into the most diversified adventures, inventing for them menaces and enemies of all kinds, whether external like the brigands who try from time to time to steal their treasure, or internal like the would-be dictator who once sprang from their midst and declared himself *schtroumpfissimo*. All of these mishaps have a happy ending, and the Schtroumpfs go back to their happy-go-lucky life of singing and dancing.

Les Schtroumpfs' happy mixture of fantasy and adventure, delightful drawing and clever narrative have made the strip into a favorite of European readers (in recent years Peyo has left more and more of the writing to Yvan Delporte, who has managed to maintain the strip's unique poetry and appeal). *Les Schtroumpfs* has gone through numerous reprints in both hardcover and paperback form; they have been made into toys and used for advertising. In the 1960s there was a series of nine *Schtroumpfs* animated cartoons produced by Eddy Rissack and Maurice Rosy with more than a passing assist by Peyo.

In the United States the Hanna-Barbera studios brought the *Smurfs* (as the little blue elves are known here) to NBC-TV in 1981. In parallel with the weekly show, which ran until 1990, there were a number of specials and one theatrical feature. After Peyo's death in 1992, his son, Thierry Culliford, took over the characters.

M.H.

SCHUITEN, FRANÇOIS (1956-)

Belgian cartoonist born in Brussels on April 13, 1956, François Schuiten, the son of architect parents, had his first comic strip story published in *Pilote* at age 17. While studying art at the Institut St. Luc in Brussels, he contributed to the art magazine published by the school. In 1977 he decided on a career as a freelance artist, and his work (sometimes done in collaboration with his brother, Luc) started appearing in the major French and Belgian comics magazines of the time.

His break came in 1980 when *Aux Médianes de Cymbiola* ("At the Medians of Cymbiola"), a tale of mysticism and initiation entirely rendered in pencils, saw print in the pages of the comics magazine *Métal Hurlant*. After a brief stint as art director on Just Jaeckin's 1983 movie *Gwendoline*, he finally realized a long-deferred project when, again in collaboration with his brother, he published *La Terre Creuse* ("The Hollow Earth," 1984), a complex story mixing elements of science fiction with sociological musings.

In the meantime he had begun the work he is best noted for, the cycle he calls *Les Cités Obscures* (meaning both "dark" and "obscure") on scripts by Benoit Peeters. Started in 1983 with *Les Murailles de Samaris* ("The Walls of Samaris"), this monumental saga has unfolded to date over three more titles: *La Fièvre d'Urbicande* ("Fever at Urbicande," 1985), *La Tour* ("The Tower," 1987), and *Brusel* (1992). In all of the titles the characters are dwarfed by the futuristic, tentacular, recondite cities which, perhaps reflecting the artist's parental heritage, are the real protagonists of the tales. Schuiten has also written and illustrated a string of more conventional prose stories related to the cycle.

In addition to his work on the "Cities" cycle, Schuiten is also the author of a number of unrelated comics stories, sometimes on texts by others. He has also realized sculptures, serigraphs, and lithographs, and has overseen the decoration of the Luxembourg Pavilion at the 1992 World Exposition in Seville. He is only in his early forties and even more should be heard from him.

M.H.

SCHULTHEISS, MATTHIAS (1946-   ) One of the new breed of German comic artists, Schultheiss was born July 27, 1946, in Nuremberg but grew up in Hamburg. He spent four years at a country boarding school in Franconia; the first action of the new principal was to confiscate Schultheiss's cornet. After high school and a stint in the army he was taken into the High School for Graphic Design and allowed to skip the first four semesters because of above-average talent. His hopes to get the artistic education he craved was not fully realized at this school, so he went on to educate himself by copying comic strips like *Rip Kirby*. He left school after only three semesters in 1969 with the grudging admission that he had enough know-how to make it professionally—which he did. For

Matthias Schultheiss, "Trucker," © Matthias Schultheiss.

about ten years he worked in advertising as a freelance artist.

During this time he worked on his storytelling technique and developed comic strips of his own, which he offered to Bull's Pressedienst, the German affiliate of King Features Syndicate. A series about the St. Pauli district of Hamburg did not meet with much interest, but Bull's picked up his strip about a trucker done in a style that perfectly copied the style of the British *Modesty Blaise* strip. However, the series was never sold to a newspaper. In 1977 he was asked to do comics about historic events. Once again, the finished product did not see print.

Schultheiss's interest in comics did not diminish. He decided to try his truck driver story once again and offered the series to *Zack* magazine. The publishers picked up an option on the series, but for publication in color, everything had to be redone completely with fewer black areas. Hence he prepared *Trucker*, the story of a truck driver going the length and breadth of the United States and getting into all kinds of adventures. To do so he gave up his advertising work to devote himself entirely to comics. Then he was informed that the editors felt his material was not aimed at a general mass market, and his comic story was axed.

Trucker was published in 1981 in *Comic Reader*, a book printing work by German comic artists not published by regular comic publishers. Schultheiss had the last laugh, as *Zack* magazine folded soon after. Schultheiss for a time worked shifts as a loader at the airport to forget about the frustrations of trying to do comics in Germany. But finally, due to his interest in literature and his penchant for exceptional stories, he got permission to adapt several stories of Charles Bukowski into comic album format. These met with critical acclaim although they were not published by a comic book publisher but by a "normal" publishing house. The German market was still slow in giving him more comic work.

In the mid-1990s Schultheiss had some of his own comic short stories published in *Special USA* and in *L'Echo des Savanes* in France. The most interesting comic novels produced by Schultheiss since then are *Le Théorème de Bell* ("The Truth about Shelby") and *Le rêve du requin* ("The Sharks of Lagos"). They were highly dramatic and graphically satisfying comic novels. When they turned out to be a success in France as well as in the United States they were picked up for publication in Germany.

Schultheiss is the epitome of the saying that the prophet isn't thought to be worth anything at home. For while his comic debut was published in Germany and his literary adaptations were well received, there simply wasn't anyone daring enough to want to risk publishing comics by a German artist at first. Only when Schultheiss's qualities had been recognized by French publishers was he reimported for publication at home. When these books proved successful on the German market, he was finally asked to do comic albums that were to premiere in Germany. Still, Schultheiss was not completely happy with German comic publishers and left for the United States in 1993, having conceived comic projects for publication in America and in Japan.

W.F.

SCHULTZE, CARL EDWARD (1866-1939) Carl Edward Schultze, creator of the widely popular turn-of-the-century strip, *Foxy Grandpa*, was born in Lexington, Kentucky, on May 25, 1866, into a lower-middle-class German immigrant family. As the family prospered, Schultze was sent from Kentucky to study in German schools during his teens, where he perfected his simple but fetching comic style sufficiently to obtain a job on the *Chicago News* at $16 a week in the late 1880s. Among his colleagues of the time were such later famed figures as R. F. Outcault and George Barr McCutcheon. After a number of years doing general newspaper art and cartoon work, Schultze moved to the *New York Herald*, where in the early heyday of comic strips he was asked to develop a strip, and introduced his initial concept of a shrewd old man who turns the tables on the Katzenjammer-type pair of kids who plague him. Schultze just called the old man Grandpa, but an assistant editor of the *Herald*, William J. Guard (later press agent for the Metropolitan Opera), said he was foxy, and suggested the full name for the strip, which Schultze used. Introduced as the leading strip in the Sunday *Herald* comic section for January 7, 1900, *Foxy Grandpa* was an almost immediate hit with the paper's readers.

Like other popular comic strip artists of that period, Schultze was hired away from the *Herald* by William Randolph Hearst for his *New York American* and *Journal* combine. In the powerful Hearst Sunday array, however, the mild and repetitive Schultze strip did not shine notably, and Schultze, although well-paid and a notable New York figure with a Park Avenue home and a string of saddle horses for most of the first two decades of the century, was dropped by Hearst and moved at a lower income to the *New York Press*, where *Foxy Grandpa* was folded as a regular comic strip in 1918.

Trying other approaches, Schultze fielded a nature story series in prose, with a daily one-panel drawing accompanying the text (usually featuring *Foxy Grandpa* and a bunny enlarged from Schultze's bunny signature trademark of the *Foxy Grandpa* strip with a variety of animals), to newspapers in the 1920s, but this did not do noticeably well, and was folded in a few years. After this, Schultze, plagued with debts and personal problems accentuated by the death of his wife of many years, dropped from sight, to reappear in January 1935

Carl Schultze, "Foxy Grandpa."

at the offices of the Association for Improving the Condition of the Poor (AICP), in New York. This organization, responding to his desperate appeal for help, got him a WPA position working on a government reading-materials project at $95 a month. Here he illustrated school books, one of the most popular of which was titled *Julia and the Bear*.

Now an aging man, Schultze lived in a $4 a week room at 251 West 20th Street in New York, popular with neighborhood kids for whom he would draw pictures of Foxy Grandpa and his other characters and other nearby inhabitants, but apparently forgotten by the newspaper publishing world and his old cartoonist conferees. Here he died of a heart attack near the door of his room on January 18, 1939. He was buried in Ward Manor Cemetery, in Dutchess County, near New York City, through the aid of one of his West 20th Street neighbors and the AICP.

B.B.

SCHULZ, CHARLES MONROE (1922-   ) An American cartoonist born November 26, 1922, in Minneapolis, Minnesota, Charles Sparky Schulz graduated from a St. Paul high school and took art lessons from a correspondence course offered by Art Instruction, Inc., of Minneapolis. He was drafted in 1943, served in France and Germany, and was discharged in 1945 as staff sergeant.

After the service, Schulz returned to St. Paul, where he got a job lettering cartoons for a religious publication. Later he became an instructor at Art Instruction where he met his first wife, Joyce Halverson. At the same time he freelanced and had his cartoons published in the *St. Paul Pioneer Press* and the *Saturday Evening Post*. In 1950 he started making the rounds of newspaper syndicates with a child feature tentatively called *Li'l Folks*. After a number of rejections, the strip was finally accepted by United Feature Syndicate, and made its debut on October 2, 1950, under the new title of *Peanuts*. The rest is comic strip history: unnoticed at first, *Peanuts* was to become the most successful comic feature of all times. For the material of his strip, Charles Schulz has been drawing on childhood memories (Charlie Brown, the leading figure in *Peanuts,* has a barber for a father, just like Charles Schulz), and from his raising of five children. Schulz has made many disclaimers about the philosophical content of the strip, such as stating that his chief purpose is to "get the strip done in time to get down to the post office at five o'clock when it closes"; yet he was to comment on another occasion: "It has always seemed to me that the strip has a rather bitter feeling to it, and it certainly deals in defeat." It is clear that the ambivalence in the man is reflected in the curious ambivalence of the strip, which makes *Peanuts* one of the most fascinating creations in American comic literature.

Charles Schulz is also the coauthor (with Kenneth F. Hall) of a child study, (*Two-by-Fours: A Sort of Serious Book About Small Children* (Warner, 1965); and he has illustrated a few books by others (notably Art Linkletter's *Kids Say the Darndest Things*), but most of his career has been devoted to the *Peanuts* strip (on which he does everything himself, including the lettering) and to *Peanuts*-related material. His personal life (except for his divorce and remarriage in 1973 to a woman much younger than himself) has been uncommonly stable. Charles Schulz has received the Reuben award twice, in 1955 and 1964, the Peabody and Emmy awards in

1966, and many other distinctions too numerous to mention. A documentary on Charles Schulz was produced for CBS-TV and broadcast in 1969. He was made a Knight of Arts and Letters by the French government in 1990.

M.H.

SCHWARTZ, JULIUS (1915-   ) American comic book editor born June 19, 1915, in the Bronx, New York, Schwartz was a science-fiction fanatic. He and Mort Weisinger founded *The Time Traveller* (1932), the first generally distributed science-fiction fanzine. Later, the duo founded the Solar Sales Service, in which they served as agents for the work of such science-fiction writers as Ray Bradbury, Robert Bloch, Edmond Hamilton, Alfred Bester, Otto Binder, and H. P. Lovecraft to pulp magazines.

When the pulp field collapsed, Bester introduced Schwartz to National and he began editing comic book stories in 1944, and was later instrumental in introducing many science-fiction writers to the comic book market. During this time, Schwartz was editing stories in many titles, including *Sensation, All-Star, Flash*, and *Green Lantern*. In the 1950s, Schwartz's major work came on two science-fiction titles, *Mystery in Space* and *Strange Adventures*. There he helped writers like Gardner Fox, Binder, Hamilton, and John Broome produce some of the finest science-fiction tales in comic books. Sy Barry and Carmine Infantino were his top artists. Infantino, Murphy Anderson, and Fox teamed up with Schwartz to produce *Adam Strange* in *Mystery in Space*, perhaps the best sci-fi hero strip ever to appear in comic books.

In 1956 it was Schwartz and his writers and artists who revived the superhero concept by revamping the defunct *Flash* feature for *Showcase*; they later helped launch what is commonly known as The Second Heroic Age, and it was under Schwartz's guidance that Fox wrote the landmark "Flash of Two Worlds" story, which lead to the revival of many 1940s superheroes. The flagging sales of two of National's mainstay books, *Batman* and *Detective*, both of which featured the Batman character, precipitated moving Schwartz in as editor in 1964. He immediately initiated the New Look with Infantino and Anderson, and this revamping eventually led to the *Batman* television series and its attendant camp style that Schwartz personally detested, but which catapulted National to unheard-of sales heights.

Schwartz eventually moved on to edit the highly acclaimed *Green Lantern/Green Arrow* series of relevant stories, a short-lived series that garnered favorable press but no appreciable sales boost. In recent years, he was also handed the major *Superman* family books, which he also revamped after his friend Weisinger resigned. It was Schwartz who presided over the national revival of the original *Captain Marvel* in 1973. Since his retirement in 1982 he has been a popular fixture at comic conventions throughout the country.

J.B.

SCIUSCIÀ (Italy) After the success encountered by *Il Piccolo Sceriffo*, publisher Tristano Torelli tried his hand again with a product which, while seemingly different, was actually similar to his earlier ones—it featured the same size publication, same editorial formula, same basic topic. The new feature got its theme (and its name) from Vittorio De Sica's 1947 film, *Sciuscià*. As in the movie, the hero was a juvenile waif, one of the numerous war orphans then roaming the streets who were called *sciuscià* by American soldiers (a deformation for the term for shoe shine).

The sciuscià, Nico, was a 15-year-old boy and a fugitive from a little town in southern Italy. He had been chosen by Captain Wickers of the American Secret Service to bring a coded message to Rome, which was still occupied by the Germans. Nico's adventures went on from there. He was accompanied by the ever-present Fiametta, his fiery girlfriend, and by Pantera, his loyal lieutenant. After the war ended (in comic books), Nico traveled to Burma, China, Africa, and Canada.

The first *Sciuscià* comic book came out on January 22, 1949, drawn by Ferdinando Tacconi and Franco Paludetti. In a matter of months its circulation had doubled. The reasons for this success are not too clear; it could not have been for the artwork, which was primitive or for the stories, which were stereotyped. It must have been due to giving its readers a dose of cheap escapism. At any rate a flood of comic books featuring the exploits of brave young boys hit the newsstands, and Torelli himself issued a kindred product in 1951: *Nat del Santa Cruz*, drawn by the ubiquitous Tacconi.

The publication was discontinued in the late 1950s but resumed again in 1965 with Lina Buffolente as the artist; it did not last long. *Sciuscià* was reprinted in the short-lived publication *Evviva* (1973) and is now being republished by Edizioni De Miceli of Florence. In 1952 Giana Anguissola and Tristano Torelli authored a novel based on the strip.

G.B.

SCORCHY SMITH (U.S.) *Scorchy Smith* was Associated Press News's most exemplary comic strip. It was one of the original group of strips and the only memorable one fielded by A.P. in March 1930; it suffered the checkered career and miserable direction characteristic of all A.P. comic features, and it finally folded along with the entire line of A.P. comics (or what was left of it) in 1961.

Scorchy Smith was the creation of John Terry, brother of famed animator Paul Terry, and himself a former animator and editorial cartoonist. Modeled after Charles Lindbergh, whom he was supposed to resemble, Scorchy had an uncertain personality and identity, somewhere between that of an earnest aviation pioneer and a devil-may-care barnstormer. Terry's line did not help the often muddled plot: the faces were chiefly blurs, and the action depicted with such incredible sloppiness that a lengthy narrative was

always needed just to keep the readers informed of the goings-on. With all its faults, *Scorchy* was A.P.'s best-selling strip.

In 1933 Terry became sticken with tuberculosis and a young staff artist, Noel Sickles, was called upon to ghost the strip (after Terry's death the following year, Sickles was allowed to sign his own name, starting in December). Sickles literally turned the strip inside out, making it into one of the most sophisticated features of the time, with his airy brushwork, his atmospheric effects, his perfect setting of mood and action, using only a few simple lines and impressionistic shading. The plot and dialogue (ghost written by Milton Caniff with whom Sickles shared a studio at the time) also became wittier and more suspenseful. Scorchy was now a soldier-of-fortune always ready to leap into his plane in order to thwart bloodthirsty revolutionaries from taking over some South American banana republic, or to save an heiress from the hands of her kidnappers. Under the combined leadership of the Caniff-Sickles team, *Scorchy* reached new heights of popularity and readership; yet when Sickles asked for a raise he was turned down and, disgusted with it all, he abandoned the strip in October 1936.

Succeeding Sickles was Bert Christman, another young A.P. staffer. The strip remained artistically praiseworthy (Christman's depiction of planes was especially striking) and narratively entertaining. In April 1938, however, Christman decided to leave in his turn, and the strip was handed over first to Howell Dodd (who drew it for only a few months), then to Frank Robbins, early in 1939.

Robbins had served out his apprenticeship briefly with an aviation strip of uncertain merit called *Flying To Fame* (a blatant misnomer) and he turned out to be *Scorchy*'s most remarkable artist, next to Sickles. His line was forceful, virile, and quite heavy, his drawing done in masses of solid, ominous blacks. He endowed the strip with a striking reality and a palpable solidity. The popularity of *Scorchy* was so great that, early in the 1940s, a Sunday page was added, wherein Robbins was able to demonstrate that he could handle color with as much assurance and aplomb as black and white.

When Robbins left the strip in 1944, he was succeeded by Edmond Good, followed in 1946 by Rodlow Willard, one of the most hapless of comic strip illustrators, who, in the course of his eight-year tenure, mightily contributed to the strip's downfall. Limp drawing, trite situations, and insipid intrigues by John Milt Morris marked the last years of *Scorchy*'s career; when A.P. finally decided to discontinue the feature in 1961, it was less a case of murder than mercy killing.

"Scorchy Smith," Noel Sickles. © AP Newsfeatures.

Scorchy Smith is one of the great forgotten illustration strips; despite its unpromising beginning and lamentable end, it deserves to be exhumed from the dust of private archives into the light of print if only for the brief period from 1934 to 1944 when it was one of the most innovative and vibrant features of the era.

M.H.

SCOTT, JERRY (1955-) Jerry Scott, an American cartoonist, was born in Elkhart, Indiana, on May 2, 1955. After briefly attending Arizona State University, Scott became a freelance graphic artist in 1974, working in this field for a few years. In January 1981 he took over George Crenshaw's *Gumdrop*, a gag panel presenting the precocious mischievousness of children and the subsequent befuddlement of their parents. Two years later, United Feature Syndicate proposed that, in addition, he bring *Nancy*, the Ernie Bushmiller classic, back from its continuing decline during the 1970s and early 1980s.

This Scott did remarkably well while he maintained the strip's original spirit and gentle humor: under his pen, the characters are more sharply defined and subtle and speak in a modern voice, and the situations are more true to contemporary life and ways of thinking. He continued to write and draw *Nancy* until 1995 when, its mounting popularity notwithstanding, he decided to quit and devote his creative talents to a new and very funny child strip, *Baby Blues*, which he signs with Rick Kirkman and which made its debut in late 1995. It is distributed by King Features Syndicate.

P.L.H.

SECCHI, LUCIANO (1939-) Luciano Secchi is an Italian newspaperman, writer, and editor born in Milan on August 24, 1939. After studies in Milan, Secchi freelanced for different publications, contributing short stories, articles, and reviews. In 1963 Secchi (under the pseudonym "Max Bunker") and with the help of Antonio Raviola (signing "Magnus") for the drawing, created his first comic strip *Kriminal*, in the

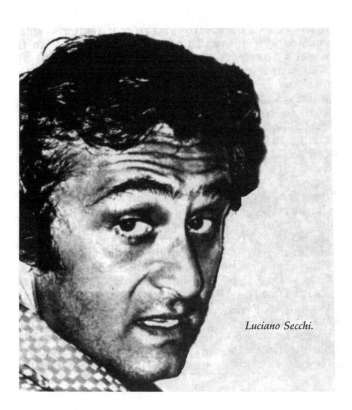

Luciano Secchi.

tradition of the Italian *fumetto nero* (black comics), followed the next year by *Satanik*, a female variation on the same theme of the antihero fighting against the blind repressive forces of society. Both of these strips enjoyed great success and earned Secchi a considerable reputation as a scriptwriter.

In 1968 Secchi created (again in collaboration with Raviola) the burlesque *Maxmagnus* about the predatory king of a mythical European kingdom. Secchi is also the author of a number of other strips, notable among them *Virus Psik*, an experimental series with drawing by Chies, and the recent *Fouche, un Uomo nella Revoluzione* ("Fouche, a Man in the Revolution"), an ambitious attempt at depicting in comic strip form the turbulent era of the French Revolution (the drawings are by Paolo Piffarerio). Also significant is *Alan Ford*, Secchi's greatest success to date.

Luciano Secchi has also been the editor of the Italian comic magazine *Eureka* since its inception in 1967. In this capacity he has greatly contributed to the appreciation of comic art in Italy; he has been instrumental in the Italian publication of *Terry and the Pirates*, *Steve Canyon*, and the Marvel stable of superheroes. He has received numerous distinctions, including top awards at the International Salon of Humor in Bordighera and the comics festival in Genoa. In addition to his achievements in the field of comic art, Secchi has also had published several of his novels as well as anthologies of his short stories, and he is a regular contributor to *Storia Illustrata*, the most important history magazine in Italy.

In 1982 Secchi left Corno to found his own company, Max Bunker Productions (now Max Bunker Press), which published all six titles of the *Alan Ford* saga and produced the first full-animation cartoons of the character as well as a few feature films. In the meantime he continued to write mystery novels with Ricardo Finzi as the protagonist.

In 1990 he started the short-lived comics magazines *Bhang* and *Super Comics*. That same year he also created *Angel Dark*, about a hard-boiled detective, that lasted only for ten issues. In 1994 another experiment, *Kerry Kross*, involving a lesbian investigator, caused the feminist press to launch a campaign against the character; the title was discontinued after 11 issues, but there are plans to revive it in 1997. In 1995 the indefatigable Secchi launched a new title written by his son Ricardo, *Gabriel*, about a nun with superpowers.

M.H.

SECRET AGENT CORRIGAN *see* Secret Agent X-9.

SECRET AGENT X-9 (U.S.) *Secret Agent X-9* made its first appearance (with much preceding and accompanying fanfare) on January 22, 1934; written by famous author Dashiell Hammett and drawn by up-and-coming artist Alex Raymond, it had been slated as King Features' answer to *Dick Tracy*.

In spite of the syndicate editors' mindless tamperings with the original script, the first four episodes (written by Hammett) remain by far the best. They established the character of the secret agent as a lone wolf, an implacable foe of crime who mingles in the midst of the underworld, adopting its habits, its jargon, and even its methods. In the first episode, the hero asks to be called Dexter ("it's not my name but it'll do") but later relinquishes even that alias to keep only his cryptic code number. X-9 moves swiftly but warily in the metropolitan jungle inhabited by gigolos, racketeers,

"Secret Agent X-9," Alex Raymond. © King Features Syndicate.

molls, kidnappers, and extortionists, amidst the trappings of a luxuriant and decadent society and in an atmosphere of cynicism and amorality. So strong was Hammett's characterization and so stunning Raymond's artwork that this is the image of *X-9* that remained in the reader's mind, long after the creators had abandoned the strip, within a few months' interval from each other, in 1935, (Hammett in April, Raymond in November).

Raymond was succeeded by Charles Flanders, the first in a bewildering array of artists and writers (who included Leslie Charteris of the *Saint* fame). Flanders tried to remain in the line of his predecessor but, although he did a creditable job, he could not sustain the character over the long haul, and he left in 1938, to be followed first by Nicholas Afonski (who drew *X-9* in a broad, grotesque style) and then by Austin Briggs.

Briggs's work on *X-9* (from November 1939 to May 1940) rivals even Raymond's in sheer brilliance. In his capable hands *X-9* became once again the enigmatic G-man of whom little is known. Aided and abetted by his talented scriptwriter Robert Storm (who had taken over from Charteris in 1936) Briggs re-created a world of shadows and menace, of bizarre intrigues and dark deeds, of dangerous and desperate men, and sultry and driven women.

When Briggs left the strip to create the daily version of *Flash Gordon*, he was followed by Mel Graff who, after 1942 (when Storm left as scriptwriter), was to betray the spirit of the strip to a considerable extent. Graff saddled *X-9* with an official name, Phil Corrigan, a family life, and even a fiancée. In 1960 Bob Lewis (pseudonym of Bob Lubbers) succeeded Graff and his cute and overmannered style drove *X-9* deeper into mediocrity. The strip would have probably gone under (it carried very few papers at that point) had it not been for Al Williamson who took over in January 1967. Williamson (helped by his able scriptwriter Archie Goodwin) restored *X-9* (now rechristened *Secret Agent Corrigan*) to something resembling its erstwhile splendor. In 1980 it was taken over by George Evans, who

did a creditable job of continuing the feature until its unfortunate demise in the spring of 1996.

Because of syndicate mishandling *X-9* misfired badly; it never even came close to rivaling *Dick Tracy* in popularity. It did inspire a radio program and two (bad) movie serials (1937 and 1945). Its influence on other strips (even police strips) has been negligible; but on the screen the dazzling and inflexible persona of the hero created by Dashiell Hammett and Alex Raymond has left a durable imprint, from James Cagney's 1935 role in *G-men* to Robert Stack's characterization in *The Untouchables* in the 1960s to Kevin Costner in the movie version of the 1980s.

M.H.

SECRET OPERATIVE DAN DUNN *see* Dan Dunn.

SEEKERS, THE (G.B.) "The Seekers" is the name given to a kind of Missing Persons Bureau run by Una Frost. It consists of Suzanne Dove, brunette and beautiful, and Jacob, blond and beautiful. This take-on-anything (and also take-off-anything) team was created in the image of the highly successful *Modesty Blaise* strip by writer Les Lilley and artist John Burns. Intended for the *Evening News*, the strip was sidetracked into the *Daily Sketch* via strip editor Julian Phipps, and began on May 2, 1966. After that paper's demise it continued in syndication and concluded on May 10, 1971. One of the first strips to reflect the permissive age, heroine Suzanne went one up on Modesty by regularly appearing naked. This happened whenever she took off her dress, for she wore no underclothes!

John Burns drew *The Seekers* in a style very close to that of the late Jim Holdaway. Born in Wickford, Essex, Burns had no formal art training, yet he has emerged as one of today's finest sex-and-violence illustrators. He joined Doris White at Link Studios as an apprentice at the age of 16, and worked on strips for such weekly comics as *Girl's Crystal*, *School Friend*, and *Boy's World*. For *Wham* he drew *Kelpie* (1964), then the fantastic color serial *Wrath of the Gods* (1964) for *Eagle*. His first newspaper strip was *The Tuckwells* (1966), a weekly serial in *Sunday Citizen*. In 1971 he adapted the television series *Countdown* for the comic of the same title,

"The Seekers," John M. Burns. © Associated Newspapers Ltd.

and did a similar strip adaptation of *Mission Impossible* (1973) for *T.V. Action*.

D.G.

SEGAR, ELZIE CRISLER (1894-1938) Elzie Crisler Segar, tragically short-lived creator of the immortal Popeye and Wimpy in his *Thimble Theater* strip, was born in Chester, Illinois, on December 8, 1894, to Amzi Andrews and Erma Irene Crisler Segar. Amzi Segar was a housepainter and paperhanger, and Chester, Illinois, was a long way from anywhere in the horse-and-buggy days of the turn of the century. Yet the Sunday papers from Chicago and Indianapolis reached even there, and the young Elzie was as familiar as any city kid with *Happy Hooligan, The Newlyweds, The Kin-Der-Kids,* and *Old Doc Yak.* More important, he was stirred to draw himself. He soon realized that his talent was minimal, yet his will to make it as a cartoonist kept him at his youthful drawing board into the small hours of night. A correspondence school course helped, and when he went to Chicago to try his luck on the papers there, his work showed enough verve to impress R. F. Outcault, creator of the seminal *Yellow Kid* and an idol of Segar's, who got him a job working on the hackneyed *Charlie Chaplin's Comic Capers,* a daily and Sunday strip running in the old *Chicago Herald.*

Segar's first *Chaplin* appeared on Sunday, March 12, 1916, and he continued with the strip until its syndicate owner, James Keeley, broke with Chaplin and scuttled the feature on April 16, 1917. The following Sunday, Segar got a crack at a strip of his own, a weekly page called *Barry the Boob* (about a young, nitwit soldier in an unnamed army on the European battlefields). *Barry* lasted a year, folding when the *Herald* was purchased by the Hearst *Chicago American* and *Examiner* combine, in April of 1918. Segar went with the *Herald*'s assets, and started his first really successful feature on June 1, 1918, in the evening *American.*

The first *Looping The Loop,* a column of small cartoons satirizing downtown Chicago (the loop district) and its theater and film attractions, was a considerable hit, and its regular appearance on the paper's theater page for the next year built the *American*'s circulation considerably. Hearst's New York syndicate officials noted the newcomer with interest, and trained him to go to Manhattan in late 1919 to start work on a comic strip for the Hearst chain. This new feature, called *Thimble Theater,* and similar in format and content to Ed Wheelan's popular *Midget Movies,* which Hearst had just lost to another syndicate, dealt with melodramatic stage themes and figures in daily gag routines. The first episode ran in the evening *New York Journal* on December 27, 1919. Public response was favorable, if not sensational, and the new feature continued, with Segar quickly shucking the stage drama trappings and concentrating on developing his own individual characters, such as Olive Oyl, her brother Castor, and her boyfriend, Ham Gravy. Drawn simply, in six small daily panels, the early *Thimble Theater* resembled Charles Schulz's *Peanuts* in style and gag structure. The strip also had the virtue of fitting into odd corners on daily comic pages, so that Segar was asked to start a companion daily strip of the same size for the Hearst morning *New York American,* to appeal to the new breed of suburban office commuter, and to be named (for a commuter train) *The Five-Fifteen.* Segar created a new character for this miniscule epic named John Sappo,

E. C. Segar, "Thimble Theater." © King Features Syndicate.

gave him a nagging wife, Myrtle, and set readers to chuckling from the outset, on December 24, 1920. (He also gave Sappo a son named Archie, mentioned in the opening episode, but never seen or mentioned again in the strip.) By the early 1920s, the Hearst syndicate felt Segar was ready to do a *Thimble Theater* Sunday page, and the first full-color page appeared in the Saturday comic section of the *New York Journal* on April 18, 1925. *The Five-Fifteen,* renamed *Sappo,* was added as a single strip of panels to the color page on March 6, 1926, and increased to an upper third on July 10, 1926.

Meanwhile, Segar himself, once he felt secure as a cartoonist, took his wife (named, like Sappo's, Myrtle) and left New York for Los Angeles, where he settled at a nearby beach city called Santa Monica for the rest of his life. It was there that he conceived the first character to give him international fame and personal fortune when he introduced Popeye the sailor into the *Thimble Theater* daily strip on January 17, 1929. Popeye took the nation by storm wherever Segar's strip was published, and within a year, orders were pouring into King Features from newspapers everywhere demanding local publication rights. Yet in the midst of this acclaim, Segar, already ill for some time, died on October 13, 1938: one of the most untimely deaths in strip history.

The earliest strip cartoonist mentioned by name in a major popular dictionary (*Webster's Collegiate,* Fifth Edition, 1941, in which he is credited with adding the words *jeep* and *goon* to the language), Segar was a devoted sports fisherman and a long member of the Santa Monica Rod and Reel Club; he loved to do carpentry of all kinds, and had his work covered in articles in such magazines as *Mechanix Illustrated*; but above all, he was one of the most naturally gifted artists and writers the strip medium ever afforded drawing board space to, and one of the major creative geniuses of the century.

B.B.

SEGRELLES, VICENTE (1940-) Spanish artist born in Barcelona on September 9, 1940, Vicente Segrelles apprenticed with the ENASA truck manufacturing company while attending night school at the School of Arts, where he specialized in advertising art. He eventually rose to the position of project draftsman, and at the same time freelanced as an illustrator with assignments that included *The Iliad* and *The Odyssey.* After his military service he devoted himself fully to advertising work as an illustrator and designer. In 1970

Vicente Segrelles, "El Mercenario." © *Vicente Segrelles.*

he left advertising to freelance as an illustrator, mostly in the field of popular science books (some of which he wrote himself) and of magazines, where he gained a solid reputation as a cover artist. Only in 1980 did he turn to comics with his series *The Mercenary*, currently published in over a dozen countries, including the United States.

A characteristic feature of Segrelles's work, which applies equally to his illustrations and to his comics work, is fantasy. He naturally chose fantasy as the main theme of his series, with some additions of sword-and-sorcery elements and a good dose of science fiction. He develops his stories in a way that allows him to display his talents as an illustrator to best advantage, composing each panel as a separate picture and maximizing its visual impact through his use of color. The adventures of the Mercenary (no name is given to the taciturn hero) have been published from their inception in the magazine *Cimoc* and later collected in book form. In the United States they have appeared in *Heavy Metal* and in a series of hardbound volumes.

In addition to *The Mercenary*—whose success from the outset was international and whose imagery was greatly admired by Federico Fellini—Segrelles has also over the years authored a number of shorter stories, most on heroic fantasy or sword-and-sorcery themes, some of which were later anthologized in *Historias Fantasticas* (1992). At the same time he never abandoned the illustration field and he has worked for many European and American publishers (notably Tor, Warner, Bantam, and New American Library).

J.C.

SERAFINO (Italy) Egidio Gherlizza created *Serafino* in 1951 in the pages of the *Cucciolo* comic book as a filler intended for the younger readers of the publication. Serafino is a cute little dog always attired in a bizarre costume made of a pair of too-short pants held by huge black suspenders, a red sweater, yellow shoes, and a soft hat sandwiched between his large ears. Serafino is

"Serafino," Egidio Gherlizza. © *Edizioni Alpe.*

ready to do anything to earn himself the sumptuous dinner of which he is always dreaming. To date he has worked as a truck driver, gardener, night watchman, fruit picker, potmaker, pantmender, and in any number of other odd jobs. His goofiness invariably gets him in hot water but his persistent good fortune always allows him to get out of it. At the end of each episode he can be seen seated with fork in hand in front of a big roast chicken.

Gherlizza has introduced into his strip good surrealistic touches that brighten and enliven the simple story line. The feature has been so well received over the years that *Serafino* was given its own monthly comic book in 1973. It lasted into 1985.

G.B.

"Sgt. Fury." © Marvel Comics Group.

SGT. FURY (U.S.) *Sgt. Fury and His Howling Commandos* debuted in its own comic book by writer and editor Stan Lee and artist Jack Kirby in May 1963. Issue number 1 introduced the gruff sergeant and his World War II platoon of Howlers such as Dum Dum Dug and bugler Gabe Jones, Dino Manelli, and Izzy Cohen. The lineup of the platoon changed from time to time but always featured a cross section of ethnic groups. The men frequently bickered over petty matters but always rallied together when confronted with the Nazi menace, usually depicted in typical B-movie tradition. A frequent antagonist was the bald, monocled Baron Strucker.

Kirby drew the feature, incorporating some of his own wartime experiences, for seven issues, returning later for issue number 13 when Fury met Captain America. Though Kirby continued to do covers for several years, the feature soon became identified with penciler Dick Ayers. Apart from occasional fill-in issues by John Severin, Tom Sutton, and Herb Trimpe, Ayers handled all the penciling. Various inkers did the strip but the issues embellished by Severin are generally considered the best in terms of art.

Scripting was done by Lee until 1966 when Roy Thomas took over for a year, followed by Gary Friedrich. The stories gravitated from gritty emotion to super heroics with Fury, his shirt perpetually in shreds, dodging a barrage of Nazi bullets. Eventually, Marvel

began a superspy strip, set in the present day, entitled *Nick Fury, Agent of SHIELD*.

Apart from the superhero influence, *Sgt. Fury* was also influenced by trends in the other Marvel books. The constant bickering among Fury's men was obviously inspired by the fights that divided groups like the *Fantastic Four* and the *Avengers*. Some issues, attempting to make a negative statement about war, depicted Fury as a frail, very human man in direct opposition to his usual image as a cigar-chewing superman.

Marvel attempted two spin-off imitations of *Sgt. Fury*. *Captain Savage and his Leatherneck Raiders* began in 1968 and lasted four years. After it ceased publication, Marvel tried *Combat Kelly and the Deadly Dozen*, which lasted a year. Both followed the *Sgt. Fury* format of a lead character commanding a team of various ethnic characters. Both imitations employed much the same creative team as *Sgt. Fury*, also.

Sgt. Fury appeared in seven annual specials (1965-1971), some featuring new material. In the 1970s, the *Sgt. Fury* comic began to fluctuate in quality with a variety of writers and inkers. Frequent reprint issues disrupted the comic's continuity and soon took over completely. Reprints also ran in *Special Marvel Edition* (1972-1973) and *War Is Hell* (1974). The series was finally canceled in 1981.

M.E.

SERGEANT PAT OF THE RADIO PATROL see Radio Patrol.

SGT. ROCK (U.S.) *Sgt. Rock* was the creation of writer and editor Robert Kanigher as the first recurring feature in National's line of war comics. The series began in *Our Army at War* number 81 (April 1959) with a story drawn by the team of Ross Andru and Mike Esposito. The title character, however, was a composite of several from earlier Kanigher stories, most notably the sergeant from *The D.I.* and the Sand Fleas in *G.I. Combat* number 56, dated January 1958.

In the first *Our Army at War* appearance, the character was named Sgt. Rocky, nicknamed "The Rock of Easy Company." Within a few issues, he evolved into the more conventional platoon leader, Sgt. Rock, and

"Sgt. Rock," Joe Kubert. © DC Comics.

was illustrated by the artist most closely identified with the strip, Joe Kubert. Other artists who relieved or followed Kubert on *Sgt. Rock* include Jerry Grandenetti, Irv Novick, Russ Heath, George Evans, and John Severin. Kanigher remained the principal writer.

The origin of Sgt. Frank Rock, as told by Kanigher and Kubert, ran in *Showcase* number 45 (August 1963). The story introduced Rock as an army private who enlisted in the early days of World War II. He subsequently rose to the rank of sergeant when he held Easy Company's position on a hill despite a Nazi onslaught that killed the other men in his unit.

The various members of Easy Company were introduced in issues of *Our Army at War* and included such supporting characters as Ice Cream Soldier, Bulldozer, Wild Man, and one of the comics' first nonstereotyped black characters, Jackie Johnson. The *Sgt. Rock* stories were mainly set in the European theater of operations, dealing with the men of Easy, their battle against the enemy, and the personal strains that each found themselves confronting in the face of war. The stories were introduced and told in the first person by Sgt. Rock, and many of them concentrated on the tremendous mental anguish endured by men in wartime.

Rock teamed with the characters of two other National war strips, the *Haunted Tank* and *Johnny Cloud*, in *The Brave and the Bold* number 52 (March 1964). He later teamed up with *Batman* in that same magazine for several stories that found Rock alive in the present-day army, still with the rank of sergeant. For a brief period, National attempted a spin-off with a series in *Our Fighting Forces* detailing the exploits of Rock's lieutenant brother, Larry. The *Lt. Larry Rock* strip achieved neither the popularity nor the longevity of the *Sgt. Rock* feature.

The comic book was officially renamed *Sgt. Rock* in 1977. Joe Kubert was again the mainstay of the series, but other talented artists, including Ric Estrada and Doug Wildey, also worked on the title. It was discontinued as a monthly in 1988 but continued as a quarterly until 1992.

M.E.

SEVERIN, JOHN POWERS (1921-   ) American comic book artist, writer, and editor, John Powers Severin was born December 21, 1921, in Jersey City, New Jersey. Although he had no academic art training, Severin began drawing cartoons for the *Hobo News* in 1932 and continued until 1936. He did not enter the comic book field until November 1947, however, when he illustrated a crime story for the Simon and Kirby team, then working at Crestwood. Severin then went to work directly for the Crestwood/Pioneer group and became the writer/editor of *Prize Western* comics, and also drew Western strips like *Lazo Kid, Black Bull,* and *American Eagle.* The first strip, *Lazo Kid,* was about a Mexican character and wasn't outstanding, but Severin's work on *American Eagle* was. A great fan of realistic Western tales, his work on the feature was one of the few serious, relatively unbiased handlings of the American Indian in comic books. Done in collaboration with Will Elder and Colin Dawkins, the strip remains unpublicized. When you get the feeling of realism, Severin once said in an interview, when *American Eagle* wasn't just tomahawks and cavalry sabres, it was about then I began taking a hand. Severin remained with the feature and Crestwood until its 1953 demise.

It was about that time he began working for William Gaines's EC group. Concentrating mainly on Westerns and wars under the direction of editor Harvey Kurtzman, Severin began developing his realistic, illustrative approach. He spent considerable time on detail and accuracy, and he once said he didn't draw comic book people, rather he drew people as they were. Some of Severin's finest work came in the last three issues of the *New Two-Fisted Tales*, for which he edited, wrote, and drew. Again concentrating on Western tales, the Severin-edited issues are among the best of the EC years, but they too folded when EC garnered too much negative publicity in 1953 and 1954. He also drew some outstanding, if somewhat static, material for the early issues of Kurtzman's *Mad.*

After EC folded in 1955, Severin began working for the Charlton and Harvey groups and began working more often for Stan Lee's Atlas group. There again he concentrated mainly on Western strips, but when Lee began the Marvel group in 1961, Severin went on to contribute fine material for the full range of Marvel comics, including *The Hulk* and a successful collaboration with Dick Ayers on *Sgt. Fury,* a war strip.

Over the years, Severin has also worked for Nedor (1948-1950), Skywald, Seaboard, National, and several others. He also contributed fine work to Warren's black-and-white magazines during the middle and late 1960s, particularly on the short-lived but excellent *Blazing Combat* title. Throughout his career, he has also contributed to Major Magazines, mostly for *Cracked,* a *Mad* imitation. Some of his noteworthy contributions in the 1980s have been *Bold Adventures* (1984) and the Marvel graphic novel *Conan the Reaver* (1988).

His sister, Marie, is also in the comic book business, and they collaborated at Marvel for a short time as the artist-inker team on the ill-fated *King Kull* book (1973).

J.B.

SEXTON BLAKE (G.B.) Britain's second greatest fictional detective (some say first; others brand him the office boy's Holmes), Sexton Blake, was created by hack writer Harry Blyth, under one of his pen names, "Hal Meredyth." Blake first appeared in a long novelette, *The Missing Millionaire*, published in Alfred Harmsworth's weekly for boys, *The Halfpenny Marvel*, on December 13, 1893. He appeared in similar stories for some 80 years, via such papers as *Union Jack, Detective Weekly*, and his own *Sexton Blake Library.*

He had already appeared in a number of films, silent and sound, when Percival Montagu Haydon, an Amalgamated Press editor, decided to include Blake in his new weekly children's comic, as a picture story. And so in number 1 of *The Knockout*, dated March 4, 1939, *Sexton Blake and the Hooded Stranger* began. "My word, this is a grand change from work," commented Blake's boy assistant, Tinker, in panel one. But then a car roared past their picnic. The man in that car is the Hooded Stranger, the most dangerous crook in Europe! cried Blake, and Pedro the Bloodhound was hot on the trail. A haystack camouflaged a lift, and down they all went to a Giant Underground Stronghold packed to the rivets with armored tanks! The game was afoot. Within weeks the strip had expanded from two pages to three, virtually unprecedented in British comics, and the villain behind the scenes turned out to be General Bomgas, dictator of Etland. (He was not the Hooded Stranger, however; his identity remained unknown.)

"Sexton Blake," Alfred Taylor. © Amalgamated Press.

The first artist to draw Blake as a strip hero was Joe (Joseph) Walker, a long-time illustrator of adaptations of Western movies starring Buck Jones and Tim McCoy for *Film Fun*. But he soon switched for Alfred H. Taylor, who continued the series until January 1, 1949. Taylor created the saga's best-remembered gimmick, the Rolling Sphere, invented by Chinese scientist Hoo Sung, and a handy thing to have during *Sexton Blake on Secret Service* (1942), when General MacRobert had to be rescued from Malaya. Then came *Sexton Blake and the Golden Lion* (1944), *Sexton Blake and the Threat of Kwang Shu* (1945), *Sexton Blake and the Atom Eggs* (1946), and so on.

Taylor was suddenly reduced to the status of lettering artist on January 8, 1949, when the artist who had done so much to establish Blake's original character and appearance in the old story papers took over the strip. This was Eric R. Parker, long a strip artist on *Knockout* for *Patsy & Tim* and other serials. The artwork took a decided leap upwards as Parker plunged his old favorites into *The Secret of Monte Cristo*, but he lasted only 14 weeks. Then the strip was given to R. C. W. Heade, then to R. MacGillivray, until Roland Davies took over from December 10, 1949. By 1954 Heade was back, but the episodes were complete each week. They stayed this way to the end (1960), with Taylor still doing lettering.

When television took up the rights to the character in 1967, *Sexton Blake* was revived as a strip in *Valiant*, the weekly comic that had, meanwhile, absorbed *Knockout*. The hawk-nosed detective was remodeled to match his television image, actor Laurence Payne. A large paperback reprint was published called *Valiant Book of T.V.'s Sexton Blake* (1968). But when the television series was dropped, so was the strip.

D.G.

SHADOW, THE (U.S.) 1—*The Shadow*, alias Lamont Cranston, first appeared in a Street and Smith pulp story called "The Living Shadow" (*The Shadow Magazine* number 1) in April 1931. Written by Walter Brown Gibson under the pen name "Maxwell Grant," the feature introduced the mysterious, crime-fighting Shadow and his equally inscrutable crew of helpers. Running concurrently with *The Shadow* radio show, the character became one of the most popular figures of the 1930s, and when comic books began making strides later in the decade, it was only a matter of time before *The Shadow* made an appearance.

In March 1940, Street and Smith issued the first *Shadow* comics, and the once invisible creature of the night became a gnarled face peering out from between a blue, low-brimmed hat and blue cloak. Most of the stories were signed by Gibson's pen name, but it is a virtual certainty that he did not write them. Artistically, most of the early stories were produced by the Jack Binder shop, but Bob Powell (1947-1949) and under-publicized pulp illustrator Ed Cartier contributed some excellent material in later years. But despite its scrupulous adherence to *Shadow* traditions and its first-rate production, the strip never matched the pulp or radio popularity the character enjoyed. *The Shadow* lasted in comic books until November 1950—a total of 107 appearances.

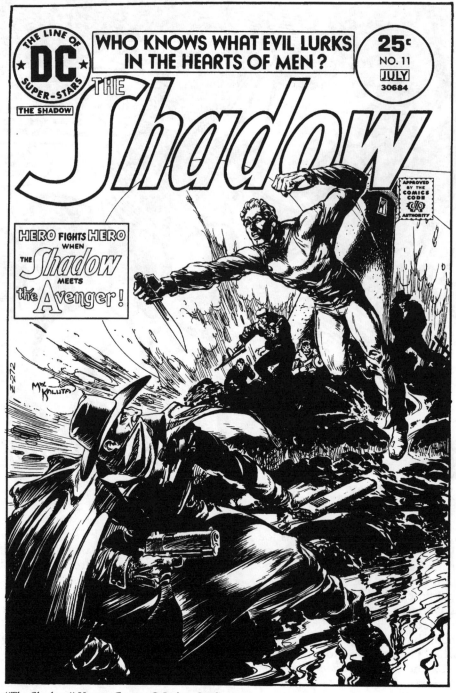

"The Shadow," Vernon Greene. © Ledger Syndicate.

2—During the superhero resurgence of the 1960s, the Archie group released a new *Shadow* series beginning in August 1964. And although this Shadow also claimed to be Lamont Cranston, the strip bore absolutely no resemblance to the old Shadow. He was a superhero, complete with green and blue tights and campy, juvenile dialogue. Doug Murray, comic writer for *The Monster Times*, counted it among the ten worst comic strips ever published. It died in September 1965 after eight issues.

3—National Comics announced plans to reissue the old *Shadow* series in early 1973 and Denny O'Neil was chosen as writer and editor. But the strip, which premiered in November of that year, has had tremendous artistic problems. Recognized talents like Berni Wrightson, Alex Toth, and Jim Steranko all quit before the first issue was published; however, young Mike Kaluta handled the first three issues and he was widely

acclaimed for his sensitive treatment and the 1930s mood of decay he portrayed. Frank Robbins began illustrating the book with the fourth issue and his version was completely different, mainly concentrating on action and adventure.

J.B.

4—*The Shadow* also enjoyed a brief newspaper career from 1938 to 1942 in a strip drawn by Vernon Greene and distributed by the Ledger Syndicate. The newspaper version was close to the original conception of the pulps, both in mood and execution. Greene proved to be a surprisingly effective action artist, and his somber and disquieting compositions, full of foreboding and menace, mark his Shadow as a forerunner of Will Eisner's Spirit.

The Shadow has known a checkered career in comic books (see above). The first version appeared in 1940, done by Greene. From 1942, when he was drafted to the end of the *Shadow Comics* run in 1949, came Jon Blummer, Jack Binder, Charles Coll, and Bob Powell, among others. *The Shadow* was brought back in the 1960s, 1970s, and 1980s, without success every time. Dark Horse Comics is currently trying to revive the crime fighter's fortunes by pairing him with other pulp heroes such as Doc Savage.

M.H.

SHAW, ERNEST (1891-197?) British cartoonist, writer, illustrator, and game creator Ernest Shaw was born in Hull, Yorkshire, on January 21, 1891. He was educated at Day Street School, leaving in 1905 to become errand boy to a printer. He studied art by copying the strips of Tom Browne from the halfpenny comics, then took a postal course with Percy V. Bradshaw's Press Art School. He sold his first cartoon to *Puck* (1910), then freelanced to his local weekly newspaper, *Hull & Yorkshire Times*. He joined the staff as general artist, drawing sports cartoons and caricatures of local celebrities, moving to the *Hull Daily Mail*, *Evening News*, and *Sports Mail* group as sports and political cartoonist.

He volunteered for war service in the Royal Army Medical Corps in 1914, and drew cartoons for the service magazine, *The Ration*. He also devised a *Lightning Cartoon* act to entertain convalescent soldiers. His sketches of details of operations on wounded soldiers as performed by surgeon Major J. L. Joyce were printed in *The Lancet*.

After demobilization Shaw raised his sights to the London market and began to submit his work to Amalgamated Press. He began with sports cartoons for *All Sports* (1919), but Tom Webster was by then king of this field. Very attracted to the American newspaper strips *Mutt and Jeff* and *Bringing Up Father*, Shaw was determined to develop in this area. He began with *Clarence* and *Cyril the Sporty Scout* in *Sports Fun* (1922), and *First Aid Freddie* and the extraordinary crazy strip *Ikeybod & Tinribs*, both in *Champion* (1923). His big break came when he was given one day in which to take over a full-page weekly composite cartoon, *The Gay Goblins* for *Family Journal*, upon the sudden death of its creator, Lewis Higgins. He succeeded and continued the feature from 1926 until the last issue. An even longer run came with *Mr. and Mrs. Dillwater*, a weekly domestic strip, which he drew for *Answers* magazine from 1923 to 1948.

Other strips include *Hector in Wireless* (192?); *Sandy in People's Journal* (193?); *Dr. Gnome of Gnomansland*, which ran for 21 years in *Woman's Illustrated*; *The Wee Macs* in *Sunday Mail* (1940); *Sammy the Scout* (1938) in *Liverpool Daily Post*; *Gingham & Polkadot* (194?) in *Home*. From the 1940s Shaw concentrated on the juvenile market and created *The Dingbats*, a group of pixies who appeared in strips, puzzle books, painting books, story books, *Dingbats Comic* (1948), and three *Dingbats Annuals* (1949-1951). He devised card and board games, including *Menuette*, and syndicated his own puzzle panels, *Tantalising Teasers* and *Problematics*. His books include *Pocket Brains Trust* (1943), *Believe It All Rot* (1945), *Daily Deeds of Sammy the Scout* (1948), *Jolly Jokes for Juvenile Jokers*, *Dr. Gnome's Annual* (1953), and the primer, *How to Be a Successful Cartoonist* (1946).

In 1973 Shaw was rediscovered by Denis Gifford, and as Britain's oldest working cartoonist appeared as a panelist on the television series *Quick on the Draw*. An honorary member of the Cartoonists Club of Great Britain, Shaw died in the late 1970s.

D.G.

Ernest Shaw, "Mr. and Mrs. Dillwater." © Answers.

SHEENA, QUEEN OF THE JUNGLE (U.S.) Because of the plethora of fine artists it has had, Edgar Rice Burroughs's *Tarzan* remains the definitive jungle comic strip. It dominated both the newspaper strip and comic book jungle market. In fact, the only worthy comic book competition was *Sheena, Queen of the Jungle*, a strip with healthy doses of sex, sadism, and items surely aimed at arousing prurient interests. S. M. Iger and Will Eisner created the feature for the Editors Press Service in 1937, but the character did not make its first American comic book appearance until artist Mort Meskin and writer William Thomas produced it for Fiction House's *Jumbo* number 1 (September 1938). There it became fabulously successful and lasted 167 issues until March 1953. The character also had 18 issues of her own title from Spring 1942 until Winter 1953.

Unlike *Wonder Woman*, which featured material aimed at a girls' audience, *Sheena* was aimed at young boys. Sheena was a beautiful blonde with an outrageous figure. She wore only the skimpiest fur-and-leopard-skin costume, certainly more than enough to attract boys just reaching the point of sexual awareness. Sheena would swing through the pages Tarzan-style, Juanita Coulson wrote in *The Comic Book Book* (Arlington House, 1974), her long blonde hair flying and her fur bikini plastered to her 42-23-34 figure. I'm sure it brought the drooling male reader back for more. And it probably did, because the feature had many imitators, including *Nyoka* (Fawcett) and *Jann of the Jungle* (Atlas).

But Sheena was always the leader. Her companion was a hapless man named Bob who functioned in

"Sheena," Mort Meskin. © Fiction House.

much the same way Lois Lane operated in *Superman*: Bob would always be caught or captured by some African interloper and Sheena was pressed into service to defeat Bob's captors and rescue her assistant.

Sheena's popularity reached into other media, as well. She made many pulp magazine appearances and there was even a short-lived *Sheena* television series starring Irish McCalla. A movie version, starring Tanya Roberts in the role of Sheena, was released in 1984.

J.B.

SHELTON, GILBERT (1940-   ) While Robert Crumb and his creations are unquestionably the best-known of the underground comix society, Gilbert Shelton certainly ranks on a comparable level. His creations, *The Fabulous Furry Freak Brothers* and *Wonder Wart-Hog*, have become ingrained in the American consciousness, and probably say more about the readers they cater to than Robert Crumb's sexual fantasies. Whereas Crumb took readers to the outer levels, and some say the basest and most chauvinistic fringes, Shelton's features reflected things as they were and as they probably would continue to be. While it was Crumb who opened the sexual vistas and broke many of the old taboos, it was Shelton who went beyond the pioneering and made the later strides.

Born in June 1940, Shelton produced his first major strip, *Wonder Wart-Hog*, in December 1961. Written by Bill Killeen, the strip made its first appearance in the University of Texas magazine, *Texas Ranger*. Both Shelton and Killeen were studying there, and, for several months, the duo continued to work together on the strip. *Wonder Wart-Hog* himself was always the sex-crazed parody of *Superman* and the whole superhero mystique. In his secret identity as reporter Philbert Desenex, an outrageous and sharp parody of Superman's alter ego Clark Kent, the Hog of Steel destroyed just about every superheroic cliché, and, in the words of one critic, virtually destroyed any validity the superhero concept claimed.

Shelton soon assumed the complete writing and drawing of the strip, but when Killeen began *Charla-*

tan, another college humor magazine, Shelton was there with *Wonder Wart-Hog*. The strip eventually found its way into *Help!*, the Harvey Kurtzman-edited magazine. Unfortunately, *Help!* folded shortly after *Wonder Wart-Hog* began, but the feature survived in car magazines like *Hot Rod Cartoons* and *Drag*.

By 1968, however, Shelton began to branch out. He had already created the *Freak Brothers* for the *L.A. Free-Press* the year before, and, when his first underground comix book, *Feds and Heads*, appeared, it was apparent Shelton was ready to move on from *Wonder Wart-Hog*. Although the Hog of Steel made several sporadic appearances throughout the rest of the 1960s and early 1970s, it was the *Freak Brothers* that became Shelton's main vehicle. Unlike *Wonder Wart-Hog*'s dogged parodies of the antiquated superhero myths, the Freak Brothers were sex-seeking, dope-hungry revolutionaries of sorts, who accurately reflected the emerging youth culture of the late 1960s. While *Wonder Wart-Hog* mirrored past values, Frankling, Fat Freddy, and Phineas were contemporary characters entertaining contemporary audiences with contemporary humor. In the late 1970s Shelton took up residence in Europe, whence he continued to send material to Rip-Off Press until the late 1980s.

As an artist, Shelton never had the effect on styles and accepted standards of quality as Crumb did. His work was always clearly done and pleasingly presented, but it was not as earth-shaking or revolutionary. While his peers were busy shaking the trees of established art worlds, Shelton continued to entertain. As a result, Kurtzman, who is seen by some as one of the guiding lights of the underground movement, called Shelton the pro of the group.

J.B.

SHENANIGAN KIDS   *see* Katzenjammer Kids, The.

SHEN PEI (1934-   )   Originally named Shen Peijin, Shen Pei graduated in 1954 from Central Art Academy, East China Branch (which at present are Zhejiang Art Academy and Chinese Art Academy). Until he moved and settled in Hong Kong in 1980, Shen had been a member of the Chinese Artist Association and worked as art editor for the *Xin Shaonian Bao* ("New Juvenile Journal"), which later became *Zhongguo Shaonian Bao* ("Chinese Juvenile Journal") and for the People's Art Publication House.

In June 1958, Shen started his long comic strip for children, *Xiaohuzi* ("Little Tiger"), published with the *New Juvenile Journal* (later with the *Chinese Juvenile Journal*). The hero in the comics, whose name was "Little Tiger," was a cartoon figure known by every young reader, even every adult, in China. In the first issue, "Little Tiger" was telling the readers: "My name is Xiaohuzi, and from now on I will be your friend. You should learn from me when you see what I am doing is good, and criticize me when you find what I am doing is wrong." Hoping to guide children to better behavior Xiaohuzi was established in Shen's comics as a good boy who was honest and warmhearted, loving, and caring of his peers, protecting the young and respecting the elderly, and was a hard-working pupil. In one such episode, Xiaohuzi gives the smaller pear to his younger brother. At the end, the unhappy younger brother realizes that Xiaohuzi is a good big brother who keeps the bigger but worm-eaten pear to himself.

Shen Pei, "Dividing Pears." © Shen Pei.

In order to make his strip even better, Shen visited many schools and talked with teachers, even disguised as a school janitor, and observed children by making friends and playing with them. After Shen left for Hong Kong, *Xiaohuzi* was continued by other artists.

It is now the oldest comic strip in China, having run for almost forty years. Since he settled in Hong Kong, Shen has published cartoons with the *Hong Kong Business News* under the pen name "Wei Chi Heng." Although they are still light, humorous cartoons in both content and style, they are quite different from his previous works.

H.Y.L.L.

SHERLOCK LOPEZ (Spain) Every country, it would seem, must have its comic strip spoof of A. Conan Doyle's *Sherlock Holmes* tales. In the United States it is *Sherlocko the Monk*, in Yugoslavia *Herlock Sholmes*; *Sherlock Lopez y Watso de Leche* (to give it its original title) is the Spanish parody of the British detective and his assistant, and first appeared in issue 229 of the magazine *Flechas y Pelayos* (April 25, 1943). The strip's author is cartoonist Gabriel Arnao (who uses the pseudonym "Gabi"), one of the best representatives of Spanish humor, a specialist of the absurd and the creator of other popular features of the 1940s and 1950s, such as *El Señor Conejo* ("Mr. Rabbit," 1944), *El Pequeño Professor Pin y su Ayudante Freddy* ("Little Professor Pin and his Assistant Freddy," 1944), *Jim Erizo y su Papá* ("Porcupine Jim and his Daddy," 1947), *Pototo y Boliche* (1948), and *Don Ataulfo Clorato y su Sobrino Renato* (1948).

After having lived numerous outlandish adventures in Flechas y Pelayos, *Sherlock and Watso* have been recently resurrected in the pages of the comic weekly *Trinca*, where they carry on in a style and an atmosphere reminiscent of a now-vanished era. The new series ended in 1982.

L.G.

SHERLOCKO THE MONK *see* Mager's Monks.

SHIELD, THE (U.S.) Comic books were fighting World War II long before Pearl Harbor, and one of the first super-patriots was *The Shield*, created by artist Irv Novick and writer Harry Shorten. Making his first appearance in MLJ's *Pep* number 1 in January 1940, the character predated *Captain America* and became one of the most popular heroes of the 1940s. There were two origins, but the most often cited appeared in the first issue: Joe Higgins, his father killed by foreign agents, vowed to spend his life fighting to protect the American way of life and constructed a shieldlike costume which gave him superpowers and invulnerability.

The Shield feature also included several outstanding supporting characters. Two of them, Ju Ju Watson and Mamie Mazda, were among the earliest attempts to inject humor into a straight superhero adventure strip. But Dusty, the Boy Detective, the Shield's youthful sidekick, eventually became the major supporting character. His 1941 premiere also predated the introduction of Bucky in the *Captain America* feature.

The strip underwent several drastic changes toward the end of 1942. Novick, an outstanding artist of rare maturity, left the strip in less capable hands; then, after a minor costume change, the Shield was stripped of all his powers and cast as an everyman champion of the people. But neither change was to help the strip fight off the postwar superhero malaise, and a once-obscure back-up humor feature called *Archie* knocked *The Shield*

Kon Shimizu, "Kappa Tengoku." © Kon Shimizu.

from its lead position; *The Shield*'s last appearance was in the January 1948 issue of *Pep* (number 65). The character also appeared in 13 issues of *Shield-Wizard* comics between Summer 1940 and Spring 1944. There was also a Shield G-Man Club, but that too was soon changed to the Archie Club.

The Shield was revived in 1965 when the MLJ (now Archie-Radio) group attempted to exhume several of their characters as high camp during the mid-1960s *Batman* craze. In this new version, the Shield was a hopelessly destitute drifter who couldn't hold down a job because his crime-fighting interfered with his work. The whole line faded the next year, but not before Belmont issued a *High Camp Superheroes* paperback written by *Superman* co-creator Jerry Siegel. The title was briefly revived in 1983 by Archie Comics.

J.B.

SHIMIZU, KON (1912-1974) A Japanese cartoonist born September 22, 1912, in Nagasaki, Shimizu's parents died when he was seven and he was brought up by his grandmother. At Nagasaki Commercial School, Shimizu became famous for his caricatures of teachers and schoolmates. After graduation, he decided to become an artist and left for Tokyo in 1931 in order to enter the School of Fine Arts. His ambition was not realized, however, and Shimizu became a sidewalk artist in order to survive.

In 1933, through the intervention of a friend, Shimizu began working for the Bungeishunjii Publishing Company, contributing illustrations, fillers, and cartoons. That same year he joined the Shin Mangaha Shudan, the cartoonists' group founded by a band of young and iconoclastic artists, led by Ryūichi Yokoyama. In 1935 he produced a comic strip for the daily *Shinseinen, Tokyō Senichi ya Monogatari* ("The Tales of 1,001 Tokyo Nights"), noted for its new and fresh style (later inspiring a movie).

Soon after the Pacific War, Kon Shimiza became the political cartoonist for the daily *Shinyūkan*; his cartoons were so popular that in 1948 he was hired away by the much more prestigious *Asahi*. In 1951 he created his famous comic strip *Kappa no Kawatarō* ("Kowatarō the Kappa") about a merry band of river imps (called *kappa* in Japanese). The strip was so successful that it was made into a television series and gave rise to countless sequels: *Kappa Tengoku* ("The Kappas' Paradise," the most famous title in the series, 1952); *Sen-*

goku Zouhyō ("Soldiers of the Sengoku Era," 1961); *Kappa Houdai* ("The Fancy-Free Kappa," 1964); *Kappa Furai* ("The Wandering Kappa," 1966); and others.

Kon Shimizu also illustrated a number of books and magazines. He wrote several picture books and short stories but was most famous for his kappas. The kappas had a traditional representation in Japanese folklore, but Shimizu, instead of slavishly following tradition, gave his own rendition of these uncanny creatures in a tender and lovely style. His female kappas were especially sexy and alluring. Shimizu's creations were used as the trademark of Kizakura sake (wine), and in television, magazine, and newspaper advertisements.

Kon Shimizu had been influenced by the works of Ippei Okamoto from his high school days. His comic universe was depicted with restraint and taste but with a fine sense of humor. He used only the brush in his drawings, with a light and expressive touch that perfectly matched the mood of the story. In addition to being a great cartoonist, Shimizu also displayed his talents as a portrait artist, illustrator, book designer, and picture book artist. He died on March 27, 1974.

H.K.

SHIRATO, SANPEI (1932-) Sanpei Shirato is a Japanese comic book artist born February 15, 1932, in Tokyo. Shirato's father was a proletarian artist and his son, soon after graduation from junior high school, started working as a *kamishibai* artist (showing and narrating sequences of cartoons which he had drawn himself). In 1952 he also concerned himself with the puppet show company, Tarōza, for which he did stage design. In 1957 he made his debut as a *kashibon manga* (a cartoonist who draws stories for rental comic books) with his work, *Kogarashi-Kenshi*.

Many more creations followed from the pen of Sanpei Shirato: *Kōga Bugeichō* (a ninja story, 1957), *Onikagejo Hishi* (1959), *Fūma Ninpūden* (1959), *Ninja Bugeichō* (the strip that made him famous, 1959), *Kaze no Ishimaru* (his first feature for a magazine, 1960), *Ōkami Kazō* ("Wolf Boy"), *Seton Dōbutsuki* (an adaptation of Seton's novels), and *Sasuke*, all in 1961; *Shinigami Shōnen Kim* (a Western) and *Haiiroguma no Denki* (an adaptation of Seton's novel, *The Biography of a Grizzly*), both in 1963; *Kamui Den* (1964); *Watari* (1965); *Fūma* (1965); and *Tsuri* ("Fishing," 1967).

"Shoe," Jeff MacNelly. © Tribune Media Services.

Shirato created a number of ninja strips, and he is most famous for those. A ninja is a superhuman being who is able to use the special abilities which he has developed into an art (called ninjutsu). But Shirato's ninjas are not simple superhuman beings: their ninjutsu is scientifically substantiated. Shirato is also famous for the violence contained in his works: scenes of battle and uprisings, depictions of cruelty and malevolence. Setting his work in the past, Shirato also severely castigates the injustice and cruelty present in modern society. His major creation, however, remains *Kamui Den*, which he picked up again in 1982 and on which he has been working ever since.

Shirato's early style was simple and basic like that of Tezuka, but it became gradually more and more realistic. His works have been reprinted often, and they have influenced a whole school of comic book artists: Haruo Koyama, Shōhei Kusunoki, Yashiharu Tsuge, Seiichi Ikeuchi, and others.

H.K.

SHŌCHAN NO BŌKEN (Japan) *Shōchan no Bōken* ("The Adventures of Shōchan") was created by artist Tōfujin and scriptwriter Shousei Oda for the illustrated weekly *Asahigraph* where it first appeared in January 1923.

Shōchan was a clever and courageous little boy who loved adventure and was always accompanied by a pet

"Shōchan no Bōken," Tōfujin (Katsuichi Kabashima). © Asahigraph.

squirrel. *Shōchan no Bōken* was a fantasy strip not unlike the fairy tales of old, in which monsters, demons, and other assorted creatures played an important role. After the great earthquake of 1923, Shōchan moved to the daily *Asahi* (November 1923) and became a very popular feature (around this time the *schōchan-bou*, a white woolen cap with a pom-pom on top, worn by the hero enjoyed a great vogue among Japanese youngsters). The strip ended in 1925 when Tōfujin left the *Asahi* staff.

Actually Tōfujin was the pen name of Katsuichi Kabashima (1888-1965), a noted and talented Japanese illustrator, who taught himself art by copying the ink illustrations of the *National Geographic* magazine. After he left the *Asahi* offices, Kabashima worked as a magazine illustrator for the Kōdansha publishing house. He drew many illustrations for books, especially for the war novels of Minetarō Yamanaka. His graphic style was very realistic and highly detailed (his drawings almost looked like photographs). He particularly enjoyed drawing ships and earned the nickname "Fune no Kabashima" ("Kabashima of the Ships").

Kabashima's artwork on *Shōchan* was not realistic, however, but simple and sharp, showing a fine eye for humorous detail.

H.K.

SHOE (U.S.) Jeff MacNelly was already an award-winning editorial cartoonist when *Shoe*, his comic strip on the trials and tribulations of the avian staff of the east Virginia newspaper the *Treetops Tattler-Tribune*, began in September 1977. It is syndicated by Tibune Media Services who also syndicates this thrice-weekly editorial cartoons and his panel *Pluggers*, which began in 1992. One of the first of the modern wave of editorial cartoonists to draw syndicated humor strips as well as their editorial cartoons, MacNelly had won the Pulitzer Prize in 1972 for his work at the *Richmond News-Leader*.

Shoe was an instant success. The antics of P. Martin "Shoe" Shoemaker, editor-in-chief, and his sloppy but lovable ace reporter and columnist "Perfesser" Cosmo Fishhawk had great appeal to the feature editors who buy comic strips. It didn't hurt that MacNelly won a second Pulitzer Prize for editorial cartooning in 1978.

In 1978 his editorial cartoons also won him the coveted Reuben for Best Cartoonist of the Year voted by the National Cartoonists Society (NCS). So highly did his peers think of *Shoe* that in 1979, MacNelly won a second NCS Reuben statue for *Shoe*. (Jeff MacNelly is the only cartoonist to ever win back-to-back NCS Reuben awards.)

MacNelly, who was born in 1947, is an alumnus of the University of North Carolina—Chapel Hill, where he drew cartoons for the student newspaper. He then worked for *The Chapel Hill Weekly*. His editor there was Jim Shumaker who taught journalism at the university, smoked cigars, and wore high-top black sneakers to work. His nickname was "Shoe," and MacNelly named the strip in his honor.

As an editor, the *Tattler-Tribune*'s Shoe is of the old school. He chomps a cigar, likes a drink now and then, and will occasionally bet on the horses. His counterpoint, Cosmo Fishhawk, is a dedicated writer who can't find anything on his incredibly messy desk; is constantly on a diet; procrastinates; and has an eye for the women.

While drawn as birds, the characters are human in every other way. The supporting cast includes Skyler, who's Cosmo's 12-year-old nephew; Roz, a tough old bird who runs the local diner; Loon, the wacked-out newspaper delivery bird; Muffy Hollandaise, a very preppy cub reporter; and U.S. Senator Battson D. Belfry, who's a laughable semi-scoundral drawn as a caricature of former House of Representatives legend Tip O'Neill.

MacNelly is one of the funniest editorial cartoonists published. *Shoe* allows him to use gags to comment on the state of everything from popular culture to politics in America. For example, Cosmo is watching an ad on television for a tabloid talk show that hypes a program about "men who sleep with daughters of their mothers-in-law." When Sen. Belfry encounters Shoe and Cosmo at Roz's diner he claims he's visiting his constituents to see what they think. Shoe responds, "Actually, we were just thinking how nice it was that you were there and we were here."

The drawing in the strip is full of detail and wild crosshatching in a style MacNelly has made his own. He acknowledged his debt to Walt Kelly by writing an introduction to *Pogo Even Better* in 1982. However, MacNelly never copied but broke new ground in the use of talking animals as he created his own cartoon world.

Big business and government and many of the subjects of his editorial cartoons appear as targets of his humor in *Shoe*. However, he also can indulge in his love of sports as nerdy Skyler is shown playing baseball, football, and basketball and even being accidentally sent through marine boot camp on summer vacation.

A cartoonist who loves to draw and loves the newspaper business, MacNelly has seemingly endless energy. He illustrates the weekly syndicated Dan Barry humor column and in 1992 Tribune Media Services debuted his cartoon panel *Pluggers*. *Shoe*, which celebrated its twentieth year of syndication in 1997, is published in more than 1,000 newspapers.

B.C.

SHŌNEN OJA (Japan) *Shōnen Oja* ("The Boy King") was created by Soji Yamakawa in 1948 and was first published in book form in the *Omoshiro Bunko* series (issues 1 through 4); when the magazine *Omushira Book* was founded, *Shōnen Oja* was among the first features that it published.

Shingo Makimura, alias Shōnen Oja, was a jungle boy brought up by Mera the gorilla in Africa. His father was a Japanese missionary who had discovered a mys-

"Shōnen Oja," Soji Yamakawa. © Omoshiro Bunko.

terious green stone, the cure for an incurable disease, but later disappeared. With his father missing and his mother killed by tropical fever, Shingo was carried away while still a baby by Mera who had saved him from the claws of a lion. Shingo grew up strong and hardy, and he battled many enemies, including the Red Gorilla, the Big Crocodile, the Monster Tree, the cannibalistic Gara-zoku tribe, Ura the Devil, not to mention a brontosaurus. When he was faced with mortal danger and no hope of triumphing by himself, Shingo was saved by the timely intervention of a mysterious stranger Amen Hoteppu (who, in fact, was none other than Yuzō Makimura, Shingo's father, who had escaped from the clutches of his enemies and was hiding under a secret identity).

Shōnen Oja was clearly inspired by E. R. Burroughs's *Tarzan* but it succeeded in creating a flavor all its own and is probably one of the more inspired variations on the ape-man theme. *Shōnen Oja* was not, *stricto sensu*, a comic strip but an illustrated story with text under the pictures, but it exerted a great influence on the post-World War II Japanese comics. Along with such other celebrated features as *Sabaku no Maō, Daiheigenji, Chikyu S.O.S.* and *Shōnen Kenya, Shōnen Oja* represents the Golden Age of Illustrated Stories in Japan.

H.K.

SHORT RIBS (U.S.) Frank O'Neal created *Short Ribs* as a daily strip for NEA Service on November 17, 1958, and it was quickly followed by a Sunday version on June 14, 1959.

Short Ribs is not the usual run-of-the-mill comic strip. The action (or what there is of it) takes place on several levels, spatial and temporal: one day in a castle of the Middle Ages, the next in Dodge City, and the one after that in ancient Egypt. There are accordingly several sets of characters who keep reappearing at intervals (although they never meet, after the fashion of John Dos Passos's novels), and who constitute the weirdest assortment of oddballs ever assembled in one comic strip. Those include a feisty witch ("fastest wand in the kingdom"), an insecure king and his nagging wife, a soft-hearted hangman, a pair of hot-tempered duelists ("I dare you to step over this line"), two self-examining Soviet commissars ("Why do they keep call-

"Short Ribs," Frank O'Neal. © NEA Service.

ing it the Party? Who's having any fun?") and an inept sheriff ("still the slowest gun in the West").

Like the contemporary *Mr. Mum, Short Ribs* utilized the incongruous, the absurd, and the nonsensical. Visual puns abound as do inside jokes (an Egyptian reading a comic strip on a pyramid wall comes upon the inscription: "to be continued on next pyramid").

Short Ribs was never been able to achieve the success it deserved, probably because of the very wealth of the artist's imagination. There was something compulsive, almost manic, in O'Neal's inexhaustible inventiveness and in his staccato but deadpan delivery; and one can well understand the bewilderment of many a reader coming for the first time upon this unorthodox comic strip. Yet *Short Ribs* is a rich lode to mine for the connoisseur who can easily find in it the inspiration for such disparate strips as *The Wizard of Id, Sam's Strip, Tumbleweeds,* and *Broom Hilda.*

In the 1960s Gold Medal reprinted a number of *Short Ribs* strips in pocket-book form. In 1973 O'Neal left the comics field in search of more lucrative pursuits, and his assistant Frank Hill took over the feature. In his hand *Short Ribs* lost much of its freshness and spontaneity, often degenerating into a patchwork of tired clichés and bad puns. It steadily lost circulation until it finally came to an end in May 1982.

M.H.

SHUSTER, JOE (1914-1992) Joe Shuster was an American comic book and comic strip artist born July 10, 1914, in Toronto, Canada. Shuster's family moved to Cleveland, Ohio, in 1923, and it was there that he met writer Jerry Siegel. Together as teenagers the pair began publishing science-fiction fan magazines. In one of the issues, they reviewed Philip Wylie's novel, *Gladiator,* and it was the basis for their biggest creation, *Superman,* which was conceived in 1933.

At the same time, Shuster was studying art and attended John Huntington Polytechnical Institute and the Cleveland School of Art. In 1936, Siegel and Shuster broke into the comic book business with New Fun Comics, Inc., later to become Detective Comics,

Joe Shuster, "Slam Bradley." © National Periodical Publications.

and later National Periodicals by drawing lacklustre adventure strips *like Dr. Occult, Henri Duval, Spy, Federal Men, Radio Squad,* and *Slam Bradley.*

In 1938, however, the company purchased the first *Superman* story from them for $130. Making its first appearance in June's premiere issue of *Action Comics*, the feature was an immediate success, and since then Superman has gone on to become the best-known adventure character in the comics.

Shuster's art was primitive, blocky, even crude, but it was beautifully designed and well conceived. For the most part, Shuster's simple work became the style of the earliest adventure comic books, but his work was generally better and more inspired than the horde of imitative artists who followed. He worked mostly in long shots which presented a full look at the character; Shuster's art was never pretentious or fancy. Instead, he settled for straightforward narrative work that critic and artist James Steranko once likened to the style of editorial cartoonists.

Although Siegel and Shuster made a considerable amount of money on a superficial basis from *Superman* (The *Saturday Evening Post* estimated their 1940 income at $75,000) they owned no part of the character. And even though they opened a shop to produce the ever-burgeoning amounts of work being requested by National and Wayne Boring was probably the best of the shop workers, they never had any rights to the character. Although Shuster drew the character through 1947 both in comic books and for the McClure Syndicate comic strip he was left with nothing.

After a stint with the Bell Syndicate on the Siegel-scripted *Funnyman* strip, Shuster left the industry completely. While Siegel continued to work sporadically in the field and kept his name in the public eye by waging a long-running court battle with National over the rights to *Superman*, Shuster vanished. According to most reports, Shuster was now almost blind in a California nursing home, and the information for this entry was obtained through the intercession of Siegel, who convinced his former coworker to respond after what Siegel called these years of seclusion. In 1977 Shuster, along with his partner Jerry Siegel, won a lifetime annuity from DC Comics, the owner of the *Superman* franchise. He died in Los Angeles on July 30, 1992.

J.B.

SHWE MIN THAR (1932-   ) Shwe Min Thar has been drawing Burmese comics since 1958, contributing both gag and strip cartoons to various magazines and newspapers since the early 1960s. He also has drawn political cartoons, although for almost all of his career, Burma has been under oppressive governments. Thus, his cartoons usually deal with social, rather than political, issues.

For three years, Shwe Min Thar studied at the State School of Fine Arts, where he won top honors; afterward he continued to learn as a student of Pagyi U Thein Han. His paintings have also been popular in Burma, having sold regularly over the years.

Since the 1990s Shwe Min Thar has been doing much caricature, newspaper, and magazine cartoons, and also produces covers of comic books and humorous novels. Like his fellow cartoonists, he works as a freelancer and self-publishes his comic books. Shwe Min Thar's work is characterized by simply executed drawings that use firm but not very bold lines, omit all backgrounds, and pertain mainly to gags.

J.A.L.

SICKLES, NOEL (1910-1982) Noel Sickles was an American cartoonist and illustrator born 1910 in Dayton, Ohio. Sickles received his only formal art training (aside from drawing lessons in high school) from a correspondence course. He started his career in the late 1920s as a political cartoonist for the *Ohio State Journal*. In 1933 he moved to New York and got a job as a staff artist for the Associated Press at $45 a week. At AP, Sickles renewed his friendship with fellow Ohio-born Milton Caniff, who was then doing *Dickie Dare* and, before long, the two men were sharing a common studio. Early in 1934, when John Terry, creator of the aviation strip *Scorchy Smith*, became too ill to work on the feature, AP called on Sickles to ghost the strip (when Terry died later that year, Sickles was allowed to sign his name to the feature).

Noel Sickles's tenure on *Scorchy* was nothing short of revolutionary. As Henry C. Pitz, himself a noted illustrator, stated in a 1949 article: "At the end of six months the technique had changed from sketchy conventional line to much more positive and realistic type of rendering; and the next step introduced light and shade, bringing the pictures into the realm of solid, pictorial, flesh and blood illustration." Soon this new method of drawing caught on like wildfire among adventure strip cartoonists, starting with Milton Caniff who had just shifted from *Dickie Dare* to *Terry and the Pirates*. By 1935 Caniff and Sickles were working closely together. At times, Sickles would pencil a whole sequence of *Terry* while Caniff would write the continuity for *Scorchy*. (In addition they were collaborating, under the pen name of "Paul Arthur" on the *Mr. Coffee Nerves* ad strip for Postum.)

In view of the soaring success of the *Scorchy Smith* strip, Sickles in 1936 asked for a raise on his $125 a week salary. When he was turned down, he quit AP and the comics field, and retired to upstate New York in order to, in his own words, meditate. He was back in New York City in 1939, however, briefly working with Caniff on *Terry* again and ghosting *Patsy* for Mel Graff. In 1940 he returned to illustration and did a series of war drawings for *Life*. These attracted the attention of the War College in Washington, and Sickles was commissioned to do instructional illustration for the armed services. Later he transferred to the Navy Department where he worked on highly classified assignments in which his skills as a draftsman were needed.

At the end of the war, Sickles went back to freelancing for magazines and advertising agencies, doing illustrations and full-color paintings for *Life*, *The Saturday Evening Post*, *Reader's Digest*, *This Week*, and other publications.

Noel Sickles has been honored many times for his work as an illustrator; yet his comic strip career, short as it was, may prove just as significant. With the possible exception of Milton Caniff, no other realistic strip artist has had as much impact on the profession as Sickles. He once summed up his artistic method in these words: "Rather than work in minute detail all over my drawing, I have found that if I take pain to use careful and exact detail in the right places . . . I can handle the balance of my drawing in a broad fashion. The eye will infer a complete statement from such indication."

Sickles retired in the late 1970s and devoted his time to painting Western scenes and landscapes in and around Tucson, Arizona; he died on October 3, 1982. It is a tribute to his stylistic brilliance that the technique he had introduced in the mid-1930s is still

"Il Signor Bonaventura," Sto (Sergio Tofano). © Corriere dei Piccoli.

widely used and emulated more than a decade after his death.

M.H.

SIEGEL, JEROME (1914-1996) Jerome (Jerry) Siegel's first comic book creation was *Superman*, the quintessential comic book character and granddaddy of thousands of superheroes that have since overrun the medium. Siegel's career was haunted by the character ever since its conception in 1933 and its first publication in *National's Action* number 1 in June 1938. Siegel and artist Joe Shuster, a childhood friend, sold the character for $130 and received little else since. In fact, Siegel spent a good portion of his adult life vainly attempting to regain some rights to what is unquestionably the most lucrative character ever to appear in comic books.

Born in Cleveland, Ohio, on October 17, 1914, Siegel loosely based his *Superman* concept on Philip Wylie's 1930 novel, *Gladiator*. *Superman's* origin has been enshrined in Americana, of course, and hundreds of imitations followed. In retrospect, however, Siegel's *Superman* was unique because it featured a superpowered being adopting the guise of a mild-mannered reporter, Clark Kent. Superman's contemporaries were usually normal humans transformed into superheroes. The psychological implications of Siegel's juxtaposition have been studied for years.

But despite its now eminent position, the *Superman* strip was originally rejected by every major newspaper-strip house of the time. Subsequently, Siegel's first published comic work appeared in an advertising supplement for the *Cleveland Shopping News* in 1936. His first comic book work began appearing shortly thereafter. Written mostly for the law-and-order oriented *Detective Comics*, it consisted of pedestrian cops and robbers and adventure material.

In 1938, the publishers of *Detective* purchased the rights to *Superman*, published it, and Siegel and Shuster's character immediately took off. Siegel continued to work on the character until 1948, his tales consisting of little morality plays and his characterization of *Superman* being more sedate than that of later writers. Litigation surrounding the ownership of the character followed almost immediately.

Although Siegel constantly claimed that he was blackballed from the comic book industry as a result of the suit, his list of credits is as long as any in the field. But many industry observers find it strange that none of his later creations were ever successful over long periods. Many believe that while Siegel may not have been blackballed, he may have been consistently punished for his attempts to regain *Superman*.

Over the years, Siegel worked on many newspaper strips, including *Superman, Funnyman, Reggie Van Twerp, Ken Winston, Tallulah*, and others. He also was Ziff-Davis's first comic book director.

Siegel had little of his comic book writing published in his later years. Until 1975, in fact, he lived a reclusive life in West Los Angeles before he began publically commenting on his many fights with National: he wrote an article on the litigation in the fourth issue of *Inside Comics*, an industry magazine, and attended his first comic convention in San Diego, where he received the conclave's Inkpot Award. Yielding to public pressure, DC (successor to National) awarded Siegel (along with his partner Joe Shuster) a lifetime annuity. He lived quietly in Los Angeles until his death on January 28, 1996.

J.B.

SIGNOR BONAVENTURA, IL (Italy) A playright, an interpreter, and finally a cartoonist, Sergio Tofano (better known as "Sto") produced one of the most celebrated characters in Italian comics for the readers of the *Corriere dei Piccoli*; a character who has been beloved by at least three generations of readers: il Signor Bonaventura. Tofano's simple line and elementary message were the main ingredients in Bonaventura's popularity for more than 50 years, during which time hundreds upon hundreds of whimsical stories were turned out.

Il Signor Bonaventura ("Mister Bonaventura"), starring a dapperly attired, clownish-looking little man, first appeared in October 1917, and ran every single week until 1955; it was again revived in 1970. An optimistic counterpart to the luckless *Happy Hooligan* (whose adventures also ran in the *Corriere dei Piccoli*), Bonaventura, whatever the calamities that befell him in the course of the story, always ended up winning the big reward (in the form of a one-million lire bill, later increased to one-billion, due to inflation).

In the course of his wanderings in search of some good deed to perform, Bonaventura is always accompanied by his very small and elongated basset hound. His son, Pizziri, always gets into trouble playing with the millions his father has won, while many other colorful characters populate the strip, such as the handsome bar-fly Cecè, the ever-present Barbariccia, Comissar Sperassai, the lugubrious Crepacuore, the meek Omobono, and many others equally as funny. Every *Bonaventura* episode starts with the characteristic verse: *Qui comincia l'avventura/ Del Signor Bonaventura . . .* ("Here begins the adventure/ Of Mister Bonaventura . . .") and then winds its merry way to a crescendo of lightheadedness and optimism, regardless of time, place, or situation.

In 1927 and again in 1953, Tofano adapted his own comic strip to the theater. In 1942 he directed a film of *Il Signor Bonaventura* starring Pablo Stoppa. In 1966 Bonaventura appeared again on stage with Paolo Poli in the title role. Since Sergio Tofano's death in 1973, the strip has been drawn by Carlo Peroni and others.

G.B.

SIGURD (Germany)

Sigurd is a genuinely German comic book feature with a young blond knight errant as its hero. The name and saga of the original *Sigurd* is almost identical to that of Siegfried. The comic book *Sigurd,* despite the fighting prowess and seeming invincibility of its hero cannot boast an impenetrable skin like Siegfried's, however.

Sigurd was created by Hansrudi Wäscher and first published in 1953 by Walter Lehning's comics group as the fifth series put on the market in the Italian or piccolo format of 6⅝ × 2⅞ inches. Each issue had 32 pages printed in black and white on newsprint plus a color cover. The books were published weekly and ran continued stories much in the manner of American movie or radio serials with an unavoidable climax and questions about how the hero could possibly escape his latest cliff-hanging predicament to ensure the sale of next week's issue which, of course, starts out with a recapitulation of the goings-on.

The adventures of Sigurd are shared by Bodo, a suave, Gawain-type knight. They were soon joined by Cassim, an orphaned boy Sigurd had saved from a house set afire by pillaging Viking pirates. The daring trio embarked on a journey with damsels in distress, crooked knights, dragons in the form of dinosaurs, and the like, waiting at each and every turn of the road. Like the original Siegfried and/or Sigurd of legend and myth, the comic book Sigurd has a run-in with Etzel (Attila the Hun).

Except for the first 40 issues, Hansrudi Wäscher wrote all the stories he drew. Although his graphic style is relatively simple (a consequence of having to draw to the same scale as the book page), even stiff or wooden, it never failed to attract a large following, for

"Sigurd," Hansrudi Wäscher. © Hansrudi Wäscher.

Wäscher managed to tell exciting stories. Wäscher's style is still emulated by up-and-coming fan artists.

The first run of *Sigurd* piccolos ended with number 324 and was followed by 87 reprint issues. Earlier, a full-sized color comic book, reprinting three of the piccolo pages to one page, had been started. With number 125, this *Sigurd* comic book switched to original material and continued to issue number 257. *Sigurd's* life ended when the Lehning group folded in 1968. The feature had a seven-issue comeback in 1971, but production was stopped when problems arose over the estate of Walter Lehning. The death of publisher Lehning brought about the end of a line of comics that is still fondly remembered as one of the uniquely German entries in the history of comic books. *Sigurd* may have been the most popular of this line of comics, as it was also reprinted in *Harry*, a magazine combining comics and text features. For some time, *Harry* even carried a specially produced *Sigurd* comic strip. And, in 1964, a *Sigurd* special containing an illustrated novel was published.

In 1976 a first short-lived series of *Sigurd* reprints was published. Finally in 1980 publisher Norbert Hethke, devoted to reprinting 1950s comic books, started reprinting the entire *Sigurd* material. Thanks to good contacts with Hansrudi Wäscher, new material was added. Some of the reprints have been done as deluxe editions.

W.F.

SILAS see McCay, Winsor.

SILLY SYMPHONIES (U.S.)

A Sunday strip created by artists of the Walt Disney Studios (Al Taliaferro most notably) and published in the 1930s, *Silly Symphonies* was named for a Disney series of musical animated shorts of the period, and first appeared together with the first *Mickey Mouse* Sunday page on January 10, 1932.

The *Silly Symphonies* strip consisted of several different narratives featuring unrelated characters, sometimes based on studio releases of the time, and running for widely varied periods of time. The first and longest *Silly Symphony* story carried no subtitle (as did the later narratives), and featured the sometimes epic adventures of a ladybug complete with antenna, whose wings had been stylized into a natty spotted jacket, named Bucky Bug. The opening Bucky Bug saga ended on March 4, 1934, with Bucky's marriage to June, and

A Silly Symphony: "The Practical Pig," Al Taliaferro. © Walt Disney Productions.

on March 11, 1934, the second *Silly Symphonies* narrative, *Birds of a Feather,* began. The Bucky Bug story was partly reprinted in a *Big Little Book* of 1934, titled: *Mickey Mouse Presents a Walt Disney Silly Symphony.*

Birds of a Feather was followed (with a one-week break for a full *Mickey Mouse* page) by *Peculiar Penguins* on July 1, 1934. Next were: *The Little Red Hen* on September 16, 1934 (in which Donald Duck made his first strip appearance on the same date); *The Boarding-School Mystery,* with Max Hare and Toby Tortoise (in which the prototype of Bugs Bunny, Max Hare, appeared) on December 23, 1934; *Ambrose the Robber Kitten* on February 24, 1935; *Cookieland* on April 28, 1935; *Three Little Kittens* on July 28, 1935; *The Life and Adventures of Elmer Elephant* on October 27, 1935; *The Further Adventures of the Three Little Pigs* on January 19, 1936; and *Donald Duck* on August 30, 1936. Beginning with *Donald Duck,* the *Silly Symphonies* feature carried a weekly subtitle for the first time, appearing as *Silly Symphony Featuring Donald Duck,* while, also for the first time, the rhyming dialogue was abandoned.

In July, 1937, the *Mickey Mouse* Sunday companion feature became simply *Donald Duck,* and the *Silly Symphony* was abandoned. (Later in 1939, it was revived for a short time as part of the title of a *Pluto* half-page, which had been running earlier as *Mother Pluto,* and then as simply *Pluto the Pup*: the elongated title was *Silly Symphony Featuring Pluto the Pup,* which ran from September 3, 1939, until November 10, 1940, when a new strip titled *Little Hiawatha, A Silly Symphony,* began and ran until November 16, 1941.) After the *Donald Duck* title addition, the single Sunday Disney page added further weekly half-pages: from 1937 on, as many as five or six different Disney-bylined half-pages could be found running at the same time, such as *Mickey Mouse, Donald Duck, Pluto, Jose Carioca,* and an animated feature serial (such as *Snow White, Pinocchio,* etc.). *Silly Symphonies,* as a strip title, got lost in the shuffle, disappearing after *Little Hiawatha.* (The Three Little Pigs, revived as strip characters in *The Practical Pig* on May 1, 1938, and Elmer the Elephant returned in *Timid Elmer* on December 4, 1938, but both ran without the *Silly Symphony* title.)

Physically, *Silly Symphonies* opened as a narrow, page-topper Sunday strip, enlarging to a full half-page on September 22, 1935, in the middle of the Three Little Kittens story. *Birds of a Feather, The Little Red Hen, Peculiar Penguins, Ambrose, Three Little Kittens,* and *Elmer* all appeared as *Silly Symphonies* animated cartoons in the 1930s. One other *Big Little Book* collection based on the strip: *Walt Disney's Silly Symphonies Stories* was published in 1936. This included *The Little Red Hen, Birds of a Feather,* and some more *Bucky Bug* adventures.

B.B.

SILVER ROY (Spain) *Silver Roy* (subtitled "The Lone Commando") saw the light of print in the first issue of the revived comic magazine, *Pulgarcito* (1947). The strip was also published in various annuals, as well as in the magazine *Super Pulgarcito* from 1949 until its demise in 1951.

The strip's creator was Bosch Penalva, who later left the comic field to devote himself to cover illustration for juvenile novels, a genre in which he excelled with his flair for color and his facility of line.

His hero, Roy Silver, was an agent for the United Nations, stationed first in the waters of the China seas, later in the jungles of India. The strip was bathed in an atmosphere of Asian intrigue and opium dens very reminiscent of *Terry and the Pirates* and *Jungle Jim.* The hero was characterized by the pith helmet which always covered his head, and by his anti-Japanese feelings, both typical of an era influenced by American war movies in which the Japanese were the villains.

L.G.

SILVER STARR IN THE FLAME WORLD (Australia) Created by Stanley Pitt, the strip first appeared in the *Sydney Sunday Sun* on November 24, 1946. Initially, the strip was given the entire tabloid centerspread and the result was breathtaking. This allowed Pitt a freedom of layout that was closer to comic books than newspaper strips. Pitt utilized this freedom by presenting sweeping panoramas; long, towering panels down the side of the page or large central panels that dominated those surrounding it. Pitt's beautiful artwork was complemented by delicate pastel tones and shades, tastefully administered by a master colorist. The sheer beauty of the early *Silver Starr* pages has never been equalled in Australia.

Silver Starr was Pitt's tribute to *Alex Raymond* and *Flash Gordon* and there is no denying that he borrowed heavily from that strip for his inspiration. Silver was an Australian soldier who had returned from the war to join an expedition into the earth's interior. Though their backgrounds were different, Silver and Flash were the same kind of dynamic hero. The trip to the earth's core was lead by a scientist, Onro, the counterpart of Dr. Zharkov. Another member of the team was Dyson, whose features were based on those of Errol Flynn. (Over the years, Flynn's features found their way into many Pitt illustrations.) As this trio ground their way through the earth's crust in a rocket-type ship with a great drill on the bow, their radar-television threw up an image of a beautiful, red-haired girl who was surrounded by lashing tongues of bluish flame. This was the lovely Pristine (De Solvo) Queen of the Flameworld and Pitt's compliment to *Dale Arden.* This was the setting for a series of thrilling adventures that was to earn *Silver Starr* a permanent place in the history of Australian comic art.

While the story line never reached the imagination heights of *Flash Gordon,* it was entertaining and provided Pitt with exotic locales on which to employ his talents. Under Pitt's deft handling, the underground caverns and rock formation scenes came to life; as did the scenes of seas of molten lava and the ship winding its way through rock and water. The earth's interior was peopled by a race of giants, with massive heads, and a race of scaly Ape-men all of whom made ideal subjects for Pitt's fertile imagination. The one weakness of the strip was that it never produced an antagonist of the calibre of *Ming the Merciless*. The sequence of villains Ungra, Tarka, and Gorla were stereotypes, who were always overshadowed by the personality of Silver.

Silver Starr suffered a series of reductions in the printed size and when it was, eventually, reduced to 6 × 6½ area, Pitt left the paper. The final *Silver Starr* strip appeared on November 14, 1948.

During the early 1950s, there were six reprint comic books published by Young's Merchandising. Starting in 1958, Cleveland Press reprinted these stories, again, along with another four original *Silver Starr* stories. Although it had only a short life and a comparatively limited circulation, the impact of *Silver Starr* was sufficient to establish the reputation of Stanley Pitt for all time.

J.R.

SILVER SURFER (U.S.) When writer and editor Stan Lee and artist Jack Kirby created the *Fantastic Four* strip in 1961, neither was aware of the fantastic following the feature and subsequent creations would garner among older teenagers and college students, a market rarely, if ever, reached by comic books. They eagerly accepted Lee's moralizations, his often sophomoric rationalizations, and even his disorganized and inconsistent theories on humanity. In response, he continued creating stranger and more confusing civilizations and races, all of them used to grind out the Lee line on civilization as we know it. There was the Watcher, a sort of intergalactic storyteller; there were the Inhumans, a race of superhumans who lived apart from humanity; there were the Kree and Skrull galaxies, two more superhuman races who constantly battled over long-contested racial differences; and there was even Galactus, characterized almost godlike by Lee.

And from Galactus came the Silver Surfer, the former's herald and top henchman. A native of another of Lee's super galaxies, the Silver Surfer was extremely powerful: his body was covered by a coat of silvery galactic glaze which would protect him from anything in the universe; he had an atomic surfboard that he used for instantaneous transport; and, to make him complete, he was almost limitlessly powerful. Premiered in *Fantastic Four* number 48 (March 1966), the character became instantly successful and Lee made him his own, personal Jesus Christ-surrogate. "I do my most obvious moralizing in the *Silver Surfer*," the writer/editor once said.

At first an occasional guest star in the *Fantastic Four* strip, Lee eventually revealed that the Surfer had been sentenced to earth permanently by Galactus for showing too much concern for humans, whom the Surfer rarely understood and always pitied. For several appearances in the *Fantastic Four*, the Surfer traveled the earth, constantly trying to be of help, constantly misconstruing a situation, constantly fighting against his will. Almost every story ended with his moralizing about his unfair imprisonment on earth and earthlings' inhumanity to him and other beings. A galactic crybaby of embarrassing proportions, comic critic

Dwight Decker once complained, claiming the feature was for those looking for spoon-fed moral instruction.

Nevertheless, the *Silver Surfer* became phenomenally popular, prompting Lee to launch the character in his own title, *The Silver Surfer*, which premiered in August 1968 with artwork by John Buscema. The book was immediately hailed by most critics as the finest and most sensitive strip of its time, although there remained a vocal minority who complained of its facile philosophizing and childish ethical values. But the strip won fan-issued Alley awards in 1968 and 1969 for best full-length stories, and the character was voted most popular in 1968. Buscema's artwork, unlike the controversial stories, was universally hailed as brilliant and innovative.

After 18 issues, however, *The Silver Surfer* folded due to poor sales, Lee blaming its demise on the general comic-reading public's inability to handle more mature features. The character has since appeared sporadically as a guest in many Marvel strips. He reappeared briefly in his own title in 1982, and again in 1988 to 1989.

J.B.

SIMMONDS, POSY (1945-   ) British cartoonist Rosemary Elizabeth "Posy" Simmonds was born August 9, 1945, in Cookham Dene, near Maidenhead, Berkshire. A farmer's daughter, she was educated at Queen Mary's School, Caversham, and studied fine art and French at the Sorbonne in Paris and graphic design at the Central School, London. After illustrating for *The Times*, she began her first regular daily cartoon feature, *Bear* in *The Sun* on November 17, 1969. In 1972 she moved to *The Guardian* as an illustrator. From May 1977, while John Kent, creator of *The Guardian's* weekly strip *Varoomschka*, was away in America for six months, her idea for a replacement was accepted. Recalling one of her childhood favorites, she started by showing what had happened to "The Silent Three," a schoolgirl mystery originally drawn in the 1950s by Evelyn Flinders in *School Friend*. This soon developed into a contemporary comedy of manners centered around long-suffering Wendy Weber and her family and friends.

Posy Simmonds pinpoints the everyday crises among suburban liberals, reflecting and satirizing *The Guardian's* own readership. In 1981 she produced *True Love*, an original graphic novel, exposing the alluring fallacies of British girl's romance comics. She left the newspaper strip to create children's books in color strip form, including *Fred* about the secret nighttime stardom of an ordinary domestic cat, which was adapted into an animated film in 1996. She has also written film scripts and television documentaries. In 1997 she completed a graphic novel to be serialized in *The Guardian*.

She is ambidextrous and has invented her own distinctive lettering font, jokingly called "Anal Retentive." She was voted Cartoonist of the Year in Granada Television's awards in 1980 and in the British Press Awards in 1981.

P.G.

SIMON, JOSEPH (1915-   ) American comic book writer, artist, editor, and publisher, Joseph Simon was born October 11, 1915, in Rochester, New York. Joe Simon began his comic book career in 1940 as an artist/writer/editor on the *Blue Bolt* adventure strip. He also helped create some of Novelty's minor features like *Hillman* and *Gunmaster*. About the same time, however, he was an editor at Fox comics and worked on their major strip, *Blue Beetle*.

In 1941, Simon and Jack Kirby began their famed partnership and created the legendary *Captain America* feature. Much has been said about the working relationship of the pair, many claiming Simon was the business genius while Kirby handled the creative end, but it was obvious that Simon had a considerable hand in creating the red, white, and blue character that made Timely a major force in the comic industry of the time. The pair also created the *Fiery Mask* and *Young Allies* strip for Timely.

They next moved to National in 1942 and created a horde of adventure features, including *Boy Commandos* and *Newsboy Legion*. They also handled characters like *Manhunter, Robotman,* and a revamped *Sandman*. Simon is credited with creating the *Real Fact* book. Harvey was the next stop for the team, and, in 1945, Simon and Kirby created the stellar *Boy's Ranch* Western feature. After Harvey, there came books for Hillman and Crestwood before the pair formed their own outfit, Mainline, with Simon as publisher. Formed in 1954, the company folded the next year, and, in 1956, Simon and Kirby split their long partnership.

In the years immediately following the breakup, Simon spent most of his time with the Archie group as an artist, editor, and writer. During his tenure, he created two superhero books of note, *Private Strong* and *The Fly*. Neither were outstanding, but they were Archie's only two nonhumor books of the period.

Simon eventually returned to National in 1968 to write, draw, and edit a new book entitled *Brother Power, The Geek*. Attempting to cash in on the peace movement of the time, the Geek was a hippie sort who was really just an animated dummy. Although it was a rare opportunity to see Simon's artwork and storytelling ability without Kirby's influence, the book was badly done and lasted only two issues. In 1973 in the midst of America's Watergate presidential crisis Simon launched *Prez*, an unlikely tale of a teenager made president with the help of an unscrupulous machine politician. Another attempt to capitalize on the political state of the nation, the book was a dismal failure and folded the next year. In the late 1970s he moved on to advertising.

Over the years, much has been said of the Kirby half of Simon and Kirby, most critics simply assuming Simon did little or none of the team's creative work. This has not been proven, however, and it may still be some time before Simon's contributions to the creative efforts of Simon and Kirby are fully known.

J.B.

SINNOTT, JOE (1926-   ) American comic book artist born in Saugerties, New York, on October 16, 1926, Sinnott, joined the navy after high school and served in the Pacific. After his discharge, he worked three years in a cement factory and finally entered the Cartoonists and Illustrators School in 1949. While there, he published his first comic book work, *Trudi*, a five-page filler for St. John. Tom Gill, one of his instructors, then hired him as an assistant for his Dell and Timely work. Sinnott began working directly for Timely in March 1951, penciling and inking everything from crime to horror to humor to superhero strips. He also produced material for Dell, Charlton, Treasure Chest, and Classic Illustrated before limiting himself to Timely/Atlas/Marvel in 1959.

One of the most outstanding inkers in comic book history, Sinnott began producing his best work when he and Jack Kirby began working together on a regular basis in November 1965. Starting with *Fantastic Four* number 44, Sinnott became Kirby's regular inker on the strip. Perhaps the greatest comic artist of all time, Kirby had a big, brawling style which highlighted exaggerated anatomy, gadgety panels, sprawling layouts, and general mayhem. Sinnott tightened Kirby's pencils considerably, smoothing out his occasional rough spots and weaknesses. He also added slickness and more blacks than Kirby had previously utilized. The *Fantastic Four* became a showcase of graphic excellence, and when Kirby abandoned the feature in late 1971, it was Sinnott who was given the task of maintaining continuity. In rapid-fire order, John Romita, John Buscema, and Rich Buckler all attempted to fill Kirby's spot, but Sinnott remained the inker and kept the strip as Kirby-esque as possible.

Sinnott remained at Marvel until 1992, working on every major title, from *The Avengers* to *X-Men*. He also illustrated the one-shot *Life of Pope John Paul II* in 1983. After his departure from Marvel he inked some *Zorro* comic books and illustrated several stories from the Bible.

J.B.

SIOPAWMAN (Philippines) What superhero can boast of having the largest nose, the most rotund body, the softest muscles, the least amount of hair on the head (without being completely bald), and buck-teeth? No one else but, Siopawman!

On July 9, 1963, *Siopawman* began in the first issue of *Alcala Fight Komix* and has been appearing for that publication every other week. This laughable, well-meaning, super-misfit was the brainchild of Larry Alcala, who devotes much of his spare time to writing, lettering, and illustrating *Kalabog en Bosyo, Tipin, Congressman Kalog, Laber Boy, Dr. Sabak en his Monster, Mang Ambo,* and a slew of other features and editorial cartoons for newspapers, magazines, and comic books. Alcala spends the rest of the time as a professor at the University of the Philippines.

Siopawman originally came from the planet Siopaw. Somehow, his big nose and unusual shape irritated the rest of the inhabitants and he was unceremoniously shipped out to the planet earth. Coincidentally, *Siopaw* is also the name of a Chinese pastry that is quite popu-

"Siopawman," Larry Alcala. © Alcala Fight Komix.

lar in the Philippines. Needless to say, the hero bears a strong resemblance to this exotic delicacy.

Siopawman can withstand the hail of bullets as well as the most devastating blows that his arch-enemies can lay upon his fat-laden body; he is as invulnerable as Superman. And like Superman he has an *S* on his uniform. He also wears a cape (to hide the patch on his shorts). His hostile opponents are among the most wickedly ingenious in the annals of comic history. Alcala's fertile imagination created a bizarre array of villains who are just as wacky as his main character. Among them are vegetable creatures, space aliens, local crooks, berserk geniuses, and the pulsating, quivering, Jello-Man! Siopawman gives no sign of slowing down after 35 years of ordeals and tribulations.

A fascinating aspect of the series is Larry Alcala's clever use of American and Filipino words, with his inventive puns and play on words, to convey a multiplicity of meanings. Alcala is also an entertaining and innovative storyteller with a great sense of humor.

His ability to control the continuity and the flow of movement in his strips, and the masterful manner in which he visualizes his ideas make him one of the foremost experts in sequential storytelling. The economy of his linework and the simplicity of his approach underlies his sophisticated understanding of the medium. He has gained the admiration of the readers and the respect of the industry and has distinguished himself in the field of education and communications. He is the recipient of the much coveted CCMM (Citizens Council for Mass Media) award.

O.J.

SI YEOO KI (China) *Si Yeoo Ki* ("The Westward Pilgrimage") was written by Wu Tcheng-en in the 16th century: an allegorical novel of fantasy and the supernatural, it has long since become a classic of Chinese literature. Its hero, Souen Wu-kong the monkey, became, through arduous training, a super-being capable of reaching up to the heavens and digging down to the center of the earth. Proclaiming himself the equal of the Celestial Emperor, he brought toil and turmoil to the kingdoms of earth and the skies. Exceeded, Buddha himself had the meddlesome monkey chained to the Mount of the Five Elements (there is a striking similarity with Prometheus). Five hundred years later, having converted to Buddhism, Souen Wu-kong escorted the monk Santsang in his westward pilgrimage in search of the sacred Buddhic scriptures.

Si Yeoo Ki is an account of this long and perilous journey in which Souen Wu-kong accomplished the most brilliant feats, fought spirits and demons, and finally achieved the ultimate goal. In their quest Santsang and Wu-kong are joined by two more of the monk's disciples: Tchou Pa-kie the pig, and Ho-chang the bearded warrior. The four travelers constitute the allegorical personifications of four different attributes of man: *Santsang* the mind, *Wu-kong* the heart, *Pa-kie* the appetites, and *Ho-chang* brute force. The Chinese theater has maintained and reinforced this tradition by giving the stage protagonists masks through which their primal attributes are expressed.

The People's Republic of China has kept these old legends alive, taking away their more metaphysical connotations. In the 1950s and 1960s a series of comic books illustrating the different stages of the westward journey were issued by the People's Institute of Art and Culture in Peking. The most interesting episode, titled

"Si Yeoo Ki," Tchao Hong-pen and Tsien Siao-tai.

81 Adventures, which tells of the pilgrims' encounters with the skeleton witch, was adapted by Wang Sunpei and drawn by Tchao Hong-pen and Tsien Siao-tai. The book proved so popular that it was translated into English and French in 1964 (with a second printing in 1974) for distribution abroad.

The drawings of the comic book version of *Si Yeoo Ki* are in the traditional Chinese manner, there are no balloons, and each panel (with a printed text running underneath) fills an entire page, making it more an illustrated book than a comic book as we know it. The story is nonetheless fascinating in its minuteness and detail. (The tale has been widely known outside China, especially in Japan where a comic strip parody, *Shifumai Yamana's Songoku*, appeared as early as 1930.)

M.H.

SJORS EN SJIMMIE (Netherlands) *Sjors en Sjimmie* ("George and Jimmy") stars two boys, one white and one black, in humorous adventures. Originally titled simply *Sjors*, it starred a boy and his friends in the tradition of *Our Gang*. *Sjors*, it must be noted, was actually named *Perry Winkle* and was the star of the *Winnie Winkle* Sunday page for a number of years. The Sunday *Winnie Winkle* enjoyed a large success in Europe in the 1930s and was published under a number of different titles in France, Germany, and (among others) the Netherlands. *Sjors* appeared in *Sjors Weekblad* ("George's Weekly"), which was first published on January 2, 1936, as a children's supplement of the newspaper *Panorama* and continued until October 31, 1941, when it became a casualty of World War II.

At the time *Sjors* was an original Dutch comic strip and had been so since 1938 when Frans Piët had taken over writing and drawing the strip when Branner was changing the tone and lineup of his Sunday page. Owning the rights to their title, the Dutch were able to continue the strip on their own, subtly changing it over the years so that its origins are nothing more than a

"Skeets," Dow Walling. © Herald-Tribune Syndicate.

long-forgotten memory today. The never-aging *Sjors* is more than six decades old.

There was a six-year hiatus from 1941 to 1947, however. But by then the weekly supplement of *Panorama* was back in print, ultimately becoming an independent publication with considerably more pages than the original four, of which *Sjors* had been the only comic feature. From 1951 to 1954 the comic book was titled *Rebellenclub* ("Rebels' Club"), from 1954 to 1968 *Sjors van de Rebellenclub* ("George of the Rebels' Club"), and since 1968, once again simply *Sjors*. By that time the strip itself had been rechristened *Sjors en Sjimmie*, incorporating Sjors' black costar, Sjimmie.

Sjors en Sjimmie was continued in 1970 by artist Jan Kruis who later on turned the artwork over to Jan Steeman, noted for also having done the semifunny science-fiction comic *Arad en Maya* ("Arad and Maya") for the *Sjors* magazine. Other originally Dutch series published in *Sjors* over the decades include *Tommy's Avonturen* ("Tommy's Adventures") by Piet Broos, *Monki* by B. J. Reith, *Olaf Noort*, *Cliff Rendall*, and other strips by Bert Bus, plus *Brammetje Bram* by Eddy Ryssack. *Sjors* and other strips serialized in the magazine have been reprinted regularly in album-sized books.

W.F.

SKEETS (U.S.) Former King Features cartoonist Dow Walling created his gentle strip about a young boy, *Skeets*, in 1932, debuting on May 1. Syndicated by the *New York Herald Tribune* as a Sunday strip only, it depicted the simple premise of the innocent boyhood adventures of Skeets, his passive parents, pals Button-Nose, Whiffle, cousin "Eggy" Hanty, Pudge Willikins, and others.

Owing much influence from and noticeable imitation of Percy Crosby's *Skippy*, the mischievous antics of the neighborhood boys mirrored a Norman Rockwell portrayal of baseball, skating, fishing, dips in the pond, and trips to the candy store. Occasionally, spirited dream sequences, visits to Santa, and poignant episodes of youthful reflection hinted at Walling's aesthetic range, but most of the time the feature remained dedicated to commonplace, domestic hijinks. Walling never developed the characters' personalities to any degree, relying primarily on formulaic, situational humor. His semicrude artistry simplified notice-

ably during the late 1940s, yet his earlier work displayed unique and innovative attention to environmental detail not seen in other strips of the genre. The strip was reprinted in the 1940s in *Peter Rabbit* comic books.

Childless himself, the cartoonist drew the charming exploits of his fictional boy with the pillbox hat until its last appearance on July 15, 1951. Walling was a charter member of the National Cartoonists Society.

B.J.

SKIPPY (U.S.) In 1919 Percy Crosby, fresh out of World War I, started his long collaboration with the humor magazine *Life*. In the pages of the old *Life* there appeared, with increasing frequency, a 10-year-old curbstone philosopher named Skippy who soon became so popular with readers that Crosby decided to syndicate his adventures to interested newspapers in the middle 1920s. In 1928 King Features took over the distribution of both the daily strip and Sunday page of *Skippy* (while Crosby wisely retained ownership).

"Skippy," Percy Crosby. © Percy L. Crosby.

"Skyroads," Dick Calkins. © National Newspaper Syndicate.

Skippy Skinner, floppily attired in a nondescript checked hat, oversize jacket, and short pants, held forth on the neighborhood curbside, flanked by the fawning court of his pals, Sooky Wayne the slob, Sidney Saunders the schemer, and a few other wide-eyed life observers. Skippy was not a nice kid (even by comic strip standards), he had none of the spontaneousness of Perry Winkle or the high spirits of the Katzenjammers. His view of the adult world was bitter and disenchanted, and there was a viciousness in his attitude to others. He was forever calculating the odds, pitting his wits against the institutions, and manipulating his little companions for his own purposes. In short, he was a fully developed adult with the appearance of a kid.

There was great humor in *Skippy*, but it was always tinged with sadness, even pessimism. More often than not it dealt in humiliation, defeat, and alienation, thus offering the readers a foretaste of the themes that Charles Schulz would later develop in *Peanuts*. Crosby's drawing style (closer to straight illustration than to the cartoon) has been praised to the skies by some critics, but it was probably a bit too academic for the purpose. (In the 1920s and all through the 1930s, a top piece, *Always Belittlin'*, was tacked on to the Sunday *Skippy*: also a child strip, it reflected even more strongly the author's misanthropy in its depiction of small tots busily engaged in putting one another down.)

Percy Crosby became seriously ill in 1942 and was soon unable to continue drawing the strip. In 1943 he formally withdrew *Skippy* rather than have it ghosted by somebody else (a rare occurrence in a profession not particularly noted for its high ethical standards). While it lasted (and with the exception of the last painfully shaky episodes) *Skippy* was a well-crafted and thoughtfully written feature, but it somehow fell short of the mark, and its potential was never fully realized. (In 1971 the old *Skippy* daily strips were being resyndicated by Windy City Features.)

Percy Crosby's strip has inspired two movies: the 1931 *Skippy* (which launched the career of kid actor Jackie Cooper) and the less successful *Sooky* (1932). The 1931 film won an Oscar for best direction (Norman Taurog).

M.H.

SKYROADS (U.S.) *Skyroads* was created in 1929 by two former World War I pilots, Dick Calkins and Lester J. Maitland, for the John F. Dille syndicate. Calkins, however, was already overburdened with the drawing of *Buck Rogers* and he turned the artwork over to his two assistants, Zack Mosley and especially Russell Keaton.

The first strip opened with a stirring address by Maitland, the first paragraph of which might be useful to quote in its entirety: "Since the beginning man has struggled to conquer his environment. The lands of the earth and the waters of the sea have come under his dominion. The air alone remained unchallenged. Earthbound man has gazed fascinated at the limitless blue above him, yearning to ride the ocean of the air. This generation has seen the age-old yearning realized."

After that soaring announcement, the basic plot of the strip (as given in the next panel) must have seemed to many a reader as something of a letdown: Ace Ames and Buster Evans find themselves owners of a new biplane. They form a partnership, Skyroads, Unlimited. In a nutshell this represented the predicament of the early aviation strips: the discrepancy between the lofty aims and the pedestrian plot. In the case of *Skyroads*, the authors tried to alleviate the situation by inserting at least one didactic panel in each strip, explaining the importance of wind factors and detailing the workings of wing flaps; this practice, however, had the disadvantage of slowing down the action considerably, without appreciably enlightening the reader, and it was soon discontinued.

Over the years, *Skyroads* featured several teams of actors playing in alternance, as it were: Ace Ames and Buster Evans disappeared around 1933 (along with Maitland) and were succeeded by *Hurricane Hawk*, a dashing and resourceful air devil. At this point Russell Keaton was the sole author of the strip (even signing his name to it) and some of the adventures he concocted were excellent in the quality of their suspense and the clarity of their drawing. The episode pitting Hurricane against a hooded legion of air pirates led by a malevolent dwarf known as the Crimson Skull was particularly memorable. In 1939 Hurricane was replaced by Speed McCloud, then by another hero, Clipper Williams. With the assistance of a score of young boys and girls known as the Flyin' Legion he cleaned the skies of foreign agents and saboteurs. Around 1942 the strip vanished into the wild blue yonder for the last time.

After the first couple of years, *Skyroads* turned into one of the better-drawn aviation strips, with Russell Keaton firmly at the controls. It cannot be ranked among the top strips of the decade but it certainly deserves some recognition for its high spirits, unflagging action, and flavorful plot.

A few of the early episodes of *Skyroads* were reprinted in paperback form by Edwin Aprill, Jr. (Ann Arbor, 1966).

M.H.

SLIM JIM (U.S.) One of the most popular of all early American comic strips, *Slim Jim* is also notable for showcasing some of the most original, though virtually forgotten, comic strip art. The feature began as *Circus Solly*, originally a daily strip in the *Chicago Daily News*. Distributed in Sunday format by the World Color Printing Co. of St. Louis in September 1910, dozens of rural papers soon carried the strip under its new title, *Slim Jim and the Force*. The artist was George Frink, an authentically funny cartoonist who is hardly remembered today; he also illustrated two Peck's *Bad Boy* books: *Peck's Bad Boy and the Circus* and *Peck's Bad Boy and the Cowboys*.

Frink's style was sketchy and filled with native humor. His art was original but reminiscent of McCutcheon, Joe Donahey, and early Herriman. There was free movement in his panels and as much slapstick as in *Opper*.

Slim Jim was an outrageously tall and thin character. His three eternal pursuers, the force, were comical constables and therein is the basic plot for years of merriment: Slim Jim each week manages to just outwit and outmaneuver his would-be captors. The hijinks take them all over the world, in cities and on farms, on airships and boats.

Frink, who signed only his surname to his work and left his first name a mystery to comic historians for years, died in 1912; had he lived longer, his name might have been remembered today as one of comics' greats instead of as a postscript. Strangely enough, his successor on *Slim Jim* is also an enigma. Raymond Crawford Ewer was a gifted penman who brought nearly as much inventiveness of art and ideas to the comics as Winsor McCay, and at about the same time.

Ewer was a comic strip innovator, even in those early days. He experimented with extra-long panels, bold colors, and treatments of the Sunday page as one

"Slim Jim," Raymond Ewer.

entity. His art was as funny as Frink's, but on a baroque, detailed order. His drawings looked like they came from sketchbooks, with many lines happily searching for the essence of a figure: Ewer's drawings were anatomically perfect and students can compare his work favorably, in terms of spirit, execution, and quality, with Heinrich Kley.

He brought a joyous spirit and some knockout visual excitement to *Slim Jim* but he, too, died young around Christmas 1913, after only one year of work on the strip. Ewer's last published drawings, except for *Slim Jim*, appeared in *Puck* magazine in the mid-1910s. Some earlier drawings—crude, on the verge of slick—appeared in *Judge*, but his *Puck* centerspreads in color are masterpieces of cartooning observation and delineation.

After Ewer, the World Company brought in Stanley Armstrong to continue *Slim Jim*. His work was pedestrian, suffering all the more from the shadows of excellence which preceded him. Jim took on a slightly crazed, funny expression and had more of a character under Armstrong, but overall, Armstrong's work was stiff.

Armstrong's service on the strip was strangely interrupted in 1915 when a succession of artists drew and signed it, each for a couple of weeks or so: Clarence Rigby, C. W. Kahles, Ernie McGee, and some reprinted Frink pages. But then Armstrong returned and continued on the strip which always enjoyed rural American popularity until the World Color Printing Co. itself died in 1937.

R.M.

SLYLOCK FOX AND COMICS FOR KIDS (U.S.)
The usually uninspired genre of children's pages added a refreshing feature in 1986 with the introduction of *Comics for Kids*, by the son of *Moose* creator and King Features' bullpen artist, Bob Weber, Jr. Originally a Sunday only syndicated strip for foreign markets, King launched it domestically on March 31, 1987. Consisting of several regular interactive features, an early component was a hog family named *The Pigglys*, since replaced by the visual puzzle *Find Six Differences*, accompanied by an elemental *How to Draw* lesson and a multiple-choice question panel. *Bonnie and Boo-Boo* is a strip within a strip, featuring a team of siblings that

"Slylock Fox," Bob Weber Jr. © King Features Syndicate.

provides pure comedy drawn with a charming simplicity, differing from the familiar Weber style used throughout the other elements.

The strip's nucleus, though, is Slylock Fox, a shrewd detective who skillfully solves cases along with his diminutive and venerating sidekick, Max Mouse. Presented in one commanding panel, a crime is described simply while a hidden clue is pictured, inviting the reader to help deduce the situation caused by regular nemeses Count Weirdly, Shady Shrew, Wanda Witch, or Harry Ape, among others. Facts about nature, health, pet care, ecology, and self-esteem mix in with the brain teasers, resulting in an educational, entertaining, and informative package. All text and dialogue are captioned, giving the piece more the feel of children's book art than that of a comic strip. Drawings by young readers are regularly published; a fraction of the 150 to 200 drawings received each week. Weber, Jr., writes all the continuities but is assisted by his father on some of the artwork, especially since the advent of a daily version.

A fine card set, *Slylock Fox Brain Bogglers*, was produced recently, showcasing 90 of the cunning Reynard's best adventures. In 1994 the feature was retitled *Slylock Fox and Comics for Kids* and currently appears in 400 newspapers.

B.J.

SMILIN' JACK (U.S.) On October 1, 1933, Zack Mosley started *On the Wing* (changed to *Smilin' Jack* in December of the same year) as a Sunday feature for the *News-Tribune* Syndicate; a daily strip was added on June 15, 1936. Smilin' Jack Martin is a pilot and in the convention of the time, that means he does everything, from searching for lost explorers to solving bank rob-

beries. In his exploits he is aided and abetted by his boy companion Pinfeathers, his faithful cook and jack-of-all-trades Fat Stuff (a reformed headhunter whom he brought back from the South Seas), not to mention his associates, the blustering Velvet Harry and the rather sinister Downwind (whose face is always hidden from view).

Smilin' Jack's aerial adventures are only half as outlandish as his romantic entanglements. With all his other responsibilities he finds time to be a man around town (even growing a Clark Gable moustache for the purpose) with an endless string of girls around his neck: the loyal Mary, the fiery Dixie, the bitchy Gale (respectively blonde, redhead, and brunette) among others. This does not prevent him from marrying his boss Joy, who later presents him with a son nicknamed Jungle Jolly, before vanishing from his life. (During the war Jack was to find Joy who had lost her memory only to lose her again.)

The artwork on the strip is uniformly terrible, but in spite (or because) of it *Smilin' Jack* remained popular through the years due in part to the accuracy of its technical details, and in part to the cheerful absurdities of the plot. In the more demanding 1960s, however, *Smilin' Jack* gradually lost his appeal and he was finally grounded in 1973 after a 40-year career, the longest of any aviation strip.

The strip enjoyed its own comic book version in the 1940s, and in 1942 Universal released *The Adventures of Smilin' Jack*, the last movie serial based on a comic strip that they ever produced.

M.H.

SMITH, AL (1902-1986) An American artist born in Brooklyn, New York, on March 2, 1902, as Albert

YES, THAT'S WOO WOO
BALI -- SHE WAS A SOUTH
SEA ISLAND DANCER
BEFORE SHE GOT
TOO PLUMP AND
LOST HER JOB!

"Smilin' Jack," Zack Mosley. © Chicago Tribune-New York News Syndicate.

Schmidt, his schooling was meager and a proclivity toward art was thwarted by lack of funds. In 1922 Smith got a job as copy boy on the old *New York Sun* but within a year he moved across Park Row to serve the *New York World* in the same capacity. It was here, in the manner so familiar to many of cartooning's greats, that the copy boy eventually was allowed to do some drawing on the stars' off days.

Smith's feature was *From 9 to 5*, a panel about office work, which had no connection with the later feature of the same name by Jo Fischer. This panel was picked up for a short time by United Feature Syndicate after the World folded. But the Depression rolled on and Smith resorted to jobs with the WPA in Closter and Demarest, New Jersey. In the early 1930s he did odd jobs with John Wheeler's Bell Syndicate, including Christmas spot drawings and a stint as ghost for sports cartoonist Bob Edgren.

In 1932 Wheeler and Bud Fisher contacted Smith about ghosting *Mutt and Jeff*, which, for approximately 14 years, had been ghosted by Ed Mack. Here began Smith's association with the classic strip which continues today and a tempestuous association with the volatile Fisher, who was notoriously tight and a heavy drinker.

Smith was forced to carry the strip without the troublesome guidance of Fisher. He soon made the strip more genteel than it had previously been; Mutt's married life was spent more by the hearth and less in the divorce court. Jeff, too, began to seriously court girls, including Encee (for n.c.: no comment) and Chlorine. Bruno the dog joined the Mutt family and *Cicero's Cat* became the Sunday top strip, borrowed from the office cat in *From 9 to 5*. Smith's art, too, was slicker and more slapstick than any of his predecessors who ghosted for Fisher (others included Billy Liverpool, Ken Kling, and George Herriman). After Fisher's death in 1954, Smith signed the strip himself, although ownership has remained in the hands of the Countess Aedita de Beaumont, Fisher's widow. He left *Mutt and Jeff* in the hands of George Breisacher after he retired in 1980; he died on November 24, 1986, in Rutland, Vermont.

In 1950 Smith founded the Smith Service, a syndicate serving weekly papers. His own features included *Rural Delivery* and *Remember When*, with other features drawn by Joe Dennett (*Down Main Street*) and George Wolfe (*Pops*).

Smith was very active in the National Cartoonists Society for many years, and served successively as founder of the placement service, general membership chairman, treasurer (nine years), and president from 1967 to 1969. In 1968 Smith won the Best Humor Strip award.

If *Mutt and Jeff* had lost its slapstick touch under Smith, it is but a reflection of the times; the strip remains a favorite with a large list of papers. Smith, in and out of the NCS, has been a help to many young cartoonists starting their careers.

R.M.

SMITH, ROBERT SIDNEY (1877-1935) Perhaps the most attentively read and relished American writer and artist of the first third of this century was born Robert Sidney Smith in Bloomington, Illinois, on February 13, 1877, almost 40 years before he was to publish the first episode of *The Gumps* in the *Chicago Tribune* on February 12, 1917; so began the great American family epic of the 1920s.

Smith's father was a dentist, and wanted his son to follow in the profession. The boy, however, showed early talent for drawing, developed it in grammar and high school, and was turning out local cartoons at the age of 18 for the *Bloomington Eye*. Within a year, college forgotten, Smith began a series of income-improving moves through a half-score of newspapers (from the *Indianapolis News* to the *Chicago Examiner*) with which he furthered his skills in sports and political cartooning. An immediate sports page hit with *Examiner* readers, Smith seized on his popularity to introduce his first comic strip there in 1908: *Buck Nix*. One of the first humanized animal strips, *Buck Nix* delighted Chicagoans, and led to his being hired by the *Chicago Tribune* in 1912 to continue the strip under a new name, *Old Doc Yak*. *Buck Nix* had been a daily strip; *Old Doc Yak* ran only on Sunday (with Smith doing sports cartoons as a daily stint), but Smith was about to undertake a regular seven-day-a-week strip.

Just after Christmas 1916, Joe Patterson, copublisher of the Tribune, outlined a strip idea to Smith that would feature a typical Chicago lower-middle-class family with problems and successes that would reflect those of the average *Tribune* reader. He remembered and liked the name, *Gump* (first used comically in L. Frank Baum's *The Land of Oz* (1904), but also an actual surname), and suggested it for Smith's new strip menage. Introduced by a short sequence of the first daily *Old Doc Yak* episodes, *The Gumps* began in February 1917. Two years later, public demand forced Smith to fold the Sunday *Old Doc Yak* and replace the still-popular strip with a Sunday *Gumps* in June 1919. By this time, *The Gumps* was being snapped up by newspapers across the country, alerted to the fact that Smith's family strip had greatly increased the *Tribune's* circulation.

The 1920s were the golden years for *The Gumps* and Robert Sidney Smith (who had begun his cartooning career with the signature "R. Sidney Smith," but soon dropped the first initial for the simple and famed "Sidney Smith"). Smith's personal fortune, of course, soared. By the early 1920s, he already owned an extensive estate, Shirland, near Trudehurst, Wisconsin, and a costly Chicago residence; commanded use of the topmost office in the Chicago Tribune tower; owned a fleet of cars, which he drove at top speeds along deserted country roads; and had hired the best talent he could find to work with him on *The Gumps* (Harold Gray, Sol Hess, Stanley Link, etc.).

The impoverishment of the country and the shattering of many dreams by the 1930s didn't seem to affect the popularity of *The Gumps*. In fact, Smith had so built the fame and value of his strip by 1935 that, on the expiration of the old contract with the *Tribune*, he was able to command a new one that would pay him a million dollars over the following three years, and he was given a Rolls-Royce as a bonus. Speeding back to his Wisconsin estate the morning after he had signed the new contract in Chicago (October 20, 1935) Smith collided with another driver at an isolated country point in Illinois and was killed instantly.

B.B.

SMITTY (U.S.) One of the few *Chicago Tribune-New York News* strips of the 1920s which was not in large part the idea of publisher Joe Patterson was Walter Berndt's *Smitty*, which first appeared daily on Monday, November 27, 1922, and Sunday on February 25, 1923 (in the *News* only). Derived to a great extent from Walter Hoban's *Jerry on the Job*, Berndt's first version of this famous strip ran in the *New York World* as *Bill the Office Boy* for a short time until Berndt was fired for insubordination. Taking the strip to the *News,* the young artist found Patterson to be interested. Having launched a strip about a working girl, *Winnie Winkle,* the publisher saw the use of one about a working kid with a similar office background, and was only inclined to change one thing: the hero's name. Trying a handy phone book for inspiration, Patterson hit the S's and found nothing but pages of Smiths. Giving up, he suggested "Smitty" as a nickname, pinpointed a cumbersome first name among the phone book Smiths, and told Berndt to get busy.

The first episode, captioned: "Meet Up With Augustus Smith," showed Smitty, a dapper little guy in cap and short pants, sauntering into a drugstore to phone his new boss, Mr. Bailey, and ask if the office boy job he had advertised the day before was still open. Told that it wasn't, and that the boy he had hired was satisfactory, the grinning Smitty strolled happily and securely out of the store, his worries over. Mr. Bailey, Smitty's genial, rotund boss, appeared in the following day's episode and costarred with the office boy hero through the ensuing 50 years of the strip.

"Smitty," Walter Berndt. © Chicago Tribune-New York News Syndicate.

A simple, but somehow always witty and amusing strip, *Smitty* had little in the way of plot in the daily strip (Smitty becomes a Golden Gloves boxer, gets involved in major league baseball, goes on camping trips with his boss, etc.) and featured only situation gags in the Sunday page, largely with the aid of Smitty's obstreperous kid brother, Herby, and his pet dog, a lop-eared mutt named Spot. Smitty's parents, Ma and Pa Smith, were the only other regular characters in the strip, until an Indian guide named George was introduced in the daily strip in the late 1930s, and Smitty (who grows infrequently over the years to young adulthood) meets a permanent girlfriend in the office named Ginny in the late 1950s, whom he eventually marries.

Never filmed in live action and animated only briefly by Pathé in 1928, *Smitty* appeared in a few worthwhile book collections in the late 1920s and early 1930s, as well as in some infrequent comic book collections a bit later, but otherwise has not been well reprinted. Berndt's only other strip work after launching *Smitty* was the addition of a four-panel Sunday companion strip named (despite his stardom in the larger part of the page) *Herby*, in 1930. Both strips were discontinued in 1973.

B.B.

SMOKEY STOVER (U.S.) What is probably one of the most outrageous comic strips ever devised saw the light of print (as a Sunday feature) on March 10, 1935: *Smokey Stover*, penned by the zany Bill Holman and distributed by the staid News-Tribune Syndicate.

Smokey Stover, as his name indicates, is a fireman and, along with his boss, Chief Cash U. Nutt, he turns the firehouse into a madhouse. Riding to the fires in a

"Smokey Stover," Bill Holman. © Chicago Tribune-New York News Syndicate.

red buggy, Smokey is likely to cause more mayhem than the cause of his alarm. The commotions are just as many within the firehouse as without: on occasion Smokey had the fire wagon outfitted with tank tracks (to tread softly) or equipped with chimes (more melodic than sirens).

Smokey Stover's chief sources of fun are the innumerable puns that Billy Holman regularly inflicts on his reading public ("carrying colds to Newcastle, the bottle of Bunker Hill, and for whom the belles toil are a few of them), and the cryptic signs which he liberally scatters throughout the strip (Notary Sojac, Foo, 1506 nixnix). Figuratively firing in all directions, Bill Holman was able to maintain a high level of spontaneity and hilarity for more than 40 years. *Smokey Stover* has had as many misses as hits, but its rapid-fire delivery and iconoclastic asides more than made up for the occasional clinkers and the inevitable duds. (For a long time *Smokey* had a companion strip, *Spooky*, about a cat as nutty as his master; when *Spooky* was discontinued, the cat became a permanent character in *Smokey*.)

Holman regrettably put an end to the zany exploits of his merry crew of firemen when he retired in 1973. *Smokey Stover* has been reprinted sporadically in the 1980s, most notably in an anthology of screwball comic strips published by Fantagraphic Books.

M.H.

SNAKE TALES (Australia) In October 1974 cartoonist Allan Salisbury (who signs "Sols") came up with *The Old Timer*, a comic strip featuring a beer-guzzling old codger, his sharpie pal the Con-Man, his nemesis the Flyin' Doc, and a couple of aborigines known as the Lost Tribesman and His Wife. The strip originated in Sydney's *Daily Telegraph* and was later syndicated all over Australia through Inter Continental Features. Sols kept adding new characters, like the Old Timer's secret admirer Lillie and Crazy Croc the lazy crocodile; and to crown it all, in 1976 Snake sneakily slithered in.

Snake is a pathetic reptilian whose only aim in his lonely and earthbound life is to acquire some friends along with a few limbs. Having once innocently asked what he didn't have that others did he got the obvious reply, "Fingers, thumbs, nails, knuckles, hands, wrists, elbows, legs, kneecaps, thighs," ad infinitum. As to his other failing, he has to resort to carrying a sign reading, "Give the snake a kiss," or to call upon a rent-a-friend service (for which he has to pay special rates).

All his shortcomings only served to endear Snake to the readers all the more, to such an extent that the feature was renamed *Snake Tales* in 1978.

Among the hallmarks of the strip almost from the beginning have been its puns. Some examples will suffice: "Why did so many turn up at the optician's party? He promised them all a spectacle." "Why did the drunk kamikaze pilot survive the war? He got smashed before he took off." "How do you stop your telly running all night? Make sure it has commercial brakes." While critics have excoriated the author for his incessant stream of bad puns, most readers appear to relish his corniness.

Sols's graphic style can charitably be characterized as minimalist, but it is nonetheless telling in its conciseness. Soon after *Snake Tales* became established, it met with growing success not only in Australia (where it has been reprinted into a number of paperbacks and has given rise to much merchandising) but also overseas, particularly in Scandinavia. In the United States it was syndicated by NEA from 1982 to 1991.

M.H.

SNOOKUMS *see* Newlyweds, The.

SNUFFY SMITH *see* Barney Google.

SOGLOW, OTTO (1900-1975) An American artist born in New York City on December 23, 1900, Soglow was educated in New York public schools and then trained at the Art Students League from 1919 to 1925 under, among others, John Sloan. Soglow's inspirations in art were Winsor McCay, George McManus, and George Herriman, although he aspired to a career in fine arts.

His first published drawing was an amateur submission to *Cartoons* magazine in 1919, but his professional career began in 1925 with Western illustrations for *Lariat* magazine. After breaking into the magazine field (Soglow had worked in New York at various odd jobs, including painting baby rattles), other sales followed, to the *New Yorker*, *College Humor*, *Life*, and *Judge*. In 1925 he also drew for the *New York World* "Metropolitan" section.

Soglow was a charter member of the zany *New Yorker* crew in those early days when camaraderie did so much to build that magazine into an institution. One can imagine the sessions when Soglow, Harold

Ross, S. J. Perelman, Thurber, E. B. White, and others thought up captions for Soglow's classic drawing of merely a city street with an open manhole; the cartoon ran literally dozens of times with different gags.

One such Soglow cartoon editor Harold Ross particularly liked, and he requested more of the Little King featured in it. Soon the Little King became as popular a magazine cartoon character as Henry, Little Lulu, or another generation's Hazel. And soon the eternal purchaser of comic genius, William Randolph Hearst, was in touch with Soglow.

Wily Ross, however, had a contract for the *Little King* full-page strips, so while Hearst waited for expiration, Soglow drew *The Ambassador* (very close to the King in flavor and style) in the Saturday feature section, with captions, and as a strip for King Features syndication. As a newspaper comic strip, *The Little King* began on Sunday, September 9, 1934. (Its companion strip was the equally funny *Sentinel Louie*.)

Soglow's stark, almost diagrammatic style, devoid of shading but always alive with action, has marked him as one of the most individualistic of modern strip artists. His contributions to the art have included services away from the drawing board. He was founder of the National Cartoonists Society, and he has been on frequent tours of bases in war and peacetime as well as devoting time and effort to other charitable causes. In recognition of his contributions he has received, among other awards, the NCS Reuben and the Elzie Segar Award.

Soglow retired from his weekly task of drawing spots for the *New Yorker*'s "Talk of the Town" in 1972 and continued to produce *The Little King* for a sadly diminishing list of Sunday papers, until his death on April 3, 1975.

R.M.

SOLANO LÓPEZ, FRANCISCO (1928-   ) Solano López is an Argentine artist born October 26, 1928, in Buenos Aires. The death of his father when he was eight delayed the future artist's avocation for drawing, which he had manifested at an early age. He briefly pursued law studies and later worked in advertising before definitively turning to comics in 1950. He worked for several publishers and later started his fruitful association with fabled editor and scriptwriter Hector Oesterheld; their first collaborative effort was *Uma-Uma* (1953) for the magazine *Rayo Rojo*. Soon afterward he took over *Bull Rockett*, which Oesterheld had created in 1952, and drew it until 1959; at the same time he also illustrated other Oesterheld creations, including *Ernie Pike* (on which Hugo Pratt was later to make his name), *Rolo, el marciano adoptivo* ("Rolo the Adopted Martian"), *Joe Zonda* (adventures in the South Seas), *Amapola Negra* ("The Black Poppy," a story of aerial war adventures), and especially *El Eternauta*. This series told the cataclysmic invasion of earth by extraterrestrial forces. Considered Oesterheld's masterpiece, it was later illustrated by Alberto Breccia in a new version that started in 1968. Oesterheld, however, wrote a sequel to the original version (just before his disappearance in 1977), which was also drawn by Solano López and which appeared in the magazine *Skorpio*.

In the late 1950s Solano López slowly developed a British market for his increased production. With the help of assistants he contributed for the next 15 years a flood of comic strips to IPC Magazines of London,

Francisco Solano López and Carlos Sampayo, "Evaristo." © the authors.

the most noteworthy being *Air Ace Library* (1959), *Kelly's Eye* (1963, in *Valiant*), *Galaxus* (1964, in *Buster*), *Toys of Doom* (1966, in *Buster*), *Raven on the Wing* (1968, in *Valiant*), *Adam Eterno* (1969, in *Lion*), and *Nipper* (1970, in *Tiger*). During his British phase he continued his collaboration with Oesterheld, drawing *Lord Pampa* (about a war pilot) for the magazine *Rayo Rojo* in 1963.

Solano López entered the latter phase of his career with a commitment to quality. It began with the second part of *Eternauta*, and continued with the artist's collaboration with writer Ricardo Barreiro. Together they produced *Slot-Barr*, a 1976 science-fiction series that aimed to bring more rational underpinnings to the genre, and especially *Ministerio*, set in a dictatorial society of the future, which debuted exactly 10 years later in the magazine *Fierro*. The duo's latest collaborative work has been *El Televisor*, a dystopian tale, also published in *Fierro*, starting in 1990.

In the interval Solano López worked for various European publishers, notably drawing *Historias tristes* ("Sad Stories") and *Ana* on texts by his son, Gabriel, between the late 1970s and mid-1980s. In collaboration with writer Carlos Sampayo, he came out in 1983 with *Evaristo*, which had as its protagonist a middle-age and disabused police commissioner in the Buenos Aires of the late 1950s and early 1960s. Building on Sampayo's splendid scripts, the visual rendition of *Evaristo* imparted to the work a climate of squalor, of things falling apart, deepening the sensation of hurt slowly oozed by the stories in their succession and foreshadowing the inexorable rotting away of life against a background of failure and defeat. Hailed internationally as a work of depth and significance, *Evaristo* is the artist's masterpiece to date.

J.C.

SOLDINO (Italy) In 1955 Renato Bianconi, a former editor of *Edizioni Alpe*, set up his own comic book publishing company in partnership with Giovanni Duga. The first title issued by this new house was *Trottolino*, followed in 1957 by *Soldino*.

Soldino was the creation of Giovanni Battista Carpi and Giulio Chierchini; they were followed first by Nicolino Del Principe, then by Tiberio Colantuoni, Motta, and more recently Dossi. Soldino is a little king, penniless but high-spirited, reigning over a mythical kingdom where thievery, corruption, trickery, and mischief are rampant. The monarch, however, is upstaged by his grandmother Abelarda, who often has to get her grandson out of some trouble of his own making. In spite of a decrepit body, Abelarda possesses unlimited strength; this super-grandma is able not only to knock out a whole gang of hoodlums, but also to split a mountain in two, lift a truck, or uproot a whole clump of trees like a hurricane. Abelarda is a highly colorful character who is the real star of the two comic books relating Soldino's mishaps: *Soldino Mensile* and *Soldino Super*. In the 1960s she was given her own *Abelarda* comic book in recognition of her popularity with the readers.

Another spin-off of *Soldino* is *Bongo*, an ape who frequently appeared in the company of Soldino and Abelarda. He has been recently promoted to full star status with an entire comic book devoted to his adventures. Soldino and company all ended their exploits in the early 1990s.

G.B.

SOLOVJEV, SERGEJ (1901-1975) Comics author Sergej Solovjev lived and worked in Serbia between the two World Wars. Born in 1901 in Kursk, Russia, Solovjev attended and finished Military Academy. As a cavalry officer he took part in combat against the Bolshevik forces during the civil war, and in 1920 escaped into Serbia. Just like many other Russians who decided not to return into the communist-controlled Russia, Solovjev opted to stay in emigration and become Yugoslav.

Solovjev worked as a manual laborer, then as a tax official, and started his studies at the Academy of Art in Belgrade. His first comic was a story of adventure and war, entitled *Legija prokletib* ("Legion of the Damned"); the first installment was in number 99 of *Mika Mis* ("Mickey Mouse") on May 21, 1937. Before the Nazi invasion of Serbia in April 1941, he had 31 comics printed in three different Serbian magazines. Some of these comics were later reprinted elsewhere. He signed most as "S. Solo" or "Moum Gey." The only Serbian comics artist more productive than he was Navojev. No less than 30 years after the end of World War II, one of Solovjev's comics episode was found and printed for the first time (in 1975), making his total production 32 comics.

At the beginning of 1939, *Mika Mis* editor Ignjačević had a conflict with Ivković and quit to establish a new magazine. Solovjev, unlike some others, continued to collaborate with both. The reason why he continued to work for Ignjačević is perhaps his good cooperation with scriptwriter Branislav Vidić. For nearly half of Solovjev's comics were scripted by Vidić; others, which were based on famous literature, may have been adapted by Vidić although they did not have his signature (including Dumas's *Three Musketeers* in 1938, Shakespeare's *Midsummer Night's Dream* in 1938,

Sergej Solovjev, "Ivanhoe." © Sergej Solovjev.

Scott's *Ivanhoe* in 1939, Shakespeare's *Romeo and Juliet* in 1939-1940, and *Robin Hood* in 1939). Whoever was responsible for the adaptations, they were done well with an emphasis on the most interesting key points, action sequences, plot overturns, and strong, dynamic characters.

Vidić actually signed only five scenarios for Solovjev's comics, in two different serials. *Crni ataman* ("Black Ataman") appeared on October 26, 1937. The serial's second episode was titled *Kapetan Leš* ("Captain Lash") in 1938, and the third episode was *Nevesta živog Bude* ("Bride of the Living Buddha") also in 1938. His settings included the mountainsides of the Caucasian Mountains, Turkmenistan, and Kirgizia. The plot involves a young cossack named Aljoša (pronounced *Alyosha*), who is falsely accused and expelled from his native village on the Caucasian Mountains and who decides it is payback time. His revenge is successful. Later he takes up the fight against injustices inflicted on others. This is an outstanding Serbian comics, extremely popular and important. According to an opinion poll taken in 1938, it was second in popularity after *The Phantom* but ahead of *Mandrake, Prince Valiant,* and *Flash Gordon*. The fourth episode, which was the last, was published without a special title. In it, Aljoša gets a loyal companion, Šućur (pronounced *Shootyur*). The other Vidić and Solovjev serial consisted of only two episodes, released in 1939. It was *Bufalo Bil*.

Vidić and Solovjev produced an excellent biographical serial, *Napoleon*, in three episodes, published in 1940. Also they produced the adventure serials *Black Mask—Lord Warwick* (1940), *Siberian Girl* (1940), and *Big Kid* (1940). Only Solovjev signed as author on three excellent comics *Put ka slavi* ("Road to Glory," 1940), *Ostrvo s blagom* ("Treasure Island" based on the novel by R. L. Stevenson) in 1941 but discontinued because of the onset of the war, reprinted entirely in 1951 in the magazine *Omladina* ("The Youth"), and *Carev štitonoša* ("Tzar's Shieldbearer") in 1940 to 1941. This last comic was strongly influenced by Foster's *Prince Valiant* and was the longest and most popular of the three. The time was the year 1330, setting medieval Serbia. Prince Dušan Nemanjić (pronounced *Dushan Nemanyich*), son of King Stefan the Third Dečanski, struggles after his father's death to ascend to the throne and remain on it. Through many adventures he is helped by his nephew, knight Miloš Vojinović.

The high quality of Solovjev's work was confirmed by publication abroad, mostly in France (*Three Musketeers, Tzar's Shieldbearer,* and others). His thematic range was wide. Solovjev took up all genres except science fiction and grotesque. He did Westerns, detective stories, historicals (mostly the early Russian and Serbian history), pirate stories, and biographies.

During the Yugoslav involvement in World War II Solovjev was not doing any comics. After the war he moved in 1945 to the city of Rijeka on the Adriatic coast, close to Italy; several years later (in 1953 or 1955, data on this are uncertain), he emigrated to Italy and stayed there, in the small town of Massa on the Mediterranean coast south of Genoa, for the rest of his life. After World War II many of his comics were reprinted in Serbia. Publisher and editor of the Serbian magazine *Pegaz* ("Pegasus"), Žika Bogdanović is one of the last Serbs who went to Massa and managed to talk to Solovjev there. The result of this conversation was that one of Solovjev's comics, unknown until then, *Pesma južnog vetra* ("Song of the Southern Wind"),

which he produced in 1945 but kept for himself, was printed in *Pegaz* number 3. This was in 1975, the same year as his death.

S.I.

SONOYAMA, SHUNJI (1935-   ) Sonoyama is a Japanese cartoonist born April 23, 1935, in Matsue, Shimane. While a junior at Waseda University, Sonoyama founded the Waseda University Cartoon Society, with Kineo Shitou and others. After graduation from the university and a short-lived (a few hours!) try at an advertising agency job, Sonoyama started his career as a professional cartoonist with *Ganbare Gonbe*, a humor strip that he created for the elementary school student newspaper *Mainichi Shōgakusei Shinbun* in 1958. In 1963 he published, at his own expense, a collection of gag cartoons, *Kokkyō no Futari*; in 1965 *Gyatoruzu* (his most famous adult strip, a kind of Japanese *B.C.*) appeared and was later adapted to animated film; followed in 1966 by *Hajimeningen Gon* ("Gon the Primitive Boy"), a children's version of *Gyatoruzu*. Among Sonoyama's other creations are *Hana no Kakarichō* ("The Office Chiefs Flower," 1969) and *Sasurai no Gambler* ("The Wandering Gambler," also 1969).

Sonoyama's greatest merit lies in his criticism of modern civilization, with such works as *Gyatoruzu, Hajimeningen Gon,* and the savage *Mayonakano Genshijin* ("The Primitive Man at Midnight"). In his view, primitive men were more human than modern people in that they were emotional, vital, and active, while modern people are only cogs in a huge and dehumanizing machine called the State. His strips tried to rediscover the human elements lost by modern man in our mechanized society. Those primitive men had to struggle against beasts and elemental forces in order to survive, and had to depend on their own skills for food, clothing, and shelter. Their sex urge was strong, but not perverted as in modern man and, while their lives were close to that of the animals, their human personalities came through with more strength and naturalness than the robotized humans of today.

Sonoyama is more noted for his writing than for his drawing. His graphic style is simple to the extreme, almost crude, but with a very warm and vibrant quality. In this regard he is not too dissimilar from Scott Adams, and like *Dilbert* in the United States, his "salarymen comics" (as they are called there) enjoy great success in Japan to this day.

H.K.

Shunji Sonoyama, "Gyatoruzu." © Sonoyama.